WEST AFRICAN CHURCH HISTORY II
Christian Missions and Theological Training 1842-1970

WEST AFRICAN CHURCH HISTORY II

*Christian Missions and Theological Training
1842-1970*

BY

JOHN KOFI AGBETI

E. J. BRILL
LEIDEN • NEW YORK • KØBENHAVN • KÖLN
1991

*To Da Ama and Children
for providing a peaceable family*

Library of Congress Cataloging-in-Publication Data
(Revised for volume 2)

Agbeti, J. Kofi.
  West African church history.
  Includes bibliographical references and indexes.
  Contents: [1] Christian missions and church foundations, 1482-1919 — 2. Christian missions and theological training, 1842-1970.
  1. Missions—Africa, West—History. 2. Africa, West—Church history. I. Title.
BV3540.A35   1986   266'.00966   86-149803
ISBN 90-04-07167-9 (pbk.: v. 1)
ISBN 90-04-09100-9 (pbk.: v. 2)

ISBN 9004-09100-9

© *Copyright 1991 by E.J. Brill, Leiden, The Netherlands*

All rights reserved. No part of this book may be reproduced or translated in any form, by print, photoprint, microfilm, microfiche or any other means without written permission from the publisher

PRINTED IN THE NETHERLANDS

CONTENTS

List of Abbreviations vii
Foreword ix
Preface xi

1. Introduction: Setting the Scene 1
2. Wesleyan Methodist Mission Training, 1842-1942 . . . 11
3. Basel Mission Training, 1843-1918 36
4. Bremen Mission Training, 1855-1915 49
5. Presbyterian Mission Training, 1916-1942 65
6. Baptist Convention Training, 1888-1970 74
7. Anglican Church Mission Training: Phase I, 1925-1932 . . 86
8. Anglican Church Mission Training: Phase II, 1933-1965 . 101
9. Roman Catholic Mission Training: S.M.A., 1909-1965 . . 120
10. Roman Catholic Mission Training: White Fathers—1946-1965 142
11. Towards United Missions Training: Trinity College, Legon—1943-1965 153
12. Towards United Missions Training: Immanuel Theological College, Ibadan—1958-1965 184
13. An Appraisal 196
14. Theological Education for Tomorrow 207

APPENDICES

I Plans for Establishing Mfantsipim School 215
II Report on the Opening of the New Buildings of St. Augustine's College, Kumasi, on 22/4/28 217
III Bishop's £67,000 Appeal Fund 219
IV Catechists' Institute, Osu: Time-table for July-December, 1853 220
V Ewe Presbyterian Church—Theological Seminary 1933 Time Table—Ho 221
VI Volta Region Showing German Togoland 1919 . . . 222
VII List of African Ministers trained from 1842-1965 (Ghana) 223
VIII Register of Immanuel College of Theology Students, Ibadan, Nigeria, 1958-1965 231

IX	Register of Trinity College Students, Legon, Ghana, 1943-1965	234
X	Trinity College, Kumasi, Ghana: Rate of Growth of Student Body	236
XI	The Phasings of Trinity College Plan, Legon	239
XII	The Staff of Trinity College, Ghana, 1943-1965	241

Bibliography 243

Index 251

LIST OF ABBREVIATIONS

A.A.C.C.	All African Churches Conference
A.D.A.	Accra Diocesan Association
A.M.E.Z.	African Methodist Episopal Zion
B.M.A.	Basel Mission Archives
C.A.C.T.M.	Central Advisory Council of Training for the Ministry
C.M.S.	Church Missionary Society
C.P.P.	Convention People's Party
E.P.C.	Evangelical (Ewe) Presbyterian Church
G.A.T.R.K.	Ghana Association of Teachers of Religious Knowledge
G.B.M.	Governing Body Minutes
G.C.D.S.M.	Gold Coast District Synod Minutes
I.M.C.	International Missionary Council
I.R.M.	International Review of Missions
M.B.	Monatsblatt
M.C.G.	Methodist Church, Ghana
M.M.S.	Methodist Missionary Society
N.B.M.A.	North Bremen Mission Archives
N.C.C.C.	National Council of the Churches of Christ in the U.S.A.
O.S.B.	Order of St. Benedict
P.C.G.	Presbyterian Church of Ghana
S.M.	Scottish Mission
S.M.A.	Society of African Missions (Societe des Missions Africain Lyons)
S.P.C.K.	Society for the Propagation of Christian Knowledge
S.P.G.	Society for the Propagation of the Gospel
S.S.M.	Society of Sacred Missions
T.E.F.	Theological Education Fund
U.C.G.C.	University College of the Gold Coast
U.F.C.S.	United Free Church of Scotland
U.G.	University of Ghana
W.M.M.S.	Wesleyan Methodist Missionary Society

FOREWORD

In the 1950's, the International Missionary Council (now merged with the World Council of Churches) commissioned four surveys of "the Training of the Ministry in Africa", which covered the entire sub-Saharan area. In the course of these studies it came to light that whilst, with the declared intention of establishing self-reliant indigenous churches, the crucial importance of giving somewhat adequate theological training to the future leadership of these churches was generally acknowledged, yet in point of fact only a very low priority was given to this matter in the practical policies and day-to-day decisions of the missionary bodies responsible, judging from the proportion of their resources in personnel and finance that was made available to it.

The now well-known Theological Education Fund was mainly a response to this anomalous situation and, during the years of its operation was able, through its grants-in-aid, to stimulate and induce all concerned—both missions and younger churches—to give the preparation of all levels of their workers the serious attention which it deserves.

The present trend in theological education appears to be to prefer less formal teaching arrangements and methods to the traditional institutional approach. I believe that the originality and inventiveness evident in some of the modern schemes are that fully utmost use was made of the very meagre opportunities available in the past. For example, in the complete absence of any sort of seminary, one African priest received his training for the priesthood almost entirely by private study with the three or four expatriate priests under whom he worked in different places as a full-time teacher-catechist, keeping a note-book in which each successive teacher marked the topics studied.

The West African case study here presented is thus a very valuable instalment of our ecclesiastical history. It is comparatively recent history. I was struck by the fact that most of all but the earliest personages mentioned in connection with Ghana were well known to me. But the research has thrown up several interesting and valuable facts which even those who believe themselves to be fairly conversant with this ground will find refreshingly new. A major virtue of the book is that it covers both Protestant and Roman Catholic work. We must hope for many more such documentations in the future.

Legon House, C.G. BAËTA
Ho, Volta Region,
Ghana, 1987

PREFACE

The purpose of this book is to present a historical account of Theological Education, that is, the training of Christian ministers, in West Africa from 1842 to 1970. The need for such a study has been apparent since it was called for on a continental basis in 1950 by the Rt. Rev. Stephen Neill, when he made the following statement:

> There was a very widespread feeling that this investigation was mostly timely, and that a situation had arisen in which wise planning and confident action on the strategic scale were needed, if the pressing needs of a new situation were to be met.... If the subject (training for the Christian Ministry in Africa) is to be fully represented in perspective, historical research would be needed for which at present I have not the leisure.[1]

But from 1950, however, no historical work on the subject of the present inquiry, has been made available in any adequate detail. Books that have been published concerning ministerial training in Africa or in African countries, either dealt with curricula, contents, philosophy of religious training and activities of the seminaries training the Clergy or made only marginal historical references.[2]

It is hoped that the results of this research will not only make historical information available from which other relevant themes may emerge but will also provide the desired perspective to guide the Church in West Africa in making wise plans for the future reformation of the training given to its clergy.

After the independence of Ghana in 1957 the need for over-hauling the training given to the African clergy became more urgent. It was felt in political and intellectual circles that the leaders of the Church in Ghana, and this was true of the whole of West Africa, were so concerned about ecclesiastical life that they tended to be reactionary against national aspirations; thus it was felt that the time had come to reform the Church so that its leaders might not only understand divine things, but also appreciate and appraise without prejudice the contemporary political, cultural and social revolutions taking place in Ghana and West Africa.

Two representative illustrations taken from Ghana, should suffice to substantiate the above conclusion. First, from Government circles, the Christian Church was branded: "a misnomer, a sectarian minority body operating in its own interest ... and has always been a divisive and disrup-

---

1 Stephen Neill, *Survey of the Training of the Ministry in Africa*, Part 1, (London, 1950), p. 4.
2 Such books are listed in the bibliography. A brief bibliographical essay on them could have been added, but lack of space would not permit it. In any case a cursory glance through the relevant books will affirm the conclusion that they lack sufficient historical information about ministerial training.

tive force on all recent occasions of national unity connected with independence".[3] To arrest this apparent disloyalty of the Church to the State, a Department of Religious Affairs was to be established, by the C.P.P. Government, to "control and dictate the activities of the Churches and to seal these moves, legislation was to be passed to cover the prohibited organisations including the Christian Council as subversive of democratic government and public good".[4]

The Government's attitude to the Church had been provoked by the Church's hostility to some national issues; the Methodists refused to permit their indigenous ministers to take part in Party Politics and those ministers who insisted and joined the Government Party were compelled to resign from the Christian ministry; the Churches, through the Christian Council, condemned as evil, without giving convincing and realistic reasons, some of the cherished social, religious and cultural practices namely: polygamy, pouring of Libation (explained in Chapter 1 of this book) and reverence paid to the ancestors—just to mention a few—although the Government was forcefully reviving them. Worst of all, Nkrumah's national youth movement, the Young Pioneers, founded in June 1960, "dedicated to serve the cause of Ghana's socialist reconstruction and Africa's freedom and unity, while at the same time advocating world brotherhood and peace"[5] was condemned publicly by the Church as sacrilegious because the movement hailed Nkrumah as "redeemer" (Osagyefo) and his "Messianic Majesty".[6]

The second illustration suggesting that the time had come for some reformation in the Church came from an intellectual community. One of the lecturers in the institute of African Studies, University of Ghana, Legon (whose name, for obvious reasons, will not be divulged) was once invited to preach a sermon at the Presbyterian Church, Aburi in Akwapim. Instead of wearing an European suit, he put on local traditional attire. The innovation displeased and upset the Church Elders; but they were so pleased with the sermon that they suggested to the preacher that he should offer for the Christian ministry. "Then", the lecturer told me, "in disgust I told them: 'Da a mo be gyae aborofosom no, me di sofo'"—(Twi) that is, "when you stop European-worship, I shall become an ordained minister".

The significance of these two examples for our purpose here is that they symbolize the undercurrent of the contemporary local hostilities to the Church, viz.: the fealing that traditional Christianity as it was presented to West Africa from Europe had been preventing the local Church, especially the leaders, from taking active part in the national, social and cultural revolution taking place. The crux of the matter is that to enable the leaders

---

3 *Ghanaian Times* (Accra), Vol. XI, No. 3, 483, 30th Jan., 1969.
4 *Ibid.*, However, the Government's plans did not mature before the Coup d'Etat on 24th February, 1966.
5 *Ghana Year Book*, (Accra, 1964), p. 139.
6 Lloyd Garrison, "Accra Ghana 28th February", *New York Times*, March 2, 1967.

of the Church to communicate efficiently to all sections of the community it was necessary, in the words of the University lecturer referred to above, "to stop European-worship", that is, traditional missionary Christianity should be reformed. It was not Christianity, as such, that was opposed; but the foreignness of its approach to vital national issues. The deafricanizing effect of excessive missionary control in the formation of the African clergy is too unpatriotic to be tolerated in independent Africa.

The point to examine then is how to go about the needed Church overhaul. It is the submission of this investigation that we may first of all begin with the clergy for, as it is they who disseminate Christian truth and transmit ecclesiastical tradition to posterity their training should first be reformed so that they may, in the future, revolutionize the old methods, the attitudes and the parochial collective and colonial mentality inherited from the past paternalistic missionary control. But the prerequisite of any such reformation and reshaping is an accurate knowledge of how the training was done in the past. This explains why the greater part of this book has been limited to the history of the training given to the African clergy during a period of over 125 years by Western Missionaries.

The period selected is very extensive and although a shorter one would have been easier to handle, the lengthy period will be retained for two reasons: firstly, the earliest recorded attempt, to establish a Theological Institution in West Africa solely for the training of prospective African ministers, was made by the Wesleyan Methodist Missionary Society in 1842. Secondly, the Methodist and Presbyterian Churches' experiment to cooperate in the training of their ministers together reached its culmination in 1965 when a new united college was dedicated near the University of Ghana, Legon.

It may be noted at this point, that although there were many denominations in West Africa towards the end of our period, the inquiry will be limited to only five: the Methodist, the Presbyterian, the Anglican, the Nigerian Baptist and the Roman Catholic Missions[7] because these were the denominations which had done the most persistent and extensive work on the training of their ministers locally? The emphasis is on *missions* rather than geographical location.

It would have been beneficial, however, to add a section on the training of the ministers who serve the Spiritual/Independent Churches (the

---

7 Two very large Roman Catholic Seminaries in Nigeria have not been included: SS Peter and Paul at Ibadan and Bigard at Enugu. SS Peter and Paul is run by the SMA and since SMA training has been studied in Ghana it was felt that a second SMA study would only end in an unnecessary repetition of policy.
Bigard Seminary, Enugu, is the largest Seminary in Africa. Its population has been in the region of 600 students. It is run by the Holy Ghost Fathers and its inclusion in this study is imperative. Unfortunately, however, I visited the institution in 1977 only to learn that all the relevant documents were lost during the Nigerian Civil War of the 1960's and that it was only in France or Ireland that I could have access to them. As time and funds could not permit my visit to either of these places, I have to omit my visit to either of these places. I have to omit the Bigard Seminary history reluctantly and painfully. It is hoped that its inclusion in a later edition may be made possible.

Sects).⁸ The information might, perhaps, have thrown more light on the kind of approach the older churches should adopt regarding the anticipated reformation. But owing to lack of space this theme has been hopefully relegated to a future researcher.

It will also be noticed that I have omitted the actual histories of the missions because they have been dealt with in another volume. So also, the "CALL" of the prospective candidates has been omitted because Sundkler has dealt with the various factors which have been prompting men to offer themselves for the Ministry.⁹

Finally, the criticism of the content and relevance of the various seminary programmes has been deferred towards the final chapters in order to avoid unnecessary repetition in the historical sections.

The most important fact which has emerged from the preceding paragraphs is that in Independent West Africa, indigenous, social, religious and cultural practices can no longer be brushed aside as pagan without sympathetic and objective understanding of the vital role they play in African behaviour.¹⁰ As it is of primary importance that the Clergy should be made aware of this fact and be educated to appreciate its implications for the future of the Church in West Africa, Chapter 1 of this book will discuss very briefly, the basic indigenous philosophy which has determined these practices.

In dealing with the historical sections I have drawn almost exclusively on unpublished materials such as synod Minutes, Church and Seminary Annual Reports, Seminary Diaries or Log Books, reminiscences collected from a few of the past students either orally or through letters and a few unpublished Ph.D. and S.T.M. theses.

The books, pamphlets, periodicals and newspapers consulted were valuable in either throwing more light on aspects of the investigation which were not explicit from the unpublished materials or as means whereby the problems of ministerial training in West Africa were compared with similar problems in other countries.

An examination of the footnotes and the Bibliography will reveal the extent of the sources consulted. It will also disclose my indebtedness and acknowledgment to the numerous archivists, librarians, seminary students, Principals or Rectors of Theological Institutions, colleagues and friends who in their several ways have assisted me in writing this book. I must, however, mention a few names. These are: the Archbishop of Cape Coast, the Most Rev. Kodwo Amissah, for permitting me to use the Roman Catholic records in the Archbishop's House, Cape Coast, to visit the

---

8 The term Spiritual or Independent Churches or the Sects is used in describing Churches which have broken away from the Missionary churches in Africa and are controlled by African leaders Independent of the parent denomination.
9 Bengt Sundkler, *The Christian Ministry in Africa*, (London, 1960), Chapter 1.
10 Searle Bates, et. al., *Survey of the Training of the Ministry in Africa* Part II, (London, 1954), p. 5.

two Roman Catholic Seminaries at Pedu and Amisano near Cape Coast and St. Victor's at Tamale; the Rev. Paul Wiegrabe, North Bremen Mission, Bremen, Western Germany, who helped me with the translation of the relevant documents written in German; the Rev. Fr. Anastasius Odaye Dogli, Mr. S. K. Motte and Dr. E. Amu formerly of the Institute of African Studies, University of Ghana, Legon, who freely supplied on request, certain missing links in the Roman Catholic and Presbyterian training. My thanks are due also to the Rev. Professor C. W. Dugmore, Department of Ecclesiastical History, King's College London, who directed my course and gave me useful advice; to Dr. J. R. Gray and Dr. H. Fisher of the History Department, School of Oriental and African Studies, London, who in 1968, gave me the opportunity to discuss the preliminary tentative outline with their M. A. Area Studies Class who gave me useful suggestions, to the Nigerian Baptist Theological Seminary Ogbomosho for its invaluable and generous co-operation, to Mrs. H. E. Thomas, the wife of a former Principal of Trinity College, Kumasi, who read some of the chapters and made valuable criticisms, and to Mr. Frederick Tweneboa-Koduah and other typists who, with great care and efficiency typed the revised manuscript for publication, often calling my attention to "slips" here and there in the draft. All mistakes are, however, mine and mine alone.

My researches were originally financed for two years by the Theological Education Fund, 13 London Road, Bromley, Kent, England which awarded me a generous grant including my travel expenses to study archives in Ghana, Rome, Basel and Bremen. The University of Cape Coast provided further grants which enabled me to expand the original work. To them, also, as well as Emeritus Professor C. G. Baëta who wrote the Foreword, I am grateful. Then, last but not the least, I am grately indebted to my wife whose peaceable disposition, encouragement and sacrifice enabled me to work in an atmosphere of contentment.

This book has grown out of my Ph.D. Thesis for the University of London in 1969. For publication purposes, I have revised and expanded the original material: "The Training of Christian African Ministers in Ghana: 1842-1965", to cover West Africa. This explains why most of the examples given have Ghanaian bias. To make the reading easy, I have also shortened the length of some of the original chapters by dividing them into more than one chapter. The original thesis has not, however, suffered any serious mutilation. 1965 ought to have been the upper limit but for the Baptist Training where the more appropriate point of stop is 1970.

Religious Studies Department
University of Cape Coast,
Ghana
4th December, 1982.

John Kofi Agbeti

CHAPTER ONE

INTRODUCTION: SETTING THE SCENE

West Africa, during the colonial period was partitioned among the British and the French especially after World War I. This study is limited to the so-called four former British sister colonies: the Gambia, Sierra Leone, the Gold Coast (now Ghana) and Nigeria. It would have been more comprehensive to include the French speaking countries; but that would have demanded more time and money which the author at the time of the researches did not have. It would be advantageous if such a historical study of Theological Education is carried out in the French speaking countries of West Africa also. Detailed regional studies of this kind would enable future researchers to co-ordinate a more comprehensive and accurate account of Theological Education comprising the whole of Africa.

At the beginning of the period of this enquiry, that is, by 1842, West Africa had not then been demarcated into the distinct colonial political divisions mentioned above. But the traditional linguistic divisions had been in existence together with the traditional political structures such as chieftaincy, councils of elders, village and clan headmen etc.

Above all, the people of West Africa had their own religious beliefs and practices before the advent of Europeans. These traditional beliefs and practices had been named variously by Europeans as: fetishism, idolatry, superstition, heathenism, paganism, animism, etc. It is irrelevant for our purpose here to debate whether or not these terms describe adequately the traditional religion. Suffice it to note that, irrespective of names, the nature and content of the beliefs and practices sprang from the world view indigenous to the people.

Jean Capart, an Egyptologist, wrote that: "the concept of *LIFE* alone allows the Egyptian religion to be assessed at its full worth. . . ."[1] There is, a good amount of truth in this statement, not only for Egypt, but also for Africa and West Africa in particular. Some West Africans, literates and illiterates, Christians and non-Christians, adults and young people, sometimes wear on their fingers "gatrogakpara" (a ring locally made of copper or/and black iron); sometimes "ti" (a black powder produced by traditional African doctors) is injected into the blood system of some people. When people behave as mentioned above they do so because they believe that the objects possess life-saying potency - a potency that can solve the problems of *Life*: e.g. misfortunes, sickness, barrenness, destruction, death and so on. This concern for *LIFE*, pulsating life, is the foundation upon which

---
1 Placide Tempels, *Bantu Philosophy* trans. (Paris, 1959), p. 26, Fn. 2, par. 2.

the indigenous world view or philosophy of Africans has rested from time immemorial.

In a nutshell the world view is a belief that the universe, brought into being by a Creator, comprises both supernatural and material spheres. The most penetrating feature of this *INDIGENOUS* world view is the concept that all the *beings* or forces in the universe interact one with another in such a way as to make human existence meaningful only within the group. All members of the family, the clan, the village and the town are individually and severally one another's keepers. They exist because they belong to groups.

Although these *beings* or forces are thought of as units or individuals, standing by themselves, each being a *force* apart, they have always interacted one with another. The world's forces are believed to be like a spider's web. If one single thread vibrates the whole network of the web is shaken. For example, the death of one person in a family affects the whole family, the whole clan, the whole village: sheep are slaughtered, crops in the farm are used during the funeral celebrations and so on. So also, birth, marriage etc. of a single *being* interacts with other beings. It is true that families, clans and tribes are composed of individuals; but the individual's "life is lived in a social context, within the culture that his group has built up throughout its existence; his religious beliefs and practices are a part of the complex network of social relations which make up his total life".[2]

Nothing can break this group solidarity; not even death; an unbroken link exists between the dead, the living and the yet unborn. It is this concept of the existence and the perpetual interaction of beings and its impingement on the *group* life and action that has, from the very early days, determined the religious and social life of West Africans.

For practical purposes the world view, which has determined the group life of the people, may be graphically described as in diagram on page 3.[3]

This pictorial summary is self-explanatory. At the centre of the Universe: Mawu (Ewe) - the Supreme Being - God; next in rank - the ancestors; then the other spiritual beings followed by the visible earth with its own goddess and forces.

---

2 Christian Council of the Gold Coast, *Christianity and African Culture* (Accra, 1955), p. 3. (hereafter cited as CCGC, *Christianity and African Culture.*
3 E.G. Parrinder, *African Traditional Religion* (London, 1962), pp. 24-25, represents the relationship between these beings by a triangle. Parrinder says, "at the apex [of the triangle] is the sky, which symbolizes the Supreme Power from whom all life flows and to whom all returns". It is precisely because the Supreme Power is the source of life, that it is more appropriate to describe him as the centre of the universe around which all beings exist. Fr. Tempels confirms that "Nothing moves in this universe of forces [beings] without influencing other forces by its movement. The world of forces is held like a spider's web of which no single thread can be caused to vibrate without shaking the whole network". Temples, *op. cit.*, p. 41. Although Ghanaians and Africans think of the Supreme Being as dwelling somewhere behind the skies, even though he is thought of as *Deus incertus et remotus*, he is also thought of as the very centre, but not just the apex of LIFE: "He gives existence, power of survival and of increase, to other forces." Tempels, *loc. cit.*

INTRODUCTION: SETTING THE SCENE

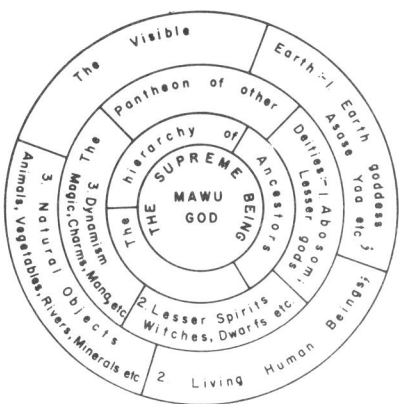

The Supreme Being, *Mawu* or God, the highest being in the hierarchy is the one who increases and diminishes life because he is the creator and the source of life. His attributes and the very lofty ideas Africans have had about Him, before the coming of the missionaries, have been extensively discussed elsewhere[4] and I need not repeat them here.

The Ancestors were the first fathers and founders of the various clans or tribes. After death, they became:

> The first to whom the Supreme Being communicated his vital force with the power of exercising their influence on posterity. [Thus] they become the most important chain binding men to the Supreme Being. They became spiritualized beings belonging to a higher hierarchy than the recent dead.[5]

In virtue of their new spiritualized status the ancestors have been profusely reverenced in West Africa, although they have neither been classified as gods nor as lesser spirits.[6] This latter point is crucial, because ancestor reverence or worship has often been vehemently condemned by the missionaries and the African ministers, on the ground that the ancestors are prayed to as gods,[7] so that some sections of the population, including some Christians, have been regarding the African ministers as isolated from vital cultural issues.

In fact, ancestor reverence has persisted in spite of ecclesiastical opposition because of the concern for *Life*. As it is believed that the ancestors or

---

4 Consult the bibiliography at the end of this book for the appropriate books dealing with the African and West African traditional religions and with the African World View or Philosophy. Other relevant bibliographies regarding African Ideas about God will be found in each of the relevant books listed.
5 J.K. Agbeti, "Missionary Enterprise, Education and Nationhood in Ghana since 1828". Unpublished Master's Thesis. New Haven, U.S.A., Yale Divinity School, 1967.
6 Temples, *op. cit.*, p. 42, especially fn.1.
7 CCGC., *op. cit.*, pp. 17-23.

the dead possess deeper and superior knowledge of *Life* it is also believed that they have the power to replenish and enhance the *Life* of the living, on condition that the living maintain satisfactorily the group solidarity. When the living eat, they should give some of the food to the dead; when they drink wine, some should be poured down for the dead. Failure in these duties is believed to incur the displeasure of the dead. Indeed, it has been believed that misfortunes, such as barrenness, drought, famine, sickness, death, in short, most diminutions of life are the consequences of displeasing the ancestors. The aversion of this displeasure of the dead or of the inimical forces is at the root of most of the social practices.

For example, when a person dies the living weep and cry bitterly; they spend a long time mourning; they are extravagant during funeral celebrations. The Church has been counselling thrift in this matter without much success. The reason is evident: the living do not want to incur the displeasure of the dead by mourning in an unsanctioned manner.

As the supernatural universe has a hierarchy of beings so also the living are in a hierarchy of progeniture. The eldest of the clan or family is the sustainer of life; he is the link between the ancestors and their living descendants. Thus, the chief, the head of a state, or a family elder is the true link between his subjects and their ancestors.

The most important symbol from which a chief derives the traditional sanction for his authority is, in some West African countries, the stool the throne, "on which the father, the grand old man of the family or tribe, sat in his life time to deal wisdom and justice to the members thereof".[8] Thus, the *Stool* is the sacred source of the Chief's power and the symbol which invokes in a people of the same lineage "a desire to perpetuate the memory of the departed father or ancestor".[9] According to Dr. Busia, in Ghana, "it is the Stool that symbolizes the people's identity, unity and continuity, and it is these sentiments that are kept alive by the festivals and rites associated with them".[10]

In all the royal festivals the ancestors are revered for the reasons already given above. Offerings of food and drinks are given to them. During the pouring of libation, the Supreme Being, the Earth Goddess and the most powerful of the ancestors are invoked, and prayers offered to them while the drink is poured bit by bit on the ground.[11]

It is not only during the royal annual festivals that ancestor worship or

---

8 J.B. Danquah, *The Akim Abuakwa Handbook* (London, 1928) p. 85.
9 *Loc. cit.*
10 K.A. Busia, *The Position of the Chief in the Modern Political System of Ashanti* (London, 1951), p. 22
11 See Christian Gaba, "Anlō Traditional Religion: a Study of the 'Anlō' traditional believer's conception of and communion with the 'Holy' ". Unpublished Ph.D. Thesis, London, King's College, 1965, Appendix B, where 'Anlō' traditional prayers offered to the Dead have been preserved. On the whole question of 'Libation' see also J.K. Amissah et. al., *Libation* (Cape Coast, 1958).

reverence is practised. The other occasions calling for the custom include funerals, outdooring and naming of a new-born baby, puberty and marriage ceremonies and worship at a local shrine. Libation is poured on all these occasions because by doing so, the *living* try to preserve "and perpetuate contact between themselves and the spiritual being and powers whose assistance is so vital for the maintenance of exuberant life on this earth".[12]

Next in the hierarchy of forces is the Pantheon of other Deities. Dr. G. Parrinder has done extensive work on these deities and we need not spend much time on them here.[13] It is sufficient to note that as they are thought of as inimical and whimsical in their interaction with the *living*, they are appeased with sacrifices. In order that the sacrifices may be offered to the satisfaction of the deities, sacred specialists, priests and priestesses are trained to take charge of the various shrines where prayers and sacrifices are offered. The sacred specialists are like liaison officers between the living and the lesser gods; through them the gods give promises, make demands, issue threats and show either anger or displeasure as the circumstances may demand.[14]

Finally, the lowest in the hierarchy of forces is the visible universe - the Earth. In Ghana, the Twi call her "Asase Yaa" and the Fanti "Asase Efua". Yaa is the name given to females born on Thursday, and Efua, females born on Friday. Thus Thursdays or Fridays are sacred to the Earth Deity, and no farming should be done on these days, or on any other day of the week regarded as sacred to the Earth Goddess by other tribes. Apart from this agricultural taboo, the Earth Goddess is also believed to abhor "wanton spilling of human blood on her, incestuous practices, burying a dead pregnant woman without autopsy to extract the unborn babe from her womb and, above all, sexual relations in the bush".[15] As she is likened to a fertile woman she is believed to be the supplier of food, rivers, water, trees, minerals, in short, all vegetables and creatures that make human life worth living. In order to get the best out of her fecundity, the taboos should be

---

12 Agbeti, *op. cit.*, p. 16.
13 Consult the bibliography at the end of this book.
14 M.J. Field, *Search for Security: an Ethno-psychiatric Study of Rural Ghana* (London, 1960), pp. 55-86. Miss Field, here, describes how the lesser deities possess the sacred specialists in the shrines. It is only after the spirit of the deity has entered the priest that the specialist will be able to communicate the deity's wishes to the supplicants. This belief in spirit possession is not peculiar to Ghana alone. G.M. Carstairs, "A view from the shrine: the Rural Priests in West Africa and India", *Listener*, Vol. 65, 2nd March, 1961, p. 385, makes the point that the most important places people turn for help during times of suffering are "certain rural shrines where the spirit of the 'obosom' or local deity would enter into the body of the priest of the shrine and through his agency would bestow magical protection on the supplicants who come before him".
15 Peter Sarpong, "Traditional Beliefs", *Ghana Association of Teachers of Religious Knowledge* (GATRK), *Annual Report*, 1966, p. 3. Sarpong does not tell us why these acts are hateful to the Earth Goddess. But what is relevant here is that the taboos should be scrupulously kept to avoid the displeasure of the goddess and the diminution of life that may result from breaking them.

scrupulously obeyed by all. One person's disobedience may result in the diminution of life for all.

In this brief sketch of West African world view, it is only the most recalcitrant beliefs and practices which defy the Churches' censure that have been dealt with. The other aspects of the indigenous philosophy such as the concepts of morality, ethics, wisdom and so on have been discussed in the relevant books included in the bibliography.

What we have said so far is that West Africans, and for that matter, indigenous Africans, centre their beliefs and practices around *life* - abundant life. LIFE derives from the Supreme Being who created the world and is the centre of the universe of supernatural and terrestrial beings. These beings interact with people to produce a world order which enables *Man* to realize the fulness of *life*. Thus, the end of all the social, religious and cultural practices is the attainment of affluent life. To achieve this end, certain customary duties are not only expedient but also obligatory. For example, priests and shrines are visited to get magical protection; "gatrogakpara" (a magical ring), charms and amulets are worn to ward off misfortunes; traditional African doctors are consulted to get protection against inimical forces such as witches; a man may be married to more than one woman to beget many children who are looked upon as the most potent evidence of prosperity as illustrated by the following adage: "vi vǫ nyo mu atifu gā". (Ewe, meaning, a bad child is more precious than wealth.) Again, funeral, puberty, and marriage customs, annual festivals and social injunctions are scrupulously kept in order to avert the displeasure of the ancestors. Above all, the ancestors should never be forgotten; when the LIVING eat they should throw some of the food on the ground for them, when they drink they should pour some of the substance drunk (water or wine) to the ancestors.

There are some points of contact between this indigenous world view and the Christian Faith. Common to both are the beliefs: in God, the Creator and centre of the world, in a supernatural and temporal universe, in life after death, in principalities and powers (the inimical and whimsical forces), in the conern for LIFE and belief in group action and solidarity as desirable human behaviour (cf. fellowship of Christians). It does not mean, however, that these indigenous beliefs are sufficient in themselves to explain the purpose of the Supreme Being for the world.

This was the cultural milieu into which the missionaries came, planted Christianity and trained African ministers to assist them in converting the traditional people. The training began as soon as the missionaries had the opportunity. For example, the Basel Mission came in 1828 and in 1843 a seminary was opened at Christiansborg, Osu, for the purpose of training local personnel to assist the missionaries even though no Africans had yet been baptized; the Wesleyan Methodist Mission followed in 1835 and in 1838, two young men were under training in the manse as prospective candidates for the ministry; similarly the Bremen Mission entering the field in 1847 started a seminary in 1864. So also when the others came towards the end of the nineteenth century and the English Church Mission at the beginning of the twentieth century, they did not hestitate to train Africans as helpers.

There was no evidence in the documents, consulted for this study to show that the Missionaries had been motivated by Henry Venn's three-self principles: self-government, self-support and self-extension, which directed that:

> ... the arrangements which [might] be made in the missions should from the first have references to the ultimate settlement of the native Church upon the ecclesiastical basis of an indigenous episcopate, independent of foreign aid or superintendence.[16]

The impressions given by the documents showed rather that the need to raise a "native agency"[16] arose in the nineteenth century as a result of the fatal experiences the Missions had suffered. For example, those which started training African personnel between 1842 and 1864, had been compelled to do so mainly because of the constant death of the missionaries in the field.[17] The disaster brought it home to them "that the only hope for really permanent results and continuous development lay in the training of an adequate staff of "African helpers",[18] and the emphasis was on "helpers".

The African assistants were entrusted mainly with evangelical work while the missionaries monoplised the administration and remained the supervisors. Because the work entrusted to the helpers was considered important, great care was exercised in selecting the men for it.

Laid down methods of selection were used by the missions, under discussion, in recruiting their ordinands though there were variations from country to country depending mainly upon the local needs. So in Ghana, for example, with the Wesleyan Mission, any "one who [had] within him a feeling of divine compulsion to share the glory of the Christian Gospel with others through the Ministry rather than through any other vocation",[19] and voluntarily offered himself to the Church for training became subjected to certain tests: he must have taken a prescribed course in lay or local preaching and must have served satisfactorily as an accredited lay preacher for at least one year; the genuineness of his call to the ministry should have

---

16 William Knight, *The Missionary Secretariat of Henry Venn* (London, 1982), p. 417 cited by J. F. A. Ajayi, *Christian Missions in Nigeria 1841-1891: the Making of a New Elite* (London, 1965), p. 175.
17 Here the phrase "native agency" is used in its widest sense to include ministers, teachers, evangelists, catechists and other lay-workers who are essential to the complete life of the Church in carrying out the spiritual requirements and effective work of conversion.
18 Noel Smith, *The Presbyterian Church of Ghana, 1835-1960* (Accra, 1966), Appendix II, p. 286. A.E. Southon, *Gold Coast Methodism: the First Hundred Years, 1835-1935 (Cape Coast, n.d.)*, pp. 37-51, and Paul Wiegrabe, *Ewe Kristo Hame Nutinya* (St. Louis, U. S.A., 1936), pp. 1-6.
19 Southon, *op. cit.*, p. 74.

been confirmed by his superintendent minister, the Leaders' Meeting of his local congregation and the Quarterly Meeting of the Circuit in which he had been residing at least during the year. After this his academic standard was tested by a written examination consisting of questions on Bible Knowledge, English, Arithmetic, General Knowledge and an Essay in the candidate's vernacular - this latter paper was not required from candidates who had qualified for University studies or post-graduate work. The result of this examination and the recommendations of the candidate's local minister and local meetings were considered by the candidates' committee of six Ministers of the Church. If he was successful this committee recommended that he should proceed to the next series of tests comprising: preaching a sermon (based on a text selected by himself) in his own vernacular before a panel of three ordianed ministers of the Church; submitting a written sermon and a list of books he had read (theological and general) to the Secretary for candidates, taking a second written examination in Christian Doctrine and English. The results of these tests were submitted to the Synod Committee appointed to deal with candidates. This Committee examined the student orally of doctrinal, ethical, social, theological and general matters and gave marks. The committee then voted on the candidate and if he won the majority vote he appeared before the Synod, gave an account of his Christian experience and answered questions that any member of Synod might ask. Finally, Synod voted on him in his absence and if the vote was in his favour, he was sent to a theological college for training.

As for the Presbyterian Church of Ghana, they selected their ministerial candidates from among teacher-catechists (certificated teachers who had successfully completed a prescribed course in theology at the training college) and from trained evangelists (elementary school pupils who had had two-year evangelistic training at a Presbyterian Seminary for training evangelists). A member of either of these categories of candidates who felt himself called to the ministry communicated his desire to his District Pastor in writing. He was then orally examined by his Pastor and his local Session (Meeting) who forwarded the written application with their comments (if they were convinced of the genuineness of the call) to the Presbyterial Committee.[20] This Committee "sounded" (interviewed) the candidate: he was thoroughly questioned about his education, life and work, special interests, marriage and family life, temperament, social standing, financial stability, interest in evangelism, participation in Church and Church organisation programmes and his personal experience of God. The findings of the committee with their candid comments about the candidate's applica-

---

20 Trinity College, "Memorandum on the Advisability of Establishing a Theological Faculty in connection with the Proposed West African University. I. Statement on the Methodist Approach to the Training of the Ministry and the Present Practice." Mimeographed. Oversight Committee File, 1940-1958.

tion were then forwarded to the Synod Committee, who authorised another "sounding" by the Moderator or his deputy or deputies. His report was sent to the Synod Committee or to the Synod Committee Executive who accepted or rejected the candidate.

Before 1943, candidates who had been accepted were formally called or written to by the synod and if they finally accepted the call, a place and date were fixed for the ordination. But since 1943, the accepted candidates have normally been sent to Trinity College, Ghana, for organised ministerial training.

In the case of the Evangelical Presbyterian Church two methods were used. In the first instance, all teacher-catechists were subjected to examinations while they were teaching. On leaving the seminary a student was employed as teacher class II. After two years' teaching experience he had to sit for a qualifying examination and he was promoted teacher class I when successful. After ten years' satisfactory service as teacher class I, when no disciplinary action had been taken against him, he became eligible to take the catechists' qualifying examination conducted by a speical Examination Board comprising: the Chairman of the local Missionary Board or his representative, the Principal and two senior African members of staff of the seminary. Those who passed the examination were recommended to the Home Committee who appointed them as Catechists to take charge of schools and congregations as vacancies arose. From among them, those "who by faithfulness in their duties, zeal and general usefulness during a number of years [distinguished] themselves and served to the perfect satisfaction of congregations and missionaries [might] on the proposal of the majority of the District Conference and the Local Committee, be mentioned to the Home Committee and recommended to them for the ministry".[21] After World War I this method of selection for ordination was modified along the lines which the Presbyterian Church of the Gold Coast has been following since 1943.[22]

As regards the Anglican Mission, any member of the Church who felt called to the priesthood wrote to the Bishop or a member of the Ordinands Advisory Committee asking that he might be considered for acceptance as a prospective candidate. He would then be asked to complete an official application form giving particulars of his marital and academic status and mentioning three priests as referees, of whom one should normally be the parish priest of his local congregation. Upon the contents of the application form and the reports of the referees, the committee rejected or accepted the candidate. The factors which disqualified applicants were poor education and improper marriage. A rejected candidate was usually encouraged by the Committee "to continue his studies or put his marriage in

---

21 The Presbyterian Church of Ghana, "The Holy Ministry", mimeographed (Accra, n.d.).
22 Basel Mission Archives, "Steps Towards Ordination," File No. 69.

order",[23] and a successful candidate was sent to a Theological Training College. So also the Baptists had their peculiar methods of selecting their candidates for the ordianed ministry.

With the Roman Catholics, Priests and Pastors selected from among primary school pupils, "boys who gave signs of an ecclesiastical vocation",[24] and sent them to a minor seminary, "to shield them from worldly contagion",[25] trained them in the rudiments of letters, fostered piety in them and protected the seed of their divine vocation.[26] From the minor seminary (i.e. at the end of their secondary school studies) those who had not lost the desire of becoming priests proceeded to a major seminary, where they were trained for the priesthood.

The subsequent chapters will now survey the history of the training which the selected candidates received in their various denominational or united theological institutions from 1842 to 1970.

---

23 E.P. Church, File CH/10, No. Since 1943, catechists in the Presbyterian Churches (P.C.G. and E.P.C.) "who have served the Church for some time, but because of age or some other limitations are not permitted to attend Trinity College, may, upon recommendation by Synod Committee, attend a pre-ordination course at the [evangelists' training, seminaries]" for one academic year.
24 A Nickles, "Recruitment and Training for the Anglican Ministry in Ghana", mimeographed (Accra, n.d.), in the possession of the Rev. Danquah, Trinity College, Legon, Ghana.
25 Canon Law 1353.
26 *Loc. cit.*
27 *Loc. cit.*

CHAPTER TWO

WESLEYAN METHODIST MISSION TRAINING
1842-1942

The first phase of how the Methodist Church, Ghana started and consolidated the training of its African ministers manifests a fluctuating and uncertain story. The history began in 1842 when a Theological institute was opened in Akrah[1] and it ended in 1942 when the students for the ministry in training at Wesley College, Kumasi, were removed from Wesley College to join hands with Presbyterian ministerial students in a new united Theological College. Prior to 1842, however, preliminary preparations had been made towards the establishment of an institution.

In March 1838, Thomas Birch Freeman selected the pioneer and prospective African candidates for the ministry. They were two: William deGraft and John Martin, "excellent young men, who had stirling piety" and who felt themselves "called by God the Holy Spirit to preach the Gospel to their country men".[2] They had both received a good and plain education at the Cape Coast Castle school.[3] Freeman transferred them from the local community and took them into the Mission House, in order to keep them "entirely beyond the reach of demoralizing influences",[4] and to shelter them from contact with the townspeople until they were capable of taking care of themselves. In pursuit of his principles of separation Freeman did not permit them any communication with the town, except that he sent them on Sundays "to teach in a Sunday school of about fifty children and adults".[5] During the week the students were kept busy with their books. It is not clear what they actually studied in the Mission House; but after three months of their stay there, it became evident that William deGraft had made tremendous progress and this, apparently, moved the quarterly meeting held on 11th June, 1838, at eleven o'clock in the morning, "to recommend to the Missionary Committee that William deGraft should be accepted as candidate for the ministry".[6] But the training of African ministers in the manse was not Freeman's ambition. His ultimate aspiration was

---

1 The terms *Akrah* and *Accra* are used interchangeably in this study.
2 Thomas B. Freeman, "Extract of a letter from the Rev. Thomas Birch Freeman dated Cape Coast Castle, August 20th 1838", MMS, *Missionary Notices,* IX, 1838-1841, pp. 39-40 F.L. Bartels, *The Roots of Ghana Methodism* (Cambridge, 1965), p. 31. The young men had belonged to the Bible group by whose initiative Methodism came to Ghana. Both were among the Foundation Class Leaders of Cape Coast.
3 For the history of this school see: C.G. Wise, *A History of Education in British West Africa* (London, 1956).
4 Bartels, *op. cit.*, p. 33.
5 Bartels, *loc. cit.*
6 *Ibid.*, p. 32

the establishment of a Theological Training Institution. But in June 1838, the project was too premature because death had depleted the missionary staff, leaving Freeman practically alone on the field.[7] The scheme had to wait until reinforcements arrived.

Meanwhile, Freeman proposed to the Missionary Committee that they should make arrangements for the two young man to visit England. It was not a vain proposition, for, in those days, (even as in these present days) people laid stress on visits to England. They paid the deepest attention to people who had been to England "while if one who had never left the shores of Guinea[8] attempted to reason with them, they would either turn away from him in disgust, or insultingly say: 'What can you know about it? You have never been to England'."[9] The main purpose of the visit was not, however, only to boost the prestige of the African prospective candidates, but also to raise funds for the progress of the work in the Gold Coast.

As it was not financially possible for Freeman to travel with the two young men to England at the same time, he went, in 1840, with William deGraft alone. deGraft justified the confidence placed in him by leaving an indelible impression on his British audience.[10]

Resulting from the visit, about £5,000 (¢10,000) was raised,[11] to enable the Missionary Committee to meet the expenses of sending out six missionaries to supply the required reinforcement. deGraft was received, also, into the service of the Wesleyan Methodist Missionary Society as a regular and accredited African teacher, and Freeman himself, was authorized to employ several other Christian "Natives" as subordinate agents in the great work.[12]

The immediate questions which come to mind in connection with the third result concern, first of all, how to recruit the several Christian "Natives" since the Methodist work on the Coast was, in 1840, barely five years old; but this was no problem to Freeman. He knew that the Castle School was a potent source of supply of such Christian young men. He had inspected that school before his visit to England in 1840. He noted with satisfaction the religious and academic progress of the pupils and stated, in concluding his report, that:

> I cannot but express the grateful satisfaction which I always feel, when I reflect on the facilities with which the school has furnished us in carrying on, under God, the great work of evangelizing this important part of the African Continent. But for this school, we should, in all probability, have found ourselves in the midst of a mass of ignorant people from whence (sic) we could have selected non to interpret for us those ground truths of Christianity which are

---

7 Southon, *Gold Coast Methodism*, Chapters IV and V.
8 Guinea was the term used for the West Coast of Africa from the Senegal to the Cameroun.
9 Freeman, *op. cit.*, p. 40.
10 *The Gold Coast Aborigines* (Cape Coast), 18:2:1899.
11 The actual sum was £4,650. Bartels, *op. cit.*, p. 48.
12 Wesleyan Methodist Missionary Society, *Report*, Vol. VIII (1841-1843), p. 82.

calculated to enlighten and bless the world—none to assist us in teaching the rising generation the rudiments of a religious education.[13]

The other question concerns how the funds for the payment of the several agents' stipends might be raised. Freeman does not tell us the salary scale of the agents that might be employed nor does he tell us the source of the income. But he was confident that the payment of the agents would not be a problem either, because he believed that the Africans did not need as much money as the European missionaries. He believed that way, for, he was convinced that since the African missionaries were used to the climate and the food of the land it would not be as expensive to employ them as it would be to employ foreigners from Europe.[14]

Thus with these assets accruing from the visit to England: the £4,650 (¢9,300) to be exact, the five new missionaries[15] and the authority to develop a "native agency", Freeman and deGraft left England on 10th December 1840, together with Mrs. Lucinder Freeman and the five new missionaries, the Rev. and Mrs. Thompson Hesk, the Rev. and Mrs. Samuel Annesley Shipman and the Revs. John Watson, Charles Walden and William Thackwray. They landed at Cape Coast on Monday, 1st February, 1841.

In December, 1841, the Missionary Secretaries wrote the Committee's annual letter to the Gold Coast District Synod of 1842. It was an epoch making letter in respect of training of local personnel for the work of the Church. The letter instructed Freeman to establish without delay a school or Seminary "for the mental improvement of any young men, who exhibit any signs of a preaching talent, or who may be useful to their country men, after a course of elementary instruction in Theology, the English Language & c.,"[16] and that the young men might be under his charge except that, if his engagements were too numerous to prevent his attending to the students, then Samuel Shipman might take charge of the Seminary. Freeman decided to place the school under Shipman's charge not only because Freeman was too busy, but because Shipman had been stationed at Akrah and the Akrah mission house was very large and could provide more suitable accommodation for the Principal and students of the Institution than the Cape Coast mission house. Moreover, the Akrah society was very small and Shipman could devote more time to the teaching and efficient training of the students in addition to his normal pastoral duties.

---

13 T.B. Freeman, WMMS, *Report*, Vol. VII (1840), pp. 79-80.
   Cf. Freda Wolfson, *Pageant of Ghana* (London, 1958), p. 122 where the Revs. J.F. Schon and S.A. Crowther confirmed Freeman's impression of the Castle School at Cape Coast.
14 T.B. Freeman, MMS, *Missionary Notices*, IX, pp. 39-40.
15 The sixth missionary was not secured, thus five were sent. See Page 21 above and also Bartels, *op. cit.*, p. 48.
16 MMS, *Gold Coast District Minutes*, 1842, Box 1842-1866, Secretaries to the Gold Coast District Synod, Dec. 1841.
   cf. S.A. Shipman, *The Missionary Child* (London, 1842), p.108.

On March 2nd, 1842, about 9.00 p.m., Shipman arrived in Akrah from Cape Coast where he had been recovering his health. Without any delay he started the school envisaged by the Committee under the title: *The Akrah Theological Institution.*

The Institution was expressly designed for the training of "Native Agency."[17] But when it was opened, in March 1842, "no definite plan relative to the education of the young men and their personal expenses"[18] was made and Mr. Shipman was left almost entirely to his own judgment and discretion in the making of temporary arrangements for carrying out the views of the Committee. The temporary plans which Shipman adopted, both as to the method of instruction and expenditure, were so satisfactory that the Synod which met in May, three months after the opening of the Institution, accorded its high approbation in these words:

> We rejoice to state that the young men already in the Institution have, considering the circumstances under which they have been placed, made respectale progress in their studies.[19]

Although the beginning of the Institution was very modest, its progress within the first year was considerable. It was commenced with no official opening ceremonies; the first students were only three, William Hanson and John Ahoomah Solomon recruited by Freeman plus Francis Grant, the headteacher of the Accra Boys' School, who received lectures in the afternoons, and there was only one instructor. The roll gradually increased to six students during the year and "the proficiency which the six young men made, who were placed in the Institution, entirely under the care of Mr. Shipman, not only in their learning, but in their piety, was a wonder to all who knew them".[20] This was not a flattering comment when we consider the seriousness with which Mr. Shipman trained those pioneer students. He recorded in his Journal on 1st September, 1842 thus:

> My forenoons and afternoons are now pretty well occupied with the young men, who are improving, I believe, in their acquaintance with the English Language, grammar & c. and whom I am instructing, as I can, in the first principles of the doctrine of Christ.

The initial course of studies within the first three months of the Institution's life was:

9-10 a.m.	(a)	Spelling for all.
	(b)	2 pupils wrote copies.
	(c)	2 pupils—translation into Fante.
10-11 a.m.	(a)	2 elder ones wrote copies.
	(b)	2 younger ones had English Grammar and Arithmetic.

---

17 See note on "Native Agency" in Chapter 1, Footnote 17.
18 MMS, *Gold Coast District Synod Minutes*, 1842, Box 1842-1866.
19 *Ibid.*
20 Shipman, *op. cit.*, p. 117.
   Also cited by Bartels, *op cit.*, pp. 60-61

11 a.m.-12 noon	Reading the Scriptures.
2-4 p.m.	(a) The elder ones with the school master attended class. They first repeated English Grammar, then spent some time in parsing. This was followed by the reading of one of John Wesley's Sermons and the students asked questions.
	(b) The younger ones attended to the cleaning of the school.
	(c) The two elder ones, sensible and good young men acted as interpreters alternately in class.
Home Work	All the students took to school every morning exercises which they had written previously on their slates.[21]

The basic course of studies was gradually expanded. By the end of 1842 Geography was added to the general course and English Composition to the scheme pursued by the two senior pupils. The expansion continued, as we shall see later,[22] in a more copious manner in order to lay the foundation for a more thorough training of the agents of the Church.

Mr. Shipman was not, however, fortunate to see the further development of his school. On 2nd February, 1843, just when the Institution was eleven months old, Shipman died. He was succeeded by three other missionaries consecutively: the Rev. B. Watkins arrived in Akrah in 1843, but he died early in 1844; he was followed by the Rev. Timothy T. Greaves who arrived in Akrah on 3rd March, 1844; but "the Great Head of the Church has also seen fit to remove his servant from the sphere of usefulness to a world of spirits".[23]

These deaths might have been very disheartening, but the Committee in England was not dismayed. The fourth missionary, the Rev. John Martin was appointed to take charge of the Institution, then, with eight students in residence. He arrived in Akrah, in July 1845, and on July 7th, he paid a glowing tribute of praise to the students as follows:

> Great praise is due to the students in the Institution; with their conduct generally I am delighted. They are deligent in their studies, humble and zealous in the cause of Christ. One of them has translated into the Akrah language the Commandments with the responses of the Communion Service. They are read at the close of the school, the children responding in their own tongue.[24]

Mr. Martin did not, however, remain in Akrah for a long time. On 11th July 1845, he was transferred to Cape Coast to start a second Theological Institution for the Western section of the District. He was succeeded at Ak-

---

21 MMS, *Gold Coast District Synod Minutes*, 1842, Box 1842-1866.
22 See pages 27-28 of this book.
23 Shipman, *op. cit.*, p. 118.
24 MMS, *Missionary Notices*, Vol XI (1845-1847), p. 170.
25 Southon, *op. cit.*, p. 89.
   See also, MMS, *Missionary Notices*, Vol. XI, p. 71.

rah by Henry Wharton, who had arrived in the country on 23rd June 1845.

Although the Institution at Akrah was interrupted by the decease of the missionary tutors, the quality and behaviour of the students did not deteriorate. This impression was forcefully asserted by the Rev. Henry Wharton in his report to the 1846 Ghana District Synod in these words:

> With reference to the conduct of the young men, we can speak in terms of the highest praise. They have hitherto manifested a kind and respectful demeanour towards those who have been placed over them. Combined with a readiness of disposition to be instructed in those things which are intended to fit them for future usefulness in the Church. During the year two of the students have been removed from the Institution and are now sustaining subordinate offices[26] in the mission works. There are at present only five young men in the Institution, four of whom are acceptable Local Preachers and Interpreters.[27]

But Wharton too did not remain in charge of the Institution for any length.of time. In 1846 he was succeeded by the Rev. Edward Addison. He attended the Theological Institution during the day and in evening he went out to talk to large groups of people who used to gather around him in the streets and market places.[28] By Addison's time, however, the Institution was only a "little Theological Institution".[29]

That the Institution did not grow large may be due to the fact that the Instructors divided their attention between the congregation and the Institution. Thus, gradually, the Akrah Institution ceased to function because of poor numbers. Indeed, at the District Synod held on 18th January, 1847, the Akrah Annual Report on the Institution showed that there had been only three students on the roll during the year 1846. One of the three had been removed at the end of 1846 and employed as an Agent in a circuit. That is, at the beginning of 1847, there were only two students in residence at the Akrah Theological Institution. As it was hoped that the Institution would continue to prepare students to be a blessing to the Church and to the heathen in Western Africa,[30] the project was not suspended in spite of the poor roll. The Institution continued to struggle on until 1853, after which nothing is heard of it again in the annual reports to the District Synod. It seems that the project had died out in Akrah.

The Akrah Theological Institution existed for nearly 12 years (1842-1853). Its life was short; but its contribution justified its existence. As an Institution "expressly designed for the training of 'Native Agency'[31] it produced an efficient local nucleus, most of whom could do 'credit to an

---

26 These subordinate offices were not defined, but they seemed to represent the lay offices referred to in Chapter 1, Fn. 22.
27 MMS, *Gold Coast District Synod Minutes*, 1846, "Akrah Report," Box 1842-1866.
28 MMS, *Missionary Notices*, Vol. XI, p. 178.
29 *Loc. cit.*
30 MMS, *GCDSM*, 1847, Akrah Report, Box 1842-1866.
31 Shipman, *op. cit.*, p. 118.

English pulpit', and were willing to go anywhere 'to publish the glad tidings of Salvation'. "³² This might not be an exaggerated estimation when we examine, carefully, how the students of this embryo Institution were trained.

In the morning, between 9 and 10, they were made to translate English passages into Fante; this was followed by English Grammar and then Arithmetic. In the afternoon from two to four o'clock, Reading and Textual study: selected sermons from Wesley's Sermons were read—the instructor endeavouring to explain as plainly, familiarly and fully as possible—Methodist doctrines by answering students' queries and referring the students to the texts of scripture. Apart from these daily exercises weekly assignments were also given. The students were required to prepare two sermon outlines each week during their leisure hours and the instructor gave them, from his own library, several introductory books to guide them: for example, Watson's Conversations, Todd's students' Manual, Stoner's Life and Gregory's books.

In addition to the academic programme, there also existed a very well planned scheme for practical training. There were four services of worship of Sunday: at 7.00 a.m. the students took the service in the Fante Language; the second service began at 11.00 a.m. and it was conducted in English by the resident minister for the "respectable inhabitants"³³ and soldiers of the garrison. The third service was held at 3.00 p.m. and conducted by the minister in English and interpreted into Fante and occasionally into the Akrah Language by the students. The last Sunday activity was an evening service which the students organized at 7.00 p.m. in the Institution and was conducted in the Fante and Akrah Languages.

On week days the evenings were pretty well occupied. For example, on Monday there was a class meeting; Tuesday, preaching; Wednesday, class meeting conducted by the students; Thursday, night school conducted by the students and on Friday a prayer meeting.³⁴

The problem of recruiting adequate number of students for this pioneer Theological Institution did not deter the Gold Coast District Synod from making persistent efforts to promote efficient training of its African agents and ministers. The Akrah Institution ceased to exist but the project lived on in the *Cape Coast Training Institution.*

This Institution, as already hinted at above, was started by John Martin in 1845. On 5th December in the same year, he wrote a letter from the Cape Coast Castle to the Committee in Britain. An extract from that correspondence reads:

> We have now in this place an Institution of training native agents. The students at present are four in number. Their studies are Arithmetic, English Grammar, History, Geography and Theology. With them I spend three or four hours every day, when health will permit.³⁵

---

32 *Loc. cit.*
33 The Phrase was not defined. Perhaps literates were meant.
34 Bartels, *op. cit.*, Appendix B, p. 350.
35 MMS, *Missionary Notices*, Vol. XI, p. 71.

It is not clear what happened to this School after 1845. Apparently, the project did not make much progress because the statistical records do not include the name and roll of the Cape Coast Institution between 1846 and 1866.[36] It seems private training was given to the prospective candidates at Cape Coast until 1862 when W.E. Davies and J.P. Brown were sent to the Methodist Training School, at King Tom's Point, Sierra Leone, for the training of West African Methodist teachers and preachers.[37]

1867 was the turning point in the history of Methodist education and their training programme in the Gold Coast District. On March 6th of that year a letter was addressed to the Editor of the *African Times* in Lagos.[38] In that communication, the Wesleyan Missionaries were charged with neglect of their work, want of interest in the welfare of the people and oppressive exactions in the form of "contribution after contribution". The Synod held at Cape Coast on 8th February, 1868, denied the charges as "false and calumnious being utterly without foundation".

It was admitted, however, that the District had not been able to give its "Native Agents" so good a training as that which the Agents of the Church Missionaries received. The reason for this state of affairs, the Synod felt, was due to the fact that, though the ordinary schools belonging to the Wesleyan Methodist Church in the District compared favourably with similar schools belonging to other Missionary Societies on the Coast, "the Grammar schools belonging to the Church Missionary Society, and the large educational staff maintained, and the numerous and costly buildings erected by the Basel Missionary Society"[40] placed the Wesleyan Missionary Society, in that respect, at a disadvantage. The meeting decided that a normal school should be established for teacher and "native agency" training, "in which a higher class education might be given".[41] But there was no suitable man immediately available for the position of Master of such a school. It was, therefore, decided to turn to the West Indies or elsewhere for a man who should be both intellectually and constitutionally qualified to take charge of such an establishment. No action was, however, taken and in 1870 the need for such a higher school was reiterated.

The need was made more urgent when it was reported to Synod in February 1871 that Governor Usher had opened a superior school, not long ago, to be taught by a master from Sierra Leone and to be superintended

---

36 MMS, *GCDSM*, Cape Coast Reports, Box 1842-1866.
37 Bartels, *The Roots*, pp. 61-62 and 76-77.
   Bartels seems to be confused about the Accra Training Institution and the Cape Coast Institution. He gives the impression that the Accra Institution was closed "during 1861-2". He perhaps means the closing down of the Cape Coast "In-service training" he has referred to on p. 61, since the Accra Institution had been closed already in 1853.
38 At that time the Gold Coast and Lagos were administered together as the Gold Coast District.
39 MMS, *GCDSM*, 1868, Box 1867-79.
40 *Ibid.*
41 *Ibid.*

by the Colonial Chaplain. This threatened the District's educational work in two ways: first, whereas the Methodists had introduced a small fee of a penny per week, the tuition at the new school was free. Secondly, the Church felt that religious emphasis might be neglected in the Usher School. In view of this the Synod noted that:

> Although a superior school established by the Government, and conducted on liberal principles would be of some benefit, it would not in our opinion meet the wants of the District. We think it important that the rising generation of these settlements receive a decidedly religious training, which they would not do in such an establishment. What we want are schools under our own control. We regard it as a serious reflection on us as a body that among the only people whom we may be said to have entirely to ourselves we have no educational establishment beyond those of the elementary kind.[42]

The greatest problem that confronted the establishment of the proposed higher class school was the recruitment of the right type of teachers. There were academically qualified teachers who had applied to become teachers in the Methodist Elementary Schools, but "the brethren have repeatedly rejected the offers . . . on account of the absence of religious principles".[43] Those that had been employed because they were felt to be religiously suitable were not, in the majority of cases, adequate to the academic demand. Thus it was the more felt by Synod that by the establishment of a Higher School it was likely to build up a supply of a superior staff of teachers. Accordingly, at the Synod of 9th February, 1875, it was agreed that "four youths of a suitable age should be selected as early as practicable, two from the Western division[44] and sent to the High School at Sierra Leone to be trained to act, in future, either as masters or assistants in the proposed High Schools".[45] The proposal was immediately implemented and two students, Messrs. Kofi Assam and Ernest J. Hayford, left the Gold Coast in April 1875 for Sierra Leone.[46]

A year later, in April 1876, the proposed High School was opened at Cape Coast. Its aim was to give secondary education to young men, some of whom might later enter the Christian ministry. The pioneer students were seventeen in number, but by the end of the year the roll increased to twenty-eight boys. They were drafted from the elementary schools where the medium of instruction had been the vernacular. As a result, the students were "very deficient in their knowledge of English subjects".[47] Thus the first Headmaster, James Picot, gave them a good foundation by teaching them in the English subjects before they were introduced to the higher

---

42 *Ibid.*, 1871, Box 1867-79.
43 *Ibid.*, 1873, Box 1867-1879.
44 The District at that time was divided into Eastern (from Akrah to Lagos), and Western with Cape Coast as the seat of Administration.
45 MMS, *GCDSM*, 1875, Box 1867-79.
46 Bartels, *op. cit.*, p. 94.
47 MMS, *GCDSM*, 1877, Box 1867-1879.

branches of study. For example, during the first session all the scholars were instructed only in the most elementary subjects; but during the second session the first class was sufficiently advanced to begin studying geometry, mensuration, and physiology. At the end of the year they were examined and the examination results were so satisfactory that the Headmaster became convinced that the school would ultimately be a success.[48] Consequently, in June 1876, the two young men who had been sent to Sierra Leone to train as assistants for the new High School, were recalled to continue their studies at the Cape Coast School.

The school had the Normal and Theological Departments. The Theological students were, as a rule, among the Boarders. But as boarding arrangements had not been satisfactory the Synod resolved in 1879 "to reorganize the boarding system under the supervision of the resident native minister assisted by the Rev. Timothy Laing, a supernumerary and subject to the control of the Principal".[49]

James Picot had retired during the second year of the school's life and was succeeded by James Jenkins in 1879. It was under Jenkins that the new Boarding School was reorganized along the lines suggested by the Synod at the beginning of 1879. The boarders were classified as Ordinary and Special: the special students were the youths in training as Agents for the "Master's Work".[50] The roll in 1879, for the Day and Boarding Departments was 32, of which five were special students. Under the Rev. T.W. Winfield, the successor of Jenkins, the roll continued to increase because the people of the Colony were beginning to "appreciate the present advantages of the High School".[51]

The general increase of students in the School was also true of the special or mission students. There were 14 mission students in 1880 who were trained specifically as teachers and preachers. In the following year, however, the usual problem of lack of candidates for the mission work began to beset the Theological Department.[52] The other coastal towns were not enthusiastic in sending forth their children for training as mission agents, possibly because secular jobs were becoming more lucrative. In spite of this problem the Superintendent, the Rev. M.W. Mountford, was determined that the few who entered the institution should be trained thoroughly so that they might manifest to their neighbours the superiority which education could give.[53]

Nevertheless, in 1882 it seemed that the Government Education Act was going to arrest the danger of the Theological Department dying out

---

48 *Ibid.*, 1879, Box 1867-79.
49 *Ibid.*
50 *Ibid.*, 1880.
51 *Ibid.*, 1881, See also.
52 MMS, *GCDSM*, 1882; the general roll was 53 of which only eight boys were in the Mission Department.
53 *Ibid.*, 1882.

again as a result of poor numbers. In that year a new Government Education Act was passed.[54] By its terms, the Government was not only to participate financially in general education but also in the training of mission agents "provided they pass the Inspector's examination and sign an agreement to work either for us or for the Government for five years".[55]

Unfortunately, the bright attendant hopes of the Act were not eventually realised by the Church. The requirements of the Act made it imperative to recruit only maturer students who were somewhat advanced in education and to keep back those who had to start from the beginning, if justice was to be done to the Inspector's examination. But this was not practicable because there were no such maturer students available in sufficient numbers from whom future agents could be recruited for training under the new scheme. This was the case, for, parents used to remove their children from school prematurely and send them for employment in the commercial field, and this made it difficult for most of the boys to remain in training for three or four years.[56] As a result, the Mission could not benefit by the new Government Act.

The experiment whereby the Mission gave scholarships for the training of its agents was therefore continued.[57] In 1884 three boys, R. Attee, S. Hammond and E. Laing, were recruited. Attee and Laing were to "have merely their education given to them free of charge by the Mission, but their boarding fees would be borne by their friends in the town".[58] When these students completed their courses, the project of training agents seemed to have been discontinued once more, for, no reports appeared in the District Minutes on the Training Institution from 1886 until 1890. In 1891, however, the work was resumed and four students were reported to be in training at the Cape Coast Institution.[59] The Synod felt disappointed

---

54 D. Kimble, *Political History of Ghana: The Rise of Gold Coast Nationalism 1850-1928* (Oxford, 1963), p. 73.
55 MMS, *GCDSM*, 1883, Box 1880-1890.
56 See Chapters III and IV of this book.
   The Presbyterian Schools also suffered similarly. Although the Cape Coast Press welcomed the 1882 Education Ordinance, Kimble, *loc. cit.* it later condemned the Ordinance as worthless because no clause was added to make it compulsory for the pupils to remain in the schools for certain number of years. See *The Gold Coast Times* (Cape Coast), 9th September 1884, and *The Gold Coast Methodist* (Cape Coast), December 1886.
57 The experiment was begun in 1880 when three boys from Apollonia were given full scholarships. See MMS, *GCDSM*, 1883, Box 1880-1890.
58 *Ibid.*, 1884.
59 *Ibid.*, 1892, Schedule VI, Box 1891-1897.
   It seems that the secondary section was also closed down in 1889 owing to the lack of funds. Kimble, *Political History*, p. 85. It was also re-opened in 1891, and renamed the Collegiate School. At first it was controlled by the native gentlemen, J.W. deGraft Johnson Snr., John Sarbah, J.P. Brown and W.E. Pietersen, who re-opened it. The Principal then was the Rev. F. Egyir Asaam, *The Gold Coast Methodist Times*, No. 2 Vol. 1, 30:4:1894. In 1892, however, the Wesleyan Mission took over its control, and the Principal of the Theological Institution, the Rev. James Fletcher, became the Principal of the Secondary Section also in addition to his normal work as Chairman of the District.

in the paucity of the roll and, in consequence, the following intelligence was sent to the Missionary Committee in England by the Chairman of the Gold Coast District, the Rev. James Fletcher, who was also the principal of the High School and Training Institution:

> the Training Institution will be greater help to our future work when we have a greater number of young men in training. We might offer greater inducements to candidates but I very much fear that it would result in attracting young men who merely seek temporal benefits.[60]

In Addition to the paucity of numbers, the progress of the students in residence was not quite satisfactory. None of the four students scored an aggregate of 50% in their final examination.[61] This was attributed mainly to the sickness and consequent removal of two successive Principals.[62] In the following year, 1892, the three students in residence also made poor progress because their attention was divided between part-time teaching or work in the bookroom and their studies; moreover, the Principal was not able to devote himself entirely to his work.

Two factors were deemed necessary for improving the performance of the students: the recruitment of suitable students and of a full-time Principal entirely set aside for the training of Agents. These, it was hoped would make the Institution a splendid factor in the education of the rising Ministry.[63]

Hitherto students had been admitted into the Institution to train as Teachers and or Catechists or Ministers. But in 1894 this policy was revised and it was resolved at Synod "that only intending candidates for the Ministry be received into the Training Institution".[64] In accordance with the new policy two candidates, B. Appiah from Aburi Circuit and J.R. Addo from Accra Circuit, were received at the 1894 Synod. They studied the Catechism, Theology, English History, Geography, Grammar and Arithmetic. In the first year they were orally examined in all the subjects except in Arithmetic, where the Examination was written.

Their examination results in the second year, the final year of their training, make an interesting study. One of them was very good while the

---

60 MMS, *GCDSM*, 1892, *op. cit.*
61 *Ibid.*
62 *Ibid*
63 *Ibid.*, 1893.
64 *Ibid.*, 1894, Appendices: No. 21.
   It seems that the Synod decision was influenced by the new Education Ordinance of 1887 which replaced that of 1882. This new Ordinance provided for a department with a regular schedule of inspection which facilitated the keeping of continuous systematic records. Kimble, *loc. cit.* The impingement of these changes on the Theological Institution of Mfantisipim was that more attention was paid to the secondary section in order to satisfy the Government inspectors. As the Theological Institution was not qualified for Government Grants, the Mission was financially responsible for the students. But the financial burden would be greatly lessened, if the lay students were set free to join the secondary section where the Government gave grants-in-aid.

other was exceedingly incompetent. For instance, the examination marks and the examiner's remarks were pleasing in one case but entertaining in the other:

Student	Catechism	Theol.	Gram.	Geog.	Hist.	Arith.
A	80	75	93	86	100	50
B	24	5	36	19	0	0

The seriousness of B's incompetence was recorded by the examiner, William F. Somerville, in his 1895 report in the following words:

> Mr. B. is thoroughly incapable. There does not seem to be any mental power to grasp the meaning of the questions and if there is a wrong way of doing things that way seems to be chosen. In Arithmetic, in a compound subtraction, the lines are turned upside down but that does not hinder the subtraction: a simple long division becomes multiplied by twenty and twelve as it goes on. The History was a mere recital from the beginning of the book onwards with the numbers of the questions inserted at intervals. In Theology Mr. B was entirely at sea. Grammar was the only subject where there was not an entire failure.[65]

Thence, until after 1898, no mention was made of any Training Institution in the District Reports. Apparently the effort to train ministers separately was suspended to make more ambitious plans for the future training of indigenous ministers, not only for the Gold Coast, but to serve the whole of West Africa.

The Missionary Committee had sent a letter in 1896 to the West African Districts suggesting that a common Training Institution for the West African Methodist Districts be opened in Sierra Leone for the training of Local agents. The Gold Coast District Synod discussed the suggestion at the 1897 Synod and came to the following conclusion:

> It was felt that with the progress of secular education at the Gold Coast, it is of the utmost importance that our young ministers be more suitably equipped than present advantages offer. This Synod respectfully suggests that the Gold Coast, as being the central part of our missionary operations in West Africa, and as having the greatest number of ministers and probationers, will be found the most convenient situation for such an Institution.[66]

In response, the Committee intimated to the Gold Coast through the missionaries in 1898, that plans had already been finalised for the establishment of a Training Institution, solely for the training of ministers, in Sierra Leone, and that the training of Teachers and Catechists should be carried on in the Gold Coast. The Synod consented and requested that the £50 0s. 0d. (¢100.00) granted for the training of Agents be increased to £100 0s. 0d. (¢200.00). By these decisions the scheme whereby ministers were trained in the Gold Coast came to an end for awhile.

---
65 MMS, *GCDSM*, 1896, Box 1891-1897.
66 *Ibid.*, 1897.

Negotiations for opening the new Institution went ahead and the Central Institution for the training of Methodist ministers in West Africa was opened in Freetown, Sierra Leone under the title: *Richmond College.*

It was started in October 1902 with the Rev. W.T. Balmer, B.A., B.D., as the Principal. The first Gold Coast candidates to be admitted in that year were: A.W. Stanhope, J. Hayford and G.E. Barnes. They were joined by John A. Assan in October 1903. In the following years, 1904, Frederick Emmanuel Ekuban (aged 25 years), and Joseph C. Mensah (aged 28 years) were admitted. The last student to be admitted from the Gold Coast was Isaac Larbey Thompson who entered the Institution in 1905. Unfortunately, he did not complete the course because he died in March, 1906. In all, during the five years of its active existence, the Richmond College, Freetown, trained seven men from the Gold Coast District, for a period of two years each.

The greatest problem encountered was inadequate enrolment, although the College was opened for the three West African Districts, Sierra Leone, the Gold Coast and Nigeria. For example, of the three students in the College in 1903, two were from Sierra Leone, one from the Gold Coast, but none from Nigeria.

Although the roll had not been rising appreciably, the expenditure for running the College continued to climb up and the levy upon the Districts became larger than had been originally anticipated. In consequence, the Gold Coast Synod of February 1905 recommended to the College Board that it was advisable to open the Institution to lay-students also so that the school's usefulness might be increased and the assessment for the working expenses reduced.

From 1906 to 1909 the Gold Coast no longer sent candidates to Richmond College, Freetown, and the project of training Gold Coast indigenous ministers was suspended again owing to certain developments taking place in Cape Coast as described below. That the Gold Coast might not continue to incur debts for a College to which no Gold Coast students, were sent, the Districts gave notice, in 1908, that the Richmond College, Freetown, should be closed down until its position was finally determined.[67] The notice was not heeded and the College continued to exist in spite of poor enrolment and mounting expenditure. As a result, when the Chairman of the Sierra Leone District requested the Gold Coast District at the beginning of 1910 to contribute to the expenditure, the Gold Coast Synod of that year "was of opinion, that the College should have been closed and no expenditure, therefore, incurred and could not accept any responsibility in relation thereto".[68]

The Gold Coast position had been precipitated by certain activities in

---

67 MMS, *GCDSM*, 1909, Box 1898-1906.
68 *Ibid.*, 1910.

Cape Coast since 1900. The Cape Coast High School, then called the Collegiate school, had also not been functioning satisfactorily. Therefore, some Fantes, W. Sam, R.A. Harrison, J.E. Biney, D. Myles Abadoo and Mensah Sarbah, zealous "to work for education on Ghanaian lines",[69] formed a Company 'Fanti Public Schools Ltd.', and opened its first school, Mfantsipim, on Monday, 3rd April, 1905, with the motto: "Dwen Hwe Kan" (Think and look ahead).[70] Unfortunately, the anticipated prospects fell below expectation and the new school was amalgamated with the Collegiate School, for efficiency, under the name Mfantsipim. It seems that the Company did not find the management of the united school easy, so in 1908, the secretary, Mr. D.M. Abadoo, sent the following letter to the Chairman of Methodist Church, Cape Coast:

Cape Coast,
27th Feb., 1908.

The Rev. A.T.R. Bartrop,
Chairman & Gen. Supt.,
Wesleyan Mission,
Cape Coast.
Dear Sir,
I beg to inform you that at a meeting of the Directors of the Fanti Public Schools Ltd. held yesterday the following resolution was passed.

'Resolved that the School be handed over to the Synod and that the same be communicated to the Chairman of the District.'

On the question of School plant representation of the Company may be considered later on.

I am,

Dear Sir,
Yours sincerely,
(D.M. Abadoo)
Secretary.[71]

Synod resolved to take over the School under the then existing name, Mfantsipim, and a management board was appointed.

This decision was influenced considerably by the visit of the Rev. W.T. Balmer, B.A., B.D., of Richmond College, Freetown, to the Gold Coast in 1907. In that year he was directed by the Missionary Committee in England to proceed to the Gold Coast District to examine its educational affairs. In his report, he requested that the Principal of Mfantsipim should always be a European, as in the Girls' High School and Training Home.[72]

---

69 Bartels, *The Roots*, p. 165.
70 *Ibid.*, p. 166.
71 MMS, *GCDSM*, 1908, Box 1907-1911.
72 *Ibid.*
    One would have liked to know the reasons why Balmer made the request that a European should *always* be the head of Mfantsipim; but the records did not reveal Balmer's reasons supporting the request. In 1915, however, the Rev. W. Goudie, then the General Secretary of the MMS, made a statement after his West African tour and that assertion is significant for explaining the reason behind Balmer's demand. Goudie wrote, when com-

Following on the report, the Missionary Committee wrote, among other things, in their annual letter to the Gold Coast at the end of 1908 for the 1909 Synod, the following paragraph on the subject of a Training Institution in West Africa:

> The question that at the present moment calls of special attention is that of a Training Institution in West Africa in which Africa's sons can be trained with efficiency and in adequate numbers for work amongst their own people. We can never hope to evangelise West Africa save as we are able to increase the numbers and efficiency of Ministers, Evangelists, Teachers and voluntary workers, also, from amongst the natives of the country. Hitherto such training as exists has been fragmentary, insufficient and in many respects unsatisfactory. To meet this need two proposals have been placed before the Missionary Committee. First, the Church Missionary Society has invited us to co-operation on equal terms in the work of training and education, having as its centre Fourah Bay College at Freetown, Sierra Leone.[73] As an alternative a scheme has been eleborated by the Rev. W.T. Balmer, B.A. B.D., for a Central Training Institution at Cape Coast, well organized and equipped, at which it may be possible to train agents of various degrees for the West Coast Districts. We enclose a paper in which the two proposals are set forth, and it will be for the Synod to consider them and declare their mind. Of course, it will be free for the Synod to recommend some other method of dealing with the question which may seem more desirable. It is a matter of supreme interest and should be considered with careful thought and earnest prayer.[74]

After careful and prayerful consideration the Synod rejected the Fourth Bay proposal and accepted Balmer's suggestion to establish a Central Training Institution, "which shall combine under one roof the training of

---

menting on the work of the Methodist native agents in West Africa, that: "The fact remains that a weak spot in the Negro character is a lack of fitness to bear responsibility and the development of that gift in the individual or in the race, in Africa as elsewhere, must be a slow process". W. Goudie, *Report of Visit to West Africa* (London, 1915), p. 63. That is the crux of the matter. For a very long time some Europeans have believed that the African is of inferior human character, and that what a European can accomplish an African is incapable of achieving. See Edward W. Blyden, *Christianity, Islam and the Negro Race* (London, 1877), p. 66, where Blyden made the point that such a pernicious European view of the African character led some of the missionaries in West Africa to evangelise the natives under the belief that: "The African mind is regarded as a great blank, or worse than a blank, filled with everything dark and horrible and repulsive. Everything is to be destroyed and replaced by something new and foreign". Goudie and Balmer might have been graduates of this type of philosophy. In fact, it will be shown in Chapters III and IV of this investigation that the Presbyterian missionaries were similar to the Methodists in this matter.

The reluctant attitude which the Protestant Churches adopted in the Gold Coast in relation to the devolution of leadership to the natives in the Theological institutions, was only an aspect of the general West African post-Crowther controversy, viz: the failure of African leadership. After the death of S.A. Crowther, in 1892, Africans were considered to be inefficient for leadership in the Church. See Sundkler, *The Christian Ministry in Africa*, pp. 44-76; J.F.A. Ajayi, *Christian Missions in Nigeria: The making of a New Elite* (London, 1965), pp. 235-261, and C.M.S., *Intelligencer*, 14:11:1892.

73 C.M.S., "Resolutions adopted by the Committee of correspondence of July 17th, 1906". Box G3 A1/L13, 1900-1907, Sierra Leone Letter Book, Vol. 13, p. 398.

74 MMS, *GCDSM*, 1909, Box 1907-1911.

African teachers, agents, catechists and ministers, and that the Institution School be now known as Mfantsipim School".[75]

Balmer preferred Cape Coast to Freetown because on his inspection tour of the Gold Coast he discovered that young men in Cape Coast were thirsty for education and the strong wind of nationalism blowing over certain prominent people in Cape Coast made them anxious to give financial support for the development of education in Cape Coast.[76] This nationalistic feeling probably considerably influenced the Synod's decision in support of Balmer.[77] Having thus resolved to build the Central Institution of Cape Coast, the Synod proceeded to make plans for its establishment.[78]

Soon after the 1910 Synod the new Institution was opened in its temporary buildings in the Cape Coast Castle under the name: "The Richmond College and Mfantsipim School"[79] with the Rev. W.T. Balmer, B.A., B.D., as the Principal, assisted by the Rev. Gaddiel Acquaah, the senior indigenous teacher. Under these men the training of ministers was resumed again in Cape Coast with a good beginning.

The first theological students to be admitted were five, of whom two were ministerial candidates, and the remaining three, agents. During the year one agent-candidate worked so well that he was recommended to be accepted for the ministry. This increased the ministerial candidates, in 1910, to three namely, Odartei, Portuphy and W. Acquah the latter promoted to the status of ministerial candidate. Although the students were "men of varied attainments",[80] all of them showed "evidence of piety and good character".[81]

Their studies included certain prescribed books of the Bible, viz: Old Testament—Genesis, Judges, II Kings, and Isaiah; New Testament—St. Mark, Acts, Philippians; Elementary lessons in Philosophy and Theology; Homiletics and Sermon Criticism; English Language and Literature; Elementary New Testament Greek and Hausa. In all these they showed "commendable industry".[82]

For practical training the students held services every Sunday afternoon at the Boating Company for the benefit of the Liberian nationals who were employed there. They attended the services regularly and preached in turns.

In spite of the good work Balmer had begun at Cape Coast, he was compelled on health grounds to leave the coast by the end of 1910.[83] On

---

75 Bartels, *op. cit.*, p. 168.
76 *Ibid.*, pp. 164-168.
77 *Ibid.*, p. 165.
   Most of those nationalists were practising Methodist laymen.
78 See Appendix 1 below.
79 WMMS, *Reports*, Vol. XXXII, 1911-1912
80 MMS, *GCDSM*, 1911, Box 1907-1911.
81 *Ibid.*
82 *Ibid*
83 Mfantsipim, "Log Book", 29th Nov., 1910, and Bartels, *op. cit.*, p. 170.

his retirement the Missionary Committee appointed, in February 1911, the Rev. Alec A. Sneath, M.A.(Mancs) as the Principal and Mr. S.J. Gilbson, B.Sc.(Lond.) as Vice-Principal.[84] Under their supervision, with the help of the African members of staff, the Institution continued to grow. In 1911 nine candidates were received as theological students for training as agents.

About this period, the Rev. W.R. Griffin published an article "A great call from the Gold Coast"[85] in the 1910-1911 Foreign Field of the Wesleyan Methodist Church. He pointed out how "on every hand Muhammadanism [was] advancing with wondrous rapidity" and was "sweeping down through the Northern Territories of the Gold Coast to Cape Coast and Accra and through Northern and Southern Nigeria to Lagos". He suggested that it was "incumbent upon Christianity to occupy, at once, strategic points" to counteract the advance of Islam. He felt confident that by establishing a Training Institution on the Coast for local agents and ministers and by opening a girls' school at Accra, the coastal base would be made secure to serve as a springboard of evangelism into the interior. That an army of trained indigenous workers might be guaranteed to perpetuate more aggressive evangelisation of the coast, the Gold Coast District began to speed up more effective plans for the erection of the permanent buildings of the new Institution at Cape Coast.

A site was obtained costing at least £1000 (¢2,000)[86] for the buildings, and the Synod of 1911 decided, forthwith, to raise £3,500 (¢7,000) towards the erection of the structures. The Missionary Committee was to supplement this amount with a grant of £3,000 (¢6,000), the total estimated cost being £7,000 (¢14,000).[87] As work on the permanent buildings progressed the school continued to expand on its temporary site, the Sea View House. In 1912 there were 121 students on the roll. Five of them were theological students, three of whom were ministerial students and the remaining two were catechists. At the end of the year two boys from the top form of the Secondary Department "were accepted as candidates for the ministry at the Synod of 1913".[88]

It was also in 1912 that the theological curriculum was widened to meet the direct education needs of the students and the demands of Circuit administration. The syllabus then comprised: Theology, Greek, Christian Evidences, New Testament Criticism, Old Testament and New Testament Exposition, School Method and Management, Methodist Finance, English Literature and Sermon Criticism. For practical training, the Cape Coast, Elmina and Anomaboe Circuits, adjacent to the school, arranged for the students to embark on practical preaching in their societies.

---

84 MMS, *Reports*, Vol. XXXII, p. 173.
85 MMS, *Foreign Field*, Vol. VII, 1910-1911, p. 379.
86 *Ibid.*, pp. 380-381.
87 *Ibid.*, p. 381.
88 WMMS, *Reports*, Vol. XXXIII, 1913-1914, p. 167.

1914 was "a wonderful year in West Africa" said the Rev. W.R. Griffin, Chairman and General Superintendent of the Gold Coat District.[89] Wonderful because "the main building with the Assembly Hall of the Richmond College and Mfantsipim School for boys has ... been erected".[90] Its capacity was 100 boarders and 300 day students, some of whom would be ministerial students. The vision and the great possibilities about the future of the school were being perceptibly realised.

Meanwhile the training progressed satisfactorily; Elecution and Logic were added to the curriculum and greater attention was paid to practical training than in the earlier days of this Institution. For example, in addition to preaching in the Circuits the students conducted Bible Classes in the High School, and assisted in the Cape Coast Sunday School.

In 1916, however, although the staff was increased to four, comprising the Rev. A.A. Sneath, M.A., Principal, the Rev. R.P. Dyer, M.A., Vice-Principal, the Rev. G.R. Acquaah and the Rev. F.C.F. Grant, there were no theological students in residence,[91] because no candidates came forward for reception as ministerial candidates during the 1916 Synod. In the following year, however, S.P.Q. Ghartey and J.E. Appiah went into residence on November 3, 1917,[92] and classes were resumed on the 5th of the same month.[93] Mr. C.H. Bartels, Junior minister of the Cape Coast Circuit, joined the class afterwards. He was later relieved of circuit work so that he could do justice to his studies. Though the class was small and the students showed interest and made good progress, Synod was of the opinion:

> That a theological institution of such small dimensions denies to the men those social opportunities which are in some respects the most valuable part of College life. Their life is bound to be circumscribed and their interests are bound to be limited. They do not have intercourse with men whose outlook, attainments and social position are different from their own. The student should learn from his fellows almost as much as from his tutors, but an Institution the size of ours, in denying this advantage, fails to fulfil one of the most important functions of a College.[94]

Earlier, about the beginning of 1917, the Fourah Bay Scheme[95] had been revived and the Missionary Committee reported in the *Foreign Field* the following message:

> Several years ago it was proposed that we should join the Church Missionary Society in their fine Training College at Fourah Bay, Sierra Leone.[96] The

---

89 MMS, *The Foreign Field*, Vol. XI, p. 42.
90 *Loc. cit.*
91 MCG, *GCDSM*, 1917.
92 *Ibid.*, 1918, p. 5.
93 *Loc. cit.*
94 *Loc. cit.*
95 MMS, *Foreign Field*, Vol. XIV, 1917-1918, p. 57.
   Cf. C.M.S., "Sierra Leone Letter Book:" Box G3 A1/L14, 1908-1920, pp. 297-298.
96 See pages 26-27 above.

scheme was revived a few months ago, and has now been adopted by the two Societies.⁹⁷ The decision to unite in this work marks an important step towards closer co-operation in the mission field. The two Societies are the largest working in West Africa, and it promises well for the future that the ministers of both Churches will be trained together at Fourah Bay. By the new arrangement the C.M.S. will appoint the Principal, and the W.M.M.S. the Vice-Principal. Our Committee has appointed the Rev. W.T. Balmer, B.A., B.D., to the latter post.⁹⁸

Following this arrangement the ministerial training was separated again from lay-training in the Gold Coast and transferred to Fourah Bay, in Freetown, Sierra Leone. Once Again the bright prospects of training locally African ministers in Cape Coast at the Richmond College and Mfantsipim School became frustrated. But the Gold Coast District did not raise any objection against the Fourah Bay scheme this time, possibly because it was felt that the project would provide the students with the needed "social opportunities which are in some respects the most valuable part of College life".⁹⁹

In pursuit of the new scheme the candidates received at the 1919 Synod to be trained as ministers (S.D. Nate-Kodsi, J.E. Allotey Pappoe and S.H. Wilson) were sent to Fourah Bay College as the pioneers from the Gold Coast. They made satisfactory progress as affirmed, at the end of their two-year course in 1920, by the following report which the Vice-Principal, the Rev. W.T. Balmer, sent to the 1921 Synod;

Fourah Bay College,
27/1/21

Dear Mr. Webster,¹⁰⁰

In case you need a report of your men in College here, I beg to say that Messrs. Wilson, Nate-Kodsi and Pappoe hae continued to acquit themselves well. Their studies have comprised:—

Systematic Theology,
Christian Ethics,
N. T. Greek,
St. John in Greek,
Early Church History,
English History,
Homiletics.

In the Terminal exam. they have done well, Mr. Wilson heading the list of Ministerial students from all the Districts.

By their conduct they have shown themselves to be earnest Christian gentlemen and I confidently recommend them for acceptance as candidates for our ministry

Kind Regards,

Yours Sincerely,
(Signed) W.T. Balmer ¹⁰¹

---

97 C.M.S., Box G3 A1/L14, 1908-1920, p. 318.
98 MMS, *Foreign Field*, Vol. XIV, p. 57.
99 See p. 29 above.
100 The Rev. Webster was the Chairman and General Superintendent at the time.
101 MCG, *GCDSM*, 1921, Fourah Bay College Report.

After the first batch of students, three more students were sent to Fourah Bay from the Gold Coast before the scheme was discontinued. J.S. Aidoo was admitted in 1920 and he was followed in 1921 by C.C. Ohene and J.B. Wilson. These students also made satisfactory progress and one of them, J.S. Aidoo, successfully took the Matriculation Examination in 1921 and was "permitted to proceed with his Arts course at Fourah Bay College".[102] When C.C. Ohene and J.B. Wilson completed their studies in 1923 no new students were sent to Fourah Bay from the Gold Coast District to be trained as ministers, because a new arrangement had been completed, about the middle of 1922, for the training of Church workers, including the training of ministers, locally in the Gold Coast.

When the ministerial students were separated from the Cape Coast Institution and sent to Fourah Bay, the lay-students of the Theological Department were also removed from Cape Coast to a new Institution at Aburi. *The Aburi Institution* was opened on 9th April, 1918[103] to train efficient evangelists and teachers who would "build up the Church, filling the minds of the converts with Christian ideas, and leading the members to a full Christian experience".[104] This institution did not, however, function satisfactorily until its re-organisation in 1922. For example, in 1919 the Institution was closed down because the students "absented themselves in a body",[105] in protest against a matter concerning monthly allowances and it was not re-opened until the middle of 1922, mainly because of the negligence of the Principal, S.J. Gilbson.[106]

Before it was re-opened the Institution was re-organised as a result of the visit made to the four West African Districts by the Rev. Edgar W. Thompson, M.A., General Secretary of the W.M.M.S. and Sir Arthur Black, from the autumn of 1921 to the winter of 1922. They studied thoroughly the Gold Coast problems, especially those that related to the training of African workers. They recommended that the Training Institution at Aburi should be re-opened, "but on fuller consideration this gave place to a scheme of greater magnitude and it was decided to build a College at Kumasi",[107] a more central town than Aburi, to produce "a staff of catechists and teachers adequate to the rapid development of the work".[108] As a preparation towards the commencement of the training in Kumasi, the *Wesley Training Institution*, Aburi, was re-opened on 1st July, 1922 with 30 students in residence. This was the real beginning of Wesley Col-

---

102 *Ibid.*, 1922, pp. 5-6.
103 MCG, *GCDSM*, 1919, p. 54.
104 WMMS, *Report*, Vol. XXXIV, p. 64.
105 MCG, *GCDSM*, 1920, Aburi Institution Report.
106 *Ibid.*, 1921, p. 44 reverse.
107 WMMS, *Reports*, Vol. XXXV, pp. 80-81.
108 *Ibid.*, p. 81. See Bartels, *op. cit.*, pp. 188-189 for the rapid growth of the Church as a result of Samson Oppon's evangelisation of Ashanti.

lege, Kumasi, the new institution for the training of Church workers, both lay and ministerial.

The first Principal was the Rev. C.W. Armstrong and the Vice-Principal was Mr. L.B. Greaves, M.C., B.A. In its initial stages, the College had two sides: the normal, which was a tree-year course for teachers, and the theological, which comprised (a) a one-year course for catechists and (b) a combined three-year teacher-catechist course. The primary syllabus consisted of Bible Subjects, English and Arithmetic; for practical training the students conducted Sunday and week-night services at the Aburi Church and organised open-air preaching in the town. In addition to these acts of worship one or two services within the College had been found very inspiring, and had helped to cement the sense of fellowship and the happy relationship that existed between the then "generation of staff and students".[109] From the very outset, a large measure of self-government was enjoyed by the students, who elected officers without staff intervention. This introduction to student responsibility and initiative contributed considerably to the promotion of evangelistic activities organised by the students in later years.

The first ministerial students to enter Wesley College, Aburi, at Easter 1923, were Solomon B. Akyeampong, Ebenezer Brown, Ishmael Amonoo, Solomon Butler and Geo J. Nyarko. They worked satisfactorily as evinced by the Principal's report at the end of 1923 in these words:

> They are all men of strong individuality, above the average intelligence who have applied themselves diligently to study and made excellent progress during the year. They have taken Sunday appointments in the Chapels of the Circuit, and conducted fellowship meetings in the College. Without exception they are all men of great promise.[110]

Meanwhile arrangement for the erection of the permanent buildings at Kumasi had progressed so steadily and rapidly that the new Institution was dedicated by His Excellency Brigadier General, Sir Gorden Guggisberg, Governor of the Gold Coast, on 3rd March, 1924.

Two days after the Dedication "the first students came into residence on Wednesday, March 5, 1924".[111] The College was originally planned to be an institution of evangelists and teachers; but one of the happiest features of the day when the first students came into residence was that, of the 74 men in residence, selected from all over the District, seven were accepted to be trained for the ordained ministry,[112] comprising the five who had

---

109 C.W. Armstrong, MCG, *GCDSM*, 1923, Appendix 5, p. 36.
110 *The Gold Coast Annual*, 1927, pp. 25-26.
111 Wesley College, "Log Book", 1924-1957, 5:3:24, p. 3.
112 *Loc. cit.* MMS, *The Foreign Field*, June 1924, p. 208, recorded that the College began in Kumasi with 81 men of whom 9 were ministerial candidates. It seems that the Log Book entry is more reliable because the *GCDSM*, 1924, recorded five names as ministerial candidates, in 1923: the *GCDSM*, 1925, Appendix No. 4 recorded that two new candidates had been received at 1924 Synod, making a total of seven ministerial stu-

completed their first year at the temporary premises at Aburi and the other two were received at the 1924 Synod to begin the first year.

With the commencement of Wesley College in its permanent premises in Kumasi, the history of the training of African ministers by the Methodist Church locally in the Gold Coast entered a definite stage when the Richmond College and Mfantsipim School experiment, earlier, to train ministers, teachers and catechists together, came to be consolidated.

From the very outset of its life, the College made excellent progress. The number of resident students at the beginning of 1925 was 80, of whom five were ministerial students, two of whom were in their second and final year and the other three were new students in the first year. The ministerial roll, did not, however, rise to ten candidates for all the two or three classes together in any one year, although the general roll of the College continued to grow to a maximum of 142 in 1931.[113]

The initial course of study for the ministerial students at Wesley College comprised the Bible, Theology, Greek, Ethics and Mohammedanism.[114] During the years that followed, these subjects were expanded gradually until by the beginning of 1942 the curriculum for the ministerial students consisted of Church History, Church Organisation, English Grammar and Composition, Literature and Speech; New Testament, Old Testament, Special New Testament, Theology; Vernacular: oral and written; Greek, News Lecture, Homiletics, Methodist Law and Discipline, Psychology and Morals, Hebrew and Roman History (mainly for special students who were preparing for the Intermediate B.D.),[115] New Testament Theology and Ethics.[116]

The quality of work done by the ministerial students had been satisfactory and it gradually grew to a very high level. For instance, in 1941 two students read for the London Intermediate B.D. while two others, Awotwi Pratt and C.W. Cudjoe took the Senior Cambridge Examination in December of that year.[117]

Thus, during a century (1842-1942) of training African ministers in the Gold Coast, the Methodist Mission was able to maintain a satisfactory training only for 20 years 1922-1942. During this period the students were trained, at first, for two years between 1922 and 1931 and then for three years from 1932 to 1942, except that in 1941 one student who was preparing for the London intermediate B.D. spent a fourth year in residence.[118] In all, Wesley College trained 40 ministers who were taught by

---

dents in 1924. The were Solomon B. Akyeampong, Ebenezer Brown, Ishmael Amonoo, Solomon Butler and Geo. J. Nyarko plus the two new men.
113 *Ibid.*, pp. 8-28 and 33-76.
114 MCG, *GCDSM*, 1925, Wesley College Report.
115 S.G. Nimako and J.W. deGraft Johnson were the first students in this category.
116 Wesley College, "Records", 1938-1942.
117 *Ibid.*, 1941.
118 *Loc. cit.*

missionaries assisted by African ministers most remarkable of whom were the Revs. F.C.F. Grant and Benjamin Markin.

But during the whole period, 1842-1942, 101 African ministers were trained by the Wesleyan Methodist Mission in the Gold Coast (see Appendix VII). Under the supervision of the missionaries, these "native assistants" (as the missionaries used to call the African clergy) helped to spread the Gospel rapidly from the coast to the hinterland as far as to Ashanti and the Volta Region. Kimble was not exaggerating when he wrote about the Methodist Society that:

> After the establishment of the native ministry in 1852, the Society spread very rapidly, especially among the Fantis on the Coast, its popularity being no doubt due, in some measure, to the democratic nature of its institutions and system of Church Government.[119]

Indeed, in 1852, when John Hagan was ordained the first African Methodist minister in the Gold Coast, the Methodist Christian Community was only 6,025 adults and children;[120] but in 1942 the number was 118,559.[121]

The impact of the training was not only felt in the expansion of the Church, but also in national affairs. Some of the ministers, as we shall presently see, gave positive stimulus to the development of nationalistic movements.[122] An example will suffice: the *Gold Coast Methodist Times* was founded at Cape Coast in 1894 with the Rev. S.R.B. Solomon as the editor. Although the paper's declared intention was to remain strictly religious, "entirely innocent of the odium of controversy and such like inventions of the Evil One",[123] the editor quickly made it "the outlet of major political grievances, and made a lasting reputation by its successful handling of the Lands Bill agitation".[124] Apparently, Mr. Solomon's training gave him a measure of self-confidence and individual freedom which made him excel not only as a minister of the Gospel but also as a nationalist. It was this awareness of self-confidence and individual freedom that made the earliest Ghanaian Methodist ministers out-spoken, on national issues, and gave the training which they had received its distinctive character.[125]

But at the end of 1942 the specific Methodist training of African ministers, locally in the Gold Coast, come to an end when the ministerial section

---

119 Kimble, *op. cit.*, p. 162.
120 MMS, *GCDSM*, 1852, Statistics, Box 1842-1866. The members were distributed in only five circuits: Cape Coast, Anomabu, Dominasi, Akrah and Kumasi.
121 MCG, *108th Annual Report*, 1943, p. 4. The number of the circuits had also increased from 5 to 29.
122 Kimble, *op. cit.*, p. 161.
123 *The Gold Coast Methodist Times* (Cape Coast), Vol. 1, No. 1, March 1894.
124 Kimble, *op. cit.*, p. 162. cf. Ward, *op. cit.*, pp. 354-358 dealing with the circumstances, etc. which brought about the Lands Bill Agitation. See also *The Gold Coast Methodist* (Cape Coast), Dec. 1886, re African representation in the Legislative Assembly.
125 The Missionaries did not always take kindly to this. See pages 202 ff.

of Wesley College was transformed in 1943 to a new Institution, the Joint Theological College, near Wesley College, where the Methodists and the Presbyterians began to co-operate in the training of their ministers together.

As this united training eventually developed to embrace other Communions, the history of the Joint Theological College will be deferred until the story of the training of African ministers by the other Communions, the Presbyterian, Anglican and Roman Catholic, has been narrated respectively.

CHAPTER THREE

BASEL MISSION TRAINING
1843-1918

Unlike the other denominations, the Presbyterians did not have theological college devoted solely to the training of their ministers earlier than 1943. But the missionaries evolved an ingenious system whereby prospective candidates for the ministry were given thorough training prior to their ordination. The policy which they followed "was to gather school pupils from a number of villages and towns and give the best of them further training as teachers"[1] and catechists or assistant preachers. After many years of satisfactory service as teacher-catechists some of these trained "native agents" were selected for ordination. The pages which follow will describe how the system was carried out by the Basel and Bremen Missionaries, respectively.

The Basel Mission opened its first seminary for the training of teachers and assistant preachers at Christiansborg in 1843. A large house had been bought by the Missionaries from the Danes. It was in this house that an elementary school and the seminary were started.[2] The idea was to train a handful of mulatto boys[3] to serve as the nucleus of a "native agency" among the Ga. The seminary did not make much progress in the first seven years of its life because the mulatto boys used to leave the school after they had studied for some time and take up commercial posts. So, in 1850 there were only four African boys left in the school.[4]

The character of the seminary began to change from 1851 when J. Zimmermann was appointed to take charge of it. Within two years of his arrival the school began to make good progress. At the beginning of 1853, there were 11 students in residence of whom six were mulatto boys and five were black boys. For the first time the class was divided into two, class I and class II and the teaching staff was increased to four because of the growing numbers. There were six boys in the first class: five mulatto boys, Thomas Swanikier, Jonas Malm, Adolf Briandt, William Cleland, Carl Reindorf and one black boy, Christian Obobi. Those in the second class were two mulatto boys, Theodore Wulff and Neils Holm, plus three black boys, Isaak Akuete, Gottlieb Anang and Gottfried Ahama. They

---

1 G.G. Gunn, *A Hundred Years, 1848-1948: The Story of the Presbyterian Training College,* Akropong, cyclostyled ed.
2 Noel Smith, *The Presbyterian Church of Ghana,* 1835-1960, (Accra, 1966), p. 44.
3 "Mulatto boys": These were the male children of European and African parents.
4 Wilhelm Schlatter, *Geschichte der Basler Mission, 1815-1915, Afrika Band III* (Basel, 1916), p. 45.

were all almost young men with their ages ranging between 16 and 22 years.[5]

The fourth member of staff, Thomas Quatei, an African, was employed during the year as an assistant teacher and at the end of the year Zimmermann asked the Home Committee for an additional missionary teacher because he (Zimmermann) had started work on translating parts of the Bible into the Ga language and on writing a Ga Grammar book.

In the same year, 1853, the duration of the course was extended from two to three years and a new time-table was put into operation. The analysis of the time-table illustrates how efficiently Zimmermann organised this little teacher-catechists' seminary.[6]

Tutor	Subjects	Hours per week	
		Ist Class	IInd Class
Zimmermann	Catechism	4	
	Biblical Theology	5	
	Bible reading with explantion: N.T.	2	2
	Grammar: English & Ga	2	2
Lecher	Bible reading with explanation: O.T.	3	3
	World History	4	
	Singing	2	2
Steinhauser	Geography	2	
Quatei	Bible Stories: N.T.		4
	Ga Exercises		2
	Arithmetic		2
	Total Hours per week	24	17

In addition to these subjects it seems that the 2nd class had two periods of teaching practice in the elementary school from Monday to Friday between 8.00 a.m. and 10.00 a.m. every week.[7]

There were no lectures on Saturdays except that the 2nd class had one period of Bible Stories with Quatei from 7.00 a.m. to 8.00 a.m.

Soon after the re-organisation of the seminary the political situation at Christiansborg compelled Zimmermann to transfer the institution, at the end of 1854, to Abokobi about 12 miles inland and north of Christiansborg. In September 1854 Christiansborg was bombarded by the British Administration in the Gold Coast. In March 1850 the Danes had sold to the British all their forts, including the fort at Christiansborg (Osu). By this action the Danes transferred also to the British the vague influence they had exercised over some of the tribes, for example, Osu, Akwapim, Akim,

---

5 Basel Mission Archives (BMA), (Africa, 1851-1853), p. 183.
6 *Loc. cit.*
7 Appendix IV.

on the eastern side of the Gold Coast. Immediately after the assumption of the jurisdiction over the new places the British introduced the poll-tax[8] to support the British Administration. At first the chiefs consented to pay the tax; but in 1854 the local people defied the Government's request that they should send in their contribution for the year. It was this rebellion which led the British to bombard Christiansborg. After the local people's resistance had been brought under control the British garrison "entered every house plundering, and pulled down several stone buildings which stood close to the Castle".[9] The two houses of the Basel Mission had been damaged by shells during the bombardment and the breaches thus caused made it easy for people to enter and steal nearly all the missionaries' possessions.[10] The Basel Missionaries at first sought refuge in the Wesleyan Mission House in Accra but after some days Zimmermann removed to Abokobi with his family plus the seminary students and there a new permanent mission station was opened.

The seminary work went on smoothly in the new station and during the long vacation—August to September 1955—the staff and students went on a long evangelistic tour as part of the practical training offered to the students. They started from Abokobi on 14th August and travelled mainly on foot through Teshi, Oyarefa, Amrahia, Buademang (Katamangso), Odomiabra, Oyibi, Savabi, Bawaleshi, Shantse, Ologo Patu Village, Odumasi, Kpong, Asutsale, Milafi (Mafi) until they got to Ada by canoe from Kpong. The purpose of the tour was "to pay a visit to those places bordering at (sic) the River Volta and to furnish the people there with the knowledge of the glorious gospel...."[11] In pursuit of this aim the gospel was preached in each of these villages. The tour was very difficult and tiring; they travelled over 100 miles in and out; they were at the mercy of the heat of the sun; but these difficulties were trivial when compared with the satisfaction the party derived from the experience. They returned to Abokobi on 1st September and the concluding remarks of the report, Thomas Quatei sent to Basel about the campaign, expressed how rewarding the project had been. He said:

> I must confess we suffered very much from exposure to the heat of the shining sun and the chilling cold of the nightly dew. We are, however, not the least sorry for this and other trivial sufferings we had to undergo when we consider that our light affliction which is but for a moment works for us a far more exceeding and eternal weight of glory.[12]

---

8 Ward, *A History of Ghana*, pp. 228-231 and C.C. Reindorf, *The History of the Gold Coast and Asante*, 2nd ed. (Accra, 1966), pp. 322-335. These references discuss in detail the circumstances that led to the Christiansborg Rebellion in 1854.
9 Reindorf, *ibid.*, p. 334.
10 *Loc. cit.*
11 B.M.A., Africa, 1855, Folio VII, No. III, 12. cf. Appendix VI of this study—First Missionary Journey.
12 B.M.A., Africa, 1855, Folio VII, No. 12.

After the seminary at Abokobi had operated successfully for three years the Missionaries found that it was more expedient to train Ga and Twi agents of the church together. As a result, it was decided that Zimmermann should close the seminary at Abokobi and transfer the students to Akropong the head station. In response, Zimmermann went with his seven students to Akropong where another seminary had been functioning since 1848. Four students out of the seven that Zimmermann took to Akropong returned to their homes on the coast because they would not stay in the interior part of the country. With the three Ga students remaining and 10 Twi students recruited for the Akropong seminary both seminaries were unified in 1858,[13] in order that men of different ethnic groups might learn to live and work together.[14]

The seminary at Akropong had been started on 3rd July 1848 by the Rev. J.C. Dieterle and Rev. J.G. Widman. Its aim was the same as that of the Christiansborg seminary viz: to train local people as teachers and catechists so that they might evangelize their own kith and kin; but unlike the Christiansborg institution the training at Akropong lasted four years instead of three. In 1843 Rev. Widman had established a primary school at Akropong with the children of the West Indians who accompanied the Basel Missionaries to the Gold Coast in that year. A few local children were also admitted together with the West Indian children. Some of these boys exhibited extra-ordinary ability. So in 1848 Dieterle selected the five most brilliant boys from the top class of the Primary Boarding School and began the seminary with them. They were John Rochester, a West Indian and four young baptised men from Akropong, David Asante, Paul Staudt Keteku, William Yirenkyi and Jonathan Bekoe. It was a modest beginning, and the simple syllabus comprised: Reading, Writing, Arithmetic, Biblical History, Twi, English, Geography and Handwork.[15]

The seminary made steady progress and from 1858 when both seminaries were amalgamated the roll of students increased satisfactorily as follows: 1853: 13; 1860: 23; 1861: 32; 1862: 37, and 1863: 40.[16] It was also from 1858 that the duration of the course was raised from four years to five.

In 1863 an important re-organisation took place in the seminary. The Rev. J.G. Auer, a schoolmaster from Württemberg, came to Akropong in 1853 and was appointed to the staff of the seminary as the music tutor. After a while he conceived the idea of a new type of school to be called the Middle School, an equivalent of the "Mittel" school in Germany.[17] Its pur-

---

13 Gunn, *op. cit.*, p. 5.
14 *Loc. cit.*
15 Schlatter, *op. cit.*, p. 44.
16 Schlatter, *op. cit.*, pp. 95 ff.
17 Fred M. Agyeman, *A Century with Boys: the Story of Middle Boarding Schools in Ghana, 1867-1967*, (Accra, 1967), p. 27.

pose was to bridge the gap which had been growing between the Primary Boarding School and the Seminary. He had good reasons for making the proposal. Firstly, by 1860, the seminary was 12 years old and the standard of instruction had been rising as the years went by. The initial curriculum had been expanded and the subjects taught included: Bible Studies, Church History, English, the Care of a Congregation, Arithmetic, Mensuration, Geometry, Algebra, Isogogics, Pedagogics, Homiletics, Dogmatics, Music, Art and Agriculture.[18] Secondly, it was 17 years since the Primary School had been established. In the early days the pupils who entered the primary schools were almost young men and by the time they were drafted to the seminary they were almost mature young men.[19] But after 17 years, younger children began to enter the primary boarding schools, and on entering the seminary five years later they were far younger than those who had been admitted to the seminary in the earlier days. So, Auer thought that as the standard of teaching in the seminary had become very high, it would be better to give the primary pupils a sounder general education before they were recruited to the seminary. In fact, Auer's aim was to introduce the German Mittelschule system, whereby children were offered a general education beyond the years they spent in the primary or elementary schools. Auer and the Rev. Haruisch who supported him "stressed that they wanted the local boys to receive the type of education available in a first-class European town".[20] After some discussions in Basel concerning the proposal, the Home Committee accepted the scheme and implemented it in 1863. In that year two middle schools were opened, one at Christiansborg, Osu, and the other at Akropong.[21]

The Akropong Middle School was opened on the premises of the seminary and it remained there until 1867 when it was moved into its own buildings. The subjects taught were English Reading, Writing, Vernacular (Twi and Ga), Geometry, Natural History, Physics, Geography, History, Drawing and Bible Study, and the medium of instruction was Twi. The Middle school followed a four year course. In the early days, boys in the third year who wished to become teachers or catechists, received special coaching in the fourth year in preparation for entry into the seminary. Those who would become teachers were taught school method and those who would become catechists learnt Greek and Church History. After entering the seminary, the prospective teachers spent two years in a Teachers' Training School, connected with the Theological Seminary, and the catechists spent four years in the Seminary because they had two extra ye-

---

18 *Loc. cit.*, see also Smith, *op. cit.*, p. 58.
19 See page 36.
20 *Akropong Presbyterian Boys' Middle School, Centenary Celebrations, 1867-1967* (Accra, 1967), p. 1.
21 For a more detailed study of the story of the Middle School see Agyemang, *op. cit.* and E. Nothwang, *Akropong Middle School Jubilee Handbook, 1867-1917.*

ars studying Hebrew and Greek, in order to lay the foundation for correct interpretation of the Bible.[22]

But this practice whereby some of the seminarians were trained as teachers and others as catechists raised the question about the kind of training the seminary ought to be giving: teachers' training or catechists' training. In those early days, it was clear that both professions could not be easily delimited. No one could be a teacher who would not work for the congregation. To clarify the position the Mission authorities revised the early rules for the seminaries laid down in 1853 by the Missionary Field Conference for the Akropong and Christiansborg seminaries,[23] and the first of the revised house rules reads: "The Basel Mission Seminary at Akropong is an institution established solely for the purpose of training young men for service in the mission work. Every pupil of the seminary by his very entering the school declares that it is his intention, wish and promise to becoming a teacher or catechist of the Basel Mission".[24]

In pursuit of the spirit of this rule the students did not only engage in classroom studies but they were given practical training also. From 9.00 a.m. to 11.00 a.m. each school day, two of the students had teaching practice in the primary boarding school nearby. As regards pastoral work the tutors frequently went on preaching tours together with the students. Usually at the week-ends, the whole seminary went on preaching excursions to adjacent villages such as Abiriw or Asesieso. Twice a year they went farther afield to new stations such as Anum, Begoro or Abetifi, to help the missionaries in these places by preaching in the villages around the stations. As music is very important in evangelism, harmoniums were procured for the seminary and all the students who went through the seminary training also learnt how to play the harmonium, and this equipped them to lead singing in the chapel Sunday by Sunday.

The seminary training was very strict. It has been said that an old presbyter saw the seminary in its formative years as "a place for very hard and

---

22 Reindorf, *op. cit.*, p. 223.
23 H. Debrunner, *A History of Christianity in Ghana* (Accra, 1967), p. 148.
   The early rules laid down by the Missionary field Conference in 1853 for the Akropong and Christiansborg Seminaries were as follows: The catechist institutions at Akropong and Osu (Christiansborg) shall train God-fearing young men from among the congregations as teachers and catechists. They shall have the necessary gifts and a decent primary school standard. Later they should assist the missionaries in their work amongst the congregations and pagans.
   "Our main concern shall be the Kingdom of God and His righteousness. Each one will find the Lord and grow in His Grace through persistent prayer and faithful perusal of the Word of God. If any one of the students has something to discuss, let him open his heart in child-like sincerity to the house father."
24 Gunn, *loc cit.* Cf. Reindorf, *op. cit.*, p. 223, made the point that as the missionaries recognized that missionary work should not be confined to religious education and preaching alone, industrial establishments were opened and trades were taught to those who would not become teachers or catechists. Ward, *op. cit.*, p. 243, Fn. 16 confirmed Reindorf.

self-denying training—as a place of exceptionally strict discipline"[25] in everything including worship and dressing. For example, the students had regular church parades wearing black suits. On weekdays they had to wear suits of khaki or white drill. The first and second year students had to wear theirs without shoes; but in the third year they started wearing shoes with the suits. The seminary used to be dead silent during the Passion Week and the students wore black uniform to symbolise their sorrow for the Lord's sufferings.

There were, however, happy periods too. Christmas was an exceptionally happy and jolly time. There were two holidays during the year, the first about mid-year and the second at the end of the year, after Christmas. Christmas Eve was devoted to carol singing, and after the morning worship on Christmas Day gifts including clothes and blankets were distributed. The staff and students then enjoyed a sumptuous Christmas feast after which in a family atmosphere they would all sing the Thanksgiving song in Twi:

> Me wura meda w'ase
> Miyi me yam fitaa
> Miyi wo din aye
> Se woye m'agyenkwa pa.[26]

As the years went by the growth in the number of students began to cause the staff anxiety. They feared that with 60-65 students it was becoming impossible for them to maintain the intimate family relationship and to contribute to know them closely enough to render the appropriate individual help.[27] Consequently, in the 1890s it was decided to open another seminary at Abefifi, firstly to reduce the growing numbers and to ease the congestion due to accommodating all the students at Akropong, and secondly to reduce the distance from Ashanti to Akropong so that many more Ashanti students might be attracted to the new seminary for training to meet the growing demand for workers in Ashanti.[28] It was intended to open the new seminary in 1898 in the premises of an Evangelists' School which had been established there previously; but it seems the seminary did not actually begin in 1898 as has been traditionally recorded by Schlatter, Smith and Debrunner.[29] It seems the seminary was actually started in January 1899. This date seems to be the more likely because the B.M. report of 1900 recorded the following statement about the new seminary: "It will be remembered that this seminary has only been opened in January,

---

25 Gunn, *op. cit.*, p. 6.
26 *Loc. cit.* The verse may be paraphrased in English as follows: My Lord I give you thanks, I praise you with all my heart, for you are my loving saviour.
27 Schlatter, *Geschichte der Basler Mission*, p. 184.
28 Smith, *op. cit.*, p. 123.
29 Schlatter, *op. cit.*, p. 185. Smith, *op. cit.*, p. 180; Debrunner, *op. cit.*, p. 262. Smith and Debrunner used Schlatter as their source.

1899".³⁰ The report continued to say that because it was opened in 1899, there were only two classes at the end of 1900 and the total roll was 32. There were two more classes to follow, the third and the fourth and these would come into existence after one year and two years, respectively. The system of training at Abetifi was similar to that given at Akropong. The four years' course was devoted to the training of teachers and catechists. The only exception at Abetifi was that Greek was no longer taught and the last two years devoted to Catechists' training concentrated exclusively on theological subjects.

Schlatter tells us that Abetifi Seminary also made good progress until 1914 when it began to decline. For example, the growth of the number of students during five year periods after 1900 was: 1905: 30; 1910: 52, and 1914: 34.³¹

At the end of each year officers from the Education Department went to the seminaries and held examinations for the Teachers' Certificate. But at the end of their final year the students were examined by the Basel Local Committee, on the subjects studied in the final year including preaching a sermon on a given text. This examination lasted for a week and on the Sunday that immediately followed it the catechists were consecrated. This Sunday used to be momentous in the life of the seminaries and especially for Akropong town. The Principal usually dressed in his full academic and ecclesiastical robes and led a procession of the students to the chapel. People were invited from far and near to be present at the ceremony. The Principal preached the sermon and after that he introduced the students to the Local Committee of Missionaries and they consecrated them. The rest of the Sunday was spent by the students in parading the town and bidding goodbye to their friends. Early on Monday morning they were told of their stations and they departed from the seminary for good, singing their consecration hymn:

> Onyame asoma yen ne turom adwumaye
> Asumanfo ne akomfo asee n'afuw dedaw
> Fa wo dom so soma yen
> Abibirim aman no nkyen
> Wo nkurofo ye mmobo, ye mmobo, ye mmobo,
> Soma yen wo nkurofo nkyen.³²

Before I discuss the development of the seminary training in the Twentieth Century let us have a look at the impact the training had on the

---

30 B.M.A., Reports (Basel, 1900), p. 24.
31 Schlatter, *op. cit.*, p. 184. The decline might have been caused by the World War crisis.
32 Gunn, *A Hundred Years*, p. 6.
 Paraphrased in English as follows:
  God has sent us to labour in his garden which had been destroyed by unbelievers. Send us by your Grace to the Africans because they are doomed: send us to your people.

growth of the Church during the second half of the Nineteenth Century. It will be recalled that the Basel Mission work did not bear any visible fruits in the Gold Coast until after 1843. From that date onwards the work began to make gradual but steady progress. At the end of 1848 the Annual Report said that "at last the wilderness and solitary places were beginning to rejoice and the fruits were to be seen".[33] There were 60 Christians, including the 20 West Indian immigrants, at Akropong and Christiansborg. Ten years later in 1858, the seminaries had produced 26 local assistants (teachers and catechists) working in six stations: Christiansborg, Abokobi, Akropong, Aburi, Gyadem in Akyem and Odumasi in Krobo area. The preaching of the Gospel produced wonderful harvest, and church membership during these ten years increased from 60 to 385 and by the end of 1899 there were 17,645 Christians distributed over 11 stations and 185 outstations.[34] Reindorf was not exaggerating when he said, "the work had developed manhood through the manly work of those to whom it was entrusted",[35] and these men to whom the work had been entrusted were none other than the missionaries and the African assistants they had been training.

The happiest progress made during this period was the ordination of 31 trained catechists as pastors of congregations.[36] Before the seminary at Akropong was fully established opportunity had been offered to some of the most brilliant boys to continue their theological training in the Mission House in Basel. About 1856 David Asante was sent there. He was later joined by Nicholas Clerk in the following year, and in 1858 four other boys were also sent. The project was abandoned after 1858 because three of the four boys sent that year had to return home immediately probably because of ill-health, and the fourth one, Wilh. Oforikai, died of consumption in Europe.[37] Thus only two of the six who had been sent survived the change from Africa to Europe and successfully completed their studies. David Asante was the first to finish his studies and on 20th July, 1862, he became "the first (Gold Coaster) to receive Lutheran Orders on his ordination into the Ministry of the Basel Missionary Society in Basel".[38] Nicholas Clerk, the other survivor, was not ordained until 1888.

While these were under training in Basel some of the first fruits of the Akropong Seminary were also being groomed locally. Theophilus Opoku was ordained in 1872, becoming the second ordained local Basel Mission pastor but the first African minister to be trained and ordained by the Ba-

---

33 Reindorf, *op. cit.*, p. 220.
34 B.M.A., *Reports* (Basel, 1900), p. 27.
35 Reindorf, *loc. cit.*
36 Appendix VII.
37 Schlatter, *op. cit.*, p. 97. Smith, *op. cit.*, p. 51, Fn. 1: substitutes *Oforiba* for *Oforikai* without giving reasons for doing so.
38 H.J. Keteku, *The Reverends Theophilus Opoku and David Asante* (Accra, 1965), p. 12.

sel Evangelical Mission in the Gold Coast.[39] From 1872 onwards several of the faithful catechists were ordained as pastors to shepherd congregations, and the ministerial roll continued to increase steadily until, by the end of the century, 31 African ministers had been ordained.

These achievements did not come without their attendant problems. One of the missionaries in Akropong, the Rev. Mr. Mader, was nicknamed "Kwadjo Okoto" and the significance of this name is that it recalls one of the oppositions the missionaries had encountered in those early days at Akropong. It seems there lived at Akropong in the past a notorious person by the name Kwadjo Okoto who went about molesting people. So, Mader was probably considered to be Kwadjo Okoto redivivus because the records tell us that Mader always flogged the fetish priests who opposed the spread of the Gospel.[40] This hostility to the spread of the Gospel affected the seminary adversely from the beginning. It made some of the students nervous; it made a few of them run away and it made others fear what fate would befall them if the missionaries were to abandon the work and go away. But the missionaries were not dismayed; they went on labouring patiently and confidently until from 1899 they began to see abundant fulfilment of their ultimate aim for the theological schools viz: "to educate native Ministers, able to take care of the congregations, to feed their flock with knowledge and understanding...."[41] (Jer. III^{15}). Indeed Gunn must have been expressing the feelings of the men who started and developed the seminaries when he wrote that:

> These [years] must have been very happy, profitable years—years when the seminary was well established, knew what it wanted to do and how to do it, years when war and deportation were not even imagined.[42]

The period 1900 to 1914 was one of progress and consolidation of the traditions laid down in the seminaries during the past century. By July 1st, 1900, there were 75 students at Akropong and 21 at Abetifi.[43] The efficiency with which the students were trained was reflected in the Inspection Reports for the years preceding World War I. For example, in 1911 the Director of Education reported thus:

> Great attention has again been paid by the Basel Mission to agricultural work, and of the seven prizes awarded for the best school plantations no less than five have been given to the schools of this society. The number of teachers of this Mission who hold Agricultural Certificates is now very considerable, and judging from the excellent condition of many of the school gardens, there is evidence that the teachers have profited to a great extent by the courses of in-

---

39 *Ibid.*, pp. 5-6.
40 Gunn, *op. cit.*, p. 4.
41 Otto Schatt, *A Retrospect on Fifty Years of Mission Work* (Basel, 1879), p. 13.
42 Gunn, *op. cit.*, p. 6.
43 B.M.A., *Reports* (Basel, 1900), p. 9.

struction. ... The Carpentry in Basel Mission schools is far in advance of that done in other schools.[44]

Between 1914 and 1917 Rev. A. Jehle, a university-trained Principal of Akropong seminary attached the first secondary school class to the seminary, and under him Akropong "became a top seminary of higher standards"[45] than Abetifi.

But the period 1914-1918 was catastrophic for the Basel Mission work on the Gold Coast. World War I broke out in August 1914. Soon after that the Basel Missionaries declared their neutrality by confessing that they were not German but Swiss.[46] In spite of this declaration all the missionaries were removed to Accra in November. But after a few days they were permitted to return to their various stations. They had to report to the police regularly and their movements were restricted. With the exception of leave to visit the schools, the missionaries had to request permission before they travelled beyond a few miles from their stations. Of the 37 Basel Missionaries in the field at the time all except eight were German. Later they were permitted to visit their village congregations but official permission was to be sought from the Gold Coast Government before other head stations were visited.

In 1915 the Government's attitude to the Missionaries became hardened. On 19th August of that year the Acting Colonial Secretary wrote to the General Superintendent forbidding the Basel Missionaries on the Gold Coast to hold any meetings while the war continued, and warning that "any proved case of an attempt by a missionary to use his influence disloyally to the British administration will be dealt with severely and that any individual misdemeanour may be punished by the immediate internment of the German Missionaries".[47] In the following year the British Government requested the Basel Mission to send, in future, only native-born Swiss Missionaries to the Gold Coast; but the Mission Board in Basel refused to accede to the request on the grounds that such an action would defeat the international character of the Basel Missionary Society.[48] The British Foreign Office reacted angrily to the Basel Mission Board's view-point and notice was given that:

> His Majesty's Government have arrived at the conclusion that the Basel Mission as at present constituted, is so German in sympathy that it cannot be allowed to operate any longer in a British dependency.[49]

---

44 Gold Coast Government, *Education Report*, 1911 (Accra, 1912), p. 29.
45 Debrunner, *A History of Christianity*, p. 262.
46 *The Gold Coast Leader* (Cape Coast), 5th Sept., 1914, p. 2.
47 Smith, *The Presbyterian Church of Ghana*, p. 147 citing Scottish Mission records, Colonial Secretary to General Superintendent, 19th August, 1915.
48 Smith, *op. cit.*, pp. 19-21. "The ecumenical and international character of the Mission is illustrated by the sphere of labour entered into by men trained at the Seminary [in Basel]".
49 *Ibid.*, p. 148, citing G.A. Wanner, *Basler Handelsgesellschaft*, 1859-1959 (Basel, 1959), pp. 309-310.

After a year, on 10th December, 1917, the Colonial Secretary wrote to G. Zürcher the General Superintendent of the Basel Mission in the Gold Coast as follows:

> I am directed by the Governor to inform you that His Excellency has received instructions from the Secretary of State for the Colonies that all Basel Missionaries of German nationality are to be deported with the least possible delay and that action is being taken accordingly.[50]

It seems that this action had been precipitated by the Press in the Gold Coast. There seems to have been some trouble in Kumasi and the Gold Coast Leader published the following article:

> The rising has been caused through certain Basel Missionaries trekking up and down the country and persuading the poor ignorant people into the belief that the Hun is sure to come out victorious in the present world struggle and that he would have no favour for them if they did not kick against the veritable pricks—the allies.[51]

Although the Rev. Zürcher wrote a letter on 23rd May, 1917, to the Colonial Secretary refuting the charge[52] nothing could change the Government's decision. So, in December 1917 the missionaries were arrested.

The occasion was a pathetic spectacle at the Akropong Seminary. It was on 7th December, 1917. The usual Teachers' end of year examination was in progress. Rev. Stricker, a native Swiss and head of the Teacher Training Department was invigilating late in the afternoon. The other members of staff were conversing together outside when a District Commissioner accompanied by an escort policeman arrived in the school and enquired of Mr. Stricker. Mr. Stricker met the D.C. and the news was divulged: Stricker was made to convey to "the German Missionaries that the Government had decided to deport them, and that they were to be taken down to Accra that very evening."[53] They were allowed only one hour to pack their baggage. After that the Principal Jehle, Nothwang, Monninger and Grau were placed in a lorry without roof and conveyed to Accra. Stricker and Mrs. Grau alone remained at Akropong: Stricker because he was a native Swiss and Mrs. Grau because she was in the family way.[54] Grau was allowed to return to Akropong the following day on account of his wife; thus, he alone had the chance of disposing of his personal effects before he and his wife left for Accra. The people of Akropong did not desert the missionaries at the time of misfortune. They "crowded round [them] and everybody felt it was not easy to say good-bye with eyes dry".[55] By the 16th of December, 1917, the interned missionaries were deported.

---

50 Smith, *op. cit.*, p. 150, citing Scottish Mission Correspondence, Colonial Secretary to General Superintendent, 10th Dec., 1917.
51 *The Gold Coast Leader* (Cape Coast), No. 769, 5th May, 1917, p. 2.
52 B.M.A., (Unclassified envelope containing miscellaneous reports on the Gold Coast).
53 Gunn, *op. cit.*, p. 8.
54 *Loc. cit.*
55 *Loc. cit.*

The eight non-German missionaries were left behind. Six were native Swiss: H. Stricker in charge of the Akropong College, G. Zürcher at Aburi, and H. Henking at Abetifi; one was an American, N. Rhode also stationed at Abetifi and the other, an Australian, F. Jost, at Kumasi. To the utter surprise of these missionaries it became illegal as from 12th January, 1918, for any European alien to remain on the Akwapim Ridge. Zürcher tried to negotiate with the Government for permission to remove the seminary from Akropong to Odumase or Anum; but the request was not granted and on 2nd February, 1918, the remaining missionaries were ordered to leave the country by the next boat. Zürcher protested against the expulsion order but his protest was rejected by the Colonial Secretary[56] and the order was implemented.

"Thus after close on ninety years of dedicated endeavour, during which the mission initiated far-reaching religious and social changes ... it was thrust out of the country".[57] Seventy-five out of those ninety years were concentrated on the training of African personnel as teachers and teacher-catechists. The endeavour had not been in vain because a good number of the catechist-teachers climbed to the apex of the training—the ordained ministry. At the end of 1918 the number of catechists who had been ordained ministers since 1862 amounted to 56.[58] But at the beginning of the expulsions the future of the seminaries became obscure. However, they continued to function throughout the remaining months of 1918. Two Education Officers, Pearson and later Crankson, took charge of the seminary at Akropong but in the case of Abetifi the African members of staff were left alone to hold the fort. At the end of the year an influenza epidemic ravaged the whole country and for the first time in seventy years the seminary at Akropong was closed down and Abetifi also ceased to function.

---

56 B.M.A., Colonial Secretary to Zürcher, 8th Feb., 1918. Mr. and Mrs. Zürcher and Mr. Dieterle were permitted to remain in the country until the relevant documents on education were satisfactorily handed over to the Director of Education.
57 Smith, *op. cit.*, p. 152.
58 Appendix VII.

CHAPTER FOUR

BREMEN MISSION TRAINING
1855-1915

While the Basel Mission seminaries remained closed let us turn to the Bremen Mission efforts at the training of African ministers in Eweland. The aim of the Bremen Mission training of local personnel followed closely that of the Basel Mission, viz: "to train young men as teachers and catechists some of whom [might] eventually become ministers".[1] The first attempt to start a seminary at Keta was made by Kohlhammer in 1855 after six young men had been baptized. A primary school had been established there about 1853. From that school the Rev. Mr. Kohlhammer recruited the brighter boys for his institute for the training of African leaders. This institute did not make much progress from 1855 to 1860 because the relatives of the young men "were not interested in having them serve the mission, but wanted them trained for getting positions with the trading firms".[2] In 1857 the institute was transferred from Keta away from the attractions of the firms, to Waya in the interior. But these tactics did not change the attitude of the coastal people: only four students sought admission to the institute; when they had completed their course no other students applied for admission. It seems the opening of the institute had been premature.

The primary schools which had been opened at Keta and Anyako continued to make progress and at the beginning of the 1860s it became desirable to start a higher school for the training of the graduates from those schools. So, in 1861 Gottlieb Hess from Switzerland was sent out to open a school for the training of teachers and preachers. After his survey of the stations, Keta, Anyako, Waya, Ho and Peki, Gottlieb suggested that the training institute should be opened at Ho, the most central of all. But the students at Keta and Anyako were too young or too immature spiritually and some of them were reluctant to leave home for Ho. Some of those who had already graduated from the schools had been employed by the missionaries as interpreters. The opening of the school was therefore postponed and Gottlieb remained and taught at the Ho primary school.

Meanwhile the missionaries continued to find ways and means whereby the seminary could be opened: Johann Conrad Hauser of Switzerland was sent to the Gold Coast "to open a seminary as soon as possible after

---
1 Cf. The aim of the Basel Mission Training already quoted: pp. 36 & 41.
2 E. Grau, "The Evangelical Presbyterian Church: A study in European Relations affecting the beginning of an Indigenous Church in Ghana". Unpublished Ph.D. Thesis. Hartford Seminary Foundation, 1958, p. 165.

learning to know the country and the language".³ At the beginning of 1864 the Local Missionary Committee appointed a school commission to make investigations at each station to find out the number of boys who might qualify for recruitment into the proposed seminary. Their findings were not very encouraging because they discovered that the choice of students would be limited to only two schools: Keta and Waya. But when an entrance examination was conducted at Anyako, three students from Ho and six from Anyako passed and none from Waya and Keta. It seems, however, that one of the nine successful students dropped out before the seminary was actually opened.

Thus about the middle of 1864 the first real Bremen Mission Seminary was opened at Ho with eight students: Solomon Gudeti, Heinrich Theodor, George Johnson from Christiansborg, Josua Nyamasrọ from Srọgbe, and the four Quist brothers from Dzelukọfe: Isaac, Emmanuel, Peter and Solomon.⁴ At the end of 1864 the Rev. Mr. Vögelin joined the first Principal, Hauser and these two men gave all the lessons till the end of 1865 when Vögelin had to return home due to ill-health and Hauser remained the sole teacher. The simple syllabus comprised mainly religious subjects plus Geography, History and English. The course was intended to last four or five years. At the end of the first academic year the missionaries made it a policy that only seminary men would be employed in the future as teachers and catechists. This improved the recruitment considerably. The roll grew steadily and in 1866/67 there were 17 students in residence. The progress made by the seminary in three years was evidenced by its results: at the end of the first academic year Solomon Quist was employed at Keta; in 1867 many more graduates of the Ho Seminary were at work with the Mission. For example, Isaac C. Quist at Anyako, Solomon, Peter and Emmanuel Quist were at Keta; and Aaron Kwami, Fridrich Larson Kwami and Isaac Kwami were all in the service of the Mission at various stations.⁵

Hauser, the first Principal, went on furlough in 1868 and was succeeded by Gottlieb Zündel of Württemberg. He found the work too much for one person and so he employed the oldest student in residence, George Johnson as part-time teacher.

It was during the time of Zündel that the missionaries became greatly concerned about the results of the seminary training. Although the aim of the seminary was to train men for work in the mission some of the students refused to remain in the mission work after completing their studies. Nor was that all. Some of the pupils in the primary schools who had qualified for admission into the seminary declined to have seminary training. Others

---

3 *Ibid.,* p. 166.
4 North Bremen Mission Archives (NBMA), Register of Students: Bremen Mission Seminary 1864-1914 (File 101 (b)), Bremen. The exact date when the seminary was opened had not been recorded. It had only been indicated that the Seminary started at Ho 1864/65. Grau, *op. cit.,* p. 166, suggested that it was in "July" that the school was opened.
5 Grau, *ibid.,* p. 167.

who qualified and were willing to attend were considered by the missionaries as too immature for seminary work.

In order to help the unwilling students to be useful even if they refused to be in the mission employment or attend the seminary, a school commission was appointed to investigate the problem and suggest the right approach the mission should take. The commission decided that the primary school pupils who were qualified for the seminary but were unwilling to attend should be placed with the Vietor Trading Company where they could be helped by Christian discipline, and those who were too immature to benefit by the seminary training should either be employed at V.T.C. or be taught some trade at the Ho Station.[6]

While thinking was progressing on these proposals the seminary work was disrupted and the Rev. Zündel with his students had to leave Ho, on 18th July, 1869, and take refuge at Anyako. The occasion was the Ashanti invasion of Ho in 1869. The causes and progress of the Ashanti Wars of 1869 cannot be discussed here;[7] it should suffice to note how the war affected the progress of the Bremen Mission work in general[8] and the seminary in particular. During this war the Anlō (Keta, Anyako and the coastal towns), Adaklu and Akwamu were in alliance with the Ashanti against the inhabitants of Ho, Agotime and other inland towns. On June 12, 1869, the Ashanti captured Anum near Peki and deported two Basel Missionaries, Ramseyer and Kühne, to Kumasi. So, when the Ashanti advance towards Ho was announced, Zündel prudently transferred the seminary to Anyako probably because the pupils from the Anyako school had been showing keener interest in seeking admission to the seminary than those of Keta.[9] In September 1870 Hauser returned from furlough and resumed his seminary work at Anyako; but on 6th October, 1871, he died. Weyhe, from Keta, was appointed to take charge of the seminary but he also died on 27th November, 1871. The next successor, Bendor, also died on 20th August, 1872. The next man, Lodholz, became the Principal and worked until 1877 when he also died in December. The next two, Lungling and Bihler, died on 23rd August, 1879 and 4th March, 1880, respectively.[10] Thus during ten years, out of nine missionaries who led the seminary, six of them had died early.

After eleven years at Anyako, the seminary was transferred to Keta in 1881 because Keta flourished rapidly after the Ashanti wars. The reason is

---

6 *Ibid.*, p. 168.
7 Ward, *A History of Ghana*, pp. 228-231 and 241-243.
   Those interested in a detailed account of this war may consult these references.
8 Wiegräbe, *Ewe Kristo Hame*, pp. 31-33. Wiegräbe relates in detail the general effects of the war on the work of the Missionaries.
9 Grau, *op. cit.*, p. 167: in 1865 six students from Anyako alone sought admission to the seminary.
10 Paul Wiegräbe supplied these details from his personal papers.

that after the Ashanti wars had come to an end, the British made peace with the Anlo in 1874 and stationed a British commandant with a contingent of 100 Hausa soldiers at Keta,[11] and the district became quiet and peaceful. The population increased rapidly because the town's people, the majority of whom were traders, had migrated from various other towns.[12] Although the elementary school at Keta made good progress the seminary did not, because here too, the premium being placed on the economic values of education far outweighed the desire for theological training.[13] The period 1881 to 1893 was critical for the seminary at Keta; in some years no candidates were admitted because none wanted to be trained for mission work.[14] In fact, after the death of the Principal, Knüsli, in 1891, the seminary was closed down for three years after which it was re-opened at Amedzofe,[15] a town farther inland than Ho, because of health reasons as shown below.

The Amedzofe mission work had been started in 1876. A few men from Avatime district who had lived at Mayera and Abokobi in the Gold Coast colony (Southern Ghana) became converted to the Christian faith, and were baptized by Basel Missionaries. On their return to Eweland they introduced themselves to the Bremen Missionaries at Ho. Later they settled at Dzokpe, in the Avatime district, and renamed it Jerusalem. There they began to form a small Christian community, and as the community increased in numbers they requested the Mission Station at Ho to supply a teacher to care for the work. Amedzofe is strategic in this area; it is situated on a hill and its position makes its climatic conditions cool and extremely healthy. The missionaries acquired a large piece of land there upon which a future mission station could be built. In 1889 the community's request for a teacher was granted and Paul Ntumitse was appointed to reside at Amedzofe. In the following year, 1890, the first Missionary, Seeger, went to settle there and he found the place very healthy. Consequently, in 1894 the Seminary was transferred from Keta to Amedzofe where Seeger and his African assistant, Samuel Quist, became the pioneer teachers of the Amedzofe Seminary. From 1894 to 1914 the work of training African personnel became consolidated there and extraordinary progress was made.

At this point it should be stated that during those critical years, 1881-1893, at Keta, when the seminary work was not developing satisfactorily, the mission board permitted Pastor Binder to make an "experiment of training some negro youths in Europe."[16] The idea emeged in the follow-

---

11 H.W. Debrunner, *The Church in Togo: A Church between Colonial Powers* (London, 1965), p. 91.
12 Wiegräbe, *Ewe Kristo Hame*, p. 33.
13 See p. 86 footnote 2.
14 North Bremen Mission Archives (N.B.M.A.), *Monatsblatt, 1914*, pp. 76-78.
15 Grau, *op. cit.*, p. 223.
16 Debrunner, *The Church in Togo*, p. 128.

ing way: the Rev. C. Binder, a missionary, retired from the mission field in 1871 on health grounds. As he and Mrs. Binder were ill, they took with them to Europe a 14 year-old schoolboy, Christian Alifodzi Sedode, to nurse their sick baby, mainly to wash its napkins. Christian continued his education while serving the Binders at Wilhelmsdorf in Württemberg. After having spent two years in school, Christian was attacked by a severe lung trouble, and he had to return home to the Gold Coast where he continued his education in the seminary, then at Anyako. He became a teacher in the seminary until 1889 when he had to retire from the teaching profession on health grounds. After receiving his pension he continued to serve the mission as an Ewe language teacher to the missionaries and "up to his death he was an upright, modest, industrious man".[17] The Rev. Binder was encouraged by the usefulness of Christian to the mission work after only two years' education in Germany. It was this usefulness of his boy that led Rev. C. Binder to consider that other boys might yield similar results when trained in Europe. In 1882 Ernest Winard Kwaku was sent but he had to return without completing his studies because he did not have the ability to profit by the experience.[18]

After Kwaku, all the nineteen men who were sent from 1884 to 1897 to get a more thorough training for mission work benefited by their studies, returned home and served the mission in various capacities, though all of them as we shall presently see below, did not remain in the service of the mission for a long time.

Thus from 1871 to 1900 twenty Ewe boys including Christian Alifodzi Sedode were efficiently trained in Germany for mission work in their own country.

The students who were sent to Pastor Binder in 1884 were three: Andreas Aku, Herman Yoyo and Reinhold Kowu. Pastor Binder was still a parish priest at Wilhelmsdorf and there these three students had their training for three years. Andreas Aku, the most competent of the three, had teacher training in his last year at the Evangelical Teacher Training College of Lichtenstein near Löenstein in the district of Heilbronn. Later Pastor Binder was transferred to Westheim where the subsequent students were trained from 1890-1900. After the first set of three boys, three others were sent in 1890, one in 1891, three in 1892, two in 1893, three in 1894, two in 1895 and three in 1897.[19]

---

17 *Loc. cit.*
18 Grau, *op. cit.*, p. 258.
19 Schreiber, *Bausteine, 1936*, p. 252.
   Debrunner, *The Church in Togo*, p. 128. The 20 boys were: 1884, Andreas Aku, Hermann Yoyo and Reinhold Kowu.
   In 1890, Benjamin Onipayede, Albert Binder (married) and Samuel Quist.
   In 1891, Isaac Kwadzo.
   In 1892, Elias Kende and Theodor Martin Sedode Bebli.
   In 1893, Zacharias Deku and Nathaniel Kwami.

The subjects which they studied were:
A) Common Subjects taken by all students together: English, Drawing, Gymnastics and Music.
B) Subjects taken according to classes:

Class I. German, Bible Stories (Bible Knowledge including hymns which corresponded to some of the scripture passages), Oral German (through reading), Geography and Natural Science (Botany, Nature Study, etc.), Mathematics and Confirmation.

Class II. Left blank: no reason was given in the records to explain why no subjects were indicated for this class. Possibly, the subjects studied in Class I were introductory and were repeated in greater detail in Class II.

Class III. German History (World History), Church History, Physics, Arithmetic, Pedagogics and Methodics, Bible Knowledge and Comparative Religions.[20]

The teachers recorded as assistants to Pastor Binder were Flothmeier and Binder Jnr. Flothmeier taught English while Binder Jnr. taught German. Music was also taught by another helper whose name was not on record. He was only recorded as a Music Teacher. The idea may be that any music teacher who was available to come was accepted.

The students were made to feel quite at home in their new environment as evidenced by the contents of the following letter written by one of them in 1890 to the Mission Inspector in Bremen:

Westheim 29th Dec. 1890

Dear Sir,

I am hereby sending you my best thanks about our Christmas present by you. We have had a pretty evening on that day and I wish to relate you a little of it: at the very afternoon we are assembled together in our schoolroom, the whole family, the old grandmother, the maidservant together with us three. Firstly we have sung in the German hymn book Nro. 103 from the first verse till the third, afterward read our house-father the second chapter of St. Luke from the first verse till the fourteenth and spoke about it about 3/4 of an hour. After this he prayed and we sang the last verse of the same hymn. And as the conclusion we sang:

"Tochter Zion freue dich. . ." which we have learned before time.

Now we all were called upstairs into a certain room where a beautiful Christmas tree have (sic) stood, with many lights within. There stand two tables, on which the presents were set. Separately was ours on the little one.

In 1894, Ludwig Medenu, Elia Awuma and Robert Kwami.
In 1895, Theophil Asieni and Christoph Gebhard Mensa.
In 1897, Timotheo Mallet, Timotheo Ametowobla and Robert Baëta.
Plus the pioneer student, Christian Alifodzi Sedode.
20 N.B.M.A., File No. 66.

Oh, very joyful it was to us! On the following days we have celebrated the certain (sic) festivals.

With kind regards,
Yours Obediently,
Benjamin Onipayedey.[21]

The students were adopted into the family of the Binders and there in the manse Pastor Binder educated them and demonstrated to them, through the intimate fellowship his home accorded them, what a Christian home should be like.

The financial responsibility for the students' stay in Europe did not devolve on the Binders alone. In order to pay for part of the expenses incurred in the training, small societies and Sunday schools in Germany were encouraged by the Missionary Society to adopt students and pledge their financial support to the students they adopted. The response was encouraging and the pledges were honoured throughout the period. But in 1900 the experiment was discontinued mainly because Pastor Binder became very old and his age and health could not permit him to superintend this valuable work and secondly because by 1900 the seminary work in Eweland had been re-organized and was making good progress at Amedzofe. But the position was not as simple as that. Towards the end of the Nineteenth Century people began to express doubts about the effectiveness of the Westheim programme because of the following reasons:

First, as the years went by the cost of the programme became too heavy for the supporters to carry; the fare to and from Germany was large and the cost of the support of the students while they were in Germany became more difficult to bear. Second, the duration of the course was three years. The fear was expressed in Germany that the period was so long that the students might become so Europeanised that when they returned home they would be isolated from their own people.[22] As Zahn, the mission inspector, favoured the training in Europe, he suggested that in order to obviate the fear that the students would lose contact with their own people, a six months' course in Germany might be more profitable. Zahn also felt that too long a time spent by the African students studying in Europe could lead to pride in the attitude of some of them when they returned to Africa because "pride is the sin particularly of those who are the least gifted".[23] Third, some of the students had poor health while they were in Germany and others became ill on their return to Africa. Fourth, Zahn died in 1900 and he was succeeded by M. Schlunk. But Schlunk had been so opposed to

---

21 N.B.M.A., File No. 67.
22 Grau, *op. cit.*, p. 259, where references are also made to Bericht, 1891 in M.B., 1892, p. 68.
23 Zahn to Missionaries, June 20, 1895, translated by Grau in "The Evangelical Presbyterian Church", p. 259.

the project that when the students in residence completed their studies about the middle of 1900 no new men were allowed to go to Westheim.

There were three students in the final batch: Timothy Mallet, Timothy Ametowobla and Robert Baëta. As they were the last group to study under Binder in Germany, a special farewell service was held in their honour on 15th July, 1900, at Westheim. Each of the students gave an address in German: Ametowobla spoke on "The life story of the three outgoing students"; Baëta on "Heathenism in my country" and Mallet on "How Ewe Christians celebrate Church days and Church festivals."[24] Their talks were followed by that of Pastor Binder who spoke on "The Origin, Purpose and Result of the training of Africans in Germany". Among other things he said:

> The outcome of the Ewe School could be considered very good in the case of *all* the pupils if it were expected of the college-course merely that the students trained in it should teach others what they had learnt themselves without any regard to their life and behaviour; if all that was expected of the Mission were merely to spread European culture amongst people without a culture, and of a mission school, receiving its pupils at least partly from the German protectorate in Africa,[25] that on their return they should spread the German customs and German way of life, that they should if possible also enter the service of the German government, promote German trade and represent German interests. But this way of looking at the matter is just not correct; it is in fact too low. . . .
>
> In contrast with this expectation there is the claim that a mission school should not merely teach but also educate that it should not merely provide its pupils with a general human training, but equip them particularly for missionary purposes. Moreover it is not to be expected of a mission school in Europe, in the old Christendom, that it makes faithful use of the temporary transplanting of those committed to its care in order to clarify, widen and deepen their Christian understanding, to strengthen their character for good, and to encourage their spiritual life, often so young and immature, and the purpose of all this is that with the completion of their training period they may return to the field of work in their home not only well trained and enriched with knowledge, but sound in faith and burning with love in order to show themselves to be humble, efficient and reliable workers, as assistants for the missionaries, as wise educators for the pupils and as shining examples of all that is good to the older teachers.
>
> This it seems to me the purpose and goal of the mission school entrusted to me.[26]

In the light of the purpose and goal of the Ewe School in Westheim set forth in Binder's farewell report it could be safely concluded that the project was a great success when we consider the contribution some of the Westheim men made to the progress of the Church in Eweland. Briefly Dr. Grau says:

---

24 C. Binder, *Bericht der Evhe-schule und das letzte Neger-Missionsfest in Westheim* (Bremen, 1900), pp. 19-20.
25 Appendix VI.
26 C. Binder, *loc. cit.*, cited in English by Debrunner, *The Church in Togo*, pp. 128-129.

In 1903 nine of them were still serving the Mission. Some had died, others had left for higher paying jobs offered by the Government of Togoland and the rest had been dismissed.[27] But those who remained had made the effort most worthwhile. Together with the seminary trained men, they formed the African leadership which the Church [needed].[28]

But when we consider that from the beginning of the seminary work in 1864 until 1900 there was only one ordained African minister in Eweland, then we pause and ask why. It was in 1882, on March 19, that Rudolf Mallet was ordained as the first Ewe Minister by the Bremen Mission. It was after 19 years that the second and the third, Samuel Newell and Adolf Lawoe, were ordained at Ho on 23rd June, 1901. As for the Westheim men the first, Andreas Aku, was ordained at Lome on 6th March, 1910. It was only from that year that ordination of the indigenous ministers in the Bremen Mission became an annual tradition in Eweland.[29]

Although Zahn, the Mission Inspector until 1900, supported the view that the Christian Church in Eweland should be staffed by her own local workers and "also bravely proposed and carried out the training and education of a certain number of Ewe young men in Germany for Mission work..."[30] he was sceptical about the wisdom of ordaining Africans to be ministers. Zahn laid down certain conditions which the African assistant should fulfil before he could be considered as a fit person for Holy Orders. The conditions were based on 1st Timothy 3: 1-7 and Titus 1: 5-9,[31] a prospective candidate for the ministry should first of all satisfy all the conditions laid down in "Timothy" and in his work as a teacher the candidate should not only demonstrate ability and faithfulness but he should show that he understands the meaning of mission work. In addition he should have a good capacity to judge things independently and should acquire some scientific training in a seminary. Finally, he should constantly be studious. According to Zahn the African helpers did not reach the requirements because not all the students who had received training in the seminary remained in the mission work.[32] Zahn probably forgot that neither the missionaries in Africa nor the pastors in Germany were perfect men.

Zahn's policy was changed by his successor, Schlunk. Schlunk visited the

---

27 pp. 55 and 59.
28 Grau, *op. cit.,* p. 223.
29 Appendix VII.
30 R.D. Baëta, *The Development of Native Leadership* (Bremen, 1924), p. 6.
31 1 Tim. 3: 1-7: The saying is sure: if any one aspires to the office of a Bishop, he desires a noble task. Now a bishop must be above reproach, the husband of one wife, temperate ... moreover he must be well thought of by outsiders or he may fall into reproach and the snare of the devil. (RSV)
Titus 1: 5-9. This is why I left you in Crete, that you might amend what was defective, and appoint elders in every town as I directed you, if any man is blameless, the husband of one wife ... to confute those who contradict it. (RSV)
32 N.B.M.A., *Monatsblatt,* 1908, p. 78.

Mission field in Eweland in 1900. "By careful examination of the state of affairs he was impressed by the vital importance of Africans being gradually drawn into the sense of responsibility and to take part in the leadership of their own people".[33] Without any delay he proposed the ordination of two of the oldest catechists, Newell and Lawoe, whose ordination in 1901 abolished the unrealistic and ungrateful policy followed by Inspector Zahn. According to Schlunk the aim of the mission should be

> that each principal station should have its native pastor and those who have passed muster under the direct supervision of the missionary should be placed later at the larger outstations where otherwise the presence of the missionary would be necessary, yet hardly possible. The better the training of teachers and pastors, the more effective will be their help in theological and church work, as well as in leading the congregations, and the nearer the possibility of uniting the different station districts into synods with the natives playing their part; that is to say the goal of a self-governing Ewe Church under the leadership of the missionaries for the time being.[34]

Two factors were essential if Schlunk's policy could succeed. They were the need for increasing the number of the ministers (pastors) and improving the quality of the training given to the African assistants. To implement these needs, from 1910 to 1914, six Africans were ordained as pastors and in 1911 the seminary course at Amedzofe was lengthened from three years to four "and examinations during service and for promotion were introduced, as well as continuation courses for teachers with a full programme".[35]

The subsequent paragraphs will now trace the development of the *Seminary at Amedzofe* from 1984 when it was transferred from Keta until the deportation of the missionaries in 1918.

It will be recalled that Seeger and Samuel Quist were the pioneer teachers when the seminary was re-opened at Amedzofe in 1894. Later in the year the Rev. Ernest Bürgi, a Swiss teacher, was appointed the Principal of the Seminary. He held that post for 28 years including breaks and furloughs. During those years the seminary made remarkable progress, although youths from the coast did not patronize it very much because of the familiar economic reasons already given above. The greatest support in the supply of students came from the inland stations which were free from the commercial attractions of the coastal towns. As Fr. Bernard Clements stamped his personality on St. Augustine's College in Kumasi, so also the seminary at Amedzofe "received its Character from this Swiss missionary, Ernest Bürgi, whose output of work, from the merely physical aspect was phenomenal."[36] From 1894 to 1907 he held the post without breaks and

---

33 R.D. Baëta, *op. cit.*, p. 7.
34 M. Schlunk, *Die Nordeutsche Mission in Togo II* (Bremen, 1912), p. 139, cited in English by Debrunner, *The Church in Togo*, p. 131.
35 Debrunner, *ibid.*, p. 132.
36 *Loc. cit.*

this gave the institution stability. During this period Bürgi made some important changes. At first, the training lasted three years but in 1912 a new upper class was added, raising the duration of the course to four years. Two reasons accounted for this change. By 1912 the school age of pupils was no longer as high as it had been in the earlier days: consequently, some of the students completed their seminary training when they were still immature. The other reason was that as the educational system of the college developed and the Government made rules to govern both Government and Mission Assisted schools, greater responsibility was required from the teachers who would serve in the schools. Thus the fourth year helped the students to mature and also served to equip them more thoroughly for their work.

The subjects taught were the usual college subjects of those days viz: Vernacular (Ewe), English, Bible Study: Old and New Testaments, Catechism, Church History (Bremen Mission), World History, Geography, Singing, Symbolics, Church Dogmatics, Homiletics, Dogmatics, Music (Harmonium Playing), Practical Preaching, Biblical Theology, and Agriculture. The medium of teaching was Ewe and Bürgi wrote or translated most of the theological books used. They included books on the Old and New Testaments, Homiletics and Doctrine and were still preserved in cyclostyled manuscripts in the North Bremen Mission Archives in Bremen, Western Germany, during my research visit there in March, 1969.

Materials were dictated from the books to the students because there were no books from which the students could expand their notes if they were to take down sketchy notes from the teacher's lectures.[37]

Whatever arguments modern educationists may adduce for or against this method of teaching do not concern us at present; what is important is that the training the men received under Bürgi and his assistants was thorough and it was that thoroughness, as we shall presently see below, which sustained the Ewe Church during the critical years of World War I and after.

Of the African assistants who helped in the training of the students in the seminary the most notable were: George Johnson, Peter Quist, Stephano Kwami, Joseph Reindorf, Christian Alifodzi, Josua Böhn, Aaron Mexadzi, Samuel Quist, Theodore Sedode, Timothy Ametowobla, Ludwig Adzaklo, Gebhard Mensa, Christian Abutiate and Robert S. Kwami.[38] They themselves were products of the Bremen Mission training and together with

---

37 This information was given by the Rev. Solomon Anku Motte, during my research tour in Ghana from July 1968 to February 1969. The Rev. S.A. Motte was on pension at Anfoega near Kpando in the Volta Region when I visited him in August 1968 and January 1969. He was trained at Amedzofe Seminary and after his ordination to the Ministry of the Church in 1934, he was appointed to teach at Fifth Year Seminary at Ho in 1934. He served on the staff of the Seminary for three years.

38 N.B.M.A., *Monatsblatt, 1914*, pp. 76-78.
See also Grau, *op. cit.*, p. 267.

other contemporaries of theirs serving the Church in other ways, they formed the nucleus of indigenous leadership in the Ewe Presbyterian Church.

The system of recruiting students for the seminary and the kind of training given were similar to the Basel Mission practice described earlier in Chapter III and I need not recapitulate them here. It is sufficient to note that at Amedzofe Seminary candidates who were selected for the training had to promise that they would serve the mission for five years after they had completed their studies. On that promise room and board were free and needy students were given small allowances for which they gave some hours work to the seminary either in the college farm or at other school jobs.[39] It seems the money out of which the allowances were given was contributed in Germany where guardians (pfleger) were found for the needy students and these guardians gave definite financial aid and maintained personal contact with their wards in Africa.

In 1906 the progress of Amedzofe Seminary was threatened for political reasons. In that year it became a rule that German should be the medium of instruction in all Togoland schools. In consequence, students who hailed from the British Zone of Eweland were in difficulty and the problem was solved by removing them from Amedzofe which was in the German Zone.[40] A new seminary was opened at Keta in 1907 to cater for them because Keta was in the British Zone. But numbers were so poor that the new seminary was discontinued in 1914.

In that year seminary work in Eweland reached its fiftieth year, and the Jubilee was celebrated on Pentecost Sunday, 1914. At 8.00 a.m. the Rev. R.S. Kwami opened the occasion with a short prayer meeting based on the scripture passage: "When Simon Peter saw it, he fell down at Jesus' knees,

---

39 Grau, *loc. cit.*
40 For the sake of clarity it is best to summarise here the circumstances that led to the partitioning of Ewe country into German and British Zones.
   Togoland became a German possession as the result of various agreements between Germany, France and Great Britain in 1885, 1887, 1888 and 1899 respectively. The transactions came about in the following manner: until 1884 the German Government had been reluctant to acquire colonies in West Africa. Any contacts that the Germans had made with the West Coast of Africa had been through German traders or missionaries. But "during the spring and summer of 1884 the African situation was transformed by the initiative of the German Government". (See J.D. Hargrieves, *Prelude to the Partition of West Africa* (London, 1966), pp. 316 ff.)
   Briefly, in that year Bismarck deliberately provoked Great Britain on several occasions in his attempt to seek Government protection for German traders wherever they seemed to be threatened by foreign encroachments. The new German policy in Africa culminated in a scramble by which European powers tried to partition Africa. In 1885 an agreement was entered into by Germany and Great Britain whereby Krepi (Peki), Keta and other districts east of the Volta were included as part of the British Protectorate of the Gold Coast and a German Protectorate was established over parts of Togoland. By 1899 the partitioning had been completed and the boundaries became well demarcated putting the greater part of the Bremen Mission work in Eweland under German Protection. (See Appendix VI.)

saying, Depart from me; for I am a sinful man O Lord".[41] This was followed by the main worship during which the Rev. G. Däuble preached on the text: "Therefore, my beloved brethren, be ye steadfast, unmoveable, always abounding in the work of the Lord forasmuch as ye know that your labour is not vain in the Lord".[42] In the afternoon many speeches were delivered by different kinds of people including Mr. Grunner, the District Commissioner of Misahoe, Kpalime, who during his address handed over the Mission Bell which the Ashanti had taken away to Kumasi when Ho was invaded in 1869.

The Rev. G. Däuble's text was very appropriate in view of the achievements of the seminary during those fifty years.

The most remarkable achievement of the seminary work began after 1894. When the seminary was transferred to Amedzofe, in that year, there were only seven students in residence; before the principal, Ernest Bürgi began work there at the end of the year, three of the students had dropped out for personal reasons; later three of the remaining four were dismissed because they did not have the ability to profit by the course; thus at the end of 1894 there was only one student left in the seminary to take the end of year examination.[43] In the subsequent years the roll increased steadily year by year and in 1914 alone there were more than 100 students in residence.[44] In all, from 1864 to 1914, 400 students were trained locally in the seminaries as catechists and teachers[45] and 20 others were trained in Germany. It was from among these 420 trained African assistants that eight had been ordained ministers between 1882 and 1913.[46] That those of the 420 men, who remained in the mission work, made enormous impact on the growth of the Church is illustrated below.

In 1872, eight years after the seminary had been started, the Bremen Mission in Eweland celebrated the Twenty-fifth Jubilee of mission work in Eweland. In that year there were still only three mission stations (because Ho station had been destroyed in 1869 by the Ashanti) with a total of 101 Christians, 112 pupils and 16 seminarians. These figures were distributed as follows:[47]

	Christians	Pupils	Seminarians
Keta	40	39	—
Anyako	39	23	16
Waya	22	50	—
	101	112	16

---

41 Luke, 5: 8.
42 1 Cor., 15: 58
43 N.B.M.A., *Monatsblatt*, 1902, pp. 77 ff.
44 *Ibid.*
45 N.B.M.A., File 101 (b). All the 400 names had been preserved here.
46 Appendix VII N.B.: the number here is seven because the ministers in the French Zone are omitted.
47 Wiegräbe, *Ewe Kristo Hame*, p. 32

The most spectacular results began to be realised from 1890 as illustrated by the following statistics of ten-year periods up to the Fiftieth Jubilee in 1914.⁴⁸

	European	Native Pastors	Cats/trs	Christians	Scholars	Stations
1890	19	1	26	717	353	3
1900	33	1	62	2,616	1,296	4
1910	53	3	213	8,274	5,895	8
1913.	40	7	244	11,341	7,311	15

Just a cursory look at these figures will confirm that the labours have not been in vain. Every increase in the number of African assistants brought spectacular increases in membership. In 1910 for example, when the number of catechists and teachers increased from 62 to 213 the membership increase was nearly fourfold. The work of the trained men was becoming effective and it had justified the confidence which the missionaries, especially Schlunk, had placed in the training of the indigenous assistants. Schlunk had maintained that:

> the better the training of the teachers and pastors the more effective will be their help in theological and church work, as well as leading the congregations, and the nearer the possibility of uniting the different station districts into synods with natives playing their part; that is to say the goal of a self-governing Ewe Church under the leadership of the missionaries for the time being.⁴⁹

But we cannot measure the success of 50 years' seminary work only in numbers. There were other spheres of activity in which the training benefited the Ewe Church: some of the products notably Samuel Quist and Andreas Aku helped towards the production of vernacular literature. For example, Samuel Quist, Ludwig Adzaklo and others assisted in the translation of the Bible into Ewe in 1910 at Lome,⁵⁰ Andreas Aku and Samuel Quist helped in the revision of the Ewe hymn book and liturgy; Andreas Aku wrote a biography of Christian Alifodzi Sedode in German, the first thing written in German by an Ewe,⁵¹ Andreas Aku also translated John *Bunyan's Pilgrims' Progress* into Ewe; Hermann Yoyovi wrote on polygamy and because he insisted that it should be allowed in the Church he was dismissed.⁵² And when the crises came during World War I, as will be

---

48 N.B.M.A., *Bremen Mission Reports, 1890-1913*. These figures were compiled for me by the Rev. P. Wiegräbe from these reports while I was in Bremen in March 1969 in connection with this research.
49 Debrunner, *The Church in Togo*, p. 131.
50 Wiegräbe, *op. cit.*, p. 48 (group photograph showing the panel of the Bible Translators).
51 Debrunner, *The Church in Togo*, p. 130.
52 N.B.M.A., *Monatsblatt*, 1897, p. 36 cited in English by Grau, *op. cit.*, pp. 258-259, fn. 502.

shown below, the trained men provided independent leadership, led the congregations and united the districts into synod at Kpalime in 1922.

The success of the seminary training did not come without difficulties. During those 50 years, the work suffered many setbacks. It has already been shown above how recruitment of candidates for training had been hindered by commercial considerations and aspirations, especially in respect of students from the coastal towns. During the first decade the continuity of the work was disturbed by the decease of the principals; out of nine missionaries who had led the seminary during the first decade six died early.[53] The decade 1884 to 1893 was also disappointing; of the 10 men who had been employed after their training eight were dismissed for sexual immorality, one Benjamin Onipayede, died accidentally—(shot unintentionally by his bosom friend),[54] leaving only one in the mission work. But the contributions of those who remained in the mission work, and the results of their labours as described above, far exceeded any disappointments and problems the missionaries might have endured in connection with the training during those years. Indeed, during the Jubilee celebrations the missionaries and their African assistants might have been satisfied that those 50 years had been hard but profitable and gratifying years.

But this satisfaction was only ephemeral. A few months after the Jubilee celebrations World War I broke out between the German and the British and its conequences arrested and disrupted the development of the Seminary at Amedzofe in the same way as the Basel Mission Seminary work in the Gold Coast was disrupted during that period. The Bremen Missionaries in Eweland suffered a similar fate to that of the Basel Missionaries in the Gold Coast and I need not repeat the circumstances here. It is sufficient to say that by 10th January, 1918, all the German Missionaries in Eweland had been deported. Fortunately, Bürgi and his wife were permitted to remain in Eweland because they were native Swiss, and Bürgi supervised all aspects of the Bremen Mission work until 1921 when on account of his failing health they left the mission field and went home for good.

When the missionaries were arrested in August 1914 the Seminary was closed down and the students dispersed; but the African members of staff remained at their post until the end of the year when they also went away for a while. In 1915 the Seminary was re-opened and continued functioning until the end of the year, when it was finally closed down.

So ended also the Bremen Mission efforts at the training of indigenous ministers for the Ewe Presbyterian Church. Since 1916, the ministers of the Ewe Presbyterian Church have no longer all been trained together. The reason is that the Ewe Church itself became divided into two sections, one for

---

53 N.B.M.A., *Monatsblatt*, 1914, pp. 76-78.
54 P. Wiegräbe, Oral information (during my research tour in Bremen in March 1969).

French Togoland and the other for British Togoland and the Gold Coast Colony. The division came about as one of the results of World War I. After the war, Togoland (formerly a German Colony) was partitioned between the British and the French—the allies whose combined forces defeated the Germans in Togo. By the terms of the Paris Peace Conference in 1919, Lome and the whole of the coastline of the former German jurisdiction in Togo together with part of the interior were assigned to France as mandated territory and Britain was given mandatory powers over Kete Krachi, Yendi and Ho districts.[55] The British mandated territory of Togoland eventually became merged into the Gold Coast. So ended the history of one Ewe Bremen Church in Eweland. In any case the training of Ewe Ministers did not end here. It continued in another form.

---

55 Appendix VI.

CHAPTER FIVE

PRESBYTERIAN MISSION TRAINING
1916-1942

As we have pointed out above,[1] after the partitioning of Eweland between Germany and Britain in 1899, only two Mission stations of importance, Keta and Peki, fell within the English Zone. But as the new seminary opened at Keta in 1907 was not patronzied by the coastal people, and was closed down in 1914, students at the senior (middle) school at Blengo, Peki, who wanted to have seminary education were sent to the Basel Mission seminary at Abetifi from the beginning of 1916.[2]

Soon after that, in 1918, upon the invitation of the Government, the United Free Church of Scotland saved the Basel and Bremen Mission work from collapse. In January that year the Rev. and Mrs. A.W. Wilkie arrived in Accra from Nigeria where they had been serving the United Free Church of Scotland Mission in Calabar. They were followed later by the Rev. J. Rankin, Mrs. Moffat, Miss G.M. Wallace and Miss I.P. Ross. In the following year a reinforcement of five Missionaries was sent. They were the Rev. W. Samson, W.G. Murray, W.C. Smith, G. Reith and Neil MacKay.[3] These men and those who followed them to the Gold Coast Mission field i.e Ghana, supervised the work of both the Basel Evangelical and Bremen Evangelical Mission until the Bremen Missionaries returned to the field in 1923. In 1925 the Basel Mission also resumed its work. Henceforth the Presbyterian work in the Gold Coast was distributed among the three co-operating missionary bodies as follows: the Basel Mission became responsible for the Ashanti area; the Bremen Mission for the Ewe section of the Gold Coast and the United Free Church of Scotland for the remaining part of the former Basel Mission Field.

The first Synod under the supervision of the UFCS was held on 14th August, 1918 under the chairmanship of the Rev. A.W. Wilkie, the secretary of the Scottish Mission. During the session the African members

---

1 See Footnote 40 in Chapter IV.
2 E. Amu to J.K. Agbeti, 28th May, 1969.
  Among the boys from Peki who went to Abetifi and Akropong Seminaries from 1916 to 1923 were:
  1916: E. Amu, Gilbert Quampah, Justin Tedeku.
  1917: Seth Dzakuma, Conradt Ababio.
  1918: Hanson Dza, Winfried Addo, Gustav Tsagbey, Robert Akude Ntumi, Gilbert Ansre.
  1919: Bonifacius Atiase, Ambrosius Dey (Dei).
  1920 following:
  George Ayeh, Martin Simpri, Mathias Ayesu, Walter Obiri.
3 Smith, *The Presbyterian Church of Ghana*, pp. 159-160.

of Synod made an earnest appeal for Missionaries to be sent to the Gold Coast to undertake the training of teachers and pastors in the Seminaries at Akropong and Abetifi. Wilkie informed the Synod that the Scottish Mission regarded the work of the seminaries as supremely important and that a special appeal had been made in Scotland for suitable men. He promised that the earnest appeal of the Synod would be transmitted to the Foreign Mission Committee.

From 1919 to 1929 the character of the Seminary training underwent certain changes. When they were re-opened in 1919 after the influenza epidemic referred to above, Mr. P.G. Djoleto took charge of the Seminary at Akropong and Mr. Ofori of that at Abetifi. At that time, the first two years devoted to teacher training were spent at the Akropong Seminary and the third and fourth years, the theological years, at Abetifi. The division had been made in 1918 when teachers were sent from the Department of Education to teach in the Seminary at Akropong after the deportations, because it was feared that those officials from the Department of Education would not pay sufficient attention to Religious Instruction.[4]

Djoleto and Ofori reported to the 1919 Synod that the new arrangement of only two classes in each of the seminaries was only temporary and that it should be changed in the immediate future because the system curtailed the religious instruction to a certain extent. But the missionaries suggested that the two classes should be maintained in each of the seminaries. They argued that the separation had not been a loss because they said the number of students in both seminaries together was greater than in three years previously when each of them had run four classes respectively. The discussions developed into furious exchanges between the European and African sections of the Synod when G. Reith, the new missionary head of Abetifi Seminary, said that in the interest of the missionaries it was "not advisable to entrust Seminary work to natives alone".[5] The African section of the Synod insisted that the four classes in each Seminary should be immediately restored. It was not until Wilkie apologised on the following day for the misunderstanding caused by the missionaries' statement and promised that he would take up the request with the Home Board Committee that emotions subsided. The Gold Coast members then made clear their mind by saying that they

> were of opinion that the institutions including the Seminaries, were a part of the Church, and while they acknowledged the superiority of the Europeans in

---

4 Presbyterian Church of the Gold Coast (PCH), Synod Minutes (1916), p. 6.
5 *Ibid.* No reason was offered by the missionaries in support of this statement. It seems to me, however, that the comment made in Chapter II of this study, (pp. 25-26) in connection with Balmer's recommendation that only Europeans should be made the Headmaster of Mfantsipim school could apply to the Basel Missionaries, too: European myths about the incompetence and darkness of the African mind were not apparently discarded by the missionaries who uttered controversial statements such as those in question here.

learning and in the science of teaching and were thankful for their help and guidance, at the same time they thought it would not be good on their part to leave the Training Institutions exclusively in the hands of the missionaries, and the Synod Committee ought to have a voice in matters relating to them.[6]

In any case, the training remained in the two sections until the end of 1923, but other changes affecting the character of the Seminary took place soon after the 1919 Synod.

First, the curriculum was expanded in order to make it more comprehensive and the subjects taught then in the teacher training department comprised: Religious subjects—Bible Knowledge, Analysis of the Old and New Testaments, Church History and Greek; General Methodics, School Management, Geography, English History, Grammar, Composition, Euclid, Algebra and Mensuration. In the Catechist Department at Abetifi they included Dogmatics, Symbolics, Homiletics, Catechesis, Greek, Exegesis and Knowledge of Church Ordinances. There were four teachers, two Missionaries and two Africans, in each of the seminaries and they taught about 70 lessons a week in each.[7]

Another change which took place affecting the character of the Seminaries concerned recruitment. From the beginning of the Seminaries students had not been admitted by entrance examination. It has already been pointed out above that the best students from the various middle schools were selected and sent to the Seminaries. In 1922, however, those students who were sent to the Seminary were tested after they had arrived in residence and those who did not qualify were returned to their various homes. Obviously, the tests were introduced to limit intake because since 1919, the number of students had been rising steadily each year and this was leading to over-crowding.[8] Another reason is that as the expanded curriculum above illustrates, the standard of education had gone higher and only the most intelligent students could benefit by the training.

The third modification in the character of the seminary during the period 1919-1929 was the unification of the two seminaries. In 1921, Synod

---

6 Scottish Mission (S.M.), *Reports*, 1919-1920, p. 21.
7 S.M., *Reports, 1921*, p. 26.
8 S.M., *Reports, 1923*, p. 23.

The growth of the seminaries from 1914 to 1923 was as follows:

	1914	1919	1920	1921	1922	1923
Akropong	40	73	83	86	90	130
Abetifi	34	56	50	54	63	63
Total	74	129	133	140	153	193

From 1924 both seminaries were united again at Akropong.

expressed great concern about the two years' course for the teachers' training; it was felt that the duration was so short that the standard of the teachers was falling low. The reason is that by 1921 the character of the middle schools had changed considerably and the emphasis the missionaries had laid on the middle school as a preparation ground for admission into the seminary shifted to emphasis on training the pupils to pass the Government Standard VII Examination which neither included Geometry nor Greak as before. But it was from among the Standard VII pupils that recruitment was then made to the seminaries; and as the seminary authorities felt that the new recruits' background was becoming narrower, they made the first year in the seminary only preparatory; but because the subjects were quite new, the students developed the "cramming" habit for examinations. The pressure of the situation also lessened the emphasis on Religious Instruction.

As a result of all this a new course was prescribed, and starting from 1922 a three-years' course was required for a student to qualify as a teacher, in the hope that eventually the duration of the course would be extended to four years. This change was to have a far-reaching effect on the training of teacher-catechists. It would make it necessary for the catechist teacher candidates to take either five years or six years to qualify because as pointed out above, the catechist training had been a two-year post teacher-training course. As the Church was not prepared to sacrifice the subsequent training of the teacher students as catechists, it was decided that the two seminaries should be re-unified at Akropong. The proposal was implemented in 1924 when Abetifi Seminary was closed down and the teacher and catechist departments were unified at Akropong.

At this stage it was felt that a wider scope of training was necessary in the seminary. Mr. Charles Clerk, a Synod member, suggested that the seminary training "might not be confined only to theological and teaching subjects, but should include secular training in subjects such as Science, Physics, Engineering, etc... to secure affiliation with a Scottish university, as Fourah Bay College is affiliated to Durham".[9] This point of view is evidence that some of the Africans had "hoped that the new seminary would provide academic courses to pre-university level...."[10]

In 1925 another change took place; the fourth year was introduced and the first time in the history of Akropong Seminary, students were required to sign a bond which provided for a four years' Teachers' Training Course, and the first year students admitted in that year were the first to sign such a bond. Thus in 1925 Akropong Seminary became a teachers' training college rather than a theological Seminary. At the end of the year there were 205 students distributed as follows: first year 49, second year 56, third ye-

---

9 S.M., *Reports, 1922,* p. 26.
10 Smith, *op. cit.,* p. 175.

ar 60 and fourth year 40 students.[11] At that time the fourth class was the first year of theology. But the increase of enrolment as a result of lengthening the Teachers' Training to four years created a serious problem whose nature and solution were succinctly put down in the Principal's report as follows:

> During the year the Synod Committee had to consider whether the Fourth Class, who were in their first year in Theology, should proceed to a second years' study in the Seminary, or whether they should be sent to stations. If they were to return to the Seminary in 1926 further accommodation would require to be provided for them, a new classroom and a new dormitory. In order to avoid the expense of additional temporary sheds, it was decided that their course should be completed by private study of prescribed books. Candidates for the Catechists' Certificate will therefore come for examination towards the end of the year to the same centres and on the same date as candidates for entrance into the seminary. Both sets of tests can be supervised concurrently.[12]

In 1927 the accommodation problem became so acute that at the end of the year no students could be admitted for the Theological year in 1928 and the final year students of 1927 were therefore appointed to stations.

The changes which had begun to take place in the Seminary since 1919 came to a climax in 1929. In February the old seminary buildings were vacated and the teacher-students were trasnferred to the new buildings of the Akropong Teacher Training College. The old Seminary buildings became available for the continuation of the Theological course suspended at the end of 1927. As a result, 23 of the fourth-year students who had completed their teachers' training course in 1927 without going through the normal theological training were selected in 1929 for a Fifth Year Theological Training as catechists. They occupied two dormitories and a classroom in the old Seminary and the Rev. W. Stamm and Rev. J.A.R. Watt were responsible for their training. It was a one year course at the end of which the students were consecrated. This was the beginning of the "Fifth Year" which became very popular among Presbyterians until recently.

The Fifth Year made progress despite the fact that its students received the same salary as the four-year students. At first it was feared that since there was no financial benefit for taking the Fifth Year course students would refuse to take advantage of the opportunity. Consequently, some people suggested at Synod that all students should be compelled to take the Fifth Year Course in Theology to be sure the project did not collapse. The suggestion was rejected and although no compulsion was introduced by the Synod, in 1931, there were as many as 27 students in the Fifth or Theological Year.[13]

In 1933 and Fifth Year was re-organised and detached from the admin-

---

11 S.M., *Reports, 1925*, p. 8.
12 *Loc. cit.*
13 S.M., *Reports, 1931*, p. 8.

istration of the Teacher Training College; it had its separate Principal, Dr. Theo. E.L. Rapp; but the students continued to join the Training College in activities such as games and agriculture.

The course of study also underwent a few changes. Symbolics was re-introduced because the staff felt that as the Roman Catholic Church was expanding rapidly it was necessary for the Presbyterian Agents to know the differences between their church beliefs and those of the Roman Catholic Church. The second reason for re-introducing Symbolics was that a lot of sectarian books and pamphlets were being introduced into the country, and the Presbyterian Agents must be helped to judge the contents of the tracts in order "to give an answer to every man that asketh them a reason concerning the hope that is in them".[14] Dr. Rapp introduced the teaching of Islamic Studies "to enable agents to bear witness to the Muslims 'that salvation is only in Jesus Christ our Lord'".[15]

As future pastors would be selected from the candidates who had taken advantage of the Fifth Year Course it was felt in 1933 that one year was insufficient. Times had changed considerably and had become harder than in the past; education, commerce and civilization had brought many more problems, social, moral and economic. Under these circumstances not only a compassionate heart but good training of the leaders was essential if these problems were to be attacked in the right way.[16] Thus the annual report requested Synod to consider seriously the proposal made in 1930 that a Rural Training College should be opened to train lads for two years.[17]

In 1935 there were 39 students in the Fifth Year. In 1939 the Fifth Year work was disrupted; there was no Fifth Year in Training at Akropong. Dr. Rapp had gone on furlough and Rev. W. Stamn became the Acting Principal. Before the outbreak of World War II, the Rev. W. Stamn had been recalled home to Switzerland. But "owing to the War the Basel Mission Society was unable to supply a missionary for the Fifth Year work".[18]

In 1929 when the Fifth Year was started at Akropong, the Ewe students who wished to benefit by the theological course no longer went to Akropong. In the same year a new Fifth Year Seminary was opened at Ho in order that the Ewe students might have the opportunity of preaching in their own language. The Rev. Paul Wiegräbe was the first Principal for a few months until he was relieved of the post by Johannes Spieth who had been specially prepared in Scotland for the Fifth Year work at Ho.[19] Catechist Tamakloe was the first African member of staff at the time.

Between 1929 and 1938 the number of students fluctuated between

---

14 S.M., *Reports, 1933*, p. 6.
15 *Loc. cit.*
16 *Ibid.*, p. 7.
17 P.C.G., *Synod Minutes, 1930*, p. 47.
18 P.C.G., *Synod Minutes, 1939*, p. 5.
19 Grau, "The E.P. Church", p. 136.

eight and fifteen.[20] The curriculum comprised the Old Testament, New Testament, Church History, Dogmatics, Ethics, History of Religions with emphasis on Ewe Beliefs, Homiletics, Catechesis, Church Order and Ewe Language. Before the day's classes started, morning prayers were conducted at 6.00 a.m. by the weekly senior and after that 15 minutes were spent in manual labour from 6.45 to 7.00 a.m. The normal college activities, lectures, etc. began at 8.00 a.m. and ended at 9.00 p.m. as shown on the Time-Table.[21]

The students were free to visit the town between 12 noon and 2.00 p.m. and between 5.00 p.m. and 6.00 p.m. daily. But they were strictly forbidden to go to the town after 6.00 p.m., perhaps to save them from falling into immoral temptations.

At the end of their course they went on preaching tours through one of the Ewe Presbyterian Church districts. Such tours lasted for a week, after which the students were consecrated catechists before they were stationed.

Unlike the Presbyterian Church in the non-Ewe areas of the Gold Coast, the Ewe Presbyterian Church made the Fifth Year compulsory for all her teachers. In 1933 for example, three students from the Achimota Training College refused to attend the Seminary. They wanted to be teachers only. The E.P. Church Synod Committee refused to employ them as teachers in E.P. Church Schools. Other Churches also in sympathy with the E.P. Church refused to give the studens teaching posts in their schools. The students had no alternative but to submit to the Churches' ruling.[22]

In 1939 the Ho seminary was closed down because no students came out of the teacher training college at Akropong.[23] World War II followed in 1939 and the Principal could not return. During the interim plans were made to re-open the seminary at Akpafu in 1940. But the scheme did not materialise on account of the war because the German Missionaries were deported again.

The E.P. Church sought refuge once more with the Presbyterian Church of the Gold Coast. In 1940 the Ewe Fifth Year students were sent to join the Fifth Year students at Akropong. The roll in 1940 was 29 at the beginning of the year but only 27 completed the course. One of them had been stationed in the middle of the year to supply a vacancy and the other had been dismissed because his character was not satisfactory.[24]

As the German Missionaries were deported, the Fifth Year training for

---

20 *Loc. cit.*
21 Appendix V.
22 Grau, *loc. cit.*
23 P.C.G., *Reports, 1935*, p. 6.
  The vacuum was created because no students had been admitted for training at Akropong Training College in 1935 in order "to call the Church's attention to her serious financial position, and to make every pastor, teacher and Church member realize the seriousness of the situation".
24 P.C.G., *Reports, 1940*, p. 6.

the first time came into the hands of Scottish Missionaries in 1940, and the Rev. D.S. Elder was appointed Principal with the Rev. G.K. Ampofo from the E.P. Church as the African member of staff to guide the Ewe students. Under Mr. Elder greater strictness was maintained in allowing students to proceed to the Fifth Year. For instance, five fourth-year students who completed their teachers' training course in the year were not permitted to proceed to the Fifth Year because they were not considered to be mature in character.[25]

The combined training progressed well until the end of 1943. In 1941 there were 21 Fifth Year students in training. In 1942 the Fifth Year students became fully incorporated into the Teacher Training College again. They assumed responsibility for leadership of the training college, i.e. student officers were selected from among them. In 1944 the Ho Seminary was opened again and the Ewe Fifth Year students were no longer trained at Akropong. From this stage onwards this study will no longer concern itself with the development of the Fifth Year training because from 1943, as we shall see later, the Presbyterians started to train their men exclusively for the ministry in a Theological College designed for that purpose.

In addition to the contributions the Presbyterian training had made to the growth of the Church, already mentioned above, it should be noted also that the men trained in the seminaries were among the pioneers of education in Akwapim, Akim, the central provinces of Ashanti and in Eweland. Above all, the structure of the Presbyterian system of education: primary; middle and college, became adopted as the national pattern of education in the country.

That the trained men in pursuit of their work passed through many trying experiences without faltering is another evidence that the training had been beneficial. For us today it may be difficult "to realise what difficulties those men must have faced in times when chiefs and parents did not see the need for schooling, when those brave Christians attacked local fetishes and taboos and proclaimed the love of God".[26] Their life was lonely; their task was sometimes dangerous; but they wielded great influence which has been assessed by one of the Principals of Akropong Seminary in these words:

> Students go out each year ... to be leaders in swiftly growing townships, combating the temptations of the modern world, to be leaders in rural backwaters where animism and witchcraft still hold sway. The work of two of our old boys reveals the range of our task. One we found—the only teacher in a station in the debatable land where desert comes to meet forest, and Islam from the north meets the Christian Gospel from the coast. In this lonely station, with mere lads for his presbyters, our student must lay the foundations of the new faith.... He must declare to the people, half of whom speak tongues he can never hope to master, the power of his message.[27]

---

25 *Loc. cit.*
26 Gunn, *A Hundred Years*, p. 14.
27 *Loc. cit.*

Such was the plight of those pioneers. But the training they had received was so thorough that these difficulties did not make them fail in their duty. Those of them who remained in the mission work and became ordained as ministers of the Presbyterian Church in Ghana had been providing efficient indigenous leadership of the Church since World War I. But when the character of the training began to change as described above, it was feared that the efficiency of the future ministers was going to be jeopardized. Consequently, the Presbyterian Church began on 1st October, 1937,[28] to explore new avenues whereby a higher theological education than the Fifth Year might be secured for their prospective ordinands. The various stages in the development of the negotiations which ensued and culminated in the foundation and growth of Trinity College, Legon, are related in Chapter XI of this study.

---

28 B.M.A., "The minutes of the Conference of the Higher Education for Ministerial Students" (in English), *Goldküste Ausschuss und Konfernzen* (1936/37), Folio 4, Afrika Inspectorat D. 2102.

CHAPTER SIX

BAPTIST CONVENTION TRAINING
1888-1970

In 1982, after over thirty years of Baptist Mission work in Nigeria, the Southern Baptist Convention in the United States of America instructed its Board of Mission to

> encourage its missionaries to Africa to train and send forth native converts to act as possible evangelists 'and that as soon as possible the Board' take steps to establish a school on the field for the training of native converts for evangelistic work.[1]

This instruction apparently strengthened the training work which the Rev. W.W. Colley, an American Negro, and the Rev. W.T. David had begun in Lagos. These missionaries were appointed as missionaries to Lagos in 1875. They opened a class for training three young converts as soon as they assumed duty and in the following year, 1876, Mr. Colley wrote to the Foreign Mission Board as follows:

> Your heart would rejoice to hear the young men teach Christ. When I am prostrated by fever they preach to me in broken English, and on Sunday, they preach to the people from some texts, in Yoruba.[2]

One of these young men was Mr. Fadipe. By 1888, he was at 'Agbomosho' as pastor of Osupa Baptist Church. In that year the Rev. Mr. C.E. Smith was transferred from Abeokuta to Ogbomosho to "lead and strengthen a band of believers (of Osupa Baptist Church) and the pastor Mr. Fadipe".[3]

Mr. Smith, inspired by the 1882 instruction to the Mission Board quoted above, took three significant steps as soon as he arrived at Ogbomosho. First, he gathered a group of willing older men in the Osupa Church and taught them the Bible and homiletics. Second, he started a day school for children. Third, he opened a "Training School" for the training of both teachers and preachers in 1898. A full 3 year course was opened with 3 boys. The old Chapel of Osupa Baptist Church was used as the initial classroom. The subjects taught were entirely based on learning to write and number, and a study of the New Testament, especially the four Gospels, Romans and most of I Corinthians. Thus it was in 1898 that formal Baptist Theological Education was began in Nigeria,[4] and officially approved by the Foreign Mission Board in 1899.

---

1 Southern Baptist Convention: *Annual Report*, 1882, p. 37.
2 Elizabeth Routh Pool (Mrs.), "Growth of the Seminary", type-written history preserved in the Registrar's office (1967), p. 1.
3 *Loc. cit.*
4 Thomas O'Connor High, "A History of the Educational Work related to the Nigerian Baptist Convention, 1850-1959". Unpublished Ph.D. Thesis, Southern Baptist Theologi-

The purpose of the Seminary as specifically stated in 1910 was "to thoroughly prepare a native agency to do the two-fold work of preaching and teaching".[5]

In pursuit of this objective separate buildings for the training school were begun in 1901 and completed in 1902.[6] In 1901 the roll increased to "five boys and young men, from 15 to 18 years old, besides, two men in the adult or preachers' class".[7]

During the period 1901-1920 "the school had a nomadic and varying existence"[8] as illustrated below.

In 1904 the school for the first time was transferred from Ogbomosho to Abeokuta because Mr. Smith was away on furlough. The Rev. N.D. Oyerinde,[9] one of the pioneer students, went along with the class as the teacher. Among the students who went to Abeokuta was J. T. Ayerinde, who after his training went as pastor to Ijaiye Baptist Church in Abeokuta and worked there for more than twenty-five years.

In the following year Smith returned to Ogbomosho from furlough and the school returned to its pioneer home. In 1907 the school showed encouraging signs of growth: 21 students were enrolled and the course was no longer only Theological but also literary. At the end of that year one theological student completed his studies. Unfortunately, however, the school was closed down for a few months because of the shortage of missionary staff. In February, 1909, however, the school was reopened with 20 students and three new missionary teachers: Messrs Ward, Compere and Dr. George Green.

The school continued for roughly two years and had to close down once again from the end of 1911 until June 12, 1912 due to the usual lack of missionary personnel.

In July 1912, Dr. Green was appointed the Head of the College. The school was re-opened the same month and re-organized into (a) the Baptist Academy which gave secular education for two years, and (b) the Baptist Training School which offered theological education for a year.

From September, 1914, the Seminary was separated from the Academy and transferred to Shaki. In 1916, all graduates from the Academy entered the seminary. Among them was S.A. Adegbite. He completed the three year

---

cal Seminary, Louisville, Kentucky, 1960, p. 22. Further research has proved that the "Theological Training School" opened on 3rd May, 1898—See Ogbomosho Microfilm store, Microdex 1.

5 Paul H. Miller, "The Direction and Progress of Baptist Sunday-School Work in Nigeria, 1850-1965". Unpublished doctoral dissertation, Southern Baptist Theological Seminary, Louisville, Kentucky, 1968.

6 Letter from C.E. Smith to Dr. R.J. Willingham, on 11th March, 1902.

7 Elizabeth Routh Pool (Mrs.), *Loc. cit.* By 1901, Greek was taught beginning with the second year class. This information was given by Dr. Paul H. Miller through personal interview when I was visiting the Baptist Seminary at Ogbomosho in June, 1974.

8 *School Annual Report, 1958,* "General Information History", p. 7.

9 Oyerinde became the first formally trained Nigerian Baptist pastor. He went overseas in 1906 and later graduated there.

theological course at Shaki in 1917 and was employed as a teacher in the Seminary where he served until his retirement in 1965.

In 1919, Dr. Maclean was appointed the head of the Seminary and the Industrial Institute at Shaki. But during the year he was transferred to Ogbomosho and once again the Seminary had to move with him.

While at Shaki, the Seminary was expanded to include a teacher training course because the ministerial candidates asked for teaching method courses to fit them for their double task as preachers and teachers. So when it returned to Ogbomosho, there was the need to re-organise both the Academy and the Seminary to reflect its new character. Consequently, towards the end of 1920, the Academy and the Seminary were amalgamated to offset the problem of lack of missionary staff and designated: THE BAPTIST COLLEGE AND SEMINARY and the Rev. DR. G.W. Sadler became its Principal from 1921. The main difficulty during this period was the frequent change of leadership and location. This naturally led to lack of continuity so vital for the development of new ventures of this type. In spite of this difficulty, however, there was always a trickle of trained man going out on the Master's errand. For example, Messrs N.D. Oyerinde and S.A. Adegbite became outstanding church leaders. By 1917 at least 12 graduates were in active service. Nine students completed their course at Shaki from 1917-1918.

The period 1921-1950 saw some far-reaching developments. The first decade saw the consolidation of the new Seminary. In 1922, there were ten members on the staff and three pastors graduated. In the following year, out of 11 staff members 6 were Nigerians. The seminary continued to grow steadily both in student and staff population until the end of Sadler's administration in 1930.

In 1931, W.H. Carson became the Principal. In that year alone 100 candidates sought admission but there was room for only 25. Carson did not hold his post for any length of time because there seemed to be a disagreement between him and the students. This could not be handled judiciously, and 38 of the students went on strike and left the campus in 1933. Consequently, in December of the same year Carson had to resign as Principal.

He was succeeded by H.P. McCormick in 1934 when Prof. Oyerinde was the head of the Theological Department. Towards the end of the year the Rev. J.C. Pool succeeded McCormick as Principal. During the first five years of Pool's administration, new Seminary buildings were completed, the College Church was set up and the seminary transferred again to Abeokuta High School in 1936, as Pool was sent there to relieve Patterson, the Principal of that school, for a year. Mr. Pool was assisted in the seminary by Mr. J.T. Ayerinde of the High School, who taught part-time. In 1937, while the Pools were on furlough, the Seminary was transferred to Oyo under the supervision of A.C. Donath.

Before Mr. Pool went away on leave in 1937, the Annual Session of the

Mission met at Shaki in June, 1937. At this meeting a Committee from the Nigerian Baptist Convention presented this request,

> that the Principal, J.C. Pool, be authorised to seek out a higher institution either in Great Britain or in America, with which the Seminary could be affiliated for advanced work leading to a degree.[10]

"In 1938, both the Mission and the Nigerian Baptist Convention decided, upon the advice of Dr. C.E. Maddry, the Executive Secretary of the Foreign Mission Board, then visiting Nigeria and present at the meeting, to site the Seminary permanently at Ogbomosho".[11]

In the same year the school was divided officially: the Baptist Academy[12] section was transferred to Iwo, while the Seminary moved to Oyo with the Rev. A.C. Donath, the Acting Principal, and, as Senior Tutor, Rev. S.A. Adegbite who had taught in the seminary between 1918 and 1929. At the beginning of 1939, the seminary was finally moved from Oyo, back to Ogbomosho with Dr. J.C. Pool as Principal and Business Manager. Classes were commenced in February with two new departments: one for a three year advanced class of two men—E.O. Akingbala and G.O. Akinwumi, and the other for the training of students' wives.[13]

The request made in 1937 by leaders in the Nigerian Baptist Convention and the American Baptist Mission in Nigeria to affiliate the seminary with a school overseas was revived in 1939 after the problem of the permanent location of the seminary had been settled.

As a result of the investigations made by Dr. Pool while he was on furlough in 1937, the Southern Baptist Theological Seminary in Louisville, Kentucky, U.S.A. became interested. In 1938, the institution appointed a faculty (staff) committee, Dr. J.B. Weatherspoon and Dr. W.H. Davis, to work with Dr. Pool to set 'up the Curriculum for a course designed to lead to the Bachelor of Theology degree".[14]

The Committee was concerned first with the quality of students in the seminary at Ogbomosho. The students enrolled in January, 1939, (Mr. E.O. Akingbala and G.O. Akinwumi) were made the pioneer students of the proposed degree course of three years. A third student, Mr. A.M. Olaleye joined the class in 1940. The quality of their academic performance would be a vital deciding factor in the negotiations. Accordingly, "the final

---

10 H. Tupper, *Foreign Mission of the Southern Baptist Convention*, p. 3.
11 Letter from A. Scott Patterson to Dr. R.J. Willingham, on October 5, 1912.
12 The Academy was established in August, 1912, and officially opened on 10th September by the Rev. A. Scott Patterson at Ogbomosho. Its aim was to give Higher Education for Industrial and Commerical life and also espcially to prepare prospective mission workers for entry into the Theological Seminary. See page 75 above and also *Mission Meeting Minutes, 1912, of the* American Baptist Mission.
13 The Baptist Seminary was the first such school in West Africa to require the wives of its students normally to accompany their husbands to the Seminary, to receive education beginning at whatever level is appropriate.
14 Baptist Theological Seminary, *Catalogue 1958*, p. 8.

examinations of each class of the courses of these three students were sent to the Louisville Seminary to be graded by the faculty there".[15]

In 1947, another member from the faculty of the Louisville Seminary visited the Ogbomosho Seminary. Upon the basis of the examination results of the three pioneer students and the recommendations of Dr. Cornel Goerner, the visiting faculty member, affiliation was formally approved in 1948, with this new relationship:

> The Nigerian Baptist Theological Seminary is regarded as an extension of the Southern Baptist Theological Seminary, and all work done by the students in the advanced course in the Nigerian Baptist Seminary is credited by the [American] Seminary towards a degree to be awarded by the Southern Seminary through its extension, the Nigerian Baptist Tehological Seminary.[16]

This means that when the students successfully complete the full course, they will receive the Bachelor of Theology degree. This information was announced to the Nigerian Baptist Convention during their annual session in Lagos in 1948.

This development impelled the authorities to reconsider certain aspects of the training. Firstly, the entry qualification was raised. That is, after the affiliation only candidates who possessed the Higher Certificates (the Senior Cambridge, Higher Elementary, General Certificate of Education, etc.) were admitted for the four year degree course.

"Academic credit up to the equivalent of one year's work may be given those who previously have completed a Certificate in Theology from this institution, and who have met all other regular requirements for entry".

The consequences of raising the entry qualifications are numerous. But for our purpose we may mention only a few: higher qualification may imply a better educational background. This would place the students in a better position to criticise and analyse the training and this would enable them to distinguish between essential Christianity from its western cultural and social accretions. By this means the training might become more useful to the students who would then be in a position to minister more relevantly to the fast changing literate Nigerian society.

Another result concerns the position of the vernacular section of the seminary.[17] It was decided that the vernacular section should be discontinued due to the low educational background of the students (their minimum qualification was a standard VI fail, or a full Primary School Course). This did not, however, imply the complete discontinuation of the vernacular training.[18] The section was to be separated from the seminary and carried

---

15 *Loc. cit.*
16 *Loc. cit.*
17 See pages 12 and 45-47 of the 1965 Catalogue for a description of the vernacular section of the Seminary.
18 A Vernacular Pastors' School had not been started, however, elsewhere for Yoruba-speaking students. The schools were sponsored by Baptists for language groups in other areas of Nigeria.

on somewhere else. The advantages of the proposed transfer include the fact that the new location would make that mission-station an additional evangelistic agency and the seminary would be free to give more attention to the certificate and degree students.

The progress made in the seminary during the period, 1921-1959 came with some problems. The most important were finance and the irrelevance of the programmes. As regards the financing of the institution, the Baptist Foreign Mission Board largely provided the funds for running the institution. Local support was inadequate in all phases of Baptist life in Nigeria. It is not clear why it should be so. But it is evident that during the period, there had been "ever increasing income of the average Nigerian, particularly in areas predominantly Baptist".[19] The crux of the matter in High's estimation was that the missionaries failed to give proper education to the converts about the need for local stewardship. Indeed High maintained that the missionaries made no attempt

> to work a system by which the Convention would, over a period of years, assume gradual support.... The Convention had been conditioned to believe that much support would come from abroad.[20]

The problem of irrelevance of the programmes arose because the curricula and the textbooks used followed very closely those of the Southern Baptist Theological Seminary in Louisville.[21] Also, hitherto, the teaching in the Seminary had been heavily Western biased. There was only a "little admixture of African thought and expression".[22] As a result, the training offered at the Seminary could not altogeher meet the needs of the pastors in their local circumstances. Thus the authorities felt the need to contextualize the curricula and the textbooks. To achieve this end the need arose for a careful study leading to a reformation of the curricula. There was also the desire that the Nigerian theologians should re-write the theology textbooks using local expressions, illustrations and language.

---

19 High, *op.cit.*, p. 208 citing, *International Bank for Reconstruction and Development, The Economic Development of Nigeria* (Baltimore, John's Hopkins Press, 1955), p. 12.
20 High, *op. cit.*, p. 209. Other authorities do not agree with High's conclusion. Dr. Paul H. Miller for instance thinks that the phrase "insufficient effort" would have been a more accurate substitute for High's "no". Paul, also a member of staff at the Baptist Seminary, Ogbomosho during my researches there, said that Missionaries had "pushed" the Churches and Convention, especially since 1949, including the Seminary. Emphasis was given to financial support of Nigerians in positions of leadership in general Baptist education and in national leadership position in the Baptist Convention. Only after these were almost completely nationalised with much Nigerian Baptist support have finance been significantly increased in support of the Seminary. Whether wise or not, this apparently was what happened.
21 The Principal at that time felt this was necessary to assure the approval of the mother Seminary and the continued granting of degrees. This later proved to be no longer a significant factor, and creativity was encouraged by the parent institution. (Interview with Paul H. Miller).
22 High, *op. cit.*, p. 254.

Above all, there was the need for the American staff to engage in a much deeper study of the students' thought patterns and world view into which the doctrines of the Christian faith, as recorded in the Bible, were to be interpreted by the students. To achieve this, High argued that it was incumbent on the foreign staff to learn thoroughly one or more of the local languages and to endeavour to master the customs of the various tribes from which the students were drawn.

In spite of these problems, significant progress was made during this period. For example, by 1950 the affiliation was firmly granted and eight of the students completing their course that year were awarded, for the first time, the Bachelor of Theology (Th.B.) degree. During the subsequent years the new administration and classroom buildings were started and completed in 1955. These provided adequate facilities for three hundred students. The steady increase in student enrolment demanded an increase in the number of the teaching staff.[23] Consequently, by 1958, the faculty (staff) increased to 23, five of whom held doctoral degrees.

Improvements continued during the next period, 1960-1970. For example, in 1962, the school year was placed on the semester plan. That is, the academic year was divided into two major divisions: the first and second semesters starting from August and ending in May, similar to the practice in American Universities.

In the same year a new course, Certificate in Religious Education, was added to the programmes. The course was commenced in August, 1962, when the first students were enrolled. Gradually, by 1965, this programme developed into a separate department.[24]

This is only one example of the judicious way in which the courses have been adapted to suit the varying needs of the candidates and changing needs of the Nigerian Society.

A brief history of the evolution of the programmes will substantiate this evaluation. From the very early history of the Seminary the courses were divided into five separate categories according to the educational background of the students. The minimum qualification for admission to the Seminary then, was the Standard VI[25] pass or its equivalent. But there were other candidates who felt called to the service of the Church but whose education was below the standard VI pass. The convention could not eliminate them all on the grounds of poor formal education. Some of them were given admission, normally, fifteen of such candidates a year. A Vernacular (i.e. Yoruba) course of two years was arranged for them.

---

23 For instance student enrolment from 1955-1958 is as follows: 1955, 138; 1956, 144; 1957, 163 and 1958, 180.

24 Initially a programme leading to the Certificate in Religious Education was offered. In 1971, the Bachelor of Religious Education degree programme was begun, and in 1973, the Seminary began to offer the Diploma in Religious Education, as well as, the Diploma in Theology.

25 Standard VI in Nigeria used to be the first 8 years of pre-secondary school education.

There are four courses arranged for those who possess the basic qualifications and above: The certificate course was pursued by candidates possessing initially the Primary School pass or its equivalent.[26] It was a three year residential course, at the end of which, upon satisfactory completing the course, the student was granted a Certificate in Theology.

Then there were pastors of long experience in the field. In order to keep them abreast with the new theological developments a refresher or review course was arranged for them. The selection, based on the recommendation to the Seminary by the Ministerial Board of the Nigerian Baptist Convention (NBC) was made from among the Certificate holders. Those selected went into residence for one year.

An Advanced Course was organised for secondary school scholars, who failed the Higher Certificate, i.e. Senior Cambridge and the Higher Elementary examination. The course lasted three years and the successful candidates at the end were awarded the Advanced Certificate.

Finally, the 4 year Th.B. degree course was added from 1948. This was opened to successful secondary school scholars i.e. those who pass the Senior Cambridge, Higher Elementary, General Certificate of Education, etc. examinations. In addition to these, students possessing the regular Certificate from the Seminary could be credited with up to one year's residence, i.e. when admitted for the degree work they would take three instead of four years.[27]

But as years went by, with the educational advancement of the Nigerians, the courses were up-graded and expanded as illustrated below. The purpose of the new courses has been stated thus:

> The primary purpose of this Seminary is to provide a basic professional theological curriculum to equip students preparing for Christian ministries. Included in the larger scope of its purpose is the provision of basic and practical theological foundations for persons in other roles where such education is expected.
>
> Three levels of instruction are included in the basic programmes offered: degree, diploma and certificate. The Women's Training Department is provided primarily as a service for wives of students enrolled in the aforementioned basic programmes when these wives do not qualify as a candidate for a degree, diploma or certificate.[28]

This is why the Vernacular Course was eliminated[29] and others, such as

---

26 Later the entrance qualification was raised to a Modern School pass, or to a minimum of nine years successful academic work as a prerequisite. The Primary School pass did not involve the same number of years' study in every Region of the country, and neither did all Regions establish Modern Schools.
27 Specific credits were given in the form of semester hours for above average work done on the certificate level. However, this was usually sufficient to equal the preliminary year of work. This did not affect entrance requirements as such.
28 The Theological Seminary, "Information concerning Admission of Students, Classification of Degrees, Programmes of Instruction and Description of courses for the Nigerian Baptist Theological Seminary. Nov. 1974 (Mimeographed)", p. A7.
29 See page 75 above.

the diploma programmes and Women's Department, have been added. That is, the current course run by the beginning of the 70's are the Th.B. degree, Bachelor of Religious Education, Advanced Certificate and Certificate courses. Each of these courses is designed to satisfy a specific need.

The degree courses are designed:

> to help prepare persons for the wide spectrum within which the Christian ministry in Africa functions today, and therefore must be comprehensive and still allow for specialization. Each degree student, therefore, must complete certain basic required courses appropriate to his Programme of Instruction. He also has the opportunity to select courses in an area of specialization which will be in keeping with his particular interests and vocational objective.[30]

In the light of this, sixteen (16) semester hours[31] of credit is the normal load for one Semester. For the completion of the full course one hundred and twenty-eight (128) semester hours are required for graduation of degree candidates. Those pursuing the Bachelor of Religious Education, however, require an additional four (4) hours credit in Field Work and Practice Teaching.[32] The two degrees which are offered at the time of this research were the Bachelor of Theology and the Bachelor of Religious Education degrees.

The Bachelor of Theology degree is the basic degree for those candi-

---

30 "Information Concerning Admission", *loc. cit.*
31 The Semester system is an American arrangement of the school year. The regular academic year is divided into two semesters of at least sixteen weeks of class work in each. The unit of credit is a semester hour which represents one class period per week. Classes meet for each course from once to four times each week in periods of fifty-five minutes each.
32 The addition of courses such as African Traditional Religions, Islamic studies, the Sociology of Religion, Science and Religion, the Sociology of Education, and Religious Education in the Schools indicate the increasing emphasis on the West African context in which the students would serve. Furthermore, many individual subjects include research into historical backgrounds and current conditions in Nigeria which form a practical basis for deeper and more relevant theological and education studies. General education which will make ministers and educators more effective in their service also is included, both in subject content, in Field Education experiences and in extra curricular activities. Outstanding scholars of various disciplines, from Africa and overseas, are regularly brought to the Seminary for lectures and discussions. "Enrichment Programmes are planned at least once a month for voluntary participation and attendance in a wide-ranging series of programmes including literature, music, travel, ecumenics, local customs, etc." Every other week, additionally, the entire student body meets with qualified persons to discuss general education subjects which are intended, normally, to be shared with the communities in which they serve as student ministers. This has included series concerned with health problems, the work of government and community agencies, first aid, caring for children in the home, and other areas. The Seminary also is seeking to serve a larger segment of the churches and community by offering short-courses during the school holidays, and workshops and conferences at various educational levels throughout the year. Faculty and school facilities are also made available for Continuing Education Conferences for ministers and laymen, and the library is used frequently by qualified students and scholars from outside the Seminary community.

dates who are preparing for the Christian ministry in its pastoral and preaching dimensions.

The prescribed courses for this degree are Biblical Studies, Old and New Testament Studies, Historical Studies involving Church History, Christian Missions and World Religions; Theological Studies comprising Christian Theology, Philosophy and Ethics; Practical Studies consisting of Communication, and Psychology and Pastoral Theology.

The Bachelor of Religious Education degree is designed primarily for those who are preparing for educational ministries in a church, school, denominational agency or institution, pre-school religious education centre, or in mission work. As this is geared towards the acquiring of skills by the candidates the training programmes

> are carried out through classroom courses, library research, field education and clinical practice in local churches, public schools, other institutions, and the Pre-school Religious Education Centre on the Seminary Campus.[33]

The curriculum for this degree includes Biblical, theological, historical and practical studies in depth.[34] Formally, a student is encouraged to concentrate on one area which is appropriate to his vocational calling. This purpose is achieved through a system of Required Courses, Controlled and Free Electives.

The other courses which are non-degree are the Diploma and Certificate Courses. The Diploma Coureses lead to the Diploma in Theology or the Diploma in Religious Education. These courses cover three academic years or ninety-six semester hours of successful classroom credit. Those who work towards the Diploma in Religious Education have to fulfil certain requirements in practice teaching and practical leadership together with a pass in three semester hours additional credit in Field Education.

The curricula for these courses are virtually the same as the first three years of the Programmes for the degree courses of instruction, excepting that some adjustments may be made in consonance with the vocational aim of the admitted students respectively.

The Certificate Courses are open to anyone who has completed nine years of successful academic work including the Primary School pass. The purposes of the Certificate courses are similar to those of the programmes discussed above, but the curriculum is geared towards the training for priestly and prophetic duties of the pastor, teacher and missionary.

Finally, the Women's Training Department caters for women who do not have the requisite academic qualification for any of the courses de-

---

33 "Information concerning Admissions", *ibid.*, p. A9.
34 The latter area includes as its major areas: administration, teaching, history and philosophy of education, sociology and psychology of education, understanding and working with people, and specialized ministries. Music courses are also included, *ibid.*, pp. B9-B17.

scribed above but who want to prepare for religious Vocations. This department is primarily for wives of those who are enrolled in the various seminary courses. They are classed according to their previous education and experience.

All these programmes have been skilfully worked out to fulfil the objective to which the seminary was dedicated. That is:

> To the glory of God and the training of Ministers of the Gospel [and to the training of] pastors of Baptist Churches in the Nigerian Baptist Conventional and workers in other convention fields.[35]

When we consider that between 1934 and 1967 about 900 men and women completed their courses and were serving Nigeria, Ghana, Cameroons, Togo, Sierra Leone and even in Kenya in East Africa, then it may be concluded without hesitation that the Seminary has been fulfilling its purposes. This may also be evidenced from the fact that these men and women have been serving as pastors, missionaries, Sunday School and Training Union[36] workers and directors and teachers etc. Even the Churches appreciated the value of the trained men and many of them anxiously invited the men,[37] and the effect of the labours of the African pastors among their kith and kin has been expressed by Dr. High as follows:

> Local maturing Baptist Churches continued to be organized. In 1958, three hundred and nineteen out of 340 Churches were self-supporting and self-governing. Over six thousand baptisms in 1958 brought the total Church membership to 44,405.[38]

These successes were not achieved without difficulties, the most prominent being recruitment, staff and contextualization. The reasons for the lack of vocation, generally, have been discussed below and I need not rebearse them here.[39] Rather I wish to point out the fact that the spiritual life of congregations is vital in awakening the spirit of vocation among the youth of a church.

Lack of finance was the main reason why the Seminary had not been able to maintain an adequate number of African members of the teaching staff.[40] The other factors, such as the lack of proper qualification of Africans, were only possible because as the local churches found it more con-

---

35 1956 and 1958 *Catalogue*, pp. 8-9.
36 Pool (Mrs.), *op. cit.*, p. 4.
37 Pastors are not transferred by the Church Administration to congregations. Rather congregations interview pastors of their choice and invite whom they will to serve their members.
38 High, *op. cit.*, p. 262 citing *Annual of the Southern Baptist Convention, 1959*, p. 195.
39 See Chapter XIII of this book.
40 Additionally, there is strong competition from local churches, universities and the denominations who want well-trained and experienced pastors to serve them. Since in Baptist Policy the individual minister is free to serve wherever he feels God wants him to be, nationals do leave the Seminary teaching staff to serve elsewhere in Nigeria.

venient to use the free financial services of foreign missionaries in teaching and administrative positions they did not normally encourage higher education for the African staff. It is, however, satisfying to note that this attitude had been changing for the better and towards that end the seminary had planned and was carrying out accelerated Africanization of the staff. The proposal was to give the highest academic training to at least one African member of staff in every three years.[41] Other proposals for improving the Seminary include the expansion of the library which might be enlarged by 50% in 5 years, the development of African Church Music, the further provision and production of teaching-aids including Audio-Visual, and the introduction of post-graduate studies.[42]

All these proposals were geared towards "the needs of the modern Nigerian society, conditioned by all the old and new forces of tension, change and conflict".[43] It is hoped that by this new aspiration, the Seminary may later

> come more and more to reflect Nigerian thinking and culture and to take on more of an African personality.... These ends must be and can be gained without sacrificing anything of the Academic excellence already attained.[44]

This new vision is a challenge to theological education for tomorrow—not only in the Baptist Theological Seminary in Nigeria, but a challenge to all institutions concerned with the training of Christian Ministers in West Africa. The Baptist vision of today's training can serve as a significant springboard for the development of theological education tomorrow in West Africa.

---

41 Other nationals may be sent yearly for higher studies through the Convention Scholarship Scheme of the Nigerian Baptist Convention. Although heavily subsidized from overseas Baptist sources, this is directed completely by the Scholarship Board of Nigerian Baptist Conventions.
42 All but the last of these efforts named were already being undertaken with some success, and the last named was under further study, possibly to arrange a co-operative undertaking. (Inerview with Dr. Miller.) Six new buildings were also being completed in 1970 to help improve the physical facilities for a better teaching/larning environment.
43 Carlton F. Whirley, *Inaugural Address* (Ogbomosho,1971), p. 6.
44 *Ibid.*, p. 15.

CHAPTER SEVEN

ANGLICAN CHURCH MISSION TRAINING: PHASE 1
1925-1932

It has been shown in Chapter I of this study that of all the Missions under discussion the English Church Mission was the latest to engage in organised evangelistic work in the Gold Coast during the period of enquiry. The lateness did not, however, prevent the Mission from realizing as other Missions had done before it, that a local agency was vital to the proper evangelization of indigenous peoples.

Thus in less than six years after the Society for the Propagation of the Gospel (SPG) had resumed their work in the Gold Coast a Grammar School was opened on 4th January, 1910, at Cape Coast by Bishop Hamlyn "in the hope that it would be a nursing ground for the future school teachers, catechists and African Clergy".[1] Four years later it became evident that this early promise of the Grammar School as the nursing ground especially for catechists and African Clergy was not going to be fulfilled.[2] In consequence, separate arrangements had to be made for the training of catechists and clergymen. In pursuit of this plan the Rev. Gresham Wynter Morrison, M.A., was appointed in the same year, 1914, to train Ordinands in the Diocese and he settled in Kumasi as the Priest-in-charge.[3]

Two catechists, E.D. Martinson then stationed in Kumasi, and W. Hutton Mensah, catechist/Head Teacher of the Grammar School, were selected immediately to be prepared for the ordained ministry. The training they had was informal and individual; they remained at their respective posts and

---

1 S.P.G., *Reports* (London, 1914), p. 133.
2 *Ibid.*, The school quickly developed into a Secondary School rather than a training and Theological College. The reason is summed up by Herskovits' statement that the African believes that "it has been the ability to read and write that has given the European his controls over man and nature. It is this, therefore, that he seeks for himself and, above all, for his children so that they will have more adequate control of this power, and, to an extent not vouchsafed him, will be enabled to apply it in solving their own problems". Cited by D. Kimble, *A Political History of Ghana: the Rise of Gold Coast Nationalism 1850-1928* (Oxford, 1963), p. 63 footnote 1.

    Indeed parents in Ghana regarded secondary education as "the open sesame to increased authority, prestige and the royal road to economic prosperity without manual labour", J.K. Agbeti "Missionary Enterprise, Educational and Nationhood in Ghana since 1828" (Unpublished Yale Divinity School Master's Thesis, 1967), p. 49. The Methodists had established Mfantsipim School at Cape Coast in the same town. The products of this school were entering the Civil Service and were enjoying the economic benefits. It was natural for the Anglican parents too to seek for their children, in the new Cape Coast School, secondary rather than theological Education.

3 C.H. Elliot, *Some Historical Events of the Diocese of Accra from 1752-1937* (Cape Coast, n.d.), p.4.

had a kind of correspondence course. Certain books were prescribed by Mr. Morrison for the students to be read; occasionally he met each student at the candidate's station and questions based on the reading were discussed. The subjects included in the reading lists were: Theology, Canon Law, Bible Study, Pastoralia, the Prayer Book and Homiletics.[4] The training lasted for two years at the end of which the two candidates were ordained to the Priesthood on 1st October, 1916 by Bishop O'Rorke in Christ Church, Cape Coast.

This type of training was meant only to be a temporary measure until a Theological Institution could be established in the Diocese. But nine years were to elapse before the idea of a Theological Institution could mature. During the interim three more candidates, Messers. O. Renner, J.R.C. Yalley and C.H. Elliot underwent a similar informal training for ordination, with the exception that Mr. O. Renner, a Sierra Leonean, had had additional training at Fourah Bay College, Freetown, Sierra Leone, prior to his coming to settle in the Gold Coast.

By 1921 the need to increase more rapidly the number of African clergy in the diocese was becoming more and more urgent. This was just after World War I and at that time, in the 1920s, the value of cocoa was very high and there was much money about. This made it easy for people to move about very much for trading purposes, in search of good lands on which to grow cocoa and in pursuit of education and so on. Some of the emigrants who had been Christians at home established little Christian communities wherever they settled, and some others who had not been Christians at home became converted during their sojourn and they also took home with them, to their relatives, the new faith. It was a lad belonging to this latter category that invited Fr. Martinson to visit the Church he was building in his village. Fr. Martinson was then the African Priest-in-Charge of Tarkwa. During his visit to the village Fr. Martinson was so impressed by the opportunities opening in the country for evangelism that he sent the following report to the S.P.G.:

> I was called in June 1921 to visit some Christians at a village 160 miles from my station, but it was not possible for me until early in August. I travelled 126 miles by train, and then walked thirty-six miles. When I arrived I met about hundred converts waiting for baptism. A young man, from one of our stations, who was no teacher, had managed to learn to read a little of the New Testament and the Prayer Book in Fanti. He went to this village, where some of his realtions lived, early in 1920. There he started teaching his own people, and the good news spread.
>
> They built a little Church, and for a year he laboured hard, teaching them as much as he could every morning before they went to their farms, and in the evening before they retired to rest. When he thought that they were ready for baptism, he heard of our scarcity of clergy and encouraged them to wait.

---

4 This information was received orally on 5th February, 1969, from Canon Elliot, one of the pioneer African Anglican Priests, then retired and residing in Cape Coast.

After careful examination on my arrival, I baptised forty-five adults, among whom were two fetish priests and a fetish linguist. There was no other fetish priest left.[5]

Indeed, similar calls had been pouring in to the Bishop before 1921: for example, since 1915 the Western Frontier had been sending calls which could not be effectively answered. In fact, it was possible to forecast that after 1921 more calls would be sent in. But the problem about the lack of ministers was becoming more acute. In 1920 the English Missionaries had left the mission field. The reason for their departure has not been documented as far as my investigations have gone; but it seems the English Missionaries felt themselves humiliated to take instructions from an Irishman.[6] There seems to be a grain of truth in this suggestion because it was not until after the resignation of O'Rorke in 1923 as the Bishop of Accra and the appointment of an Englishman to succeed him that the Missionary strength began to improve again. Thus at a time when more demands were being made upon the Mission for expansion, between 1921 and 1923, there were only four Priests in the Diocese: One Bishop, O'Rorke, and three African Priests, Martinson, Hutton Mensah and O. Renner.

The immediate effect of this problem concerning the lack of personnel upon the Missionary strategy was that the Diocese decided to suspend multiplying bush stations, and to form radiating centres along the Coast and at Kumasi in Ashanti in order to establish in the Centres deep and enlightened religious spirit and tone.[7] While these ideas were being formed in the Gold Coast, two members of the Pershore Brotherhood[8] in England, Father Peters and Dom Martin Collett, O.S.B., were contemplating taking up Missionary work with the Accra Diocese. They arrived in the country in 1923 when O'Rorke was getting ready to quit. Originally it was intended that they should remain in Accra to assist the Bishop to make Accra the major radiating centre. But when they arrived there they were sent to Kumasi in Ashanti, possibly because Kumasi was being considered by O'Rorke as the most suitable place for a Theological Training Institution.[9] O'Rorke did not stay to see the establishment of that school. At the end of the year, as already pointed out, he had to leave the country, having relinquished his post.

His successor, the Rt. Rev. John Orfeur Aglionby, D.D., M.C., was consecrated in Westminster Abbey on the Feast of the Purification of the Blessed Virgin Mary, 2nd February, 1924, by the Archbishop of Canterb-

---

5 S.P.G., *Reports* (London, 1921), pp. 84-85.
6 Canon C.H. Elliot gave me this information.
7 S.P.G., *Reports* (London, 1922), p. 90.
8 *The Pershore Brotherhood*: Was an Anglican Religious Community at Pershore, Worcestershire, England. For the life and activities of the Brethen at Pershore, see E.M. Almedingen, *Dom Bernard Clements—a Portrait* (Lond, 1945), pp. 37-62.
9 It will be recalled that when Wynter Morrison was appointed to train the pioneer priests he was sent to reside in Kumasi.

ury as the third Bishop of the Accra Diocese.[10] Aglionby arrived in Accra on 24th March, 1924 and tackled almost immediately the problem of training Africans for the ministry. Barely six months after his arrival in the Diocese he recruited twelve prospective candidates for the ministry and put forward a firm plan for the establishment of a Theological Institution in Kumasi. The English Church Mission Infant School in Kumasi was old and plans were being made to build a new one. Bishop Aglionby recognised during the maiden visit to Kumasi that that old Infant School could be adapted and used as temporary accommodation for the proposed College. There and then he appointed the Rev. Dom Martin Collett, O.S.B., previously posted to Kumasi by Bishop O'Rorke, as the first Rector of the College and set October 1924 as the time when the College would be opened under the title *St. Augustine's Theological College, Kumasi.* The necessary alterations to the old Infant School were ordered; but the work was more complicated than had been expected: furniture must be supplied; the infant pupils must be rehoused and the adaptation of the school to suit college accommodation was not easy. As a result, the initial preparations took more time than had been anticipated and the College could not start operating in October 1924, but three months later, in January 1925.

The alacrity with which Aglionby and his colleagues effected these arrangements may be due to various factors, the most important of which may be summed up as follows: O'Rorke's concern for increasing the number of African Ministers to guard against any future wholesale withdrawal of the missionary staff as has been the case in 1920 and the silent preparations O'Rorke had made in training young men to offer for the Preisthood when the opportunity arose: the presence of the Pershore men in the Diocese; Aglionby himself had faith that the African could benefit by the training and he discovered when he visited Kumasi that £1,300 (¢2,600), mostly from the Pan-Anglican Thank-Offering Fund, was in hand, so he decided that it must be used to start the College.

Thus 1925 became a turning point in the history of the English Church Mission in the Gold Coast. But what happened at the beginning of 1925 is meaningless if we do not accord an equally important place to 1924 also. The importance Bishop Aglionby gave to both of these years and to the future of the College came out clearly when in January 1925 after the opening of the College he wrote in his 1924 report to the S.P.G. these words:

> The opening of St. Augustine's Theological College, Coomasie[11] though actually belonging to January 1925, is the great event for the diocese, and has been the chief subject of interest, work and prayer among our people during the year. The Rev. Dom Martin of Pershore Community has come out as Princi-

---

10 S.P.G., *Reports* (London, 1923), p. 888. See also Elliot, *op. cit.*, p. 5, and "Note on the Pan-Anglican Thank Offering Fund", *The Golden Shore*, Vol. 1, No. I, July 1924, p. 10.
11 The modern spelling is "Kumasi".

pal, and the College opened with thirteen students. It is true that our temporary building is only converted infant school, but we have a splendid site, at present covered by bush, on outskirts of Coomasie, where we shall train not only clergy but also catechists and teachers for our Church Schools. . . .

We realise that, humanly speaking, the whole future of the Diocese depends upon St. Augustine's College. Without a well-trained African priesthood, West Africa can never be won for Christ, and mission stations could be started in a hundred places tomorrow if we had catechists to send.[12]

The pioneer students who actually came into residence at the beginning of the College's life were 12, and not 13 as mentioned in the report quoted above. It seems that the 13 candidates consented to come into residence, but one of them dropped out at the eleventh hour due to family reasons.[13] In any case the 12 who were actually admitted were drawn from different walks of life such as from the teaching field, commercial work and from those who had just left elementary schools.[14] Their ages varied between 16 and 30 years and they were recruited from more than one tribal group, but the majority of them were Fanti.[15]

Characteristic of most new schools in the country then, and even now, many problems beset the College from its very beginning. The converted buildings were insufficient. The old Infant School referred to above consisted of three main rooms: there were two long and narrow rooms and a third room just about half the size of the others. In the alteration one of the long rooms was partitioned into two equal parts, one part to be used as students' Common Room and the other part as the Chapel and Lecture room combined. The third smaller room was the students' dormitory, supplied with iron camp bedsteads ordered from England and with mosquito curtains. The remaining long room was altered to house the staff of the school. As for kitchen and bath-house, they were erected with blocks. The kitchen was not modern and elaborate and the bath-house had no roof. There was no room left to be used as a Library. The insufficiency of the rooms did not bother students and staff very much for they were aware that the present arrangement was only temporary. The most serious problems concerned furniture and books. The furniture was inadequate and the books were insufficient. In the meanwhile appeals had been sent overseas for books such as good theological works of catholic character, good books on English Literature, on both Ancient and Modern Church History, preferably those dealing with the Church in Africa, i.e. in Abyssinia.

These difficulties did not deter the staff and students from doing the best they could in the circumstances. Work began in earnest, as the pioneer

---

12 S.P.G., *Reports* (London, 1924), pp. 94-95 and Elliot, *loc. cit.*
13 See Footnote 17 in this Chapter.
14 See p. 91 below.
15 "St. Augustine's College Kumasi", *The Golden Shore*, Vol. I, No. 3, January 1925, pp. 61-62.

daily routine shows: there were three lectures a day—two in the morning when the following main subjects were taught: Dogmatic Theology, History and Principles of Liturgical Worship, History of the Christian Church with special reference to the Ancient Church of Africa, Greek and Latin, Biblical Studies—Old Testament, New Testament, Elementary Scriptural Exegesis and Biblical History. The Biblical studies were taught in order to "provide for that intimate knowledge of the Bible which every priest should have, especially in view of an extremely good working knowledge of Holy Scripture possessed by many in the Gold Coast." The one lecture in the afternoon was devoted to Music and Latin. There were no lectures on Saturdays, in order that the students might clean up the College grounds.

It would be of immense interest if we know how much of these great subjects the students understood and absorbed. It is apparent that they did not make much headway with the subjects. The Rector himself did not expect much from them in their accademic attainments because their background was poor. By July 1925 eleven, but not twelve students, were in residence.[17] Of them the Acting Rector, Dom Francis, wrote that they were:

> Men taken from varying walks of life, all with one or two exception, possessed a very elementary and incomplete education, there are clerks, store-assistants, catechists, school-teachers and boys straight from the seventh standard of our own school. Quite obviously it would have been absurd to expect much in the way of scholarship from men who had so little chance in the way of education.[18]

Poor background, of course, produced its undesirable results. The students were not selective with the facts they needed; they read materials indiscriminately. The tutors tried to exercise rigid censorship of students' private reading; but even this was difficult to accomplish because, as their background was defective and no solid foundation of more important truths had been laid, the students were fascinated by long terms without endeavouring first to grasp the simple truths of Christian Doctrine. For instance, the Acting Rector continuing his report, said:

> I have had questions put to me with regard to Positivism and Nationalism in general, by men who had not yet grasped the simplest truths of Christian doctrine. It need hardly be said that we do not wish to train our students with a narrow-mindedness and rigidity, which will in the end leave them powerless to grapple with problems of modern life, which even in so elemental a country as West Africa often attain to a very complicated nature.[19]

The idea that the first concern of the tutors was to train the students to

---

16 "St. Augustine's College Kumasi", *The Golden Shore*, Vol. I, No. 5, July 1925, p. 129.
17 "St. Augustine's College Kumasi", *The Golden Shore*, Vol. I, No. 4, April 1925, p. 88.
18 "St. Augustine's College Kumasi", *The Golden Shore*, Vol. I, No. 5, July 1925, p. 127.
19 *Ibid.*, p. 128.

be open-minded and flexible in order that they could meaningfully grapple with the problems of modern life is worth noting. In fact the problems of modern life involve the whole personality, material and spiritual. Therefore, the function of a Theological College should not only be academic but also spiritual and pastoral. The tutors of St. Augustine's College in those early years recognized these functions and in addition to teaching the academic subjects enumerated above they also provided for spiritual and pastoral training. As regards the spiritual training the College met in worship daily: morning and evening prayers were said at St. Cyprians Church from Sunday to Friday; on Saturdays Evensong was sung in the College Chapel to Plainsong from the English Hymnal and a manual of Plainsong by Briggs and Frere. Pastoral training was imparted under the subject entitled Moral Theology—this was given to the deacons. It dealt with the principles that would guide the students to lead their parishioners according to the moral obligations which the Church imposes upon all her children alike. Under Apologetics, Pastoral and Ascetic Theology, the students were introduced to the right use of medicines and the treatment of minor ailments and accidents by medical doctors, if they were free to give the lectures.

In spite of the few initial problems already mentioned the future of the College was looked upon with great promise. Accordingly, as soon as life in the College began to take shape the authorities turned their thoughts to the erection of permanent buildings for the institution. A new site for this purpose had been acquired on a prominent point in Kumasi about January 1925.[20] The buildings were to be arranged in such a way that the advantages of the common life of both staff and students might be combined "with something of the intimacy of home life, and to avoid the harshness and rigidity of barrack-like dormitories".[21] The Chapel was to be the central building from which the College would derive its inspiration. All the other buildings would be clustered around it and they would comprise: a lecture hall, classrooms, a dining hall, the Rector's bungalow and cottages to house twelve students each. The capacity of the Chapel and the dining hall was to be about 60 to 70 students. At this stage it was difficult to forecast how many cottages would be required altogether; it was therefore decided that while the other blocks should all be built complete from the start only one cottage, estimated at a total cost of £1,400 (¢2,800) should be erected at the beginning; other cottages would be added as the roll of students and staff increased, and that any donor who would give the whole cost of one of the cottages would have the cottages named after him.

It was not in the case of the cottages alone that the assistance of donors was enlisted. Appeals were sent out to invite people to participate in the

---

20 "St. Augustine's College Kumasi", *The Golden Shore*, Vol. I, No. 3, January 1925, p. 129.
21 *Ibid.*

furnishing of the Chapel and in stocking the Library with books. The furnishings required included: two altars besides the High Altar and the Rector's Oratory, a carpet 18 ft. by 14 ft.—Indian or Persian for the High Altar, a pipe organ, stalls for the choir, presses for the sacristy and three statues of Our Lady, of St. Augustine and of St. Peter, after whom the Chapel would be dedicated. The appeals did not fall on deaf ears; many friends co-operated and gave generously; for example Her Highness the Princess Mary Louise donated red and white frontals for the Altar, an unnamed European friend presented vestments—red and white sets and a white cope—in memory of her soldier brother who died and was buried in Ashanti in one of the Ashanti-European wars,[22] and Mrs. Bogg gave two cases of books to the library, just to mention a few of the donors. Collection in cash for the whole project also progressed steadily and by October 1927, £4,186 (¢8,372) had been collected and £1,000 (¢2,000) promised towards the College Building Fund.[23]

The actual work on the buildings did not start until January 1928. The contractors worked speedily but carefully and by the beginning of April the same year the work was completed. On the 1st Sunday after Easter, 22nd April, 1928, the College was dedicated in a very impressive manner in the presence of a huge audience which included among other dignitaries the Mohammedan Head in Kumasi and Major Jackson, C.M.G., then the Acting Chief Commissioner of Ashanti. Four detailed accounts of the Dedication are now extant: three in The Golden Shore[24] by a European Archdeacon, a lay European and a lay African respectively, and the fourth by a local newspaper.[25]

1928 was not significant for the English Church Mission alone but it was

---

22 Ashanti-European Wars: cf. Ward, *A History of Ghana*, op. cit., pp. 232-312.
23 "The Bishop's Letter", *The Golden Shore*, Vol. II, No.6, October 1927, p. 110. This sum was made up of gifts and contributions for overseas sources:

The Congregation of St. Peter's Swinton, inspired by their Vicar Lord Mountmorres after he had returned from a visit to the Gold Coast contributed	£1,869	(¢3,738)
Fr. Martin with the help of a certain Mrs. Powell collected	£1,150	(¢2,300)
A.D.A. Members subscribed	£1,167	(¢2,334)
	£4,186	(¢8,372)
In addition to this the S.P.G. promised	£500	(¢1,000)
and the S.P.C.K. also promised	£500	(¢1,000)
	£1,000	(¢2,000)

24 "Opening of St. Augustine's College", *The Golden Shore*, Vol. III, No. 1, July 1928, pp. 7-16.
25 *The Gold Coast Independent* (Accra), April, 1928 (See Appendix II).

also significant for the whole country. Nearly three weeks prior to the opening of St. Augustine's College in Kumasi, the huge Takoradi Harbour was formally opened on 3rd April, 1928 by the Rt. Hon. J.H. Thomas.[26] Although the nature of both events was different, one fraught with unknown possibilities for the spiritual life of the Gold Coast and the other for material prosperity, both had hidden within them results which would impinge upon their respective developments. The harbour would invite labour from various parts of the country and the concentration of diverse peoples in a small harbour town would carry with it sociological, economic and moral problems. To meet the moral problems the Missions—in this instance all the Missions involved in Evangelistic Work in the country, not the English Church Mission alone—would have to accelerate the training of Africans in order to cope with the inevitable social and moral problems of a harbour life.[27]

The task was not going to be an easy one. The size of St. Augustine's College and that of the Harbour were of incomparable dimensions: the one was small and the other huge; the number of students in the one negligible when compared with the number of workers and passengers and cargo that would pass through the harbour. In spite of smallness of size and numbers the ideal that St. Augustine's College stood for should match competently the heavy task of handling the impending harbour problems. Beyond every material progress, the Gold Coast and indeed the whole of Africa needed indigenous leaders in all walks of life, but above all, "men of spiritual power of lofty aim and driving force".[28] This is the type of leader St. Augustine's College was built to supply. With the production in the seminaries of Church leaders with strong spiritual conviction the Churches could wield an influence that could permeate society with spiritual ideals and help to mitigate the corruption and problems that attend material prosperity. In time to come this lofty aspiration would be tested by the impact which the indigenous priests would have on the community.

Indeed, before the College was officially opened its first products had already been ordained into the priesthood. In March 1927 six students from the College had been made deacons and they remained in the college, at the temporary site, for their Diaconate, which lasted for a year, and they were ordained into the Priesthood on 4th March, 1928, a month prior to the dedication of the College. The importance of this first ordination, in the words of the Bishop, "lies in the fact that these were the first men who had ever received a systematic training in theology: they were the first fruits of St. Augustine's College, founded in 1924 and now housed in its new

---

26 Gold Coast Government, *The Gold Coast Handbook* (London, 1928), pp. 120-121.
27 K.A. Busia, *Report on a Social Survey of Sekondi-Takoradi* (London, 1956), pp. 106-114. Some of the social and moral problems are discussed.
28 "The Bishop's Letter", *The Golden Shore*, Vol. III, No. 1, July 1928, p. 2.

buildings at Kumasi".²⁹ They were Benjamin Tawiah Quartey, Ambrosius Manukure Asare, Theodore Immanuel Frederick Asiedukofiaw, William Edward Cobbah Yalley, John Francis Appiah and Samuel Augustus Christian Lutterodt.

The ordination itself took place, not in Kumasi, but in Accra. No reasons have been recorded to explain why this event took place in Accra. But it seems the authorities of the Church felt that the glory of St. Augustine's College should be equally shared between the two sections of the Diocese, the coastal and interior sections. Kumasi is the headquarters of the hinterland and barely a month after the ordination the permanent buildings would be dedicated in Kumasi. It would only be fair if the first ordination were carried to the capital of the coastal diocese, so that the people along the coastal areas could also have a foretaste of the contribution St. Augustine's College would be making to the progress of work in the Diocese.

So the staff and students of the College left Kumasi on Friday, 2nd March, 1928 by train for Accra. When they arrived at the Railway Station in Accra, they were surrounded by a large crowd of people who had assembled there to welcome them. Among them were three different choirs with their banners; the Bishop dressed in his cope and mitre and holding his pastoral staff was also there to shepherd the crowd. The students and their teachers made their reverence to the Bishop and stood around him. The whole crowd then burst into the singing of the TE DEUM. This was followed by exchanges of greetings; the Chancellor, arrayed in his wig and gown, greeted the students first on behalf of the laity, and presented each of the new deacons, with a morocco-bound copy of the Book of Common Prayer; the Bishop then greeted the guests from Kumasi and the throng marched in procession to Holy Trinity Cathedral, High Street, and there, outside the Temple, the Bishop blessed and dispersed the crowds for the night. After warm exchanges of hand shakes, lasting for about half-an-hour, the St. Augustine's College men retired to their lodgings for the night.

On the next day, Saturday, 3rd March, the morning was spent in rehearsing the ceremonies and after that the Bishop had private interviews with each of the prospective ordinands. In the evening, at about 5.30, the Bishop delivered his solemn charge to the Ordinands in Holy Trinity Church.

The climax of the event came on Sunday, 4th March, 1928. The celebrations began at 9.00 a.m. with Matins, and at 9.30 a.m. the Lord Bishop of the Diocese and the clergy entered the Cathedral from the West end in solemn sacerdotal procession with two Masters of Ceremonies between the clergy and the Bishop. The clergy were followed by an impressive company of people: the cross, lights and acolytes, followed by the six deacons,

---

29 S.P.G. *Reports* (London, 1928), p. 116.

"two and two, in alb, amice, girdle, stole and maniple, carrying chasuble on their left arm".[30] Bringing up the rear were the Rector of St. Augustine's College, Fr. Fisher representing the Education Department and Government Service and Fr. Martinson, the Priest-in-charge of Holy Trinity.

When all had taken their places the candidates were presented to the Bishop by the Rector of St. Augustine's College, Fr. Dom Bernard Clements.[31] Fr. E.D. Martinson, then preached the Sermon, after which the Oath of Allegiance to the Sovereign, and of Canonical obedience to the Bishop were administered in the Chancel by the Chancellor of the Diocese.

The Ordination then followed. The Litany was said and the Bishop went up to the altar and proceeded with the Mass. What followed is best described in the words of Fr. Clements as set down below.

> After the Gospel the Bishop came dowm from the Altar to his faldstool, and the ordination proceeded, the 'tradition of the instruments', and the vesting of the new priests with the Chasuble being included, as is the custom of the Diocese. It all passed—as such days will—like a dream, but one or two moments of the dream remain fixed in one's memory. One such moment, perhaps, was while the Bishop was censing the oblations at the offertory, and one could almost see the six newly consecrated lives there being censed with the host in unison with which they were about to offer them. Another was the moment of the Communion of the new priests, painted as it was in the splendour of their own vestments of every colour, and surrounded by all the brilliance of the Bishop's Mass all hushed into stillness by the Presence there where the Bishop moved.[32]

The great event had been completed and the long procession moved out again through the West door to greet the large crowd outside. The new priets returned to the Chancel where they received their Letters of Orders respectively. The day was rounded off at a public gathering at St. Mary's Church, Horse Road, Accra. At 4.30 p.m. a great crowd had assembled together and greeted the new priests most affectionately. After speeches[33] were made by the guests from St. Augustine's College the function was

---

30 "The Bishop's Letter", *The Golden Shore*, Vol. II, No. 8, April 1928, p. 243.
31 Under normal circumstances the Archdeacon should have presented the Ordinands to the Bishop; but on this occasion the only Archdeacon in the Diocese was unable to come down to Accra from Sekondi because he was ill in bed. Elliot, Oral Information.
32 "The Bishop's Letter", *The Golden Shore*, loc. cit.
33 These speeches have not been preserved. One of the most serious problems I encountered during my visits to the Seminaries in Ghana was that speeches delivered on important occasions in the Seminaries had not been preserved. When Trinity College was officially dedicated in 1965 two addresses were given by Dr. Hopewell of the T.E.F. New York and Dr. Baëta, Head of the Department of the Study of Religions, Ghana, respectively. Not even a summary of the important points made was entered into the daily record book of the College. I think that in the future not only the Seminaries but the Institutions of learning should make it a policy to preserve speeches and addresses given within their walls. The value of the speeches is that through reading them more accurate and unbiased assessment can be made of the impact the Institutions make on different people at different periods.

ended with a closing act of worship at Holy Trinity, and included among the worshippers were the Governor and Lady Slater.

This event was another important landmark in the history of the expansion of the English Church Mission in the Gold Coast. The experiment whereby an organized theological training was given to African priests by the Mission for the first time in the Diocese had been successful. The ceremony of ordination was an encouragement not only to the Bishop and the devoted Rector of St. Augustine's College, but also to the whole Diocese. It was too soon, in 1928, to assess the impact which the new priests would exert in their various parishes; but it was evident that with a regular training of indigenous priests by competent tutors the quality of the priesthood would be raised and the quantity would also gradually grow to meet the calls for priests that had been coming to the Bishop from various parts of the country.

The years immediately following these events, the ordination of the pioneer students and the dedication of the permanent buildings of St. Augustine's College, were years full of brilliant prospects for the College. Nine students remained in residence after the first ordination and by the first term of 1930 the total number of students in residence was 14.[34] This increase in numbers was not surprising in the light of other events taking place in the country at the time. In 1925 the Government had put forward its Education Reform which emphasized, among other things, the need for providing more secondary schools and raising the standard of education "to fit young men and women to enter a university".[35]

As a result of the premium the Government had put on Education, the English Church Mission put at the top of its priorities the need for building up more quickly an advance guard of African Clergy and Catechists, to do definitely pioneer work. The force of this need became more prominent then than before because it was recognized that the Missionary staff was not likely to be increased owing to the following reasons: the missionaries had to go on furlough after a short duration of 14 months according to government regulations for expatriates and the disrupted continuity of the work, moreover the cost of passages to and from overseas was so high that the furloughs tended to exhaust a large proportion of the income that should have been used on extension work; above all the hot climatic con-

---

34 S.P.G., *Reports* (London, 1929), p. 112. See also Bernard Clements, "St. Augustine's College: Two Years' Memories, *The Golden Shore*, Vol. III, No. 8, April 1930, pp. 271-275, where we are told that the students did not all enter the College at the same time. Six of them namely, Okwabie, Labi, Sakyiama, Armah, Quarm (Kwamie) and Ward were admitted in April 1928. George Laing, one of the pioneers who were admitted in 1925, had not completed his course at the end of 1927 because of illness; he returned from hospital and joined the 1928 class as the Senior student. John Quartey and Wilberforce joined the class as new students in July 1928. In 1929 Nelson, Poku and Ankrah were admitted, and in 1930 Andrew Ben-Smith and Yebuah went into residence.

35 McWilliam, *The Development of Education in Ghana*, pp. 53-54. The Sixteen Principles of Education Guggisberg proposed are tabulated by McWilliam.

ditions made it difficult for some of the missionaries to return to Africa. As the new missionaries who might be recruited would engage in the training of African priests but not in any definitely evangelistic work, it was imperative to accelerate the recruitment of the African personnel to cater more effectively for the literate society that might emerge as the result of the Government's educational policy.

As the institution was the first of its kind in the diocese it did not have any traditions behind it. So with the increase of students came definite efforts at consolidating the College traditions, among which may be included the following: agriculture, St. Augustine's Day Celebrations Re-union, initiation—in the first week of the last term, August to December—when a new Rector and new students were initiated and the spiritual traditions of prayer, penance, spiritual reading and worship.

It was not long afterwards, however, when dark clouds began to overshadow the College. In the first place, from the end of April 1931 Fr. Bernard Clements, the man who for five years laboured as the Rector of the College and built up its rich traditions, could no longer be spared by his community at Pershore (Nashdom Abbey) to remain in the Gold Coast. This loss was made more severe because Fr. Dominic, the other missionary in Kumasi who could act in the absence of Fr. Clements, also left about the same time for England due to family reasons. The value of their contribution to the growth of St. Augustine's College and the Diocese is best summed up in the words of the tribute paid them by the Bishop:

> Father Bernard with his gifts of sympathy and understanding and with his wide experience as a director soon won his way with the students of the College, and there is no doubt he has left his mark on the first men who went out as priests from St. Augustine's College and on those who are there now preparing for the Ministry. He was also of great service to us in the planning and building of the new College and in developing its life along wise and helpful lines. It is safe to foretell that he will never be fogotten by many of those whose paths have crossed his own. In bidding farewell to these two missionaries I cannot disguise the fact that it is a serious loss to our Mission to be deprived of men who have acquired that knowledge of the country and people which should have been invaluable to us in years to come.[36]

These were the men whose dedicated services were to change the course of the history of the young English Church Mission in the Gold Coast.[37]

The second problem that faced the College at the beginning of the 1930s concerned the recruitment of students into it. In 1930 seven of the students, Okwabi, Labi, Sakyiama, Quarm, Ward, Quartey and Armah were due to be made deacons but the ceremony was deferred[38] and in 1931 no

---

36 "The Bishop's Letter", *The Golden Shore*, Vol. IV, No. 3, January 1931, p. 37.
37 For further information about Fr. Clement's life see Almedingen, *Dom Bernard Clements, op. cit.*
38 "The Bishop's Letter", *The Golden Shore*, Vol. IV, No. 7, January 1932, p. 1.

new candidates were recruited. In fact it was not only in the Theological College that development had to be suspended. In the Diocese itself "all building of Churches and schools had had to be held up and his sending of new clergy to evangelise the Western Province had to wait till better times".[39] The reason for this anxious and worrying time for the Church is not hard to find. The difficulties arose as the result of the Cocoa Hold-up. From 1930-1931 the cocoa farmers refused to sell their produce to the European buying firms in order to resist the European firms' attempt to depress the price of cocoa for their own selfish ends,[40] and this resulted in fiscal strain. Notwithstanding the financial depression the Bishop and his African colleagues continued to hold the fort until better days returned.

It was not very long before there were signs that the better days were imminent because the cocoa hold-up had collapsed earlier then had been anticipated. In anticipation of that hope the seven students whose ordination had been deferred in 1930, were made deacons, on the 2nd Sunday in Lent, 1931 and to the priesthood on 20th September, 1931. The hope was not, however, realised and in 1932 after the last batch of five students at St. Augustine's College had been ordained to the priesthood at the end of the year, it became so difficult to find adequate financial support for the trained men that St. Augustine's College was closed down at the beginning of 1933 because the Bishop felt that to "go on training a large number of men without a reasonable expectation of providing for their support, would not be a venture of faith but a policy of rashness, which might lead us into serious difficulties".[41]

During the interim the course of training so far pursued in the College was re-evaluated. The College, within the initial nine-year period 1925-1933, endured many difficulties in addition to pecuniary problems. It was not easy to select the right stamp of men for the training, because many parents wanted their children, after leaving Adisadel College, to enter more lucrative jobs than to enter the ministry; in the process of selecting mainly from among Elementary School leavers some of the willing candidates were rejected as not being able to benefit by the studies. The building of the College, both in its temporary and permanent houses, had its attendant obstacles: the ground had to be prepared; there was the trouble of finding good teachers and guides who would work out a suitable course of training and there were difficulties concerning the choosing of parishes to which the African clergy could wisely be sent after their training to satisfy the linguistic demands of the tribes. The ethnic problems in the words of the Bishop "were constantly limiting the selection and the preparation of

---

39 S.P.G., *Reports* (London, 1930), p. 99.
40 Ward, *A History of Ghana, op. cit.*, pp. 398-400.
  This boycott did not succeed but in 1937 it was better organized and the hold-up continued through January, February and March.
41 "The Bishop's Letter", *The Golden Shore*, Vol. IV, No. 2, January 1933, p. 337.

other places years ahead so that an advance might be made on the right line".⁴² But in spite of all these difficulties, the College was able to justify its existence and but for the evil effects of the Cocoa Hold-up it would not have been closed down. So 1933 ended the first era of systematic theological training of indigenous priests in the English Church Mission of the Gold Coast and began another era of training destined to suffer fluctuating fate.

Here it should be appropriate to re-appraise the efforts made during the first decade by the S.P.G. to give organized theological education to its local priests. At the time that Fr. Bernard Clements resigned, i.e., at the end of April, 1931, there were 20 African Ministers in the Diocese. With the exception of the initial five African priests who had had private tuition prior to the opening of the College the rest of the priests had been carefully selected and given good training at St. Augustine's College. This shows that within seven years—1925-1931 both years inclusive, the Theological College produced 15 well-trained African priests. From the very beginning of the College project the Bishops had confidence that with a staff of well-trained African priests there should be spectacular progress. The confidence placed in the candidates was more than justified: Rev. J.N. Armah founded 11 congregations in the Denchera District in 1931; Rev. J.K. Yebuah made converts in 25 villages in the Anwiaso District with the help of only two catechists; there were confirmations in about 70 centres in the Diocese and almost all the candidates were prepared by African priests; out-stations were increased and indeed the central stations increased to about 11 in 1928 viz. Accra, Kumasi, Sekondi, Cape Coast, Tarkwa, Dunkwa, Bekwai, Bodi, Axim, Koforidua and Winneba.⁴³ The work in Ashanti also progressed during the period because the increase in the number of African priests coupled with the efficiency and reliability with which they worked set the English Missionaries free to accelerate pioneer evangelistic work in Ashanti. Thus Fr. Evans with the co-operation of two African priests, six catechists and eleven teachers, opened new grounds in Ashanti.⁴⁴

---

42 "The Bishop's Letter", *The Golden Shore*, Vol. IV, No. 2, January 1933, p. 336.
43 Gold Coast Government, *op. cit.*, p. 42.
44 We must not imagine, however, that every new ground was easy to open; some were so hard that it tasked the patience of the priests and their helpers to win unflinching response. See pages 42 and 43 of this study.

CHAPTER EIGHT

ANGLICAN CHURCH MISSION TRAINING: PHASE II
1933-1965

The training of ordinands was not, however, completely discontinued in 1933. It had been one of the original aims of St. Nicholas' Grammar School (Adisadel) to serve as the recruitment ground to the Anglican Priesthood. Though its character changed quickly and emphasis was laid on Secondary Education owing to the rapid growth of the Civil Service and the need to train men for it. St. Nicholas' Grammar School did not hesitate in coming to the aid of the Mission in the time of crisis. In March 1933 a limited number of prospective candidates for the priesthood was permitted to take residence at St. Nicholas' Grammar School. Three boys selected by the Bishop to be trained for the priesthood were put under the fatherly care of Mr. Alan J. Knight, the headmaster of the School.

The three students lived in the Headmaster's house. Their lecture room was the sacristy. The new College Chapel served as the centre for the little Theological Institution. In it the students and their director, Mr. Knight, said their daily Divine offices together. The influence the small theological group had on the secondary school population was tremendous. The fact that three boys felt called by God to accept the priestly vocation, instead of pursuing the secondary course with all its financial prospects, was a great source of spiritual impact on the boys.[1] Their training lasted about three years; but it was painful that they could not be ordained priests immediately.[2] They would serve for some period as catechists but when a priest was removed either by death or any accident then they would be ordained to fill the vacancies as the opportunities occurred.

In 1937 there was a glimpse of hope after the end of the 1937 Cocoa Hold-up referred to earlier in this book. At Synod the Parishes pledged to raise in the ensuing year £480 (c560) for an African Fund for paying the stipends of African Priests. Prior to the Synod of 1937, in November

---

1 Alan J. Knight, "Report on St. Nicholas April 1933", *The Golden Shore*, Vol. IV, No. 12, April, 1933, p. 385.
2 The effect of the financial slump still lingered on. There was general poverty due to poor cocoa prices and the Bishop felt that the clergy and workers would lose their true sense of proportion vis-a-vis uncontrollable financial stringency. In their difficult effort to maintain the material and spiritual balance of the Diocese, the priests and their assistants must have adequate means of subsistence because "a priest who is constantly worried by poverty in his own home, and by the shadow of debt, is not at his best in preaching the good news of the Kingdom of God"—S.P.G., *Reports* (London, 1938), p. 65. In order to safeguard this danger it was better not to increase the number of the priests so that the limited funds available might be used in maintaining the already ordained priests to enable them to preserve the work during the lean years of the country's history.

1936, the Rev. W.G. Harward had come out to the Gold Coast as chaplin to the European community and was stationed in Accra. As he was ready to share fully in the activities of the English Church Mission in addition to his chaplaincy work, students were no longer sent to Adisadel College in Cape Coast but a Hostel for Theological Students was opened in the Bishop's house in Accra, and Fr. Harward was put in charge of it. Six candidates mainly teachers and catechists were recruited and lodged in the hostel.

Formerly, there used to be a book store under the priest's house at Holy Trinity Church in Accra. It was that bookstore which was converted into the Hostel. The store was one long room which during the alteration was partitioned into a living room and a dormitory. Originally the front of the bookstore was built in glass plate fashion and so it did not allow in much fresh air. The students, recognizing the value of a well-ventilated room, decided to have the whole store extended. They received a gift of 15/- (¢0.75) from some unnamed unemployed men in north-eastern England[3] and they also raised a loan of £15 (¢30). With these amounts they paid for the cement and wood used and for the labour of the brick-layers they employed. The students themselves took an active part in the work and in the end the glass-plate was removed, the store was extended and the living room and the dormitory became much larger, about half as large again as previously. No space was allowed for a Chapel in the hostel because the Holy Trinity Chapel was nearby and its chancel served as the College Chapel. The completion of the work was celebrated with a dinner and a debate at the end of the term.

Despite the fact that the College was an improvised venture definite College routine was maintained. Prime was said at 5.30 a.m. and compline at 9.00 p.m. As the chancel was not always convenient for devotion it was felt that a separate College Chapel would be required. The lectures were given by Fr. Harward and Fr. J.R.C. Yalley, then in charge of Holy Trinity. The subjects taught were Greek Testament, the Bible, Church History, Liturgiology and Doctrine. There were no books at first; but the S.P.C.K. gave a grant of books to each student and afterwards other gifts which were received built a Library of about 40 books.[4]

Practical work was encouraged in addition to the ordinary academic pursuits; weekly services were conducted and sermons were preached at the James Fort Prison nearby, and at the week-ends the students went to adjacent villages to gain experience in pastoral work. At other times they travelled outside Accra as far as to Kumasi and preached in villages around

---

3 "Theological College, Accra", *The Golden Shore*, Vol. VI, No. 7, January 1938, p. 232.
4 S.P.G., *Report* (London, 1937), p. 83. The books from the old Theological College, Kumasi, were not transferred to the hostel in Accra because catechists were being trained there by Fr. Nelson about the same time that the hostel started functioning as a theological college.

Kumasi. They did not always find the village preaching work easy: at times they had to walk many miles only to learn that some of the village Christians had gone back to indigenous worship. For example, in 1938 the students went to villages near Kumasi and the following report of one of the students is of more than passing interest:

> September 14. Walked four miles from Bontomoroso to Adiembra. Found some members including the leader and the Church Keeper gone to fetish. Called on the Chief. Decided to return and report to the Archdeacon.[5]

A few days later another student gave the following report about another village:

> I was sent to investigate and persuade them to denounce all their heathen practices and return to Church to undergo discipline. Some of them were convinced and came to Church during the four days I spent with them and the rest promised to go back to the fetish and finish with him before they return to the Church.[6]

The promising beginning of the hostel training was short-lived. At the end of 1939 the little Theological College was discontinued; the ordination of the candidates who had been trained was suspended and the students were dispersed; four of them went into schools to teach and the one who was a catechist and a Yoruba from Nigeria[7] went back as catechist to the Yoruba in the country.[8] This sad disappointment arose in consequence of two almost simultaneous catastrophes, one local and the other international. There was an earthquake in the Gold Coast on 22nd June, 1939. It was felt all over the country; but in Accra it was most devastating; parts of the city were ruined; many people were injured and about 25 people died. In September the same year World War II broke out between the Germans and the British with her allies. The Gold Coast, then a Colony belonging to the British Empire, became directly involved in the declaration of War. The impact of these incidents on society was great: the earthquake brought financial losses as property, especially in Accra, was destroyed and needed replacement; the War brought financial strain not only to the country but to the whole Empire. Formerly, friends of the English Church Mission liv-

---

5 "Village preaching in Kumasi", *The Golden Shore*, Vol. VIII, No. 4, April 1939, p. 417.
6 *Loc. cit.*
7 "The Bishop's Letter", *The Golden Shore*, Vol. IX, No. 3, January 1942, p. 35. The Bishop wrote that "the Yorubas are a restless nomadic people and they have percolated in every district of the Gold Coast. They are hard working, active and thrifty. Some making a living by petty trading, and they itinerate from place to place; others are employed as servants, but for the most part they are to be found in the neighbourhood of the mines where they are engaged on firewood cutting to supply fuel for the engines. In dress, habits, and appearance they present a great contrast to our people, and their faces are usually scored and cut with tribal marks".
8 It has been said that six students were admitted for training at the hostel college—page 102 above. It seems one of them had dropped out before the completion of the course. This explains why five students but not six went out to their posts.

ing in England sustained and supported the stipends of the African clergy and catechists. The War reduced the resources of the donors and the overseas contribution to the diocese fell. In the Gold Coast itself the price of cocoa began to fall very low, because during the War there was greater demand for products such as palm kernel and rubber for war purposes rather than cocoa for chocolate. Lord Swinton who was the Resident Minister in the Gold Coast during the War years put forward forcefully during his New Year Message at the end of 1942 the need for concentrating on the growth of other products in West Africa rather than cocoa. He said:

> Of Cocoa, which is used principally for the manufacture of chocolate, we have more than we now need. Cocoa will recover its place of importance in the Exports from the British West African Colonies when the war ends, but until then some of the time and labour spent on its production could profitably be diverted to the cultivation of other crops. We must make ourselves self-supporting in foodstuffs.[9]

The whole situation was worsened in the Gold Coast because of black marketing: the prices of basic commodities rocketed very high, and the common people who formed the bulk of the congregations of the Churches became poor.

These circumstances explain why the little Theological College was closed and no students recruited during the War and new ordinations suspended. In fact the Bishop felt that that was the most expedient step to take when he wrote to the S.P.G. as follows:

> At such a time as this I dare not undertake fresh responsibilities, for the newly ordained men would go to parishes where they would set free clergy to do pioneer work, and that is always a matter of expense to the Mission in the early days.[10]

As new priests were not ordained immediately after the commencement of the War, clergymen who died during the period of the War could not be immediately replaced. As a result some of the parishes were combined and placed temporarily under one priest giving more work to the ministers concerned; moreover the number of catechists was reduced because there was no money to pay their salaries, and this increased, still more, the burden of the ministers.

Owing to the pathetic plight of the ministers the Diocese could not wait until the end of the War before ordination of priests was resumed. In 1941 Andrew Agyemang, an Ashanti and School Master and Joseph Adeseko, the Yoruba mentioned above, were ordained. The ordination of Adeseko was significant: the Yoruba, though superficially humble and submissive,

---

9 Gold Coast Gazette No. 84 of 26th November, 1942.
10 S.P.G., *Report* (London, 1939), p. 95.

were not easy to get on with; there used to be constant friction between them and the neighbours among whom they lived; among the Yoruba themselves there existed bitter disputes and feuds which a non-Yoruba could not amicably settle and above all they were very clannish. In spite of these characteristics the Yoruba are very religious; wherever they settle they usully build up some sort of place of worhship. A people of this type of behaviour need a priest of their own kind, a person who can understand, guide and control them. Joseph Adeseko was such a man and so he was ordained to fulfil a special ministry to a peculiar group, a ministry which would hopefully weld the Yoruba and the indigenous group into one fellowship within the English Church Mission of the Gold Coast.

In 1945, four years after these ordinations, St. Augustine's College was re-opened in Kumasi. It seemed that when the decision was taken in 1941 to ordain those two men to relieve some of the ministers who were being over worked it was also found prudent to continue to give training to only two men at a time to serve as reserves who might be ordained in times of emergency. So in 1943 two men were recruited and sent into training under the care of the Rev. G.E.F. Laing who was then the Parish Priest at Tarkwa from 1938 to 1945. The scheme progressed satisfactorily for two years, but it soon became more difficult for Fr. Laing to run the extensive Tarkwa parish efficiently and carry on at the same time the training of the students diligently. At that time the War was drawing to its end and the Diocese, forecasting better times ahead, made a more ambitious plan for the training of more students than just two men. The training was thus removed from Tarkwa and in January 1945 St. Augustine's College was re-opened in Kumasi.

Fr. Laing was transferred from Tarkwa and made the Rector of the College. He was born in 1907 in a devout Methodist family. At the time that he was being educated at Kumasi in the Government Elementary School, Fr. Elliot was the Parish Priest in Kumasi. It is believed that Fr. Elliot took special interest in young Laing and "won him over to the Anglican Church with a cup of tea".[11] He grew up an Anglican and entered the St. Augustine's College, Kumasi, in 1925. Dom Bernard Clements, the first Rector of the College, left an indelible influence on him.[12] He thoroughly imbibed the rich traditions Dom Bernard transmitted to the students. This seems to be the reason why Laing was entrusted with the training in order that he might perpetuate the highly honoured traditions of the first St. Augustine's College.

Four students were recruited to join the two students transferred from

---

11 This informtion was given by Mr. G.E. Laing, a brother of the late Provest Laing. Mr. G.E. Laing, at the time of writing this paper, was the Education Secretary of the Anglican Educational Unit, Accra, and also a lay-member of the Accra Diocesan Synod.
12 For a detailed study of the depth of the influence Dom Bernard Clements had on Laing see G.E. F. Laing, *Dom Bernard Clements in Africa*, (London, n.d.).

Tarkwa. With these six the College resumed its work again. Although the College was residential as before the character of the instruction changed almost completely. The students were now led through a correspondence course ordered from England because it was felt by the Bishop that such a scheme would enable the students to be more adequately prepared in order to raise their standard of attainment. The theological course was received from "Wolsey College", Oxford and that of English from another College. It seems the basic policy was to enable the African clergy to take the same courses of study as the Anglican Priests in England take because the students in Kumasi were to take the same General Ordination Examination at the end of their studies as the students in Britain. In fact the purpose of St. Augustine's College at this stage was to prepare the students in order that they might qualify for admission to St. Augustine's College, Canterbury, England, to take a further course of studies before ordination.[13]

By 1947 a strong feeling was developed in the Diocese that all the Anglican Clergy in the Gold Coast should be sent to England for their entire training. It is not documented anywhere as far as my investigations have gone why this feeling was developed; but it seems to me that two factors were responsible. In the first place, the Diocese became very much concerned about raising the standard of its priests. The policy that all ordinands should pass the General Ordination Examination had been accepted. A correspondence course might not be as adequate as when the students sit under the feet of experienced tutors in England. The second factor concerned the Methodist/Presbyterian co-operation in training their ministers together. As we shall see later in this study, the united training was started in Kumasi. Perhaps the Anglicans felt compelled to seek a wider Anglican fellowship in the training of their African ministers too.

But the new scheme was not easy to implement; considerable expense would be involved: the students' fares to and from Britain; their maintenance in England; allowance to their dependants while the students were away. Despite these problems the Diocese was not dismayed; it was determined to see the proposal through and to make it the normal policy for the future training of its priests.

While thinking was proceeding along these lines the correspondence course continued in Kumasi. On 21st November 1948, four students, E.A.B. Sackey, T.A. Annobil, A. Dawson-Ahmah and G.A. Quao were ordained priests. In 1950 eight students, including Williams and Thomas from the Gambian Diocese, were in residence at St. Augustine's College, and in 1951 there were nine students. Of these nine students four were

---

13 This scheme was inspired by a gift of £600 (c1,200) which was donated to the Accra Diocese for the training of African Clergy in the Diocese. It was raised by All Saints, Margaret St., from Dom Bernard Clements Memorial Fund.

admitted in February 1949.[14] From these figures it could be deduced that in 1950, four students were admitted of whom only two were from the Accra Diocese and in 1951 only one candidate was recruited. The picture from 1949 looks as follows:
  1949: four candidates recruited.
  1950: four candidates recruited (two from the Gambia).
  1951: one candidate was recruited.
This picture illustrates a serious decline in vocation. It seems that what Fr. Brewer had said in his report of 1949-50 concerning the recruitment of catechists could equally account for this lack of vocation. He wrote that "the ambition of present-day school boys to make their education a stepping stone to well-paid jobs raises difficulties for the future of such work, and village catechists appear to be dwindling".[15]

During 1951 the lack of vocation became so critical that at the end of the year St. Augustine's College once again ceased to function as a Theological Institution and the College buildings were lent by the Diocese to the Government to house the students to be trained as teachers.[16] The few ordinands who had been in residence were sent again to the Bishop's House in Accra in 1952.

The return of the students to the hostel in Accra was meant only to be an interim measure until more positive arrangements could be explored to continue the training in a well organized Theological College. It was not difficult before the new line of approach was discovered. In 1950 Bishop Stephen Neill had visited the Gold Coast as part of his Theological Survey of English-speaking West Africa. In his report on the survey he suggested that the Churches should unify their theological work by moving it all to a site near that of the University College.[17] In 1951 the Bishop of Accra appointed an ad hoc committee to discuss the Neill suggestions and recommendations. In August the same year the Diocesan Conference also discussed the proposals and was "entirely in favour of Bishop Neill's suggestions".[13] Three main reasons determined the decision of the conference.

First, such a college it was believed would give the Anglican Ordinands a

---

14 "The Bishop's Letter", *The Golden Shore*, Vol. XI, No. 7, January 1949, p. 310.
15 S.P.G., *Report* 1946-1958 (London, 1958), pp. 31 and 36. Compare with Footnote 2 of Chapter VI.
16 Ministry of Education Ghana, "A brief sketch of the History of Education", (Accra, n.d.), p. 8. In February 1951 the Gold Coast had its first General Election after which Mr. Kojo Botsio became the country's First Minister of Education. One of the first steps taken by the new Government was to draw up an Accelerated Development Plan of Education. In order to meet the proposed expansion of primary education under this Development Plan it was necessary for the Government to open a number of teacher training colleges. As the Government had not made previous accommodation arrangements to house the new Colleges, temporary houses were used. Hence the loan of St. Augustine's College to the Government.
17 Stephen Neill, *Survey of Training of the Ministry in Africa Part I*, (London, 1959), p. 63.
18 "The Bishop's Address", *The Golden Shore*, Vol. XII, No. 9, July 1952, p. 151.

wider and richer Christian fellowship. In the second place such a step would be a legitimate and practical step towards Church Union and finally the cooperation in training Protestant and Anglo-Catholic priests together would be a legitimate witness for all to see that Christians do love one another in spite of denominational affiliations.

In the following year, however, at the Synod of 1952, this position was reversed. The question of the united training was put again but it did not win approval. The reasons for the rejection have not been preserved in the Synod Minutes.[19] I have learnt, however, that two factors influenced the African members of the Synod to vote against the proposal: the problem of Apostolic Succession and the problem of finance. It seems the African members of Synod both ministerial and lay believed that it would not be proper for Protestant tutors, whose ordination was outside the Church of England with its doctrine of Apostolic succession, to train Anglican Ordinands.[20]

The Diocese, however, continued to make alternative arrangements for an exclusive Anglican training for their ordinands. First of all definite policies were laid down to guide the recruitment of future candidates. In view of the fact that the Anglican Ordinands in the Gold Coast were sitting for the same General Ordination Examination (GOE) as in Britain the policy was laid down that from 1952 only candidates who have passed the West African School Certificate Examination with at least Grade II would be accepted for the training which would henceforth last for four years. The first year would be devoted to general education and the last three years to theological training. Before his admission, a candidate would have to pass before an Archdeaconry committee after which he would go into residence in the Bishop's house for a few days. During that period he would meet the Bishop's advisory committee whose duty would be to assess the spiritual capacities of the candidates and the genuineness of their Christian living and vocation.

The immediate problem relating to these policies, especially the one that raised the entry qualification, concerned the question whether those who were willing to train for the priesthood at that time would have the basic entry qualification. In 1952 for example, there were 37 men who expressed the wish to offer for the priesthood. 12 of them were boys in secondary schools; 15 were young men and 10 were older men in the Diocese; but the Bishop was sceptical about the basic qualification of most of them.[21] The other problem concerned the staff who would take up the training. If the basic qualification of the students was required to be high, then those who would teach them must also be well-qualified. Accordingly, the Bishop suggested that the Principal should possess at least a Second

---

19. Accra Diocese, "Synod Minutes", August 1952.
20 G.E. Laing gave me this information. See Footnote 11 of this Chapter.
21 "The Bishop's Letter", *The Golden Shore*, Vol. XII, No. 11, January 1953, p. 192.

Class Honours Degree with experience in training Ordinands. None of the African Priests were qualified to hold that post then, and the Bishop had to turn to England for the supply of the Principal. While negotiations were going on in England to secure a Principal, two Anglican lecturers from the University College of the Gold Coast offered their services to assist the Bishop and the Advisory Committee in recruitinig suitable candidates.

About the end of 1953 while these plans were maturing for the reorganization of the ministerial training on a sounder basis, the Rev. Fr. Nickles arrived in the country. He was charged with the responsibility of starting a Pre-Ordination School. The purpose of the School was to give two years' general education to prospective candidates who fell below the basic qualification set down. The School was commenced on 29th April, 1954, in the Bishop's house, Accra, with six students of whom two were from the Gambia.[22]

The daily routine was as follows:— The day started at 5.00 a.m. when the students woke up. At. 5.30 a.m. they attended Matins in the Cathedral and at 6.00 a.m. there was the Service of Holy Communion. Breakfast was at 7.00 a.m., private meditation at 8.00 a.m. in the Chapel and at 8.15 a.m. the Rector joined the students of corporate Bible Study. The students often asked numerous questions about the Holy Scripture during this period and the Rector "sometimes nearly 'talks his head off' in explanation".[23] Lectures began at 9.00 a.m. until 12.30 p.m. with 15 minutes' break at 10.30 a.m. Lunch was at 1.00 p.m. after which 30 minutes were devoted to Latin Grammar. The rest of the afternoon was free for the students until 4.30 p.m. when they gathered for Evensong. This was followed by supper at 7.00 p.m., compline at 9.00 p.m. which was immediately followed by the bell for lights-out.

The subjects studied were Latin, Scripture, History, English and English Literature. The Rector taught Latin and Scripture whilst two visiting lecturers, Miss Muriel Bentley from Achimota School and Dr. Wilson from the University College of Gold Coast took English with Engligh Literature and History respectively.

The students did not engage in academic pursuits only. All of them were members of the Accra Community Centre where they occasionally went for recreation and entertainment. At other times the Bishop invited them to feasts attended by priests and their wives from other parts of the Diocese. The Gambians among the students were sometimes invited to give talks on certain aspects of life in the Gambia to Church groups such as the Holy Rosary Guild and the Friday Class Meeting at Adabraka. At other times some of them accompanied the Bishop when he went on trek and

---

22 See page 107 ff
23 "The Anglican Pre-Theological Course", *The Golden Shore*, Vol. XIII, No. 4, April 1954, p. 7.

excursions were organized to Tema and to the University College of the Gold Coast, Legon.

At the end of the first year's work it became evident that the Standard VII young men among the group would need not two years, but four years' preparation before they could qualify as Theological students. This would mean spending more money on the Qualifying Candidates. Apart from other expenses it cost £70 (¢140.00) to feed each of the candidates during the year. It would be very difficult for the Diocese to bear this cost for as many as four years. It is true that by 1954 the economic conditions of the country improved considerably,[24] and the financial position of the Diocese would have been better than during the War. But at the same time the Diocese had greater responsibilities than previously. The Diocese of Accra had ceased to be a Missionary Diocese in 1952 when its name was changed from the Gold Coast English Church Mission to the Anglican Church of the Gold Coast.[25] This new situation implied that the financial support that had been coming from the Mission in England would be reduced considerably; but the Diocese must carry on evangelizing the people.

In the light of all this it was necessary to find a less expensive way of training the candiates. It was therefore decided that the students must get into part-time employment simultaneously with their studies. Consequently, they were removed from the Bishop's house during the year, i.e. 1954, and were sent as missionary team to Sefwi under the leadership of their Rector, Fr. Nickles. The idea of the project in the Bishop's own words, is that:

> Half-a-dozen of them shall live in community with Fr. and Mrs. Nickles in a village in Sefwi, that they shall spend the mornings in prayer and study and in the afternoons they shall evangelize their village and three other neighbouring villages. In four or six months we trust that they will have made a real bond of friendship with every soul in the four villages and have brought them the challenge of Christ, and that they will have trained a body of leaders to carry on the work. The villages that we have in mind already contain some Anglicans. Then the team will move on to another group of four villages nearby to do the same work and give occasional visits to their first group of villages.[26]

The Pre-Ordination training problem having been settled, attention was focused on the Theological College itself. From 1951 to 1954 only makeshift

---

24 Ward, *op. cit.*, p. 404, give the quantity of cocoa exported and the value from 1949 as follows:
   1949: 263,000 tons £34.018 millions (¢68.036 millions)
   1952: 212,000 tons £52.533 millions (¢105.066 millions)
   1954: 214,000 tons £84.509 millions (¢169.018 millions)
25 Accra Diocese, Synod Minutes, 23rd August, 1952, p. 2.
26 "The Bishop's Letter", *The Golden Shore*, Vol. XIII, No. 6, October 1954, p. 104. According to Fr. Nickles "the Sewfi project proved impracticable"—he did not say why—"and the students were advised to enter the teaching field to improve their academic standing". One of the students, D.O. Adeloye (Yoruba), was trained by Father Nickles at the Bishop's House after the collapse of the project.

arrangements had been afforded for the training of the priests. In 1955 the makeshift position could no longer be tolerated because since 1952 when the Diocese ceased to be a Missionary Diocese it was becoming more and more urgent that the Accra Diocese should fulfil more effectively her real task of self propagation and the supreme means of doing so was the training for the ministry. Thus the Synod Standing Committee became greatly concerned when the arrangements for re-organizing the training of priests did not show positive signs of maturing even in 1955, despite the fact that in that year there were a number of young men, of the type required, offering themselves for Holy Orders. After the rejection of the Joint Training Scheme, it was thought that a Provincial Training College for the West African Province would be the best arrangement for the training of West African Anglican priests. But this was not possible because the other Dioceses already had satisfactory Colleges; St. Andrew's College, Oyo in the Diocese of Lagos and in Sierra Leone, Fourah Bay College. This was the position in 1956 when Bishop Daly left the Diocese for good; but he was convinced that Joint Training with the Protestants in the Gold Coast was the right solution and he recommended the scheme to his successor.[27]

But when Roseveare succeeded Daly, he implemented the proposal made a decade earlier in 1947 "that all the Anglican African Clergy in the Gold Coast should be sent to England for their entire training".[28] Without any delay four students were recruited to be sent to Kelham in September 1956 for a five-year training course. They were: William Nobleman Kwame Amamoo, John Francis Akoto Appiah, Francis Kwesi Buckman and Albert Willington Yamoah Mensah. The arrangements was possible due to the generosity of a Religious Community in England. Bishop Roseveare bolonged to the S.S.M. and possibly through him, this Society had consented to help the overseas training of the men at no cost to the Diocese, apart from the return fare to and from England and other incidental expenses covering clothing, books and holidays. So in September 1956 two of the selected four, Albert W.Y. Mensah and John Appiah, left Ghana for Kelham as the pioneers under the new policy. The other two could not go forward because of family reasons.

1956 was another milestone in the training of indigenous ministers for the Anglican Church in the Gold Coast. It was an epoch in which an entirely new form of training for ordination was anticipated; a training that would be thorough and worthy of the expense. Besides this overseas training, new avenues were opening in the country for higher studies. The University College of Gold Coast was established in 1948 and a place had been given to a Department of Divinity within its structure. At the end of 1955 Professor Noel King was appointed head of the Divinity Department. He was

---

27 "The Bishop's Letter", *The Golden Shore*, Vol. XIII, No. 8, April 1955, pp. 149-150.
28 See page 106.

an Anglican and he took a very keen interest in the training programme for African priests in all the Churches under discussion. With his assistance, the Synod Committee explored other avenues whereby those prospective candidates who had already attained high preliminary intellectual qualifications, such as London Matriculation or the G.C.E. 'A' Level, could seek admission to the University, then at Achimota, to take a London B.D. Course locally. Nor was that all. As the new programmes would require five years training overseas and four years at the University College of the Gold Coast, for a prospective candidate to be due for ordination, an interim measure was also considered whereby seven of the experienced Catechists who had expressed the desire for ordination in the past could be tested and given a two-year course in the Bishop's house leading to ordination. These then were the plans at the beginning of the 1956 epoch. These plans at the time they were formulated were believed to be sufficient to insure an even and generous flow of well-trained priests; to increase the number as well as to encourage vocation to the priesthood; and to help in selecting for training only the very best men available.

This last point about training only the best men could not be over-emphasized at a time when the Gold Coast was seriously agitating for Independence. Already in 1951 internal self-government had been granted with an African majority in the Legislative Assembly. The need to train African personnel rapidly to assume different types of responsibility when the British finally handed over power to the Africans became urgent. The Government accelerated its educational policy and owing to the high qualifying requirements needed for entry into the University, educational standards continued to rise year by year. Consequently, it became "obviously essential" as the Bishop put it, "that our priests should be not only of a very high moral standard but also thoroughly well educated and trained for their special task".[29] The Diocese once again had discovered how to handle the problem of the training of its ministers; the policy was specific, viz: to train less qualified men overseas at Kelham for five years and to train matriculant candidates at Legon for a four-year course leading to the London Bachelor of Divinity Degree, to be followed by a year or two of pastoral training at an English University.

This programme, in spite of the generosity of S.S.M., would involve a considerable amount of extra expenditure. Apart from the expenses to be incurred by the families of the Kelham men in respect of the return fares of the students to and from England, of clothing, books and holidays, it was estimated that each Kelham man would cost the Diocese an additional £400 (¢800) for the five years; the Achimota men would cost about £1,000 (¢2,000) each for the four years. These figures, however, did not dissuade the Diocese because the parents of all the students were prepared to help

---

29 "The Bishop's Letter", *The Golden Shore*, Vol. XIV, No. 1, July 1956, p. 13.

in defraying part of the costs; other grants would come from the S.P.G., the S.P.C.K., special local resources through appeals in the Diocese and from special subscriptions through the A.D.A. But when we consider that an average of about four or five men would begin training each year if the new policy was to be followed strictly then we can appreciate that the total cost of the programme would be formidable.

This position was made more serious by the emergency non-repeatable two-year course at the Bishop's house for the catechists referred to above. Instead of six as originally proposed, seven catechists were selected for this training and it was estimated that the project would cost £3,000 (₡6,000) exclusive of tutors' salaries. In any case, there was no going back; the need for priests was desperate and promising candidates were many. To raise money quickly to meet the urgency of the situation appeals for special subscriptions both locally and abroad was necessary. In the past, appeals for financial support were only sent to the A.D.A. and other people in Britain. But now the position demanded a local appeal, not only to the Anglican members and their sympathisers but the whole nation. Arrangements were quickly effected and on 29th October, 1956, the Bishop launched the "Bishop's Special Appeal" at a well-attended meeting.

Among the audience were very important personalities such as His Excellency the Governor, the Minister of Housing representing the Prime Minister, Sir Leslie McCarthy, the Chairman of the Central Committee of Laymen and about at least 500 people. The Bishop outlined in his speech the purpose of the meeting and launched the appeal for £67,000 (₡134,000). After that a Local Accra Committee was elected and the Appeal was given in Gā, the vernacular of the area, by Canon Okwabi who was at the time the Diocesan Treasure. Gifts and promises then began to pour in and at the end of the meeting an amount of about £6,000 (₡12,000) was collected or promised.[30] With this result many of those who attended the meeting might have returned home with great satisfaction and optimism.

Kumasi also organized a similar appeal later and there too the response was great: £10,000 (₡20,000) was given or promised on the spot. Just within a month of the launching of the Appeal the sum total of the fund both in cash and promises was £23,000 (₡46,000) by the end of November.

But the actual cash in hand ten months after the appeal was only £6,634 11s. 0d. (₡13,269.10). This was just sufficient to clear the clergymen's arrears; but it would not be realistic to devote the small cash in hand to that purpose only; the other major concerns—the training of Ministers and the extension of the work—must be kept going somehow. Indeed, the result of

---

30 "Bishop's Special Appeal (Gold Coast)", *The Golden Shore*, Vol. XIV, No. 3, January 1957, p. 62.

the £67,000 (¢134,000) Appeal was so disappointing that the Bishop could not help but voice his feeling loudly and bitterly:

> But I am deeply shocked by the failure of so many (they are numbered in hundreds) who have so far failed to honour promises to subscribe annually to the "Bishop's Special Appeal Fund". I cannot too strongly stress that more than any other single factor, this shameful failure is the cause of our clergy stipend arrears and also of the failure to complete or to undertake the extension work to which we are committed.[31]

Despite the lack of money the overseas and University training of future priests was maintained steadily from 1956 until 1965, when the project seems to have deteriorated again. The reason why the training was maintained is simple. We have said above that the cost of training students overseas and at Legon was borne mainly by students' relatives and external organizations. These sources continued to honour their promises. What the Appeal had intended to achieve in respect of the training scheme was to double the number of priests in ten years. It was this aspiration which receded into the background when the appeal failed to reach its target.

In any case the result of the training during the years 1956-65 is worth noting: in 1956 the seven ex-catechists in training at the Bishop's house satisfactorily completed their first year and proceeded to the second year in October, 1957; in the same year, one more candidate, Theophilus Annobil, the son of Fr. Annobil, joined the two men at Kelham; two candidates, John Pobee and Emml. Abban who had matriculated, began their B.D. course at the University of Ghana in October. In 1958, on September 28, the biggest ordination in the history of the Diocese took place, when eight Africans and two Europeans were ordained priests in Accra. The African priests were the seven ex-catechists trained in the Bishop's house plus Rev. Joseph Dadson who was trained for several years in the U.K. at Wells Theological College and also took a course in Oecuminism at Bossey in Switzerland. The others were: Ephraim Arkorful, Benjamin Bewaji, Seth Erskine, Clement Obeng, Albert Opoku, Edward Mends and John Sams. The joy on that day for such a great harvest in spite of storms might have compensated partly for the pains of disappointment.

1958 was not, however, all joy. It was a year when joy and sadness alternated. It was sad when during the year it was found expedient to recall two of the Ordinands at Kelham with their courses uncompleted. At the same time it was encouraging when another candidate, Robert Okine, an old boy of Adisadel, brought up by Rev. Lamaire, was recruited and sent to join the only one Accra Diocesan Ordinand left at Kelham; also another candidate, Bernard Armah, a son of another Anglican Priest, Canon Armah, was admitted to the London B.D. Course at the University of Ghana. October 1959 saw the fourth Anglican Ordinand, Philip Aggrey, en-

---

31 S.P.G., *Report* 1956-1960 (London, 1960), p. 27.

tering on the B.D. course at the University, Legon, and at the same time a fifth candidate, Richard Adjaaye, who was a member of Synod, also entered the University to pursue the courese leading to the London Diploma in Theology.

And so continued a steady trickle of good quality candidates offering themselves for ordination through the troublous times until 1961 when no new ordinands were recruited to begin training. It seems that the reason for suspending the recruitment was due, again, to financial causes. Ministerial stipends were still in arrears and since the financial position was not recuperating hopefully, it would be suicidal to train men who would not be paid to meet their mundane necessities. Those who were already in training were ten in number, viz: Albert Mensah (Kelham), Richard Adjaaye (Diploma Course, U.G.), William Awumah (Kelham) who would continue for two years in Germany; John Pobee (due to complete his B.D. at U.G. and to begin a research course at Selwyn College, Cambridge), Emmanuel Abban (U.G.), Bernard Armah (U.G.), Philip Aggrey (U.G.), Robert Okine (Kelham). In 1965, however, John Ackon (Kelham), Thomas Brient (Edinburgh) and Leopold Ankrah (Huron College, Canada) were permitted to study abroad. These 13 men would continue their studies to the end and perhaps by the time they would all have been ordained the financial position would have improved.

So, by the end of our period, the organized training of African Anglican priests in Ghana ceased to exist. It seems, however, that the training was not abandoned altogether. We started this story with the informal training of the pioneer African Anglican ministers. It is ironical that after 40 years' labours at organizing ministerial Training Institution in the Diocese we should close our study just as we had began it. In 1965 the Rev. Maurice Manderville was stationed at Tema in charge of St. Alban's Church. At that time a prison officer called Nicholas Dartey was accepted as a prospective candidate for the ministry; as no training was being organized locally in the Diocese he was asked to stay with Father Manderville in his manse. There he was prepared for ordination. In addition to private studies, Dartey travelled with Fr. Manderville, helped him with housework, taught confirmation candidates and helped Fr. Manderville to improve his Gã. This type of training could only be an interim measure and during the period of suspension of training locally the Diocese continued to explore avenues whereby effective training in the country could be resumed.

So we see that the Anglican training of African ministers in Ghana had suffered many interruptions. The life of St. Augustine's College, was very short. It existed for 27 years, from 1925 to 1951. It did not, however, function continuously within those 27 years. It was closed down in 1933, and was not re-opened for the training of priests until 1945. That is, the College did not function as a ministerial training institution for 12 years out of the 27 years. In spite of its very brief active life of only 15 years it made a tremendous impact on the life of the Church.

Prior to the opening of the College in 1925 there were only five African Priests in the whole Diocese of Accra. When it was finally closed down in 1951 there were 33 African Priests in active service and six had died, including Annan Sey.[32] This rapid growth of African clergy in the Anglican Church was no small achievement when we compare this result with the results of other denominations within a similar period of 27 years.[33] We cannot, however, measure the achievement of the College only in numbers, but also in how other people saw it. A well of information is available in the Visitor's Book of St. Augustine's College, Kumasi, illustrating people's complimentary impressions of the College.[34] Two examples, one by a layman of distinction and the other by a clergyman of international repute, will suffice.

In 1947 Mr. Magnus Sampson, the Secretary of the Joint Provincial Council of Chiefs, visited the College and made the followinig entry:

> I am very happy to have had the privilege of spending three days in the magnificent premises of St. Augustine's College. The tone of the College in excellent. There is indeed an air of Christian outlook and efficiency for which Rector and students should be proud.

Then, in 1950, Bishop Stephen Neill, a representative of the World Council of Churches, came to Ghana in connection with his Theological Survey. He spent a brief period at St. Augustine's College and on his departure he recorded the following statement:

> I have been very happy to share for a short time in the life of the Rector and students of St. Augustine's. I felt that much of the spirit of Dom Bernard Clements remained about the place, and trust if it were possible for him to return, he would find himself perfectly at home.

---

32 The Anglican Church in Ghana had no extant records about Annan Sey, to show that he had been an Anglican Priest. The information presented here was collected from Mr. Paul Jenkins, Lecturer, History Department, Legon, Ghana and Canon Elliot. Mr. Jenkins had been compiling a list of Ghanaian Anglican Ministers. His list up-to-date included Annan Sey. No file had been opened for him in the Anglican Head Office, Accra. Fr. Elliot, however, remembered Annan Sey very well when I was in Ghana during my research in 1968/69. According to Fr. Elliot, Annan Sey was trained at Oxford as an Evangelical type Anglican Priest. As a result of this when he returned to Accra he was not well-received because the Accra Diocese was high Anglican. He was, however, welcomed in the Niger Diocese where he laboured for a time. He later returned home and died in service.

33 See Appendix VII

	Period	No. of Ministers
Methodists	1842-1869	12
Basel Mission	1848-1875	6
Bremen Mission	1864-1891	1

34 The Original Visitor's Book of St. Augustine's College, Kumasi, was not traceable during my researches in Ghana. Fortunately extracts from the Book have been preserved in *The Golden Shore*, Vol. XII, No. 7, January 1952, pp. 108-111.

It is clear from these entries that under the first African Rector, Fr. G.E.F. Laing, St. Augustine's College continued to train priests to the satisfaction of those among whom they would labour. The endeavour had not been easy; the College endured numerous difficulties from the very beginning of its life: it could not be started by O'Rorke before 1925 because it was not easy to get the right man to begin the College and guide, in the right direction, the studies of the students; the number of educated young men who had a vocation from among whom to select to start the institution was pitifully small; the temporary accommodation which housed the pioneer students was grossly inadequate; owing to lack of funds the College had to close down intermittently and a few men trained elsewhere; for the same financial difficulties the ordination of trained men was at times delayed and the Ordinands had to go back into lay employment as teachers; at times some of the students were withdrawn because they were judged to be incapable of becoming priests; there was no background nor tradition to build on. But these difficulties did not alter the impact the College was built to make. It was through the efforts of the products of the College that the work and influence of the Anglican Church of Ghana expanded through the length and breadth of the country, so that by 17th June, 1959 there was an Anglican Christian community of 21,774 members.[35]

It seems that the successes achieved by the Priests in their parishes depended to a very large extent on living their theological training among the people they served. Dom Bernard Clements planted indelibly the spirit of community living and cordial fellowship among the students and between the students and himself. The first African Rector, the late Provost G.E.F. Laing, perpetuated these sterling qualities of Seminary life—the qualities which made St. Augustine's Theological College worthy of its name. Indeed, the community spirit is one of the great assets of a Theological College and "without an awareness of that deep fellowship between the students and, in many cases, between students and staff, one does not begin to sense the atmosphere of the theological school".[36] St. Augustine's College, Kumasi, epitomised the CACTM definition of a theological school as pri-

---

35 Accra Diocese, Synod Minutes, August 1959.
36 B. Sundkler, *The Christian Ministry in Africa* (London, 1960), p. 198. Sundkler discusses a Tanganyika word "ukwangala" which the Nyakyusa tribe in Tanganyika translates "good company". According to Professor Monica Hunter Wilson, whom Sundkler quotes, the highest value among the Nyakyusa is "the enjoyment of good company", because it is believed that it is "by conversing with our friends that we gain wisdom". Although in an institution of learning students are not considered the contemporaries of their teachers, a friendly attitude could be developed between the teacher and the taught. The significance of this type of friendly relationship cannot be over-emphasized in connection with the training of priests, because in their Parishes the priests should not lord it over their parishioners, but should maintain a friendly fellowship embracing the youngest and the oldest, the poorest and the richest. For further study of this interesting word "ukwangala" see M.H. Wilson, *Good Company, A study of Nyakyusa Age—Villages*, (O.U.P., 1951), p. 66, quoted by Sundkler, *op. cit.*

marily a "community of devotion".³⁷ But it was not the kind of devotion which departmentalizes life into the sacred and the profane; it was a devotion which embraced both the material and spiritual aspects of the students' college life. They studied, they worked, they worshipped together and they served one another. There is no doubt that these qualities transferred from College into the Parishes would greatly enhance the work of the priests.

In spite of the foregoing paragraphs there is one weakness which can easily escape notice and that is the problem of one-man staff. When a theological school is controlled by one-man staff, as happened in St. Augustine's College, students tend to become intellectually and spiritually dependent upon one man. One obvious disadvantage is that the students may become narrow-minded when compared with students in a multi-staff theological school where there is the possibility that the different members of staff are likely to approach their subjects differently. The problem becomes detrimental when the tutor of a one-man-staff theological school approaches his subjects mythically without any attempt to substantiate facts with sufficient evidence. For example, Sundkler tells the story of a Western teacher in an African theological school (non-Anglican). The teacher had formed the "idea that most of the individuals with whom Jesus came into contact in his ministry later turned up as Bishops".³⁸ The teacher had read in his New Testament, Matthew 19: 13-15 that Jesus blessed a child. In Church History he probably learnt that the little child blessed by Jesus became Bishop Ignatius at Antioch. He tried to correlate New Testament and Church History teaching. There is nothing wrong with correlation in teaching; but what was wrong with this one-man-staff in question was that his conclusion did not have adequate documentary evidence and there were no other tutors in the School from whom the students could learn different ideas.

There is no evidence that Dom Bernard Clements and Provest Laing were teachers of this type. Under them St. Augustine's College, Kumasi, achieved remarkable results; Dom Bernard Clements himself was a teacher of extraordinary qualities. At least, that was how Fr. Laing saw him and he expressed his impressions of his master in these words:

> Father Rector came to us as our teacher. At lectures we drank deep from his knowledge. He made all subjects interesting and easily understandable. He would make us laugh one minute and not very long afterwards carry us to another world; and when he brought us back into this one you could hear every student sigh. His knowledge of Latin was thorough. He would go either to his hall or to the college library and bring a volume of Moral Theology in Latin, and would read it to us as if reading an English version. His favourite subject was Ascetic Theology. This subject was as easy to him as it was delightful to

---

37 CACTM, cited by Sundkler, *op. cit.*, p. 199.
38 *Ibid.*, pp. 202-203.

us, because we saw in the life of the teacher, the practical expression of that branch of theology.[39]

All this does not, however, rule out the fact of the weakness mentioned above regarding the one-man-staff. It is not my intention to underrate the work done by the staff of St. Augustine's College, Kumasi. I am only underscoring a problem to guide small theological schools and my purpose for so doing is summed up in these words of the I.M.C.:

> These things are not said in a critical mood, but simply to emphasize the enormous importance of the teacher in these rather small and closely knit schools.[40]

In the light of the foregoing survey it is rather pathetic that in its search for a better and more efficiently conducted theological school, the Anglican Church in Ghana rejected the invitation to co-operate with the Protestant Churches in training their Priests together in one Institution. If in this search the Diocese were eventually to reverse its decision and consent to participate in joint training, history might show that it had taken the right decision.[41]

---

39 Laing, *op. cit.*; p. 23.
40 M. Searle Bates, et. al., *Survey of training of the Ministry in Africa, Part II* (London, 1954), p. 55.
41 It was rewarding to learn when I was at Trinity College during my research tour from July 1968 to February 1969 that the Anglicans had now accepted the Protestant invitation and were participating in Joint Training. The Rev. Fr. Albert Nickles was on the staff and four Anglican Ordinands were in residence at Trinity College at the time when this paper was being written.

CHAPTER NINE

ROMAN CATHOLIC MISSION TRAINING: S.M.A.
1909-1965

The training of African Roman Catholic Priests in Ghana has been in the hands of two religious communities of priests namely, the Society of African Mission (S.M.A.) and the White Fathers. They are only two out of very many World Roman Catholic ecclesiastical communities of priests.[1] The main purpose of all the communities "is to enable their members to work collectively toward the goals of the church".[2] The founding of each community and the inauguration of its rules had to be approved by the Vatican. Broadly speaking, the communities have been classified into two groups as follows: (a) the orders and congregations whose priests take formal and public vows of poverty, chastity and obedience, perpetually or temporarily binding and (b) the societies of secular institutes whose members do not take vows but make simple promises (perpetual or temporary) which are not as stringent as the vows[3] because it is not as difficult for the members to withdraw from their societies, if they so desire, as the members of the former group. Members of both groups, however, lead a collective life.

The S.M.A. have often been called Lyons Missionaries because it was at Lyons in France that the venerable Founder of the African Missionaries established the first seminary of the Society, and Lyons had remained the Society's headquarters for a long time. The S.M.A. had been active in French Colonial Africa until World War II when it became difficult for French missionary agencies to continue supporting all their missionaries in the field. Consequently, much of the sphere where the Lyons Missionaries had been working was re-assigned to other religious communities; and part of the Gold Coast especially the Vicariate of Accra, was allotted to the Divine Word Fathers (S.V.D.), from the United States of America.[4] But as the S.V.D. did not engage in seminary work, we shall no longer concern ourselves with them.

The White Fathers (W.F.) had been established in Algiers in the latter part of the 19th Century by Cardinal Lavigerie. Their main aim was to

---
1 York Allen, *A Seminary Survey*, (New York, 1960), pp. 299-300. Allen gives two lists showing the Principal Roman Catholic Religious Orders and Communities of Priests and Women engaged in Foreign Mission activities in 1950.
2 *Ibid.*, p. 301.
3 *Ibid.*, p. 302. The historical development of the Religious Orders and Societies, in the Roman Catholic Church since the Fifth Century A.D., and their main classifications are discussed here.
4 Helen Pfann, *A Short History of the Catholic Church in Ghana*, (Cape Coast, 1965), pp. 97-100.

convert the Muslims and pagans of Africa. They wore white vestments so that their dress might be similar to the clothing of the Muslims whom they sought to convert. Cardinal Lavigerie required the fathers to speak, read and write in the vernacular of the local people and so he forbade them to teach the French language to the natives. By 1957 the White Fathers had 1,599 of their members working in French Northwest Africa, West Africa and British East Africa, especially in Uganda.[5] With the exception of the Jesuits, the White Fathers have had more Missionaries in the field than any other community.[6] From the Sudan, they entered Northern Ghana and established a Seminary at Wiagha which later transferred to Tamale in the 1940s. The stories of how the S.M.A. Seminary at Amisano and that of the White Fathers in Northern Ghana were started and developed respectively are narrated below.

The training of Roman Catholic African Priests in Ghana was started by the S.M.A. at Amisano on 9th August, 1909. Amisano was, at the time, a small secluded village, about ten miles west of Cape Coast and four miles north of Elmina. The story of how such an isolated village became the focus of the local Seminary in the Gold Coast began in the following manner: before 1906, the indigenous Roman Catholic converts in the Gold Coast had not been educated by the Missionaries to pay dues for the upkeep of the mission work. The whole work had been maintained by the countries which sent the missionaries and by an annual subsidy of 20,000 francs (£1,000 or ¢2,000) from the Congregation of the Propagation of the Faith in Rome. But these contributions had been sorely inadequate to pay for the feeding of 27 missionaries in the field, the numerous journeys made by those of them who became sick, the salaries of teachers in the elementary schools and for the construction and upkeep of the church and school buildings and so on.

The Diocese of Nigeria had experienced similar difficulties and had solved them by establishing a coconut plantation at Tokpo, near Lagos. Consequently, the missionaries in the Gold Coast decided to adopt the Nigerian method in solving their financial problems.[7]

The Rev. Father Prefect, Joseph Pellat[8] bought a large piece of land

---

5 Allen, *op. cit.*, p. 319.
6 *Loc. cit.*
7 I have drawn here on an account written in French and preserved in the Amisano Diary (1930-1954), pp. 1-7. I do not read French; but the staff of the French Department at Achimota School, Achimota, Ghana, kindly helped me with the translation of the document entitled: "Coutumies de la Mission d'Amisano reletant au jour les faits saillants de l'Histoire de la station".
8 John van Heesewijk, "St. Teresa's Seminary Amisano—Notes". (Archbishop's House, Cape Coast n.d.), p. 1. Hereafter cited as Heesewijk, "Amisano Notes". The material contains notes on the history of this seminary. I could not lay hands on the original copy preservd in the Archbishop's house, because the documents there had not all been properly catalogued. But the Vicar General, the Rev. Fr. J. Ennoo, who was in charge of the Archives, kindly permitted me to read a type-written copy of the notes.

consisting of 143 acres at a village called Afraboadzi in the vicinity of Amisano. It was fertile, watered by a rivulet and supposed to be good for growing rubber, coffee, pineapples and certain other crops. It was bought in three sections: the first on 24th September, 1892 and the deed of conveyance was made between Kwaw Ewul, Kodwo Esuman, Kofi Akwa and Akosua Kobinaba, and the Rev. Fr. Joseph Pellet, Catholic Mission, Elmina, Trustee and representative "De la Societe des Missions Africaines de Lyon, France", and £60 0s. 0d. (¢120) was paid to the vendors who made the conveyance in these words:

> The vendors do hereby grant, sell and convey unto the purchaser, his heirs and successors . . . all that piece of land . . . described in the plan shown at the foot of these and bounded by the property or land in possession of Kobina Emisa, Kodwo Ayity Abuagdie and Termeulen. East = Ayity or Etive — West = Kwamina Abuadwi.[9]

The second and third section of land were acquired on 9th October, 1895. Unfortunately, however, the agricultural project did not make good progress because sickness and death so depleted the missionary strength in 1895 that the scheme had to be abandoned when Father Martini, the only survivor on the farm, left Amisano for Cape Coast on 1st March, 1896. Apart from occasional visits to Amisano by the Fathers, and school children on picnic days nothing more was heard about the village until 30th March, 1909. On that day two carpenters from Cape Coast who were also prospective candidates for the priesthood went to settle on the farm at Amisano. They were Joseph Michael Binly and John Andrew.

With these young men the first attempt was made by the Roman Catholics to set up a seminary in the country for the training of African Priests. The experiment was started on 9th August, 1909. On that day, a Seminary at Amisano was opened by Bishop Francis Ignatius Hummel. The foundation students were the carpenters named above and the only member of staff was John Fletcher Smith. The purpose of the training then was to give the students a good elementary school education, at the end of which they would be out as catechists and later, after some years of experience in that office, they would be given further training leading to ordination.[10]

The building which housed the Preparatory Seminary is illustrated below.[11] It was very simple. The walls and roof were made of corrugated iron sheets and the remaining parts of wood. It contained four rooms, a hall and two small verandahs. The students and their teacher occupied a room each and the fourth room was used as a chapel.

---

9 *Ibid.*, p. 2. A copy of the Deed of Conveyance No. 726/92, stamped 19. X. 1892 has been preserved in the Archbishop's House, Cape Coast, Ghana.
10 Heesewkijk, "Amisano Notes", p. 3.
11 *Ibid.*, p. 5.

	Verandah	
John Andrew		Chapel
	Hall	
Joseph M. Binly		Teacher J. Fletcher Smith
	Verandah	

The hall served both as the classroom and the dining room. Empty wine barrels were used for storing water and a filter was provided for purifying it. The beds they used were made of wood and supplied with mosquito nets fixed to each of them.

The daily routine they followed was also very simple. The rising bell was at 5.00 a.m. and after getting up they went to the rivulet and had their bath. This was followed by morning prayers at 5.30 a.m. Other prayers were also said during the day at 11.30 a.m., 1.30 p.m. and 7.00 p.m.: these included the Rosary and matins of our Lady of the Immaculate Conception. Classes were started at 8.00 a.m. and ended at 4.00 p.m. with two hours' break at 11.30 a.m.

The pioneer curriculum consisted of Reading, Writing, Arithmetic, the New Testament and Manual Labour (Gardening). One of the Fathers at Cape Coast, Fr. Goeller, visited the seminary at the end of each year and gave the pupils a promotion examination. The Bishop too, occasionally visited Amisano and gave them and their teacher encouragement.

It cost the mission £1. 10s. 0d. (¢3.00) a month to feed both students. There was no residential matron to cater for them; but a convenient boarding arrangement was made on the school grounds: the mission had employed one Gidigago Afeni, an Ewe-man, as the caretaker of the Amisano land and his wife kindly consented to prepare the meals for the students, each of whom fetched the food in turns, from the house of the cateress.[12] She was paid 10/- (¢1.00) per month and the students used their grant of £1. 0s. 0d. (¢2.00) to buy fish, oil, cassava and other ingredients for her to use in preparing the meals.[13]

At the end of three years, they successfully completed their course to

---

12 *Ibid.*, p. 6.
13 *Loc. cit.*

Standard VII level in 1912 and hoped that they would be sent somewhere else to start learning Latin.

In order to clarify how it was possible for them to complete their elementary education up to Standard VII in three years, I shall insert an extract from an account John Andrew gave to Fr. Heesewijk in 1925 concerning their background and their recruitment to Amisano in 1909. He said:

> I was staying at Green Latice Lane (Cape Coast) where I learned carpentry at my grandfather's shop. I went to school and reached Standard I. I had a companion Joe Michael Binly, who had reached Standard IV and was learning also carpentry. We were friends and spoke together about leaving the world. We were then about 20 years. We wanted to be free to serve God away from our relatives and we thought of going to Nigeria and at the same time do some job for a living. we decided to see Bishop Father Ign. Hummel who had been for a long time in Nigeria and would surely be able to help us. Bishop Hummel encouraged us, and told us to pray that God may grant us what we are asking for. After some time we came back and Bishop Hummel said: 'There's a place not far from Elmina, very quiet, where you could lead such a life'. We agreed. Gradually it dawned upon us that what God wanted us to do was to become priests, although the Bishop never spoke of the priesthood. He was preparing us gradually to this vocation and he did not want to scare us away. We went to see the place, as the Bishop had told us to go and see. 'Go now', he said, 'choose a suitable place for a home and build yourselves a house to stay in, study and pray'.[14]

Although their ultimate aim of becoming priests was not realised, the three years' experience they had at the Preparatory Seminary at Amisano had been worthwhile. At the end of the course they were not asked to go anywhere else to study Latin as they had hoped. It seemed some of the mission stations needed agents urgently. Accordingly, they were stationed in 1912. J.M. Binly was sent as teacher-catechist to Abakrampa and Yamfu Ekroful. One week after his employment he resigned from the mission work and joined the Agriculture Department, got married and was transferred to Aburi where he died on Easter Monday, 1914.[15]

John Andrew was appointed teacher-catechist to Agona on 15th May, 1912. He was determined to rise to become a priest eventually. Consequently, on Saturdays he used to go to Elmina for confession, communion and instruction from Fr. V. Berg. At other times he went to Cape Coast to take lessons and tests in Latin. Every hope of his becoming a priest faded away in 1914 when he also got married.

John Fletcher Smith, their teacher, was recalled to Cape Coast in 1912 because no other candidates were available to take advantage of the preparatory course at Amisano. He continued his education and became employed in the Government Civil Service where he served for the rest of his

---

14 *Ibid.*, p. 5.
15 *Ibid.*, p. 7.

life. He remained a faithful and prominent Roman Catholic member in Cape Coast until his death.[16]

The Preparatory Seminary at Amisano had existed for only three years, from 9th August 1909 to 6th May, 1912, during which period the two young men[17] completed their elementary education. Due to lack of vocation, the scheme was abandoned in 1912, and was not revived until 1924.

During the interim, however, the first indigenous Roman Catholic Priest, Fr. A.O. Dogli, was ordained into the Priesthood at Cape Coast on 2nd July, 1922.[18] He had worked as a Roman Catholic teacher in the Vicarate of Keta in the Volta Region and taught at Kpalime, Hohoe, Lome and Keta. His training took place in each of these stations. Fathers who were in the stations where he had taught took part, respectively, in training him for the priesthood. There were five Fathers altogether who taught him: Dr. H. Schoeder, Surry, Cockers, J. Strebler and J. Fisher.

After school hours his teachers gave him lectures on "subjects to the Priesthood"[19] and prescribed books on them for him to read. Periodically, he was given written examinations. It seemed that when he was transferred from one station to another, his tutor forwarded his scheme of work to the next tutor under whom the student was going to study. The training lasted nine years after which Dogli stayed at Cape Coast with Bishop Ignatius Francis Hummel who gave him the final instructions and ordained him priest.

Apparently, this ordination kindled great enthusiasm for the priesthood in the hearts of some of the African young men. In 1924 three young men offered themselves for training as priests. The first of whom was George Ansah. He made his wish known to father Joseph Stauffer in August, 1924. He had already asked in 1909 to become a priest after he had finished his elementary education at Elmina. But he could not enter the seminary then because it appeared he got married while he was working as a pupil teacher. But, by 1924, his wife had died and though he was about 35 years old then he resigned from his position as Secretary to the General Manager of Railways, Nigeria, in order to have training for ordination.[20]

The second and third candidates who offered to have training as priests were Francis Menyah and Joseph Sanny. Francis had been the houseboy of

---

16 *Loc. cit.*
17 *Ibid.*, p. 3. A third student, John Morgan, an Ashanti, was admitted from Cape Coast. He stayed for 18 months and dropped out for personal reasons.
18 Fr. Dogli had retired from active service and had been residing at Baglo-Buem, Volta Region, Ghana, and taking care of Christ the King Roman Catholic Church there. On learning he was the first "native" Roman Catholic priest to be ordained in Ghana, I wrote to him asking if he could tell me how he had been trained as a priest. The information here supplied is based on his reply to my letter and on the information supplied the division of supplied is not proper. Better to separate it thus: supplied. on request by the Rev. Fr. G.v.d. Weijden, Secretary, Diocese of Keta.
19 Dogli to Agbeti, 13th February, 1969. Fr. Dogli did not name the subjects but they might include the subjects mentioned in connection with the training in the Major Seminaries.
20 Heesewijk, "Amisano Notes", p. 8.

Fr. Joseph Strebler and Sanny that of Fr. Stauffer. Francis was in Standard VII then but Sanny who had already completed his elementary education, "was intelligent, pious and filled with an apostolic fire".[21]

Without any hesitating another seminary was started in October 1924[22] with the three candidates as its foundation students. They were housed at first, for a short while, in the Bishop's house at Cape Coast. There, Father de Jong, who was put in charge of the seminary, began to teach them the elements of Latin, English, Mathematics, History and Geography. Later the Seminary was transferred to the Elmina Mission when Fr. de Jong was put in charge of Elmina and its outstations. The students occupied a very small room in the Mission house and there they lodged, studied and ate. After six months there, they were transferred into a more spacious room which had been used as the Standard VII classroom. To make it suitable as a seminary it was partitioned into two parts: one section was used as the classroom and dining hall and the other section as the dormitory.

Between 1925 and 1928 the future prospects of this second attempt at training Africans for the priesthood became very slim because since the admission of the three boys in 1924 no other applicants had offered themselves for the priesthood. But from 1929 hopeful signs began to appear. On 19th January five candidates were admitted. They had been prepared by Fr. Wilh. Meelberg in a small preparatory seminary he had started at Sekondi in 1928. Meelberg had been an enthusiastic promoter of the policy that Africans should be trained for the priesthood. As a result, when he arrived in Sekondi as a Parish Priest in 1928, he collected a handful of schoolboys to stay with him in order that he might sow the seed of the priestly vocation in them and prepare them to enter the seminary at Elmina. "They formed a kind of religious community and followed a strict timetable, in which duty, prayer and work alternated harmoniously". The first fruits of this experiment were the five boys, Insaidoo, James Kwami Takyi, Joseph Braidoo, Francis Yankey and Alex Castel whom he transferred to the Elmina seminary.[24]

At the seminary, they were taught English by Fr. Kelly from 7.45 a.m. to 8.45 a.m. and from 4.30 to 5.30 p.m. Fr. Smets took them in Latin from 3.30 to 4.30 p.m.

In the following year, 1930, the intake was greater than in the previous year. Seven students were enrolled of whom five, Peter Morrison, Daniel Tawiah, G. Tukpui from Keta, Joseph Desbordes and John Ankrah were for the Minor Seminary and the other two, G. Ansah and F. Menyah who

---

21 *Loc. cit.*
22 J.V. Heesewijk, "St. Teresa's Seminary Report, January 29, 1937", Amisano Diary (1930, 1954), (on loose sheets of paper). Hereafter cited as Heesewijk, "Amisano Report, 1937".
23 Heesewijk, "Amisano Notes", p. 11.
24 Heesewijk, "Amisano Report, 1937".

had been admitted since 1924 were enrolled as the pioneer candidates for the Major Seminary.²⁵

This encouraging growth in the number of candidates for the priesthood, from 1929 to 1930, seemed to suggest that the impulse which the ordination of the first African priest in 1922 had created in a few young Africans to offer themselves for the Priesthood in 1924, had begun to gather greater momentum. The position is not, however, as simple as that. There was another undercurrent which also contributed immensely to this growth.

On 28th February, 1926 Pope Pius XI, in the Encyclical "Rerum Ecclesiae" on the promotion of the missions gave clear-cut instructions to the missionary apostolate to form an African clergy rapidly and with enthusiasm.²⁶ Through the declarations, the minds of the missionaries and of the local people had been prepared for vigorous recruitment of Africans into the priesthood. One of the immediate results of this Encyclical in the Gold Coast, as will be seen presently, was that some of the prejudices²⁷ people had had about the priesthood began to fade away gradually and some of the Africans were beginning to realise that it was no longer totally impossible for an African to become a member of the Roman Catholic celibate Priesthood.

Another result was that the missionaries themselves modified the hesitating attitude they had had concerning the ordination of Africans as priests.²⁸ It should be pointed out, however, that 1926 was not the first time that Papal directives concerning the training of African priests had been given. As early as 30th November, 1919, in the Apostolic Letter "Maximum Illud", missionaries were told to "orientate the training of [their] clergy towards the Missions";²⁹ but they were not told how to go about it. This

---

25 Heesewijk, "Amisano Notes", p. 14. See p. 186 below. Peter Morrison was apparently promoted to First Year Philosophy.
26 Pierre Veuillot, *The Catholic Priesthood: Papal Documents from Pius X to XII* (1939-54), Book I, 2nd ed. (Dublin, 1962, Vol. 1, p. 169 and Vol. II, pp. 224-225).
27 Heesewijk, "Amisano Notes", p. 6. In 1925 when Fr. Heesewijk was conversing with John Andrew one of the pioneer native candidates for the priesthood who started the Amisano Seminary, Andrew gave him the following information: "When we left for Amisano people at Cape Coast had an idea that we were sent to Amisano to become priests. But they could not believe that Africans could do so and they thought that we were crazy or dreamers".
28 *Ibid.*, p. 10. The missionaries were children of the Roman Catholic tradition and as such had believed with Rome that "there is *one* clergy in the *one* Christ". Hence prior to the Twentieth Century emphasis was not laid on the development of national clergy because there were many Western Roman Catholic missionaries to do the work in the mission fields. Thus the hesitating attitude the missionaries had had about the ordination of natives as priests seemed to be the result of the general policy referred to above rather than of doubts about the competence of the African. This comment is important because, as we have already seen in this investigation, any time the Protestant missionaries showed a similar attitude, theirs seemed to be the result of derogatory beliefs Europeans had had about African mentality viz: "that the Negro or the African is in every one of his normal susceptibilities an inferior race...." Blyden, *Christianity, Islam and the Negro Race*, pp. 75-76.
29 Veuillot, *op cit.*, Vol. I, p. 134.

vagueness disappeared in the 1926 Encyclical, and the missionaries were given definite directions about how to start the training.

These circumstances led the missionaries to take far-reaching steps. In the first place, they decided to improve the quality of future candidates. In pursuit of this decision a new College was opened at Amisano in 1928. On 23rd November that year, Fr. Maurice Kelly arrived in Cape Coast from Keta and started it, under the title, St. Augustine's Training College and Secondary School.[30] Its primary purpose was to supply trained teachers for work in the primary schools because the efficiency of the elementary schools, where candidates would be recruited to the secondary school and the seminary, depended on the efficiency of the teachers who would teach in them.

In the second place, arrangements were effected speedily to put up permanent buildings to house the Training College, the Secondary School and the Seminary. On 13th October, 1927, Bishop Hauger, the Vicar Apostolic and Fr. Heesewijk selected the eastern side of the Amisano property, a flat piece of ground, and decided that the future College and Seminary should be built there, and Fr. Hauger later drew a plan for the Training College.[31] The whole Amisano land had been surveyed by Mr. Joseph Anu Esuman on 25th September, 1927, and on 9th April, 1928, Mr. J. Hopper, a Roman Catholic P.W.D. man, submitted an estimate for the new buildings to the tune of about £8,000 (¢16,000).[32] The plans having been finally approved by the Departments of Education and Sanitation, the scheme was placed under the supervision of Fr. John Heesewijk, the superior of Elmina and the work was started in February, 1929 by Papa Andrew Ashun who did all the mason's work together with Fr. Danyame. On 23rd March, 1929 the whole project was taken over by a contractor called J. Aggrey on a daily wage of 8/- (¢0.80) plus a bonus of £100 (¢200) when the entire project was completed. The work progressed so vigorously that by the end of the year, the seven new buildings which constituted the Training College were completed and officially opened by His Excellency the Governor, Sir Ransford Slater, on 15th January, 1930.[33]

Father M.B. Kelly was appointed Principal of the Training College and Fr. E. Robbens became the superior of the 12 seminarians. Fr. Kelly assumed his new office at Amisano on 13th February, 1930. On the following day, Friday, 14th February, 1930, the seminarians were transferred from Elmina to Amisano.[34] At the new site, Fr. Kelly remained the spiritual director and confessor of the seminarians, in addition to his work as Principal of the Training College, until 1936, when the Training Department was transferred from Amisano to Cape Coast.[35]

---

30 Heesewijk, "Amisano Notes", p. 11.
31 *Ibid.*, p. 12.
32 *Ibid.*, p. 13.
33 Amisano Seminary, Diary (1930-1954), p. 7.
34 *Ibid.*, p. 10.
35 *Ibid.*, p. 11.

The Seminary began to take on a definite character from the time it was transferred to Amisano. The 12 seminarians were grouped in three classes as follows in 1930:

Form I: Joseph Ankrah
Form II: J. Braidoo, A. Castel, Fr. Insaidoo, James Kwami Takyi, Daniel Tawiah, Fr. Yankey, G. Tukpui and Joseph Desbordes.

First Year
Philosophy: G. Ansah, Francis Menyah and Peter Morrison. This was the beginning of the minor and major sections of the seminary, the details of which are discussed below.

Father L. Vermulst taught Latin from 24th February until 17th April, 1930 when he was transferred to Sekondi and Fr. Walter Boumans replaced him as the Latin teacher. For all the other lessons, meals, games, worship, etc. forms I and II joined the students of the Training College because these forms represented the Secondary section which later became the minor seminary. Their dormitory remained different from that of the teacher students. The First Year Philosophers did not join the teacher students for their subjects because as the foundation pupils of the major seminary, that is to say, having completed their preliminary general education, they had now embarked on an exclusive training for the priesthood. Starting from 16th May, 1930, the seminarians regularly visited the villages around Amisano, during their walk periods, to make contacts and prepare the way for evangelizing the villages later.

There were two terms: the first began on the first Tuesday in February and closed at the end of June, and the second lasted from 1st August till 18th December.[36]

At the beginning of May (1930), the Council of the Vicariate and the staff of Amisano had a meeting which sought to sever completely the common life that had been existing between the seminarians, especially those in the lower forms, and the students of the Training College. At the meeting, "it was decided that for the common good of the seminary and the Training College, the two institutions should be considered as two separate entities, governed by the Superior of the seminary and the Principal of the training College, respectively, each being fully responsible in his own department".[37] Other decisions taken included students' allowances and the appointment of confessors for the seminarians. The monthly allowances were fixed at £1. 10s. 0d. (¢3.00) for a student's maintenance, transport and upkeep of the property, and Fr. Robbens, the Superior of the Missionaries, was asked to administer the allocations and be responsible for the upkeep of the Fathers. As regards the appointment of the confessors

---

36 Heesewijk, "Amisano Notes", p. 15.
37 Amisano Seminary, *op. cit.*, p. 11.

for the seminarians, Fr. Kelly was nominated and the Rev. Fr. Superior of Elmina was made the Extra-ordinary Confessor. The seminarians were free, however, to choose, occasionally, any priests to be their personal confessors, according to Canon Law, 1361.[38]

In pursuit of the policy of separation decided upon at the meeting, arrangements were made to put up new buildings for the exclusive use of the seminary. The foundation stone was laid on 20th May, 1930, by His Lordship Bishop Herman from Keta. The ceremony had a double significance: it took place "exactly 50 years after the first Catholic Priests had arrived at Elmina"[39] in the 19th Century, and with it, in the words of Fr. Strebler, "a new era has set in for the evangelisation of the Gold Coast. The first saw the seed planted and the tree of faith develop. The second will see it expand in its full beauty in the priesthood".[40]

The work on the building progressed rapidly and was completed by the end of September. On 4th October, 1930 the rooms of the seminary were dedicated and consecrated to St. Teresa of the Child Jesus, patron saint of the indigenous clergy of the missions. The new seminary cost £51,600 (¢103,200) through the kindness of the apostolic work of St. Peter the Apostle of Holland and the work of St. Peter Claver Solidarity which paid £1,150 (¢2,300) and £250 (¢500) respectively.[41]

The seminarians were transferred from the old site to the new seminary on 2nd February, 1931, when the school re-opened after the Christmas holidays. That date was the real beginning of St. Teresa's Seminary, Amisano. The new house was big and spacious enough to accommodate 50 students. It consisted of two storeys. The classrooms and the dining hall were on the first floor. But, at the beginning of the term, no more than the 12 students, who had been in residence at the end of 1930, reported for admission.

As the new seminary buildings were not all completed before the students moved to the new site, and as the seminary did not have its own complete staff, the separation which the authorities had anticipated could not be absolutely realised at this stage. The seminarians slept and studied in the new seminary; but they continued to eat, play, pray and follow most of the lessons with the students of the Training College.

From January 1932, the seminary had its own staff and the students, now 14 in number, no longer joined the Training College for any lessons.

The seminary was then distinctly run in its two sections: the minor which was equivalent to a secondary school course and the major which was exclusively a theological course leading to ordination. In 1932, the minor

---

38 John A. Abbo and Jerome D. Hannan, *A Concise Presentation of the Current Disciplinary Norms of the Church*, 2nd rev. ed. (London, 1960), Vol. II (Canons 870-2414), p. 593.
39 Heesewijk, "Amisano Notes", p. 15.
40 *Loc. cit.*
41 Amisano Seminary, *op. cit.*, p. 12.

seminary had two classes: Forms II and III. There were four students in Form II: Robert Yankah, Joseph Desbordes, Joseph Ankrah and Evaristus Williams (Liberian). Fr. Kelly taught them English and Fr. Derickx taught Latin. In Form III were Jos. Essuah, Allexis Castel, Francis Insaidoo, Bernard S. Mensah, Jos. Kwami, Daniel Tawiah and Francis Yankey.[42] They were taught by four tutors: Fr. P. Derickx taught them Latin and History, Ernest Ekuban of the Training College, English and Vernacular (Fanti), Jos. Essuah, Arithmetic, Algebra and Geometry and Essilfie taught Geography.

There was only one class in the major seminary: the First Year Theology. The students in this class were George Ansah, Francis Menyah and Peter Morrison. Morrison was, however, asked to leave the institution at the end of the year because the sincerity of his vocation became doubtful.[43] Father Strebler taught them Dogma, Moral Theology, Canon Law and Scripture while Fr. Peter Derickx taught English and History.

At the beginning of the year, that was at the end of January 1932, George Ansah and Francis Menyah received the clerical habit from the hands of Fr. J. Strebler who preached on a text from Genesis 35: 2-3.[44]

During the year Jos. Desbordes and Daniel Tawiah left for personal reasons but Tawiah returned once more in July 1933.

In 1933 there were 12 students at the beginning of the session. In the major seminary, George Ansah and Francis Menyah were in Second Year Theology. In the minor seminary, there were six in Form V, Jos. H. Essuah, Alexis Castel, Francis Insaidoo, Bern. Mensah, James Kwami, Francis Yankey; in Form IV, Joseph Ankrah, Robert Yankah, and Evaristus Williams, and in Form I, Jos. Daniels who had arrived in January but owing to ill-health had to give up the training later in the year. On 11th July seven new students were enrolled. They had only finished Standard V, and when they came in Mr. Amonoo taught them Standard VI subjects as well as the rudiments of Latin. They were Francis and John Arthur (Sekondi), Ignatius Taylor (Half Assine), Francis Couston and Dominic Nyema (Axim), Bartholomew Swanzy (Eikwe) and Francis Aisnah-aleo (Nzimaland).

By the end of the year there were 18 minor seminarians in all and for each of them an allocation of £10. 0s. 0d. (¢20.00) had been asked, from the Work of St. Peter the Apostle, for their maintenance. The students used to send group photographs and letters to their benefactors yearly in appreciation of their kindness, and the Superior also sent them annual reports on the seminary.

---

42 Heesewijk, "Amisano Notes", p. 17. It is not clear how the forms were organized. These same students had been recorded as being in Form II in 1930, (*Ibid.*, p. 14) and now in 1932 (January) they were recorded as being in Form III. Possibly Fr. Heesewijk meant Form IV because in 1933 the very students were recorded as being in Form V. *Ibid.*, p. 19.
43 *Ibid.*, p. 17.
44 For a fuller account of the ceremony see the *Catholic Voice*, 1932, p. 41.

From July 1933, the staffing conditions of the seminary improved considerably: there were six members of staff: Fr. Strebler (the Superior), Fr. John Heesewijk (once a week from Elmina), Fr. Andrew van den Bronk, Ernest Ekuban, Essilfie and Fr. James Geurts. As a result, from that time, all classes, except the classes for Science, were separated from the Training College classes, and were given in the seminary; but the seminary staff continued to teach in both institutions. This practice put a great strain on them and the seminarians did not get the desired attention. As this arrangement did not work for efficiency, on 15th January, 1934, the seminary obtained its complete independence.[45] The Training College was allotted all the land to the south of the institution and the seminary all the land to the north; but the playing fields continued to be used by both institutions. The seminary now had three priests and one lay-teacher, exclusively set apart for the training of the seminarians. Religious services were no longer held in the College chapel, but in one of the rooms in the seminary temporarily improvised for worship. The Fathers and students had their own kitchens and stores and began to take their meals in the seminary dining hall.

The attainment of the independence of the seminary had far-reaching effects on its progress between 1934 and 1941. During that period, the seminary of the Lower Volta, at Keta, was closed in 1936 and the seminarians were transferred to Amisano, purely for economic reasons.[46] It was deemed expedient to maintain one seminary in the Diocese so that capital costs for running two seminaries might be reduced. In that year, the seminary at Amisano counted 41 minor and 10 major seminarians.[47]

At this stage it is expedient to treat the minor and major seminaries separately because during the period 1934 to 1941 it became necessary to separate their organization. The minor seminary will be discussed first and then the major.

The Minor Seminary underwent some important developments described below. The recruitment age of the students was definitely fixed: candidates were now to be recruited only from Standard IV and they should not be older than 15 years of age, because the authorities felt that the best moral and intellectual results would be obtained with students who were admitted young and of good catholic families.[48] They followed a six-year course

---

45 Heesewijk, "Amisano Notes", p. 22.
46 Weijden to Agbeti, "Ref. Your letter of January, 1969". Fr. Weijden, Secretary, Diocese of Keta, confirmed that Bishop A. Herman had opened a minor seminary at Dzelukofe near Keta in the 1930s. "Due to lack of qualified staff and to the limited number of students it was considered better and also more economical to close down and send the students to Amisano Seminary which became an interdiocesan seminary catering for all the dioceses of [the Gold Coast]".
47 Mathew P. Wouters, "Particulars on St. Teresa's Seminary, Amisano (Gold Coast), 1937" (mimeographed and kept in Amisano Diary, 1930-54).
48 See page 149 below for comments made on taking boys to the seminary when they are too young.

similar to that of St. Augustine's Secondary School at Cape Coast. The prime subjects taught were: English, Latin, Mathematics, Science, History, Geography, Vernacular and French. English was used in teaching both the Latin and the French lessons. The aim of the course was to give the prospective candidates for the priesthood a general education and to prepare them to pass the Cambridge School Certificate Examination after Form V or the London Matriculation Examination after Form VI.

The textbooks used in the minor seminary were the same as those used in the other institutions of secondary education in the country.

They included:

English: Nestfied's Aids to the Study of English Matriculation, English Course, Tipping's English Grammar and Herman's English Pronunciation.
Latin: Longmann's Latin Course.
Mathematics: Hall and Stephens.
History: Brendan, Ancient History; Gense, English History.
Religious
Knowledge: Hart, Bible History.[49]

However, in Form VI, Logic was introduced in preparation for Philosophy in the major seminary.

The number of new students fluctuated considerably during the period. The largest number of admissions was in 1935. After that, only a little trickle of students came in year after year as illustrated by the following figures:[50]

Year	Admissions	Year	Admissions
1934	10	1938	9
1935	20	1939	12
1936	13	1940	5
1937	10	1941	8

The number of new students admitted during the period 1934-1941 plus those admitted from 1924 to 1933 totalled 111; those admitted in 1924 being 3; 1929: 5; 1930: 7 and 1933: 9. Of the total number, 49 left the minor seminary by the end of 1941 on account of reasons to be given later in this chapter. Most of those who had left without reaching the priesthood sought employment as teachers or clerks.

Owing to the decreasing number of students in the minor seminary and the high expense of maintaining it, the following question was raised on

---

49 Wouters, *op. cit.*
50 *Ibid.*, Cf. Heesewijk's figure for 1937 conflicts with Wouters'. See Heesewijk, "Amisano Notes", p. 41. Heesewijk recorded that the new admissions for 1937 and 1938 were nine respectively: Wouters' figure 10, for 1937, seems to be the more accurate one: Heesewijk, *Ibid.*, p. 35 reporting on the state of the seminary in 1937 wrote that "there were now 55 studets: 11 in Philosophy, 10 in Form IV, 11 in Form III, 13 in Form II and 10 in Form I. Ten of these were new comers".

14th December, 1940: "Shall the minor seminary owing to the small number of its students and in order to save expenses and staff—shall the seminary be now removed and taken to St. Augustine's secondary school?"[51] The idea did not have popular support therefore no transfer was made.

By the end of 1941 there were 45 students and 11 members of staff in the seminary. But it was not expedient to maintain 11 tutors for only 45 students, (30 minor and 15 major seminarians) when debt was mounting,[52] and in view of the fact that World War II had depleted the mission staff. Therefore, arrangements were finalised during the second half of the year (1941) for the transfer of the minor seminary, and in January 1942 when schools re-opened, the 30 minor seminarians were transferred to St. Augustine's Secondary School, Cape Coast. They took their beds, desks, books and all that they had possessed at Amisano along. The transfer did not interrupt the study programmes of either institution. The seminarians had been following the same lessons as the secondary school students because the programmes of both institutions were very much the same. Thus they were easily absorbed into the relevant secondary forms at Cape Coast. For the other activities the seminarians had their separate commiunity life under the spiritual guidance of Fr. P. Cruts who accompanied them from Amisano. Five of the members of staff at Amisano were then released for parochial work, and the remaining six were left with the major seminary at Amisano.

The change did not bring about any substantial reshuffling of the staff in the secondary school. The only exception was that Fr. Beckers was appointed the rector of the seminarians. The seminarians settled down without difficulty and gained substantially. For example, of the 30 seminarians who had joined the secondary students in 1942, John K. Amissah, now (in the 1980's) the Roman Catholic Archbishop of Cape Coast, obtained the Senior Cambridge School Certificate and entered the major seminary in January, 1943; John Patrick Akoi also obtained the Senior Cambridge School Certificate and entered the major seminary in 1946. Others in the group who entered the major seminary were: Joseph Adams in January, 1943, and John Buckman in 1946.

The next period, 1942-1955, was one of mixed experiences in the history of the minor seminary. 1942 to 1945 was a blank period, because the minor seminary was integrated into St. Augustine's Secondary School, and no records were left in the Amisano Diary about its fortunes.[53]

1946 to 1955 was a period of growth, decline, and consolidation. In January, 1946, the 19 new recruits for the minor seminary did not go to St.

---

51 Heesewijk, "Amisano Notes", p. 41.
52 See page 138 below.
53 The students and tutors who were at St. Augustines Secondary School then should now be approached to supply materials to fill in the gap between 1942 and 1946.

Augustine's Secondary School at Cape Coast; with them, the minor seminary was re-opened at Amisano because the financial situation had apparently improved. Generally, the number of admissions increased, but the decline in some of the years was very heavy as shown by the figures below:[54]

Year	New Admissions	Year	New Admissions
1946	19	1951	18
1947	12	1952	33
1948	20	1953	34
1949	8	1954	17[55]
1950	14	1955	34

The heaviest decline came in 1949. This was significant because 1949 was the year which immediately followed the 1948 Disturbances in the Gold Coast. Briefly, the disturbances came about in this way: a genuine boycott campaign, against European and Asiatic-owned stores in the country, had been organized in January, 1948, by one of the chiefs in Accra called Nii Kwabena Bonne III, to resist and force down the high cost of imported goods. But the political ferment at the time quickly gave the genuine boycott a political slant and resulted in looting, rioting, incendiarism, civil disobedience and in accelerated agitation for self-government.[56] The rector of the seminary, Fr. O'Shea, stated that the unstable political condition in 1948 was one of the reasons why vocations decreased so severely in 1949; but he did not explain how.[57] However, it seemed that the extreme nationalism, which had created the political situation, had also revived some of the cherished national ideals which had been pushed to the background, during the British rule, but had not been entirely destroyed. For example, in the family system, a son was expected to earn money and contribute to the support of his parents and other relatives; education of a son was considered an investment, which would yield dividend after the training. Moreover, as has been shown in Chapter I above, a son was expected to perpetuate the family by getting married and raising children for the family. The idea of the priesthood did not promote these family ideals, so some of the parents refused to allow their sons to go to the seminary. Indeed, "it was not uncommon that a pagan parent would protest with all

---

54 Heesewijk, "Amisano Notes", p. 47-58.
55 *Ibid.*, p. 57: 60 boys had applied for admission but only 30 were selected and of these only 17 could enter the seminary because the parents of those who failed to report were either unable to afford the necessary outfit for their sons or were opposed to the idea of the priesthood for their children.
56 Ward, *A History of Ghana*, pp. 329-349, and F.M. Bourret, *The Gold Coast—A Survey of the Gold Coast and British Togoland, 1919-1951*.2nd ed. (London, 1952), pp. 197-220. These pages give detailed account of the causes, progress and results of the disturbances.
57 Heesewijk, "Amisano Notes", p. 51.

his power against the decision of his son to become a priest. The latter would resist for some time, and then give way finally".⁵⁸

From 1950 to 1955, however, the increase in the number of admissions was dramatic when compared with 1949. Two factors seemed to influence this growth. First, as a result of the great lack of vocation at the beginning of 1949, the seminary authorities had made an intensive campaign for recruitment. For example, through sermons and articles published in catholic papers and leaflets,⁵⁹ emphasis was laid on the importance and need for African priests. Parents were specially appealed to, to encourage their sons to offer for the priesthood. In the light of the political development towards independence and the greater responsibilities that would soon devolve on the indigenous priests, parents had been made to appreciate how imperative it was for the Church also to "have numerous, holy and capable African priests to assume responsibilities" ⁶⁰ in the stations, schools and colleges.

The second factor concerned the National Eucharistic Congress which took place in Kumasi from 19th to 26th February, 1951.⁶¹ Its purpose was to bring all the Roman Catholics in the country to meet in Kumasi and "pay homage to God in the Holy Eucharist".⁶² The inspiration derived from the congress awakened in the participants a new awareness of the need and value of increasing the number of African priests. The impact which the congress had on the recruitment of candidates for the priesthood was summed up by Fr. O'Shea in his report to Rome in these words:

> This made a deep and lasting impression on all people and not least upon our seminarians. The sight of so many priests and bishops, the inspiring sermons and the deep devotion everywhere manifested to Our Blessed Lord in the Holy Eucharist, brought home to them as never before the high dignity of the priesthood and what a happiness and privilege it is to stand before the alter of God.⁶³

The roll continued to increase year by year until the seminary became crammed⁶⁴ and over-crowding resulted, especially in the major seminary. But in order to maintain a high standard of training it was essential that the students should be satisfactorily housed because the tutors believed that unsatisfactory accommodation "did not make for good results and serious work and sustained effort".⁶⁵ Consequently, a scheme was drawn up to establish a new and separate seminary where the major seminarians should

---

58 *Ibid.*, p. 18.
59 *Ibid.*, p. 52.
60 *Loc. cit.*
61 Pfann, *A Short History*, pp. 102-103.
62 *Ibid* p. 102.
63 Heesewijk, "Amisano Notes", pp. 53-54.
64 *Ibid.*, p. 58. In 1955 there were 115 students: 27 in the major and 88 in the minor seminaries.
65 *Ibid.*, p. 59.

be trained again separately from the minor seminarians. Pedu, near Cape Coast, was chosen as the site and without much delay the work on the buildings was started in 1955. On October 20th the same year, the Commemorative Plaque was unveiled and blessed. [66] The work was completed early the following year, and on 11th March, 1956, the major seminarians were transferred from Amisano to the new Regional Seminary at Pedu, christened, *St. Peter's Regional Seminary*.[67]

During the period, 1956 to 1965, the minor seminary remained at Amisano and developed into a fully fledged secondary school, running six classes Forms I to VI. The Form I class, which had been abolished in 1949 because the Fathers had felt that four years were sufficient for the students to pass the Senior Cambridge Examination,[68] had been restored in 1955 for the following reason: the Accelerated Development Plan of Education had been introduced in 1952 by the Gold Coast Government[69] and as a result the standard of knowledge in the primary and middle schools began to fall. This was due to the fact that many untrained teachers had been employed to teach in the elementary schools because trained teachers were not sufficient to cope with the increased number of schools opened by the Government in pursuit of its new Accelerated Plan.[70] Thus pupils entering the secondary schools from Middle Forms II and III, (the former Standards V and VI) were not all competent enough to continue their education from Form II in the secondary schools. The weaker ones had to start from Form I.

Although during this period the minor seminary developed like any other secular secondary school in the country and took the same examination, the West African School Certificate or the General Certificate of Education, as did the other secondary schools, the tutors did not alter its function as the place where prospective candidates for the priesthood were given efficient general education combined with Christian formation of character. In order to maintain the double function of the minor seminary the tutors followed a well-planned scheme of work which made provision for scripture teaching in all the forms. The other subjects taught were: Mathematics, Additional Mathematics, Science, English, French, Geography, History, Ancient History, British History and Vernacular. In spite of the care the staff had taken to awaken the desire for the priesthood in the students most of the graduates of the seminary did not offer to go to the major seminary. In any case, St. Teresa's Minor Seminary, Amisano, remained the constant feeder of the major seminary at Pedu.

The historical development of the major seminary until 10th March,

---

66 Pedu Seminary, Log Book (1955 ff.), 20th October, 1955.
67 *Ibid.*, 11th March, 1956.
68 Heesewijk, "Amisano Notes", p. 51.
69 The Ministry of Education Ghana, *A Brief Sketch of the History of Education*, p. 12.
70 McWilliam, *The Development of Education in Ghana*, pp. 83-96.

1956, was practically the same as that of the minor seminary surveyed in the preceding paragraphs and I need not rehearse it here. The only exception was that when the minor seminary was transferred to St. Augustine's Secondary School at Cape Coast in 1942, the major seminary remained at Amisano. It was only between 10th June, 1942 and 3rd November, 1943, that it was also transferred to St. Augustine's Secondary School, when the Royal Air Force temporarily occupied the seminary buildings at Amisano during World War II. The major seminary, however, returned to Amisano on 4th November, 1943, after the Air Force had evacuated the premises.

The aspect of the history of the major seminary which should be treated separately is the organization of the training itself. For the sake of convenience this section is divided into three periods: 1930-1938, 1939-1955 and 1956-1965.

During the first period, 1930-1938, 15 students had been admitted into the major seminary from the minor seminary: three in 1930; eleven in 1936 and one in 1938. Four of the total number could not persevere to the priesthood: one each dropped out in 1932 and 1938 respectively and two in 1937.[71] Those who remained had seven years training which was divided into two years' course of Philosophy, four years Theology and one year Probation.

The first two years, spent in the Philosophy Class, were devoted to the study of the *Theologia Foundamentalis Moralis et Dogmatica* and *Spirituality.*[72] The textbooks used were: Mercier, *Manual of Modern Scholastic*

---

71 Wouters, "Particulars on St. Teresa's Seminary Amisano .... 1937", *op. cit.*
72 The content of the *SPIRITUALITY* is specified in the document "De Relatione Singulis Quinquenniis S.C. Propaganda Fide Exhibend. Caput V. De Seminaries 44 (b) (1953)" which the Rector of St. Victor's Seminary, Fr. Pageault, showed me when I was in that Seminary in the second week of January, 1969. The content of the Subject was as follows: The seminarians were to be taught the Principles of St. Ignatius Loyola in the following manner:

    Daily: 45 minutes of mental prayer.
    15 minutes of examination of conscience.
    15 minutes of visit to the Blessed Sacrament or to the Benediction of the Blessed Sacrament.
    30 minutes of Spiritual reading or those who wished could assist at Mass and Holy Communion. This was followed by 15 minutes of Thanksgiving.
    5-decades Rosary should be recited every day.
    Weekly: Confessions: the students should go on any day during the week to any Father of their choice.
    Monthly: Retreat, i.e. spiritual preparation for a few hours (similar to, but shorter than, the retreat scheme shown on page 147).
    Yearly: There should be six days' retreat every year.
    General: On Sundays or Great Feast days—Solemn High Mass and Vespers should be practised in the afternoon in order to teach the students how to perform the various sacred ceremonies.
    They should also be taught the Bishop's Statutes for the Clergy, the methods of the Apostolate and how to take care of their exterior, manners and clothes in a way convenient to their own class of people.

Philosophy; Stebbing, *History of Philosophy*; and Tanquerey, *The Spiritual Life* (for Spirituality). At the end of the Philosophy course the students went on probation for a year during which they stayed with parish priests and gained some experience in the practical aspects of the priest's work. They helped the parish priest in all types of work ranging from preaching and teaching to manual work.[73]

The students returned into residence at the end of the year and commenced the Theology course at the beginning of their fourth year. The textbooks used for this course were: Canon Law: *Notes of the Professor*; Church History: Stebbing, *the Story of the Church*; Liturgy: Hausman, *Breviary*; Muller, *Handbook of Ceremonies*; Morals and Theology: Tanquerey, *Moral and Dogmatic Theology* and scripture; *Notes of the Professor*, based on *Codex Juris Canonici* (Code of Canon Law).

The training went on smoothly until the beginning of 1938 when the seminary was hit by staff shortage. In 1937 there had been six members of the seminaries (minor and major). They were Frs. John v. d. Kooy, John Bullen, Adrian de Kok, Corn. Bodewes, John van Heesewijk and Henry Schoen. At the beginning of 1938 most of these tutors were invalided home and during the first five months the institution was left in the hands of only two Fathers, Math. Wouters, the Superior, and L. Moonen and several of the seminarians on Probation had to teach in the minor seminary until after May when reinforcement was sent. In October of the same year five new priests arrived from Holland solely to teach in the seminary. They were the Rev. Frs. Antony van Hout, Andrew Suykerbuyk, Peter Cruts, Corn. Elbers and Corn. Hulsen who arrived on 18th January, 1939.[74] With the increase of tutors the major seminary entered the subsequent period hopefully.

From 1939 to 1955 many changes took place in the structure of the major seminary at Amisano. In the first instance, four of the 11 members of staff at the beginning of 1939 taught mainly in the major seminary. The subjects they taught were: A. van Hout, Dogma and Church History; H.v.d. Ven, Moral Theology, Canon Law and Liturgy; John Kooy, Philosophy; H. Schoen, Spiritual Director, Spirituality and Religious Knowledge. The teaching staff continued to improve, both in numbers and quality until at the beginning of 1954, "a complete staff of highly qualified priests, experienced and capable, each of them expert in his own subject",[75] were engaged in the training of the prospective priests. They were six in number, five of whom were university graduates, specially prepared for their sub-

---

73 This information was gathered through conversation with some of the final year students at Pedu and Tamale during my visits to these places in October, 1968 and January, 1969, respectively.
74 Heesewijk, "Amisano Notes", p. 39.
75 *Ibid.*, p. 53.

jects and the sixth, Fr. John Heesewijk, was experienced in his field though he was not a university graduate.

As the staffing position improved the curriculum was expanded by the addition of two new subjects, Missiology and Sociology.Thus, by the end of 1954, Fr. G. Hulsen was teaching Dogma, Nico Pronk, Moral Theology, Sociology and Missiology, Hans Steemers, Scripture, lectures in Theology and Philosophy, John v. Heesewijk, Spirituality, John K. Amissah, Canon Law, Latin, Sports and Music and Fr. G. Lieben, Philosophy and Eloquence.

The other changes which took place during this period included, first, the spending of the terminal holidays. In the early days of the seminary the major seminarians spent their holidays, mainly, in the seminary. Occasionally, some were sent to the outstations to assist parish priests who needed help. Later on, they spent only Christmas holidays at home with their relatives. In 1947, however, the students went home three times a year, during each of the terminal holidays. This new arrangement became necessary because the tutors had discovered that, under the previous system, the students had not been sufficiently refreshed during the holidays because they did not change their environment.

The second change concerned overseas training. On 23rd February, 1947, the Archbishop, David Mathew, visited Amisano and, among other things, recommended that some of the students in Philosophy might be sent to the University of Rome to continue their training. Therefore, at the end of the year, Patrick Akoi was sent to Rome to study Theology.[76] In the following year, in June, two others, J.A. Essuah and K. Buah, were also permitted to take Arts degree courses in the National University of Ireland. Since then other students and priests had been getting permission to study in overseas universities.

These changes which had begun to take place in the structure of the major seminary came to a head during the period 1956 to 1965. It has already been pointed out above that the major seminary was transferred to its new home at Pedu, near Cape Coast, on 11th March, 1956. There, the Seminary, now called St. Peter's Regional Seminary, completed its re-organization.

The staffing position was greatly improved during the period and by the end of 1965, there were six highly qualified members of staff namely, C. Hulsen, D.D., (Rector), Piet Schols, S.M.A., D.Sc., Lic. Phil., Robert Barret, S.M.A., Lic. in Re Biblica, H.V. Hoof, S.M.A., Lic. C.L., Lic., Phil., N. Pronk, S.M.A., Lic. Miss. and Joseph Ennoo, D.C.L., part-time lecturer.

As the members of staff were highly qualified the standard of admission was raised accordingly and only Sixth Formers became eligible for admission. The curriculum was also expanded and included the following sub-

---

76 *Ibid.*, p. 49.

jects: Propaedeutics, Sociology, Economics, Social Economics, Scripture, Comparative Religion, Philosophy, Ascetic Theology, Canon Law, Liturgy, African Studies, Dogma, History, and Morals. The duration of the Course remained seven years for those who had not passed their 'A' Level Examination in the Sixth Form; but those who had their 'A' Level before entering spent only six years.

CHAPTER TEN

ROMAN CATHOLIC MISSION TRAINING: WHITE FATHERS 1946-1965

Meanwhile, another major seminary, St. Victor's Seminary, Tamale, had been making progress in Northern Ghana. It had been started by the White Fathers of Navrongo in January, 1946. Prior to 1946 a minor seminary had been opened there in 1933 by Fr. Gagnon, assisted by Fr. P. Haskew.[1] Selection was made from among Standard VII boys for the minor seminary where the students were trained for three years and then sent to the major seminary at Amisano. Between 1933 and 1945, six students had been sent from the Navrongo minor seminary to the major seminary at Amisano. From the beginning of the 1940s the cost of training students at Amisano had been growing very high.[2] Thus in 1945 the White Fathers decided that they would open a major seminary in the Northern Vicariate to save at least the cost of the long journey to the coast. Arrangements were made without delay and at the end of 1945 the six Northern students training for the Priesthood at Amisano were withdrawn. With them the new major seminary was opened at Navrongo in January, 1946. At first the students were housed temporarily, for two months, in the Navrongo Senior School. After that a more convenient accommodation with a peaceful and quiet environment was secured in the resident Father's house at Wiagha, about 36 miles west of Navrongo, and the seminary was transferred there to occupy the ground floor of the manse.

One of the six students brought from Amisano dropped out but the remaining five persevered to the priesthood. They were Alexis Abatey, Richard Pwamang, Rudolf Akanlu, Peter Dary and Lawrence Kyemalo.[3]

Fr. A. Richard was the first Rector and he was assisted by Frs. Lalemand, Lamaire, Le Bel and Ouellet. The students had two years of Philosophy during which they studied Church History, Sociology, Asceticism, Singing, Liturgy and History of Philosophy. The Philosophy course was followed by five years of Theology during which the following subjects were taught: Holy Scripture, Pastoralia, Public Reading and Talking, Canon Law, Liturgy, Asceticism and Singing. The Theology course was fol-

---

1 P.K. Asamoah, "Notes from Mr. P.K. Asamoah of the History of St. Victor's Seminary Tamale", (MS: preserved in St. Victor's Seminary, Diary.) (1954 ff).
2 Heesewijk, "Amisano Notes", p. 47.
3 G.A. Ouellet, was the Vicar General in Tamale in January 1969. He had been on the Staff of the Seminary at Wiagha. He supplied these names when I went to him on 17th January 1969, for information about the beginnings of the major seminary at Wiagha.

lowed by a year of Probation when the final year students stayed in parishes to gain practical experience. Thus, in all, the training at St. Victor's Seminary lasted nine years instead of the seven years spent in the south.

The explanation of the difference in years between the two institutions is this: at Amisano, the minor seminary students spent at least five years in the secondary school before they were recruited into the major seminary; but at St. Victor's Seminary, the minor seminarians had been spending only three years in the minor seminary before entering the major seminary. In effect, the students from both seminaries spent 12 years in their training for the priesthood.

The progress St. Victor's Seminary had made at Wiagha, between 1947 and 1952 was not encouraging in respect of the admissions. The number of students who were enrolled fluctuated between three and one as illustrated below:[4]

Year	Admissions
1946	6
1947	3
1948	3
1949	1
1950	2
1951	1
1952	2

It seemed that the declining roll during these seven years made the authorities reconsider the suitability of Wiagha as a seminary town. Originally, Wiagha was chosen because among other considerations, its remoteness promised peace and quiet.[5] Now it became obvious that the desired remoteness was hindering the progress of the seminary. As Wiagha was far in the "bush", away from the main towns, Navrongo and Tamale, it was difficult for the authorities to provide the necessary modern facilities for a thrifty running of the institution. For instance, in those days there were no good lorry roads to speed up transportation of food from Tamale to the bush village seminary; there were no good stores at Wiagha from which other things could be conveniently purchased without making long journeys on bad motor roads. Consequently, in 1953, the authorities transferred the seminary from Wiagha to Tamale, the capital town of the Northern and Upper Regions.

At first, St. Victor's Seminary, Tamale, consisted of one main building and five smaller ones. One of the smaller ones contained a dispensary, a library, a kitchen for the Fathers and store rooms. Another smaller building contained the student's kitchen and a room for laundry; and the rest

---

4 St. Victor's Seminary Tamale, Annual Report (1955).
5 See page 142.

were, the cook's and steward's house, a bath house and a toilet. The main building, blessed by the the Lord Bishop Champagne in October 1953, consisted of two dormitories occupied by 12 students in that year, one dining hall for the Fathers and the students, one recreation hall, four classrooms, two study halls and four Fathers' bedrooms.

Early the following year, on 19th February, 1954, at about 5.00 p.m., this main building was destroyed by fire,[6] and most of the valuable records, including the original Diary or Log Book and the Council Minutes Books, were destroyed.

As the Bishop was very much concerned that the work in the seminary might continue in spite of the misfortune, he made arrangements immediately to rebuild the house. Just a week after the fire, Brother Fr. Lorenzo, the diocesan builder, started the rebuilding and within six days he had re-roofed the main building, 170 feet long.[7]

The accident did not cause any substantial disorganization of the study programme. Eight days after the fire, temporary alterations were made in the carpenter's workshop, in the store rooms and in the kitchen to serve as the Fathers' rooms and classrooms. The verandah became the refectory and the room for spiritual reading. Classes were resumed as soon as these alterations had been completed.

In 1954, three new philosophers were admitted. One of the students who had been admitted from Accra had to return home for health reasons, thus leaving 14 students instead of 15 in residence. Three of them were in first year philosophy, one in the second year, two in first year Theology, two in the third year, one in the fourth year and three in the fifth year Theology. There were no students in the second and sixth years Theology; but the remaining two students were under Probation.

No new candidates were admitted between 1955 and 1957. This had nothing to do with the fire. It had been decided in 1954 by the seminary authorities that the entry standard to the major seminary should be raised. The three years minor seminary training had been found to be inadequate. Accordingly, it was agreed upon that from 1955, all minor seminarians would have to complete the regular secondary education course before seeking admission to the major seminary.[8] The first set of students to benefit by the new policy did not complete their secondary education until the end of 1957.

From 1958 to 1965, the character of St. Victor's Seminary became distinctly formed, traditions fully established and the training programme consolidated. In 1959 also no new candidates were admitted because the minor seminary course was extended again by a further two years—Lower and Upper Sixth Forms to be in keeping with the Government's expan-

---

6 St. Victor's Seminary, Annual Report (1953-54).
7 St. Victor's Seminary, Annual Report (1954-1955).
8 Asamoah, "Notes", *op. cit.*

sion of sixth-form work.⁹ After the 1959/60 academic year onwards, however, yearly intake of new candidates became a normal feature of the seminary tradition. In October 1962, ten new students were admitted. This was the highest number of admissions in the history of the seminary during the whole period of this study.¹⁰

This large increase in the number of the admissions was possible because a new and more spacious building had been put up in the previous year. It was 215 ft. by 40 ft. There were four classrooms on the ground floor for the use of the Theologians, a reception room for all, two classrooms and a dormitory for the Philosophers. The first floor contained the Chapel, the sacristy and eight rooms for the members of staff. The Chapel and the Fathers' rooms were built in such a way as would permit their alteration into ten rooms when the need arose. In addition to the building, two water tanks, holding 42,000 and 10,000 gallons of water respectively, had also been built. The original main building had also been transformed into a dining hall, a recreation hall, a library, two classrooms and an oratory.

The promise of increased vocation in 1962 did not last long. In 1963/64 and 1964/65 there was a great lack of vocation to the priesthood. In the former year only one student was admitted and in the latter only four. The reason for the decrease seemed to be due to the attractions of university education. Sixth Form education had become the stepping stone to admission into the universities of the country. After having passed the Sixth Form, the minor seminarians seemed to be attracted more to a three years' university degree course rather than a seven years' seminary training.¹¹ Thus at the end of this period of investigation there were only 21 students in St. Victor's Seminary, preparing to become priests, distributed in the classes as follows: Fourth Year Theology—6, Second Year—4, First Year—3 and in the Philosophy class, Second and Third Years—4 each excluding 3 in the First Year Preliminary.¹² Fifteen of them came from the Diocese of Wa and six from Navrongo.

There were six members of staff, all expatriates, teaching an expanded curriculum as follows:

R. Tremblay	Sacramental Theology and Canon Law;
R. LaRoche	Theology, Liturgy, and Spiritual Reading for Philosophy;
M. Pageault	Philosophy and Sociology;

---

9 McWilliam, *The Development of Education in Ghana*, p. 101.
10 St. Victor's Seminary, Annual Reports (1962-63 to 1964-65).
11 St. Victor's Seminary, Annual Report (1963-64).
12 St. Victor's Seminary, The Bishop's Report (15th July, 1965. The Preliminary year was arranged to improve the standard of Form V entrants. The subjects taught were: scripture readings (Introduction to Spiritual Life), Introduction to Philosophy, Holy Scripture, Liturgy and Latin. As this class was not regarded as the first year of the major seminary the three students following the course were not included in the total role of 21.

J.M. Beaulieu	Latin and he was also the Bursar;
M. Targett	Holy Scripture and Church History, and
E. Beyer	Ascetic Theology, Pastoral Theology, Introduction to Philosophy, Spiritual reading for all the Theologians.

St. Victor's Seminary also suffered from the problem of drop-outs. From 1933 to 1946 six students had entered the seminary; but only five persevered to the priesthood. In 1947, all the three new candidates admitted persevered to the end. From 1948 to 1954, out of the 13 new candidates who had been recruited, only nine completed the course. During the next decade, 1955 to 1965, 30 more students had been admitted, some of whom were still in training at the end of the period of this research, and so it would be difficult to say exactly how many would drop out on the way. In any case, from the figures quoted above it might be concluded that from 1946 to 1965, 52 students had been enrolled in the major seminary at Tamale, of whom only 24 had been ordained priests by the end of 1965.[13]

The reasons why the students had been dropping out at St. Victor's Seminary were practically the same as those for Amisano and Pedu and they are dealt with together below on pages 148 ff. It should be observed, however, that the overall small number of admissions between 1948 and 1954, at Tamale, was due mainly to the re-organization of the minor seminary on a secondary school basis and not necessarily to the lack of vocation. After 1954 the re-organization created a gap of four years in the recruitment and just when the first group was ready to be admitted to the major seminary, two more years were added to the secondary school course, as already mentioned above.

The other aspects of the training at Tamale were similar to the practice at Amisano or Pedu, therefore what now follows for St. Victor's Seminary is also true for the Seminary at Pedu.

In addition to the year of probation mentioned above, the students had practical training throughout the whole course of their training. They visited the neighbouring villages, helping the inhabitants to be better people. The Fathers normally ran night schools and modest dispensaries for the neighbouring villagers. The students assisted the Fathers by either teaching the catechism to the villagers or helping at the dispensary to treat the sores or other ailments of the patients.

Apart from academic work, the students had time for extra-curricula entertainments. They used to inivite people from various walks of life to give them talks. For example, during the 1959/60 academic year,[14] the students of St. Victor's Seminary had the privilege of listening to two White Fathers from the German Province, who spoke on "My experience in a

---

13 Appendix VII.
14 St. Victor's Seminary, Annual Report (1959-60).

Russian concentration camp" and on "The religious situation in Germany with special reference to Eastern Germany", respectively.

A third lecture, in the same year, was given by a journalist and observer for U.N.O. on "The general religious situation in the world and the social role the Church is called to play". At the other times, the students organized internal entertainments when plays were staged especially in honour of candidates who were ordained.[15]

The ordination to the priesthood had always been the climax of the training. The ordinands passed through two major stages before qualifying for full ordination to the priesthood. The first stage was the ordination to the minor Pontifical Orders: the Holy Tonsure which introduced the students to the nature of the priestly vocation and was received after the years of Philosophy; it was followed later by the Ostiariatus (Porters' Order), Lectoratus (Readers' Order), Exorcistatus (Exorcists' Order) and Acolytatus (Acolythes' Order). The major orders which followed the minor ones were (in the order in which they were received) the Subdiaconatus (subdiaconate), Diaconatus (diaconate), and the Presbyteratus (the Priesthood).

The ordination to the priesthood is preceded by a retreat which is a spiritual preparation. A typical retreat followed a pattern similar to the one set below:[16]

5.30 a.m.	Rising.
6.30 a.m.	Morning Prayers, meditations and Mass.
7.30 a.m.	Breakfast in silence—House duties.
8.15 a.m.	Study.
9.00 a.m.	Instruction followed by study or Chapel.
10.00 a.m.	Stations of the Cross.
11.45 a.m.	Particular Examens.
12.00 noon	Lunch.
1.30 p.m.	Rosary—Study or Chapel.
3.00 p.m.	Instruction.
4.00 p.m.	Bread.
5.00 p.m.	Bath.
6.00 p.m.	Instruction.
7.00 p.m.	Bendiction and Supper.
9.00 p.m.	Night Prayers.
9.15 p.m.	Lights out.

The ordination followed immediately on the first Sunday after the retreat. It usually took place in the presence of the seminarians and as many people and priests as could be present at the service. During the ceremony, the Archdeacon presented the ordinands to the Bishop who duly ordained them.

An ordination used to be followed by a luncheon given by the Bishop to

---

15 Heesewijk, "Amisano Notes", p. 57
16 Amisano Seminary, Diary (1930-1954), 7th July, 1935.

the newly ordained priests and their relatives. This used to be followed by entertainments such as football or play.[17]

From 1909 to 1965, the Roman Catholic Province of Ghana made persistent efforts to create an indigenous body of priests. During that period 90 students from the major seminaries, had been ordained into the priesthood. That was no mean achievement when we consider that many problems had been endured during the course of the training.

The foremost among the problems concerned recruitment. It has been shown already on some of the preceding pages that some of the students admitted did not persevere to the priesthood; it has also been pointed out that at times vocation had been lacking. What is of interest at this point is the examination of some of the factors which led the students to drop out and the forces which made the acceptance of priestly vocation difficult.

As regards the drop-outs, the most common factors which made prospective priests give up their call were: loss of vocation, family opposition, ill-health, weakness of character, and inability of the student to derive benefit academically from the course. As for the lack of vocation, the problems of celibacy and the indigenous view of assessing prosperity in terms of procreation have been mentioned above and we can only draw attention to them here. But as the problem of the lack of vocation is common with all the denominations under discussion in this study, further consideration of it will be postponed to the last chapter where it will be discussed as a common problem.

Many other problems also threatened the continuity of the Roman Catholic seminaries in addition to that of recruitment. From the very beginning of the projects, the major seminaries had not been satisfactorily housed until St. Peter's Seminary was built in 1956 and St. Victor's in 1961. The financial problem also had been discouraging at times. In general the major seminaries had been supported by individual scholarships from overseas sources. The benefactors were, St. Peter Apostle from Holland, Belgium, Abbe Sutter, Alsace and the Association of St. Peter Claver of Madam Falkenhayn, whose grants had also supported the minor seminary at Amisano. The grants were not always adequate and at times deficits accumulated. For example, in 1934, at St. Teresa's Seminary at Amisano, £560 (¢1120) had been asked for, but only £500 (¢1000) was received; in 1935, out of the £680 (¢1360) required only £235. 16s. 0d. (¢471.60) was granted, leaving a deficit of about £837 (¢1674) for two years.[18] St. Victor's Seminary, too, was not free from similar troubles. In the course of time, however, conditions got better and the problems became less acute.

The other problem of importance concerned how the quality of the recruits could be improved. In tackling it, the authorities increased the num-

---

17 *Ibid.*, p. 191.
18 Heesewijk, "Amisano Notes", p. 47

ber of their minor seminaries. Between 1955 and 1965 five new minor seminaries were added to the older ones at Amisano and Navrongo, increasing them to seven, scattered all over the country as follows: St. John's Seminary, Koforidua, St. Peter's School, Nkwatia-Kwahu, St. Francis Seminary, Wa, Notre Dame Seminary, Navrongo, St. Mary's Seminary, Lolobi, Volta Region, St. Charles' Seminary, Tamale and St. Teresa's Seminary, Amisano.[19] It had been hoped that in these seminaries more students would be encouraged to think seriously about the priesthood, in order that not only the quality of the recruits but also their number might be improved.

In evaluating the place of the minor seminary in relation to the recruitment for the major seminary, Adrian Hastings had this to say:

> Perhaps there is no other institution in the contemporary Church which is as difficult to evaluate as the minor seminary, and in which there can be such a full-scale clash between old and new forms of approach. Basically, the minor seminary is an anachronism, for it aims at providing a vocational and professional training for children at an age when in the past such training was given but today is not.[20]

Hastings had taken for granted, apparently, without sufficient evidence, that the minor seminary was anachronistic everywhere on the continent of Africa in 1964 when he published his book. Since the 1950s the minor seminaries in Ghana had been overhauled and brought in line with the secondary schools in the country. All the seven minor seminaries enumerated above were built to give general secondary education to at least the General Certificate Examination and Ordinary Levels, just as had been the practice in the other secondary schools. Thus the minor seminary could not be described as anachronistic in Ghana.

This conclusion does not, however, eliminate other possible problems relating to the minor seminary even in Ghana. Since independence, children in Ghana had been entering the secondary schools, in many instances, at between the ages of 12 and 13 years. At such tender ages, a student might be attracted to offer for the priesthood without actually understanding what it meant to be a priest. Even the staff, according to Hastings, might find it difficult to decide suitability for the priesthood when the pupil was immature because "boys who are very troublesome at 17 may be excellent priests at 26; boys who are meek and docile at 17 may either be so because they are weak, passive characters, not truly suited to be priests, or they may explode into total rebellion later on".[21] These are genuine criticisms which the minor seminary authorities should take particular note of.

As regards the major seminary, it had been said that in Africa it was so

---

19 Peter Sarpong, Rector, St. Peter's Seminary to Agbeti, 29th Jan., 1968.
20 Adrian Hastings, *Church and Mission in Modern Africa*, (London, 1967), p. 198.
21 *Ibid.*, p. 199.

much isolated from general life that its "atmosphere and discipline have tended to be semi-monastic, too much concern for what is actually happening in the world is practically—if not theoretically—discouraged, very few visitors come to speak to or meet the students, and rather little responsibility or freedom is accorded them".[22]

This criticism also is not entirely true of the major seminaries in Ghana partly because of the extra-curricular activities described above and partly because of the following further examples. It is true that the distances of the seminaries from the towns made it difficult for the students to have visitors very often; but they did receive visitors, both male and female. In addition the staff endeavoured to integrate the students into the local congregations. Illustrations from St. Victor's Seminary in 1954 given below represent the general practice in both seminaries.

On important feast days the students were allowed to go to the mission stations to join the congregations in worship. For instance, on Palm Sunday, 11th April, the students went to the Tamale Mission and served during the worship. On Monday, Thursday and on Good Friday, both the staff and the students joined the congregation again in worship.[23] On 15th August, Fr. Tryers sent to the seminary a lorry full of teachers, who had come from all over the Northern Territories to take a preaching course in Tamale. The visit was recorded as "a very interesting meeting and contact for both teachers and seminarians".[24] At other times the seminarians attended purely secular functions. On 26th August, three of the final year students represented the seminary at the opening of the N.T.'s Council.[25]

But the criticism that only a little responsibility or freedom had been accorded them should be taken seriously. As late as 1955 the Rector of St. Victor's Seminary testified to the validity of this criticism in these words:

> I have the impression after a year and a half that they (seminarians) were treated too much like boys. Decisions and everything were too much taken by the Fathers.[26]

It should be noted, however, that paternalism in the training of "natives" for the ministry—in fact, in the whole attitude of missionary approach to the "native" Church—was not peculiar to the Roman Catholic Church alone,[27] therefore further comments on it are postponed until the last chapter of this book.

---

22 *Ibid.*, p. 192.
23 St. Victor's Seminary, Log Book (1954 ff.), p. 1.
24 *Ibid.*, p. 0.
25 Bourret, *The Gold Coast*, p. 105. The Northern Territories' Council was established in 1946.
26 Fr. John M. Connolly, Rector to Rev. Pere H. Cote, Assistant General, 12th August, 1955.
27 Michael Hollis, *Paternalism and the Church: a Study of South Indian Church History*, (London, 1962), pp. 23-26.

In spite of these problems and criticisms, the Roman Catholic Province of the Gold Coast succeeded in building up an efficient body of African priests. In 1935 when the first two African priests were ordained, there were about 60,000 Faithfuls in the Vicariates,[28] scattered in four central stations, Cape Coast, Keta, Kumasi and Navrongo with their outstations. In 1965, there were 749,795 Faithfuls in Ghana distributed in 103 central stations and 2,053 outstations, and were being cared for by 305 priests including the 90 African priests of whom six had retired and three had died.[29]

The rapid growth of the Roman Catholic work in Ghana should not be attributed solely to the increase in the number of the African priests because the growth of the work since 1880 had already been spectacular before 1935, when the first African priests were ordained. Take for example, during the first six years of the coming of the Roman Catholics in modern times, 600 catechumens were baptized by Fr. Auguste Moreau.[30] At the end of the second decade, in 1901, there were nearly 5,000 converts in the four resident stations: Elmina, Cape Coast, Keta and Saltpond together with their outstation.[31] Therefore, the distinctive impact the training of the African priests had made on the development of the Roman Catholic Church in Ghana might be found in a factor other than in the growth of numbers.

This factor was related to the aim the missionaries had in mind when they started to train the "natives" as priests. Bishop de Bresillac's intention, when he founded the S.M.A., was that the missionaries, in their evangelization of "natives", might "train local priests who would, one day, be able to assume responsibility for the Church in their own country".[32] This was realised in the Gold Coast in 1950. On 18th April that year, a letter from the Pope, incorporated the Gold Coast as an Ecclesiastical Province of the Roman Catholic Church: it meant that the Roman Catholic Church in the Gold Coast, from that day, "... would be governed by its own Bishops, sons of its soil ..; it would rule itself in conformity with the laws of the Church and in obedience to the Pope's decrees".[33] In consequence, the four Vicariates became the four Dioceses of Accra, Keta, Kumasi and Tamale. Cape Coast, the oldest Vicariate, was created an Archdiocese with an Archbishop of Cape Coast. On June 8, 1960, amidst a great cloud of witnesses, His Grace John Kodwo Amissah, "the first African ever to be

---

28 Pfann, *A Short History*, p. 119.
29 Appendix VII.
30 Pfann, *op. cit.*, p. 34.
31 *Ibid.*, pp. 53-54. An investigation into the reasons that led to the spectacular growth of the Roman Catholic membership in Ghana would be useful and might throw more light on the best missionary methods that should be adopted in evangelizing Ghana. Owing to the lack of space the problem cannot be explored now.
32 *Ibid.*, p. 75.
33 *Ibid.*, p. 102.

nominated an Archbishop"[34] was enthroned as Archbishop of Cape Coast by his predecessor, Archbishop Porter, in the Cape Coast Cathedral.

This early devolution of power to the "native" Church was evidence that the African priests, since 1922, had been performing their duties with competence, and that competence was a testimony to the efficiency and the success with which they had been trained. Indeed, by the end of this period of investigation, some of the products of the major seminaries had obtained very high academic qualifications.[35] The Archbishop, himself, had obtained the Doctoral Degree in Canon Law; two of them, Peter Dery and J.A. Essuah, had become the Bishops of Wa and Kumasi, respectively, and the rest, with the help of about 248 Western missionaries, had been able to guide the Church in all its fields of activities such as evangelism, education, medicine and philanthropy.[36]

And so, with these achievements, made by the Roman Catholic Church in Ghana as the result of seminary training in the country, we may now take a look at the united effort the non-Roman Catholics had been making in training their ministers together since 1943.

---

34 *Ibid.*, p. 112.
35 For example, Peter Sarpong, D.D., B. Lit. (Oxon.); Charles Lejeune, D.D.; Joseph Kpeglo, D.C.L., Dip. Ed., and Joseph Owusuansah Osei, D.Phil.
36 Pfann, *loc. cit.*

CHAPTER ELEVEN

TOWARDS UNITED MISSIONS TRAINING: TRINITY COLLEGE, LEGON, 1943-1965

1943 marked the beginning of a new era in the history of the training of non-Roman Catholic African ministers in Ghana. In that year, as already hinted at in the preceding chapters, the Methodist and Presbyterian Churches abandoned the separate denominational training they had been giving to their African ministers and started a Joint Theological College, in Kumasi, hereafter referred to as the J.T.C. Its inception was the result of some years of negotiations which had taken place in the participating Churches severally and conjointly.

The initiative came from the Presbyterian Church of the Gold Coast as the result of the thinking which had been going on among its members since 1936. The Synod of 1937 appointed a sub-committee comprising Dr. T.E.L. Rapp (convener), Wilh. Stamm, David E. Elder, A.C.T. Apo, D. Glover Akpey, P.C. Richter, F.D. Harker and W E. Parkins, to consider a scheme which had been submitted to the Synod by another committee, previously appointed in 1936, to make recommendations for the higher education of candidates to be ordained into the Ministry.[1] At its first meeting, held at Odumasi on 1st October, 1937, the Rapp Committee considered the scheme and agreed that it was valuable for the higher training of future African ministers.[2] Two other meetings were held on 27th October, 1937 and 7th July, 1938 respectively, concerning how to implement the scheme.[3]

But, in July 1939, the Synod abandoned the scheme and took a different line of action. It resolved to invite "the Methodist Mission to join with the Presbyterian Church of the Gold Coast in setting up a United College for the Theological Education of the Ministers and Catechists of the Gold Coast."[4] The Methodist Church received and considered the invitation during their Synod in January 1940. The proposal was welcomed and the following reply was sent to the Presbyterian Church:

> The Synod thanks the Presbyterian Church of the Gold Coast for its invitation

---

[1] B.M.A., "Goldküste Ausschuss und Konferenzen; 1936-1937" (Folio 4 AFRIKA INSPECTORAT), D. 2102, E. 30, Nov. 1937.
[2] *Ibid.*
[3] *Ibid.*, 1938-1942, (Folio 12, AFRIKA INSPECTORAT), E. 20, Sept. 1939, D. 2187.
[4] Trinity College, "J.T.C. Memorandum drawn by the Principal, Vice Principal and the Students, 1945", Oversight Committee File (1940-1958). Hereafter cited as Memorandum, O.C.F. 40-58.

to set up a United Theological College and suggests that a committee of five members from each Church should meet during the year to explore the possibilities of such a question.⁵

The proposed Joint Committee had its first meeting in June 1941, in Kumasi, and passed the following resolution:

> The Joint Committee acknowledges that united Theological Training is of vital importance to the Churches of the Gold Coast and unanimously urges that a Joint Theological Training College should be established. It therefore strongly urges the synods of the Presbyterian Church of the Gold Coast and the Methodist Mission to give the matter their deepest consideration as soon as possible.⁶

The committee envisaged the J.T.C. as, what they called, "The Ideal College", and outlined the factors that would make the project an ideal institution. These factors were the staff, a committee of oversight, students, the scheme of work, accommodation, location and finance.

Concerning the staff, it was agreed that a joint staff representing equally both the Presbyterian and the Methodist Churches should be chosen. Four members of staff were envisaged and they were to be composed of one African and one missionary from each of the participating Churches. It was pointed out, however, that in each of the Churches, the best men available should be appointed and that it was not obligatory to divide the African and European members of staff equally. Quality should supersede nationality in the choice of the tutors.

An Oversight Committee was to be appointed to advise the staff and the synods about the college and make recommendations concerning the staff. It was to be made up of the Principal of the College, one other member of staff whose Church membership was different from the Principal's and six other people to be appointed by the synods equally.

As for the selection of the students, the Synods should continue to adopt their own methods for accepting candidates for the Ministry.

The training was to be a three years' course with special attention to training in Youth Work, the application to Religious Knowledge of the

---

5 Trinity College, Memorandum, O.C.F. 40-58. Cf. Methodist Church, Gold Coast, Synod Minutes, January 1940.
6 Trinity College, Memorandum O.C.F. 40-58. As far as my researches have gone, no reasons have been recorded, in the sources consulted, to explain the easy unanimity between the Methodist and the Presbyterian Churches regarding the united training. It may be suggested, however, that the I.M.C. meeting at Tambaram, Madras in 1938 might have influenced, very much the decisions of both Churches. One of the conclusions made at Tambaram reads: "It is our conviction that the present condition of Theological education is one of the greatest weaknesses in the whole Christian enterprise, and that no great improvement can be expected until churches and mission boards pay far greater attention to this work, particularly to the need for co-operation and united effort, and contribute more largely in funds and in personnel in order that it may be effectively carried out." I.M.C. *The Life of the Church*, Tambaram Series, VII Vols. (London, 1939), Vol. IV, p. 211.

Principles of teaching learnt in Training Colleges and the visits of students and staff to the adjacent Churches and congregations.

The Ideal College was to be residential and the accommodation should include students' rooms and offices, three classrooms, common room, music room, Chapel, library, dining room and administration block. As the staff were to be residential also, four staff houses would be needed.

Kumasi was an ideal location for the College because the committee noted that it would offer the students both rural and urban environments for practical training. The committee, in recommending that Kumasi should be chosen as the site for the college, insisted that great care should be taken to prevent any assocation with Wesley College. It was likely that the Presbyterians were the more insistent on this point of disassociation with Wesley College because on 17th July, 1939, at Aburi, the General Council of Basel and Scottish Missions said at their meeting that precautions should be taken that when the Joint Training started, the Presbyterian Church should not be swallowed up by the Methodist Church.[7]

The determining factor that would make the Ideal College possible was finance. Thus the Joint Committee discussed it and agreed the plans and estimates of the building should be secured. As for the payment of the tutors, the Churches would be responsible for the emoluments of the staff they would respectively appoint. Every student would be on full scholarship which would be paid by the Church sponsoring him.

It was realised that the Ideal College, as outlined, could not be started without some years of preparation. But as the project was very pressing and ought to be begun without much delay, the committee considered temporary arrangements and put forward the following recommendation:

> The Committee request that the possibility of using the Mile II site at Wesley College, at present used by the Methodist Church for Ministerial Training, should be explored. The Joint College should be distinct from and should not be socially connected with Wesley College.[8]

In July 1941, the Joint Committee met again and learnt that the Mile II proposal was favourable. There was reasonable accommodation for the members of staff; but two four-roomed houses to accommodate the students, classrooms and a Chapel whould be immediately necessary. The plans submitted for the four-roomed houses, Chapel and furniture, estimated at £600 (¢1200), were accepted.

At this second meeting, a suggested syllabus was also presented, discussed and accepted. The subjects included: Accountancy, Comparative Religion, Church History, English, Greek, Homiletics, Music, New Testa-

---

7 B.M.A., "Goldküste Ausschuss und Konferenzen, 1938-1942", Folio 4 Afrika Inspectorat, D. 2102.
8 Trinity College, Memorandum, O.C.F. 40-58.

ment, New Testament Ethics, Old Testament, Pastoralia, Psychology, Theology and Vernacular.

The planning seemed to be well in hand by the end of the meeting and it was proposed that if the Synods agreed, to establish the J.T.C. as outlined, then a Joint Executive Committee of eight members, four from each of the participating Churches, should be set up to put the scheme into operation. The Synods accepted the scheme and appointed the Joint Executive Committee. Its first meeting was held in December 1942.[9]

Very far-reaching decisions were taken at that meeting. Firstly, it was decided to open the J.T.C. on 4th February, 1943 with ten students of whom six were to be Methodist and four Presbyterian candidates.[10] The Methodists had four candidates in training in 1942 and they were expecting to add two other students in 1943. The Presbyterians were expecting to start with four students in 1943.[11]

The accommodation at the Mile II site, Kumasi, was sufficient to house the ten students in 1943 without the need for additional buildings immediately. In any case, after the College had started, the proposed buildings would be proceeded with throughout 1943 under the direction of the Principal and the Committee of Oversight.

Secondly, it was agreed that a house at Mile II which had accommodated, in 1942, two members of the Wesley College staff should be loaned to the J.T.C. in 1943, to accommodate its two European staff. The furniture was sufficient for only one of them, so the Presbyterians were asked to supply the necessary furniture for their European member of staff.

Thirdly, an estimated budget for running the College was presented and accepted. It provided for Overhead Charges to the value of £213. 10s. 0d. (¢463.00), covering the cost of light, water, labour, repairs, equipment, travelling and administration. Board, textbooks and stationery were estimated at £15. 0s. 0d. (¢30.00), £2. 0s. 0d. (¢4.00) and 10s. (¢1.00) respectively per student per year, making a total of £416. 10s. 0d. (¢833.00). Students' allowances were reckoned at a total of £208. 0s. 0d. (¢416.00) for 1943[12] and capital expenditure was estimated at £600. 0s. 0d. (¢1,200.00) for buildings and £200. 0s. 0d. (¢400.00) for a car.

Finally, the Joint Executive Committee nominated the late Rev. Dr. S.G. Williamson as the first Principal of the J.T.C. and the Rev. D.S. Elder, the Presbyterian European member of staff to act as Principal when Mr. Williamson was away on furlough and agreed that when started, the College should run three sessions in a year, first, second and third terms.

With all these painstaking preparations, the stage had been set for the

---

9 *Ibid.*
10 *Ibid.*
11 *Ibid.*
12 *Ibid.* The Committee expressed the opinion that the allowances paid to the students should be uniform.

opening of the J.T.C. Accordingly, on 4th February, 1943, the *Joint Theological College* was started at Mile II, on the great North Road, Kumasi, without publicity. The Principal designate, Mr. Williamson, previously on the Staff of Wesley College, had gone on furlough in 1942, so, the Rev. D.S. Elder was the Acting Principal when the College was opened. He was assisted by the Rev. R.S. Morris, the second member of staff until Mr. Williamson returned from furlough in May 1943.[13]

The pioneer students were eight instead of the ten the Joint Executive Committee had estimated because the two new students the Methodists had planned to admit could not pass the entrance examination.[14] Of the eight, four—J.K. Clegg, S.B. Essamuah, A.N.K. Sackeyfio and J.E. Yarquah—had been the Methodist ministerial candidates in training at Wesley College; the remaining four, I.A. Amaning, G.B. Ansre, A.L. Kwansa and S.A.A. Saki, were the Presbyterian students.[15]

The period 1943 to 1945 was the Trial Period, after which the participating Churches would decide whether or not the project could be continued. Whatever decision the Churches would make then would depend very much on the progress of the College during the period.

Within six months of its inauguration, people began to have bright hopes for the future of the J.T.C. In July 1943 the secretary of the Scottish Mission, MacMillan, wrote to the Principal as follows:

> You will know what great hopes are fixed upon that Theological College. It is only a small seed at the present time, but the tree that may grow from it may be a very great one indeed. Our prayers are constantly with it and its staff and students.[16]

This hope was justified by the progress of the institution during the two years that ensued. In 1944, the staff was increased by two African members: the Reverends P.C. Richter (Presbyterian) and S.G. Nimako (Methodist). The roll of students increased from 8 to 15. One of the Presbyterian students who had entered in 1943, the Rev. G.B. Ansre, had been recalled to fill a vacancy in the Ewe Presbyterian Church at the end of his first year. Eight new students were admitted in 1944 of whom six were Methodists and two Ewe Presbyterians. So, at the end of 1944 there were 10 Methodist students, three of whom had completed their course, and five Presbyterian students (three Gold Coast and two Ewe Presbyterians).[17] In 1945, the roll increased to 22 students made up of 13 Presbyte-

---

13 Wesley College, Log Book (1924-1957), pp. 77-78. See also, Appendix XII of this book.
14 Methodist Church Gold Coast (Hereafter cited as M.C.G.), Candidates Report, District Synod Minutes, Jan., 1943.
15 Trinity College, Oversight Committee Minutes Book, 1943-1949.
16 Trinity College, MacMillan to Williamson, 22nd July, 1943. (In Oversight Committee File, 1940-1958.)
17 The intermediate B.D. programme was started in 1944 with C.K. Dovlo and F.E. Adams in 1945. cf. p. 165.

rians including one from the Basel Mission, British Cameroons, and nine Methodists.[18]

At the end of the trial period the following statement was recorded, by the Oversight Committee, about the tone and success of the College during 1943-1945:

> The committee saw that there was amongst the staff a loyal colleagueship. Each member of staff has, during the past three years, given of his best, both inside and outside the classroom and the fellowship of the staff together has been real. By its efficient work it has set the College as an example both academic and pastoral.
>
> The three years of the College's life has been a joint venture in fellowship and learning amongst the students, and through them, a similar venture for the two Churches. The students coming as they did from local branches of the two Churches with the background of indifference and misunderstanding with regard to the cause of co-operation that is to be found amongst the rank and file of the two Churches, had to learn to understand each other and to pull together. There have been occasions when the fellowship has been strained owing to misunderstandings. This was especially noticeable through the fact that ministerial training in Kumasi began as a Methodist concern and it was not easy for either the Presbyterian or the Methodist students to discover what it meant as a joint undertaking. There has, however, been a steady increase of understanding and a deepening of fellowship. This has been particularly noticeable during the third year, when, with the Head-student a Presbyterian and three out of four of the senior students Presbyterians any idea that it was a Methodist College could no longer be entertained.
>
> The trial period has served to establish the kind of fellowship which can make such a united venture a success. That this has been achieved is due in very large measure to the spirit of the students themselves.[19]

It was not only in the relationship among the staff and the fellowship between the students of both Churches that the life of the College had been satisfactory during the trial period; there had been successes in almost all the improtant aspects of the experiment. The buildings, though temporary in character, had proved adequate: there were 18 bedroom studies and a hostel large enough to accommodate 12 men, making altogether a total accommodation for 30 students. The first year men occupied the hostel; the advantage being that a variety of men from different Churches and tribes were brought together in closer fellowship to learn more about one another. From the second year, however, the students occupied single rooms.

The academic programme also had been well organized during these three years so that the tradition established has remained the basic framework, within which improvements in the curriculum of the college have ever since been made. The time-table was divided into 6 × 45 minute periods

---

18 Trinity College, Memorandum, O.C.F. 40-58.
19 *Ibid.*

a day of a 5-day week (Monday to Friday). The various subjects taught and the time-table analysis were as follows:[20]

	Class	and	Periods
	1st Year	2nd Year	3rd Year
Accountancy	—	—	1
Comparative Religion	—	1	—
Church History	3	2	3
English	3	2	2
Greek	—	3	3
Homiletics	1	1	1
Music	1	1	1
New Testament	4	3	3
New Testament Ethics	—	2	—
Old Testament	4	3	3
Psychology	—	—	1
Theology	3	3	3
Vernacular	2	2	2
Pastoralia	1	1	1
General Discussion	2	2	2
Total periods per week	24	26	26

The textbooks used for the different subjects were supplied to the students from the Principal's office provided that they were available. They included, according to the various subjects, the following:

Theology:
    The Christian Faith,   Garvie
    The Theology of the Gospels,   Moffatt
    The Theology of the Epistles,   Kennedy
New Testament:
    Introduction to the N.T.,   Clogg
    The Gospels, A Short Introduction,   V. Taylor
Old Testament:
    Critical Introduction to the O.T.   B. Gray
    Bible Manners and Customs,   Mackie
    Prophecy and Prophets,   T.H. Robinson
    Religious Ideas of the O.T.   H.W. Robinson
Greek:
    B.F.B.S. *Greek New Testament*
    Pocket Lexicon   Souter
    Elements of N.T. Greek   Nunn
Church History:
    A Short History of our Religion   Somervell
    The Presbyterian Churches   Moffatt

---

20 *Ibid.*

Wesley's Journal, I Volume
Methodist Law and Discipline
Psychology:
  Psychology and Morals   Hadfield
English:
  Modern Prose,
  Poets and Poetry BK. 3   E.S. Lay
  Oral Exercises in English Composition   Nesfield
  Two Short Plays   Dumas
  The Leaguers
  Six Reformers
General:
  Peake's Commentary
  Philip's Scripture Atlas
  R.V. Bible with Apocrypha
  Methodist Hymn Book
  Twi Hymn Book[21]

In order to carry out the daily activities smoothly the day was organized in the following manner:

6.00 a.m.	Rising bell. Students used part of the first hour for private devotions.
7.00 a.m.	Prayers in the Chapel.
7.15-8.00 a.m.	First Lecture.
8.00-8.45 a.m.	Breakfast.
8.45 a.m.-1.00 p.m.	Lectures.
1.00. p.m.	Lunch.
4.30 p.m.	Games, Monday and Thursday; Gardening on Tuesday.
	Wednesday free afternoon and students could visit the town.
	Friday, general cleaning and inspection at 4.30 p.m.
6.00 p.m.	Evening Meal.
9.30 p.m.	Evening Prayers.[22]

Saturday was a free day and students who had urgent business went to town to attend to it. The other students remained in residence and spent the morning in studying. Saturday evenings were free and entertainments, lectures, debates, etc. were arranged by the students on every other Saturday.

On Sundays, with the exception of the first and last Sundays of every term

---

21 *Ibid.*
22 *Ibid.* What the students did between 7.00 p.m. and 9.30 p.m. has been omitted. That period was, however, normally used for private studies in the students' cubicles. The source of this information was the experience of the writer, himself a past student of Trinity College.

when the students and staff attended Kumasi Wesley or Kumasi Ramseyer Memorial Chapels alternatively, the students went to outstations in the morning for practical training. There were five nearby outstations during the trial period. They were Ampabame, Suame, Tafo Kuma, Adukrom and Amakom (both Ewe and Asante). On two or three occasions each year, in addition to the Sunday evangelistic work in those villages, the students and staff went away together for a few days to an area where both Churches had work, and did concentrated evangelistic and pastoral work. The places visited were Efiduase-Ashanti, Agogo, Bekwai, Ejisu-Akyinakrom. These two types of practical training were also found by the Oversight Committee in 1945 to be satisfactory, for they awakened the interest of the Churches in the united projects.[23]

Apart from the practical training in the outstations, the College received about three or four invitations each quarter from Wesley and Ramseyer Memorial Chapels to preach. When a student preached in one of these Chapels a member of staff went to listen to the sermon and give him suggestions for improvement.

Finally, special college services were held in the College Chapel for the spiritual edification of students and staff and also as further practical training for the students. Morning prayers, based on an approved College lectionary, were taken by the members of staff, each once a week, and the fifth day was taken by a third year student. Evening prayers, based on the conductor's own choice of Scripture, were taken by the students in rotation. A member of staff was on duty each week and he conducted the Wednesday service during his duty-week. Special college evening services were held on alternate Fridays when a student conducted the service and preached the sermon for criticism by the members of staff. All the College services were obligatory for both staff and students, with the exception that evening prayers were optional for the tutors who were not on weekly duty.

Another satisfactory development during the trial period concerned students' affairs. The measure of self-government given to the students was evidence that the pioneer staff had confidence in their maturity. They ran their own student affairs: they nominated their own officers—the Head Student (Secretary), Librarian, Dispenser, Mess President (Dining Hall Prefect), Groundsmen, Chapel Steward and Time Keeper. The Principal appointed the officers just as a matter of formality. The Head Student had authority within the College to arrange and supervise students' duties and work. He was the liaison officer between the staff and students. He had a student's committee consisting of himself, the Mess President and the secretaries of the three classes. They occasionally met with the Principal and discussed matters that affected the whole College.

The members of staff, however, had ultimate responsibilities regarding

---

23 Trinity College, Memorandum, O.C.F., 40-58.

general administration, grounds, cleaning and sanitation, board, stores and the library. Other vital responsibilities such as cooking and weeding the campus were delegated to the house staff comprising a cook and her assistant, the labourers and a watchman.

The experimental period was not only a period of success for the general organization of the College, but it was also a period of success in finding solutions to a few initial problems. It will be recalled that at the second meeting of the Joint Committee appointed by the Synods of the participating Churches to consider the setting up of a Joint Theological College,[24] it was agreed that the capital expenditure for the houses, Chapel and furniture should not exceed £600. 0s. 0d. (¢1200.00).[25] But when the College started its work in 1943, the Principal submitted an additional bill of £95. 0s. 0d. (¢190.00) as an estimate for installing 31 electric lights in 1944. The Methodist Standing Committee refused to accept this extra bill which they felt was shockingly high and "maintained that when the proposals for a Joint College were put before them in 1942, it was their impression that the original vote of £600 (¢1200) for capital expenditure covered all necessary building expenses for the experimental period of three years".[26]

However, after some period of discussions, agreement was reached that it was necessary to amend the original programme and increase the capital expenditure because the rapid progress of the College required that some of the developments should be implemented earlier than had been anticipated. Consequently, it was permitted that £170. 0s. 0d. (¢340) extra should be used over and above the estimated capital grant of £600. 0s. 0d. (¢1200) to be distributed as follows:

Two houses for members of staff at £300 (¢600) each	£600	(¢1200)
Lighting for these houses, say	£ 75	(¢ 150)
Electric light in other College buildings completed in 1943	£ 95	(¢ 190)
	£770	(¢1540)

This was to be shared by both Churches equally.

The other problem during the experimental period was not financial; it concerned the integration of the entrants. Two types of students had entered the College: the majority were teachers who had had four years' training at Wesley College or four years plus a "fifth year"[27] at Akropong Training College and had done five or more years' teaching. The second

---

24 Trinity College, "Minutes of the Committee appointed by the Synods of the Presbyterian Church of the Gold Coast and the Methodist Mission to consider the setting up of a Joint Theological College, 3rd July, 1941", O.C.F. 1940-1958. Hereafter cited as Minutes of the Committee appointed by the Synods.
25 *Ibid.*
26 Trinity College, Williamson to MacMillan, 11th December, 1943, O.C.F. 1940-58.
27 See Chapter V above.

group were catechists who had had only two years' post-elementary theological studies. Usually, the academic background of this latter group was low. Moreover, a number of them had formed their habits and settled in their way of thought and outlook and did not assimilate new ideas easily when they entered the J.T.C. The English they possessed was not of a sufficiently high standard; they read slowly, "seeing words rather than sentences,"[28] and they found it difficult to listen to a lecture and take intelligible notes at the same time.[29]

This position made the teaching difficult. The tutors had to choose between either setting a high standard of work and endeavouring to cover the ground in meticulous detail knowing that much of their work would be lost, or setting a lower standard and working at a slower pace knowing fully well that this approach would never make their students benefit completely by the depth of the subject.

These difficulties were aggravated by a third type of students: there were men who read for the London Intermediate and Final B.D. Examinations. Such men were usually of good academic standard. But their progress was hindered because owing to the limits imposed by the time-table and overloading of the time of the staff, the tutors had to take all the three categories of the students in one and the same class. The wise integration of these men in order that each group might derive the best results from his training remained the problem which could not be satisfactorily dealt with during the trial period.

Towards the end of 1945 a committee was appointed by the Churches to report on the College and make relevant recommendations to them. This Committee met at the J.T.C. on Wednesday and Thursday, October 10 and 11, 1945. Those present were: Presbyterians—the Revs. E.M. Asiedu, M.A. Obeng, W.M. Beveridge, H. Buchner, S.S. Odonkor and Mr. Amo-Gotfried; the Methodists were: the Revs. T.V. Beetham, F.E. Ekuban, B.A. Markin and A.W. Banks, Messrs. I.K. Agyeman and E.O. Asafo-Adjaye. The College was represented by the Revs. S.G. Williamson and D.S. Elder (Principal and Vice Principal).[30]

The Committee joined the College for morning worship on the Wednesday and Thursday. After the prayers on Wednesday morning the College was inspected. The Committee held its main sessions on the Wednesday afternoon and on Thursday morning. During the Wednesday session, a sub-committee was appointed to consider questions of curriculum, syllabi and methods of teaching. This committee met on Wednesday night and prepared recommendations which were discussed on Thursday morning. Placed before the main Committee on Thursday morning, was a memorandum which had been prepared by the staff and students of the College. It

---

28 Trinity College, Memorandum, O.C.F., 40-58.
29 *Ibid.*
30 *Ibid.*

outlined some of the history of the College since its beginning and gave a full account of its organization, finance and syllabi during the trial period. After its deliberations, the Committee unanimously voted that the College should be established on a permanent basis for the following advantages would be derived: Fistrly, an adequate training for the ministry of the Presbyterian and Methodist Churches would be provided because the staff would be conserved, a larger followship of students would be created than either Church could create, more adequate buildings and efficient administration would be provided and to the training would be brought the distinctive characteristics of the two Churches. Secondly, closer understanding between the ministers of the two Churches would be promoted, and thirdly, more united witness to the Gospel of Christ would be presented to the country.[31]

For the future direction of the College the committee made many recommendations, the most important of which concerned the government of the College, the nature and purpose of the course, preparations of candidates and length of course, method of training, textbooks, the library, visiting lecturers, refresher courses and practical work.

Before the committee adjourned, it recorded its impressions as follows:

> The Committee wished to place on record its great appreciation of the lead given by the Principal, the Staff and the students in guiding the College during its trial period now ending. Each has shown throughout, his willingness to make the scheme a success and to create a College life and fellowship that is vital and enduring. This has been so done that the Committee has been able to make its unanimous resolutions about the future of the College.[32]

With these words, the J.T.C., henceforth to be called Trinity College, entered into the next stage of its development; a decade of growth and of the search for a permanent site, 1946-1955.

Between 1946 and 1955 the total roll of students in the College fluctuated between 20 and 26, with the exception that in 1953 it fell to 14 "probably the lowest number of students in College since its inception in 1943,"[33] because only three of the applicants passed the examinations: J.K. Foh-Amoaning (Methodist), A.K. Sah and I.A. Sowah (Presbyterians). From 1954, however, the total roll had been above 20.[34] One of the most gratifying aspects of the admissions during this period of growth was that students were admitted from Churches outside the Gold Coast. For example, from the Presbyterian Church of the Cameroons: Jeremiah Chi Kangsen (1945), A. Su (1949) and E. Modi Essoka (1954); from the Methodist District of the Gambia: E.B. Stafford (1948) and I.C. Roach (1955)

---

31 *Ibid.*
32 *Ibid.*
33 Trinity College, "The Principal's College Report, 1953", O.C. File, 1940-58
34 Appendix IX.

and from the Ewe Presbyterian Church of Togoland an ordained minister, the Rev. A.K. Abutiate, for one year's course in 1954.[35]

At the end of 1951 the Oversight Committee noted with satisfaction the progress of the first two Cameroon students[36] and placed their feelings on record as follows:

> In consideration of the good work done by the Cameroon students and of the wider fellowship which is realised through their presence at the College, the Principal was asked to invite the Basel Mission Cameroons to apply for more places for new students if possible.[37]

It seemed that during this period not only the Cameroon students, but all the students became very aspiring and wanted to learn more than they had been permitted. The students of 1947 had petitioned the Oversight Committee that Greek should be taught to all students. The Committee turned down the petition on the ground that Greek studies would hinder the theological studies of weaker students. But in 1948 among the new entrants were three students who had passed their London Matriculation Examination and were required to study Greek. But the other students now felt that the staff was practising discrimination by allowing only a few students to study a subject that might prove of value to them. In order to avoid ill-feeling the staff recommended to the Oversight Committee that all students should study Greek. To allay the fears of the Oversight Committee, the staff suggested three classes for the study of Greek: those reading for University Examination, ordinary students and students of weak academic ability who would be taken slowly through the elements of New Testament Greek.

By the end of 1947, the influence of the College was being felt within and without the Gold Coast, consequently, when the Joint Committee met at the end of the year they recommended that external inspectors should be invited to report on the institution. Their concern was expressed thus:

> At this stage of its growth, students coming from the Gambia and the Cameroons[38] and requests from other Churches (e.g. the A.M.E.Z.), it would be of great value to the College to receive a report on the quality of its work from external authorities of high standing. The M.M.S. in London and the Church of Scotland Foreign Mission Committee be approached to send competent inspectors at their own charges. If not feasible a local board should be established.[39]

Meanwhile, other developments continued to take place in the College: in

---

35 Trinity College, "The Principal's College Reports" (for the relevant years), O.C. File, 1940-58.
36 Appendix IX.
37 Trinity College, Oversight Committee Minutes, 14th Dec., 1951.
38. Appendix IX.
39 Trinity College, Joint Committee Minutes, 17 and 18: Dec., 1947. However, the plan did not materialise.

December 1949, the participating Churches decided that students' travelling expenses to their homes and back from vacation should be borne by the Churches. The decision did not include the cost of excess baggage at the end of a student's course. This matter was referred to the consideration of the Joint Committee.[40] In 1951, as a result of students' petition, wives' allowances were increased from £3 to £4 (¢6.00 to ¢8.00) per month.

Another important development was the transfer of the intermediate students at Trinity College to the University College of the Gold Coast. Hitherto, Trinity College had been arranging a kind of makeshift preparation of some of the candidates to take the intermediate London B.D. Examination. In 1950 the Oversight Committee directed that, as the University College of the Gold Coast was "going to cater for studies leading up to Divinity work the College (Trinity) might relinquish the work of preparing students for the intermediate work and concentrate on the diploma for those who qualified".[41] The first reason for the Oversight Committee's decision was that the standard of the College was about that of the diploma because the majority of the students were not holders of the London Matriculation Certificates; the second reason was that the preparation for the diploma would not entail so much work for the staff.

While these developments were progressing, the first Principal, the late Dr. S.G. Williamson, accepted with the approval of the British Methodist Conference, an invitation to join the staff of the University College of the Gold Coast as a lecturer in Theology. He left Trinity College in August 1950 on furlough and when he returned to the country in October he started work at the University College at Achimota.

The other important development during this period concerned a better organized spiritual training in addition to the academic and practical traditions established in the trial period. On Ascension Day, 1955, all classes were called off and the day was used by the students and staff for meditation. The staff had been asked to collect suitable passages to guide the meditation and the day was planned as follows:

7.00 a.m.	Communion Service conducted by the Rev. Sintim Misa, B.D.
8.45-9.00 a.m.	Students assembled in the Chapel and were instructed by the Acting Principal, the Rev. Hugh E. Thomas, as to how the day was to be spent, especially about the best use of the period set aside for meditation.
9.00-10.30 a.m.	Meditation. Students remained in their cubicle-studies and spent the time in reading the prepared Bible passages and in praying.
10.30-10.45 a.m.	Students met again in the Chapel for prayers and the meditation was rounded off with an appropriate act of worship.[42]

---

40 Trinity College, Oversight Committee Minutes, 3rd Dec., 1949.
41 *Ibid.*, 1 and 15 Dec., 1950.
42 Trinity College, Staff Meeting Minutes, 13th May, 1955.

It was a rewarding exercise and in the yearly report the Principal noted that the day "was much appreciated by the students and [had] done us all good".[43] Since then the Quiet Day has become one of the most cherished traditions of the College.

Finally, at the end of 1955 the Oversight Committee accepted the suggestion of the Rev. H. Haller that at the end of their course, the students should be given a Trinity College Certificate, to be signed by the Principal, and referred the matter to the Joint Committee for approval. They also agreed to increase students' allowances to £2. 10s. 0d. (¢5.00) a month for the nine months they were in College and 3/- (¢0.30) a day for the three months' holidays during the year and £36. 0s. 0d. (¢72.00) general allowance per annum instead of £30 (¢60.00) per annum in response to the students' appeal for an increase.

The problems that the growth of numbers during this period would pose in the near future would be such that in 1956 there would be room for only three new students after the finalists had left at the end of 1955.[44] In view of this the Oversight Committee recommended, forcefully at the end of 1954, that something should be done in 1955 to meet the difficulty.[45] Thus, early in 1955, the Joint Committee discussed the Oversight Committee's recommendation and asked the Principal, Rev. W. Stamm "to prepare a detailed scheme of changes and renovations, . . . at an average low cost to cover an intake of 45 students for 20 years. . . ."[46] The Principal's scheme was discussed in March 1955 and it was agreed that the more expedient and economic step to take was to build a new Theological College during the next five years at a new site because the present site had become too noisy.[47]

Negotiations had already been going on since, 1947, in search of a permanent site for the College. By the end of the period 1946-1955 such a place had been selected. The choice lay between Kumasi, "on the ridge running from the Broadcasting Station towards the Accra Road"[48] and Accra, in the vicinity of the proposed new University College of the Gold Coast.[49] In 1949 a planning Committee was set up "to watch the University College developments"[50] and to advise the Oversight and the Joint Committees whether the permanent site for Trinity College should be in Kumasi or near the University. This decision was inspired by the results of an interview between the Principal of the University College and the Chair-

---

43 Trinity College, The Principal's College Report, 1955.
44 Trinity College, Oversight Committee Minutes, 11th Dec., 1954.
45 *Ibid.*
46 Trinity College, Joint Committee Minutes, 6th January, 1955.
47 *Ibid.*, 11th March, 1955.
48 Trinity College, Minutes of the Committee appointed by the Synods, 2nd Meeting, 3rd July, 1941.
49 Trinity College, Joint Committee Minutes, 17-18 December, 1947.
50 Trinity College, Oversight Committee Minutes, 19th Dec., 1949.

man of the Methodist Church on 5th April, 1949.[51] The Chairman was assured that a faculty of theology would definitely be incorporated into the structure of the University, and that the Department would welcome some form of affiliation between Trinity College and the University College in respect of the Intermediate London B.D.[52]

In 1950, when Bishop Neill was on his Theological tour in the Gold Coast,[53] he sent out a questionnaire to the Christian Council on the Faculty of Theology and a proposed Churches' College.[54] Out of the questionnaire the Joint Committee recommended to the participating Churches that the permanent site of Trinity College should be selected on or near the University College grounds.[55] The Churches accepted the recommendation and the following sub-committee was appointed to prepare a detailed memorandum showing how the recommendation could be implemented: the Revs. F.R. Ametowobla, J.W. de Graft Johnson, S.G. Williamson and W. Stamm (Convener).

In 1951, Williamson wrote to the Principal of the University College saying that the Churches had approved the scheme of developing Trinity College at the University site and asked if Mr. Balme could indicate a specific site, or possible sites that might be available.[56] Mr. D.M. Balme replied that he had discussed with Mr. Hubbard the architect the question of reserving a site at Legon for Trinity College and Mr. Hubbard had said that there would be no difficulty in finding a suitable area up to 30 acres, provided that Trinity College Authorities would "be able to employ the same architects and build in the same style as the rest of the University".[57]

The Rev. S.G. Williamson reported the result of his consultation with Mr. Balme to the Joint Committee on 18th December, 1951 and details of the proposed buildings, studies and other relevant matters on the scheme were entrusted to another committee of eight comprising four members from each Church as follows: Methodist: the Revs. S.G. Williamson (Convener), A.W. Banks, G.R. Acquaah and J.W. de Graft Johnson; and Presbyterians: the Revs. W. Stamm, F.R. Ametowobla, E.V. Asihene and C.H. Clerk.[58] This sub-committee was also empowered to undertake discussions with the Principal of the University where necessary.

---

51 Trinity College, "Notes of an interview between the Principal of the University College and the Chairman of the Methodist Church of the Gold Coast on the question of the Theological Faculty. April 5, 1949" Joint Committee File 1954-1961.
52 *Ibid.*
53 See Preface Fn. 1 and Chapter VIII of this book.
54 Trinity College, Joint Committee File, 1945-1961. Copy of the questionnaire has been preserved in the J.C. file.
55 Trinity College, Joint Committee Minutes, 6th Dec., 1950. For the main reasons why they decided to have a site near the University, see pp. 248-250.
56 Williamson to Balme, 15th October, 1951. University of Ghana File No. 4004/6.
57 Balme to Williamson, 1st November, 1951, *ibid.*
58 Trinity College, Joint Committee Minutes, 18th December, 1951.

While this committee was carrying on its work, it was suggested that the opinion on building the permanent Trinity College at the University site might be deferred because the idea was gradually growing "that the right place for the theological College would be on a site adjacent to the University College but not within it".[59] It seemed that two main factors influenced this line of action: first, the University's condition, that Trinity College Authorities should employ the same University architects and build Trinity College in the same style as the University, might be too costly for the two Churches to bear.

The other factor concerned the refusal of the Anglicans to participate in the project. In October 1951 the Anglican Church had applied to the Joint Committee to be permitted to participate "in a Joint Theological College in the grounds of University College".[60] At its meeting in December 1951, the Joint Committee welcomed the approach made by the Anglican Church of the Gold Coast with high hopes that plans could be made which might be acceptable to all parties.[61] The eight-man Presbyterian and Methodist sub-committee mentioned above, was empowered to study the Anglican application together with Anglican members and to make recommendations to the Churches. The Anglican Church was represented by the Bishop of Accra, the Rev. Martinson, the Rev. Canon G. Laing and Prof. J.P. Hickinbotham. The 12-man committee had three full meetings between April and June 1952,[62] and discussed reports of the sub-committees on site, buildings and syllabuses. As a result of these meetings the committee was unanimous that the Anglicans should participate in establishing a joint theological college at Legon and the following outline plan was recommended to the Churches:

> It should be clearly understood that this proposal has no connection with any scheme of reunion between the Churches; throughout its deliberations the committee has acted on the principle that any plan for joint theological training must be limited to that object, and that within a joint College the distinctive spirit, beliefs and ways of worship of each Church must be safeguarded, and the students of each Church must be trained in full loyalty to the tradition of their own Church.
>
> When this has been realised it may be suggested that there are three main reasons why the proposals of a joint college should receive the support of the Churches. First it offers to the Churches an opportunity of co-operation in providing a theological training which will be of higher quality than could be provided by any one of the Churches acting individually. Secondly, to have the college life in close touch with University life is to place the calling of the Ministry in a wider setting and to provide opportunities of drawing upon the academic life and standards of the University, and possibly of using some of its

---

59 Williamson to Balme, 26th June, 1952, University of Ghana File No. 4004/6.
60 Daly to the Secretary, Joint Committee, 15th October, 1951, Trinity College, Joint Committee Files 1945-1961.
61 Trinity College Joint Committee Minutes, 18th December, 1951.
62 *Ibid.*, 2nd May, 1952.

amenities. The joint college will always, however, be self-contained and administered separately. Thirdly, a joint college of the type proposed by the Committee will be more costly to build, equip, maintain and staff than any one Church can afford.

In short, the committee sees no reason why the hopes expressed in the resolution of the Methodist and Presbyterian Joint Commitee should not be fulfilled, provided that the Churches can raise the money.[63]

But when the scheme was presented to the Anglican Diocesan Synod in August 1952, it was rejected,[64] and this turn of affairs was destined to change the course of the deliberations concerning the building of the Joint Theological College on the University site.

Although the Methodists and the Presbyterians were disappointed they were not daunted; they went ahead with their plans to build the College at the University site. On 10th May, 1955 the University architects wrote to the Vice-Principal of the University College of the Gold Coast to say that the most suitable land for the proposed Joint Theological College would be between Little Legon and the Forest Reserve on the south side of the Legon-Achimota link road.[65] In response the Vice-Principal pointed out that the proposal to build Trinity College at the University had not been put on any official basis therefore the University had no official standing in the question and had received no formal proposal from the body sponsoring the idea though there had been unofficial discussions.[66] In conclusion Mr. Smith wrote:

> If this project is to be pursued it would seem necessary, before any other action is taken, for the College to be given an official opportunity to express its views and to negotiate the general principle and the necessary conditions.[67]

Even this did not dismay the Joint Committee and while negotiations were officially opening with the University authorities on the proposal for granting a site on the University campus for Trinity College, it appointed a sub-committee to consider estimates and plans of the buildings and to deal with all matters of a constitutional nature that might arise. The members of this building sub-committee were: the Rev. S.G. Williamson (Convener), the Moderator of the Gold Coast Presbyterian Church, the Chairman of Methodist Church, the Rev. D.S. Elder, T.W. Koomson, W. Beveridge, H.H. Buatsi, P.K. Dagadu, A.L. Kwansa, Messrs C.D.K. Lokko, J.S. Annan, the Principal and Vice Principal of Trinity College.[68]

This was the position at the end of the second period 1946-1955. The

---

63 *Ibid.*, 24th July, 1952.
64 Accra Diocesan Synod (Anglican), Minutes of 23rd August, 1952. Cf. Chapter VIII of this book for the factors which inspired the Anglican decision.
65 Harrison, Barnes and Hubbard to the Vice Principal, 10th May, 1955, University of Ghana File no. 4004/6.
66 Smith to Harrison, Barnes and Hubbard, 20th May, 1955, *Ibid.*
67 *Ibid.*
68 Trinity College, Joint Committee Minutes, 21st December, 1955.

search for a permanent site for Trinity College had not been completed. A definite decision had been taken to build the College near the University; but whether or not the site was going to be available on the University Campus or outside it remained a problem to be solved during the third period 1956-1965.

In response to Mr. Smith's direction mentioned above an official request for a site for Trinity College was sent to the Principal of the University in April 1957 by the Churches.[69] In the letter of application the Rev. G.T. Eddy gave four reasons in support of the request which read: "We think the time has come to bring the matter to you as a definite request so that it may be considered by the Council of Senate."[70] The reasons were as follows: first, although most of the candidates had not been holders of the London Martriculation Certificate, the small supply of Trinity men who had been admitted into the Faculty of Theology had been doing so well[71] that a closer association of Trinity College with the University would be stimulating to both sides; moreover, the increase in secondary education would probably enhance the supply of similar capable candidates for the Christian ministry. Second, the other category of ministerial candidates was drawn from teachers and catechists and they might be comparable with the associate students in the University in their academic standing. Third, proximity of the University would stimulate the academic life of Trinity College; for example, public lectures and other functions opened to the general public within the University would be attended by the students of Trinity College. And, four, arrangements might be made to make the University Library open to suitable Trinity College students.

The University Council responded favourably to the application and "agreed to invite the views of the General Board, the Financial Board and the Halls on the application...."[72] With the exception of the Finance Board which declined to make any comments on the application, the General Board and the Halls "had no objections to the proposal of the Methodist and Presbyterian Churches to build a new college for their Ministerial Training at Legon".[73] But Akuafo Hall saw no reason why the Churches should be required to employ the College architects and Legon Hall was concerned that as only two Churches were involved, similar requests might come from other denominations.[74]

As a result of 'the University Council's response the Principal of the

---

69 Eddy to Balme, 1st April, 1957, University of Ghana File No. 4004/6.
70 *Ibid.*
71 One of the students, K.A. Dickson, had a First Class Degree in the London B.D. Examination in 1956.
72 University of Ghana, File no. 4004/6: Ach 4217 [Item 18 of C. of S. 97 (1)].
73 University of Ghana, File No. 4004/6: F.B. 97[(10)] 11th May, 1957; GB 90[(9)], 13th May, 1957; Hall Councils: Akuafo Hall, 4th June, 1957; Commonwealth, 28th October, 1957 and Legon Hall, 17th October, 1957.
74 *Loc. cit.*, cf. Akuafo Hall and Legon Hall.

University, R.H. Stoughton, asked the Rev. G.T. Eddy to get in touch with the Provost of the University M.G.I. Smith the development officer, to discuss with him the possibilities of finding a suitable site. At the meeting between the Provost and Mr. Eddy in December 1957, the following four possible sites were proposed: (1) West of the Little Legon housing area on the south side of the Achimota link road; (2) On the west side of the Dodowa road between miles 7 and 8; (3) On the east side of the Dodowa road between the north end of the staff village concession, and (4) On the west side of the Dodowa road to the north of the Power Station. The area would be between 20 and 25 acres.[75]

In 1958 the Churches informed the Provost that they had chosen site (2), the west side of the Dodowa road between miles 7 and 8.[76] The area was approximately 24 acres and the Churches were informed by the Provost that Trinity College would "be responsible for the maintenance, not only of the area specifically allocated to it for building purposes, but also for any part of the College land immediately adjoining it to the Dodowa road side".[77]

In 1959, however, the hopeful picture of the University's granting land for Trinity College began to change, to the great disappointment of the Churches. In October that year, the Churches requested that a draft deed might be drawn up for discussion by the Churches and the University authorities.[78] In reply, the Provost of the University informed the Churches that the matter concerning land for Trinity College within the University campus had not yet been considered officially by the University Council or the Committee of the council responsible for development matters and that no legal deeds could be drafted until the whole matter had been discussed officially.[79]

The University Council met on 4th December, 1959 and discussed the Churches' request for land within the University. The Council was divided on the matter: some felt that

> The Council would be performing a useful service in allowing the Churches' authorities concerned to build within the precincts of the University College, and if further land would be spared, similar arrangements might be made for any other denominational body that wished to avail itself of such facilities.[80]

Such an arrangement was vehemently opposed by other members especially the Cabinet Minister present, Mr. P.K.K. Quaidoo, in principle "on the ground that once the (University) College became involved in any way with denominational institutions its non-denominational character would be

---

75 University of Ghana, Notes from the Provost Legon, 24th Dec., 1957, File 4004/6.
76 University of Ghana, File 4004/6: C.D.C. 29[(3)], 24th April, 1958.
77 *Ibid.*, C.D.C. 8[(8)], 20th May, 1958.
78 Eddy to the Principal, Legon, 8th Oct., 1959, University of Ghana file No. 4004/6.
79 Provost to Eddy, 14th October, 1959, *Ibid.*
80 *Ibid.*, U.C.G. 33[(5)], 4th December, 1959.

affected".[81] In conclusion the Council refused to grant to the Churches any site for Trinity College within the University and placed the following statement on record:

> It was agreed that the Church authorities concerned should be informed that 'it will not now be possible to allocate a site for Trinity College, partly because of the amount of land for building purposes that will be required by the expansion of the College (University), including the proposed Medical School, and partly because of the conditions attached to the lease of that part of the College estate on which a site might be provided for the building of Trinity College'.[82]

The decision was conveyed to the Churches by the Principal of the University in a letter addressed to Rev. Odjidja, the Moderator of the Presbyterian Church and Chairman of the Joint Committee, as follows:

Ref: 4004/6.
Dear Rev. Odjidja,

University College of Ghana,
Legon, Accra.
February 26, 1960.

LAND FOR TRINITY COLLEGE

Since 1949, there has been correspondence with this College about the possibility of obtaining a suitable site on the College estate at Legon for the building of a joint theological College for the Methodist and Presbyterian Churches. The first approach to the College was made by the late Reverend Williamson. Later on, a joint letter was addressed to the College by Mr. E. Max Dodu, then Moderator of the Presbyterian Church, and Mr. G.T. Eddy, then Chairman and General Superintendent of the Methodist Church of Ghana. The College has been sympathetic towards the idea and, in fact, negotiations for a possible site started in December 1957.

It is now clear, after further examination of the application, that it will not be possible to allocate a site for the proposed Trinity College. This decision has been reached for two reasons, viz: (1) the proposal by the Government to build a teaching Hospital at Legon, together with the necessary residential quarters for the teaching and assistant staff and nurses-in-training, and (2) certain conditions attached to the use of the lands assigned or leased to the University College, which had not previously been taken fully into account.

I know that this decision will cause great disappointment to the two Churches, but, as I have already stated, it has been reached as a result of circumstances beyond our control.

Yours sincerely,
(SGD) R.H. STOUGHTON
PRINCIPAL

The Rt. Rev. E.M.T. Odjidja,
Presbyterian Church,
P.O. Box 1800,
ACCRA.

---

81 *Ibid.*
82 *Ibid.*, C.D.C. 33(8), 16th February, 1960, No. 7 (item 6). The condition attached to the lease says: "it will be necessary to obtain the prior permission of the Government before granting a sub-lease". Cf. *Ibid* U.C.G. 33(5), 4th December, 1959. It has not been made clear why the permission could not be sought from the Government. The real crux of the matter, I think, was the fear expressed by Quaidoo.

The reply was indeed frustrating, but the Churches were not disheartened; they could not go back on their determination to build Trinity College near the University. Without any delay the Joint Committee authorised the Rt. Rev. E.M.L. Odjidja, the convener of the property, building and appeal committee, to investigate the possibility of getting another site near the University College. His investigations were fruitful and at the Joint Committee meeting held in April 1960, he reported that a new and suitable site had been found east of the University College, adjacent to the University College Hospital, between the Hospital, on the west and Mpehuasem village on the east, La Bawaleshie on the south and Labadi Stool land on the north.[83] The news was received with great joy, and after the meeting the Committee members visited the site in the company of an Architect from the Methodist Headquarters in Accra. The Rev. A.L. Kwansa was authorised to enter into preliminary negotiation with La Mantse (the ruler of La in Accra) and his Stool Elders.

There were no hindrances in respect of Mr. Kwansa's negotiations. On 21st December, 1960, the site was provisionally inspected and demarcated in the presence of the Rev. A.L. Kwansa, representing the Joint Committee and the following representatives of the La Stool—Okyeame (Linguist) Adjei Ako, Mr. D.S. Charway (draughtsman) and Manche (Chief) Okpoti.

The provisional dimension suggested was 1,000 ft. by 1,200 ft. As this did not constitute the required acreage needed for the College it was agreed that the site could be extended later, northward, not eastward because Mpehuasem was on the east side. The provisional dimension agreed on was 1,000 ft. north, 1,000 ft. on the south, 1,200 ft. on the east and on the west 1,200 ft., bounded by La Stool property on the north and south, Mpehuasem on the east and the University of Ghana property on the west.[84]

The total expenses incurred during the negotiations amounted to £15. 17s. 0d. (¢31.70) being the cost of customary gifts to the Stool Elders who introduced the site and to the representatives who were present at the demarcation.[85]

When the Rev. A.K. Kwansa gave the report of the transactions to the Joint Committee at the meeting held on 29th December, 1960, and told the members that La Mantse and his Stool Elders had definitely agreed and resolved to lease the site to Trinity College, the Joint Committee accepted the report with great joy. There and then it was resolved to pay the expenses and Mr. Kwansa was authorised to proceed with the negotiation for the extension of the site northwards.

On 16th June, 1961, the Joint Committee was informed at its meeting that with the help of Mr. Justice Nii Amaa Ollennu, the Labadi Chief and

---

83 Trinity College, J.C. Minutes, 30th April, 1960.
84 *Ibid.*, 29th December, 1960.
85 *Loc. cit.*

his Elders acceded to free conveyance of the site to the College Board. In appreciation of the generosity of the Labadi Traditional Ruler and his Elders, the Joint Committee gave a considerable gift of £500 (¢1000) to the donors.

The way was now clear for the Churches to proceed with the building of the new Trinity College. There were no further delays with the building plans, because while negotiations had been going on to secure a permanent site, various committees had also been formed comprising: property, building and appeal, to continue making plans towards the building of the new College. The Appeal sub-committee had been charged with formulating plans for financing the buildings. As early as 1957, the Methodist Church had offered to pay £25,000 (¢50,000) into a building fund in three instalments between 1958 and 1960.[86] The sub-committee received the offer with appreciation and invited the other participants, the Presbyterian Church of Ghana and the E.P. Church, to give comparable undertakings, naming the figure and the period in which they would honour such undertakings.

As a result of the appeals sent out by the Appeal sub-committee the Theological Education Fund of the World Council of Churches made the following promise in 1959

> In view of the fact that a significant improvement of theological education can be expected to ensue from the close proximity of this theological school to the University College of Ghana: IT WAS VOTED to aid in the plan for moving Trinity College Kumasi, Ghana from its present site to the campus of the University College of Ghana by a grant of up to $75,000 on a basis of $3 for each $5 raised through local channels on condition: that the amount to be furnished through local channels be raised by January 1, 1962.[87]

The payment of the money was to be made to the legal holding body designated by the regularly constituted Governing Body of Trinity College.

Hitherto the local efforts by the Church had been encouraging: the Presbyterian Church of Ghana and the E.P. Church have also promised, respectively, to pay £15,000 (¢30,000) and £7,000 (¢14,000) payable in three instalments between 1958 and 1960. By the end of 1960 a progress report of the Building Fund submitted to the Joint Committee was as in table on p. 176.[88]

The Joint Committee accepted the report and resolved that all balances should be paid by 30th June, 1961.

By April 1962, £74,000 (¢148,000) had been collected, leaving a balance of £26,000 (¢52,000) to make up the £100,000 (¢200,000), the estimated cost of the first phase of the project.[89] The Property, Building and

---

86 *Ibid.*, 17th June, 1957.
87 Charles Forman (T.E.F.) to the Joint Committee, July 1959, *Ibid.*
88 Trinity College, J.C. Minutes, 29th December, 1960.
89 Trinity College, Minutes of the Building and Appeal Sub-Committee, 5th April, 1962, Governing Body Minutes' File (hereafter cited as G.B.M.).

Churches	Allocations	Paid	Balance
	£ ȼ	£ ȼ	£
Methodist	25,000 (50,000)	15,750 (31,500)	10,000 (20,000)
Presbyterian Church of Ghana	15,000 (30,000)	10,000 (20,000)	5,000 (10,000)
E.P. Church	7,000 (14,000)	— (—)	7,000 (14,000)
Total	47,000 (94,000)	15,750 (31,500) £750 being interest.	22,000 (44,000)

Appeal sub-committee, at a meeting held on 5th April, 1962, suggested that the T.E.F. and the Missions associated with the College through the sponsoring Churches, might be approached to share this balance among themselves as follows: the T.E.F. $25,000 (£8,900 or ȼ17,800) because the Principal of Trinity College suggested that it would make up the original T.E.F. grant of $75,000 to a round figure of $100,000; the M.M.S. £4,000 (ȼ8,000); Basel Mission and Scottish Mission £4,000 (ȼ8,000) between them and the United Church of Christ in the U.S.A. and the sponsoring Churches £10,000 (ȼ20,000) to be shared thus: Methodists £5,000 (ȼ10,000), Presbyterian Church of Ghana, £3,000 (ȼ6,000) and the E.P. Church, £1,500 (ȼ3,000).[90]

The T.E.F. accepted the appeal to pay the supplementary grant of $25,000 subject to the following conditions:

> That the total of other contributions to the construction of the College be not less than $180,000.
> That the supplementary grant be paid to the College when the Executive Committee of the T.E.F. Committee is satisfied that this condition has been fulfilled.[91]

The T.E.F. resolved also to release the initial major grant of $75,000 because the conditions governing the release had been fulfilled.

The way having been made clear, financially, tenders were invited and the contract awarded to A. Lang & Co. in 1963.

The plans and specifications had been previously prepared in the Architect's Department of the Methodist Church by Mr. K. Holgate, A.R.I.B.A., who was then the Methodist Church Staff Architect in Ghana. He arrived in the country on 27th December, 1957 and in 1958 he was entrusted with the preparation of plans for the new Trinity College. The work he had started was revised and completed by his successor, the Rev. N.L.P. Warman, who suggested, for economic reasons, the following dif-

---

90 *Ibid.* It will be noticed that the total of these assessments is £26,900. That is, £900 more than the original balance left. The reason is that the T.E.F. was asked to pay a little more in order to make its total contribution a round figure of $100,000.
91 Trinity College, G.B.M., 18th January, 1963, No. 125. Cf. T.E.F. to the Principal, Trinity College, 25th October, 1962, in the same file.

ferent lines of action: first, that multi-storey blocks should be permitted instead of the previously suggested uniform single-storey development and second, that students' accommodation should consist of single rooms but with communal, instead of individual baths and conveniences. These alterations were accepted by the Governing Body of Trinity College who also had agreed that the plans should be based on a student enrolment of 60 at first, rising to 85, then to 100, as outlined in the suggested phasing of the plan.[92]

As soon as the contract was awarded, the Governing Body approved the following work programme for the contractors on 17th January, 1964: Staff houses to be completed by the end of the first week in May 1964, both dormitory blocks by the end of May, the classroom block by the middle of June and external works to be completed by the end of August 1964.[93] At the meeting the Governing Body noted with satisfaction that work had already begun on the digging of foundations for some of the houses and on the roads.[94] Thus,

> After many years of hope deferred, early in 1964 a start was made on the new buildings by contractors, A. Lang and Co. On Easter Monday, 30th March, a large crowd assembled to participate in the ceremony of laying the foundation stone of the College Chapel. The small approach road was congested with motor transport of every kind, many people having come from far away for this festive occasion. The Stone was laid by the Rt. Rev. M.E.L. Odjidja, Chairman of the Governing Body, and a very fitting address was given by our former Principal, the Rev. W.A. Stamm.... So, after 21 years, we are in the process of bringing to an end our occupation of the site at 'Mile 2' on the Mampong Road, where the College has come so happily to maturity.[95]

This maturity was the result of the developments that had been taking place, internally, at the College in Kumasi, since 1956 while the search for a permanent site for the College had been progressing in Accra. First in 1956, on 17th November, at 2.30 p.m., the first Missionary Garden Party was held on the Trinity College Grounds. Its purpose was to interest Methodist and Presbyterian members and other well-wishers in the Missionary work the Methodist and Presbyterian Churches had initiated in Northern Ghana, and to solicit funds in aid of the project. Although the function was disturbed by showers it was well attended and the net profit in cash amounted to £120 (¢240). Since then the Missionary Garden Party has become one of the annual traditions of the College.

Second, a month afterwards, at its meeting on 16th December, 1956, the staff of Trinity College proposed to the Oversight Committee that it had become necessary to re-adjust the College calendar and Curriculum.[96] In

---

92 Appendix XI
93 Trinity College, G.B.M., 17th January, 1964, Nos. 174-194.
94 *Ibid.*, No. 180[(b)].
95 H.E. Thomas, Trinity College Annual Report, 1963/64.
96 Trinity College, Oversight Committee Minutes, 16th Dec., 1956.

respect of the calendar, it was suggested that the three terms of 12 weeks each should be shortened to 10 each; the third term's vacation should be lengthened to three months and the College year should end in June and begin in October instead of beginning in January and ending in December.

Three reasons were offered in support of these proposals: firstly, that each of the two African members of staff might have three months' leave every other year; secondly, that the students might have the opportunity of doing definite work in the Districts or Circuits during the long vacation, to be supervised by the African member of staff who would not be on leave; and thirdly, that the missionary staff's absence on furlough might be reduced to one term in alternate years instead of two. The Oversight Committee accepted the calendar proposal in 1957 and recommended that it might be implemented in 1958. But the curriculum readjustment suggestion was referred to the consideration of the Joint Commitee.

Third, in 1958, a corporate body was formed to hold the land and property of the proposed new Trinity College at Legon and a Constitution, Staff and Curriculum Committee was appointed to prepare a constitution for the New Trinity College and to deal with relevant matters relating to staff and curriculum readjustment problems.

Fourth, in the same year, long vacation work was introduced for the final year students: they were stationed in Circuits or Districts for two months to learn and practise pastoral work under the guidance of a senior pastor.[97] This also became an annual tradition of the College.

Fifth, in 1959, the Joint Committee accepted the constitution, prepared by the Constitution, Staff and Curriculum Committee, for the New Trinity College. But the work on the curriculum readjustment was not completed until the end of 1960. At its meeting on 29th December, 1960 the Joint Committee made the following recommendations on the curriculum readjustment proposal that: the normal course of three years should be lengthened to four; provision should be made in Trinity College to train graduates from the University College for the Christian ministry;[98] such students should take only the fourth year course with such modifications as would be necessary; a fifth member of staff should be appointed to be financed by the sponsoring Churches; a request be made to the Theological Education Fund (T.E.F.)[99] for either a sixth member of staff or visiting

---

97 Thomas, *op. cit.*, 1958.
98 Trinity College, J.C. Minutes, 29th December, 1960. The meeting was informed that the Government had withdrawn its financial support to the Divinity Department, but that provision had been made whereby Theology could be taken as one of the subjects for the Arts Degree Course. That is, an undergraduate might take the B.A. degree with Theology as one of his subjects or as a special subject. In view of the change it was felt at the meeting that pastoral training at Trinity College was necessary, for graduates who would offer themselves for Holy Orders.
99 T.E.F.: For information relating to the origins and functions of the Theological Education Fund, see David M. Paton, "Theological Training in the Younger Churches", *The East and West Review*, Vol. XXVI, October 1960, No. 4, pp. 125-127.

lecturers and lastly, that the Missionary Societies concerned be requested to allow annual furloughs for missionary members of staff in order that they might be present in the College during the sessions.

Sixth, in April 1961, the Joint and Oversight Committes were abolished and replaced by the Governing Body and the Standing Committee. The Governing Body then ratified the Constitution, for the new Trinity College previously accepted by the Joint Committee in 1959.[100]

Seventh, in October 1961, the new entrants began the four-year course for which curriculum had been readjusted as set down below:

NO. OF PERIODS FOR SUBJECT
(All periods 45 minutes each.)

Subject	1st Year	2nd Year	3rd Year	4th Year
Accountancy	–	–	–	2
Biblical ideas	2	–	–	–
Christian Doctrine	–	3(+1)	3(+1)	3
Church History	2	2	2	2
English	2	2	2	2
Comparative Religion	–	1	–	1
		3rd Term		
Greek	–(1)	–(2)	–(2)	–(1)
Homiletics	1	1	1	2
Music	1	1	1	1
N.T.	5	5	5	2
O.T.	4	4	4	2
Christian Ethics	1	1	1	–
Pastoralia	1	–	–	2
History of Worship	–	–	–	1
Devotional Life	1	–	–	–
Christian Education	–	–	–	1
Psychology	–	1	1	–
Philosophy	–	1	1	–
Vernacular	1	1	1	1
Total periods	21(+1)	23(+3)	22(+3)	22(+1)

Extra classes for Diploma course students in brackets.

Post-graduate students would take all the 4th year classes, with the possible exception of Christian Doctrine and Islam, depending on the course actually studied at the University. They would also take the class on the Devotional Life with the 1st year, and possibly Christian Ethics with the 2nd year (this part of the syllabus dealing with the application of Christian principles to contemporary problems in Ghana).[101]

The other change of importance in 1961 was the appointment from 1st September, of a new Principal, the Rev. Hugh E. Thomas, B.A., B.D., who unlike his predecessor, was a University graduate.

---

100 Trinity College, J.C. Minutes, 17th April, 1959.
101 Trinity College, G.B.M., 6th April, 1961 (its first meeting).

Finally, when the session opened in October 1961, the first set of graduate students, Peter A. Barker, B.A. and R.P. Nyako, B.D., were accepted for the Ministry of the Presbyterian Church of Ghana. Each occupied one of the third year students' rooms, but enjoyed greater freedom than the third year students:[102] they received Probationers' stipends of £300 (¢600) per annum[103] but paid for their own boarding, books and stationery. Mr. Nyako did some part-time teaching of Greek and Comparative Religion in the second year (three lectures per week). Both of them studied Pastoralia, Homiletics, Christian Ethics and Devotional Life plus Hebrew for Nyakc and a London B.D. Correspondence Course for Barker who also had tutorial help from the Principal.

Thus starting with recruits who had been teachers, catechists and local preachers in secular business, Trinity College had successfully experimented on post-graduate training in anticipation of its removal to the vicinity of the University at Legon.

At the end of June 1964, Trinity College was closed in Kumasi and the students went away on the long vacation which ended on Friday, 9th October, 1964. On that day, without any ceremonies, Trinity College was reopened in its new premises at Legon, near the University in Accra. The long anticipated aspiration of the sponsoring Churches had now materialised.

The fact that the transfer from Kumasi to Legon was feasible in October 1964 showed that the constructional work of the College buildings, which had been started early in the year, had progressed satisfactorily on schedule.[104]

Actually, the work had been advancing so well that, six months after it had been started, the Governing Body began to make arrangements for the official opening of the College. As early as July, the opening ceremony was fixed to take place on Saturday, 23rd January, and the Dedicatory Service on Sunday, 24th January, 1965.[105] By November, 1964 the arrangements for the opening had almost been completed and the Rev. Dr. J.F. Hopewell, the director of the T.E.F. had been invited to represent the Fund and to be one of the main speakers at the Opening Ceremony. The other speaker was to be the Rev. Dr. C.G. Baeta. As for the Dedicatory Service on the Sunday, 24th January, the Rev. Dr. J.R. Chandran of Bangalore had been invited to preach the sermon.[106]

The buildings and the arrangements, in connection with the opening of

---

102 *Ibid.*, Standing Committee and Governing Body Minutes, 23rd Nov., 1961.
103 *Ibid.*, 17th January, 1964, No. 189. Later the Governing Body resolved in 1964 "that the allowance for all post-graduate students should be £300 (¢600) p.a. with arrangements for boarding etc. as before; but that this allowance was not necessarily to be regarded as a Probationer's stipend."
104 See pp. 176-177.
105 Trinity College, G.B.M., 10th July, 1964, Nos. 203-219.
106 *Ibid.*, 6th November, 1964, Nos. 237-250.

the College proceeded without interruption and on 23rd January, 1965 "the Rev. Dr. James F. Hopewell, Director of the Theological Education Fund of the World Council of Churches [cut] a tape [and declared] open the new £120,000 (¢240,000) Trinity College of the Evangelical Presbyterian, the Methodist and the Presbyterian Churches of Ghana, at Legon."[107]

In his address Dr. Hopewell described the seminary as a centre of perception, of ecumenical insight and of service and concluded each theme with the following refrains, respectively:

> Trinity College dedicates its buildings today,
> And the World Church rejoices, and yet asks—
> Will this college accept the easy course, and allow
> Its new buildings to become a *Canning Factory*,
> Or will they become a centre of thinking
> Which finds contemporary relevances in eternal truth?
>
> Trinity College dedicates its buildings today,
> And the World Church rejoices, yet asks—
> Are these buildings to become only an *Airport Terminal*
> Which scans the skies and talks to faraway lands,
> Or are these buildings also to be centres of local perception
> Seeing clearly the local dimensions of universal issues?
>
> Trinity College dedicates its buildings today
> And the World Church rejoices, yet asks—
> Will these buildings be a palace which supports fancied prestige,
> Or will they be a centre of service,
> Faithful in its ministry to the Church?[108]

His address was followed by that of Dr. C.G. Baeta, of the University of Ghana. He stressed that for the students to derive the optimum advantage of their nearness to this University they needed bicycles which friends in Western Germany were prepared to supply to the College.[109] After emphasizing the need for a "tent making ministry", i.e. a pastoral ministry by people who were earning their income from a secular job, Dr. Baeta concluded by saying that if the future ministers would learn wisdom they would not try to do the whole of the work themselves; their business would be to see that the various organizations of the Church are kept running smoothly in order to perform the local task and finally it was the task of the ministers to continue growing in theological competence which meant

---

107 *Daily Graphic* (Accra), 25th January, 1965, p. 6.
108 Dr. J.F. Hopewell, "Address delivered at the opening ceremony of Trinity College, 23rd January, 1965". (In the possession of the owner and a xeroxed copy in the possession of the writer of this book.)
109 *Christian Messenger* (Accra), Vol. VI, No. 3, March 1965, p. 2. During my research visit to Trinity College in October and November 1968, the bicycles had not yet arrived. When I was in Bremen in March 1969, I enquired about them and I was informed by the Rev. P. Weigrabe that the matter had not been pursued again from Ghana.

knowing where the main issues lay, thinking of them continuously, maintaining good personal relationship with the Lord and helping others.[110]

The celebrations were rounded off with a Dedicatory Service, on 24th January, 1965, in the £9000 (¢18,000) Trinity College Chapel, during which the Rev. Dr. Russel Chandran, Chairman of the South India Theological College, Bangalore, and executive member of the World Council of Churches[111] preached the sermon.

So, in January 1965, Trinity College entered another era of development. Normal College activities proceeded without further excitement except that the first set of graduate students in the new Trinity College, had come in with the new entrants in October, 1964. They were A.K. Ofosuhene, B.A. (Hons.), Legon and B.K. Tetteh, B.A. (Hons.), Legon. They shared classes with the other students and the subjects they studied and the tutors who taught them were: Accountancy (Mr. J.K.A. Rockson, Methodist Church Office Treasurer), Christian Ethics, Christian Education and Pastoral Psychology (Dr. E. Grau, member of Staff), Devotional Life, History of Worship and Special Seminar on the Origins, Growth and Development of the Ecumenical Movement (the Principal), Homiletics and Pastoralia, (Rev. J.K. Andoh, member of Staff) and Principles and Practice of Youth Work (Mr. Pawelzik, part-time tutor). At the end of the academic year, the Principal sent the following report to the Governing Body about them:

> Both students expressed some dissatisfaction at the lack of practical pastoral work arranged for them, and the lack of variety in it. Preaching and pastoral work was in fact arranged, but 1964/65 was a very unfortunate year for this, when entirely new arrangements had to be made with local ministers and congregations. It should also be stressed that the staff was inadequate to deal with this situation, and that these arrangements had to be supervised by a member who may have been regarded by tnese students as no better qualified than themselves. But had there been a greater willingness to profit, both men should have profited more than they did.[112].

This report raised some of the vital problems that the new College would have to solve in order to encourage graduates to offer for training within its walls: first, there was the need for a scheme of work suitable for postgraduate training; second there was the need for adequate staff both in quality and quantity to cope with graduate work and third, there was the need for humility and sympathy on the part of the graduate students. In addition, there were also the problems of the allowance the graduate student would receive when in training and how he would be stationed by his Church after training.

---

110 *Loc. cit.*
111 *Daily Graphic*, 25th January, 1965, p. 6.
112 Trinity College, "Post-graduate work, 1964/65, Report on Ben K. Tetteh and K.A. Ofosuhene by the Principal", G.B.M. File.

There were other problems one would have liked to discuss in an investigation such as this, but because of lack of space and because they had already been discussed in the College Inspection Report in 1964[113] just before the College was transferred to Legon, it should suffice to indicate them only. They concerned: administration, adaptation of the curriculum to suit local conditions and needs, staff and their method of teaching, how students had been admitted, external examinations taken by the students and the Library.

During 22 years, 1943 to 1965, 160 students including three from British Cameroons and two from the Gambia, had passed through the walls of Trinity College.[114] Although trained as Christian Ministers, the products of Trinity had been called to a variety of offices in the State: great majority of them had remained pastors-in-charge of Circuits, Districts or congregations; a few of them had obtained University Degrees and had been serving as chaplains in the University, Secondary Schools and Colleges or as Headmasters of Secondary Schools or Principals of Training Colleges; a few had been permitted to serve as Chaplains to the Ghana Armed Forces (the Army and the Police Services); a few had entered Politics; some had resigned or had been withdrawn, by their Churches, from active ministry and a few had died.

Obviously, the influence of Trinity College has been felt in every vital stratum of Ghanaian society. As it moved from Kumasi to its new home, near the University at Legon, Trinity College would perhaps, have to face fresh opportunities, wider responsibilities and searching challenges. But whether or not its past students, in their various offices, have succeeded in identifying themselves with the problems of their flock, whether or not they have succeeded in contextualizing the Christian Faith, etc., are questions that may best be discussed in a subsequent Chapter.

---

113 Trinity College, G.B.M. This was the first inspection of the College during its life in Kumasi. It was conducted on 14th and 15th May, 1964, and the problems raised were intended for the guidance of the institution at its new home.
114 Appendix IX.

CHAPTER TWELVE

TOWARDS UNITED MISSIONS TRAINING: IMMANUEL THEOLOGICAL COLLEGE, IBADAN, 1958-1965

Immanuel College, Ibadan, in Nigeria, is a United Anglican and Methodist Theological Institution. It came into being in 1958 when two separate departments of Divinity were merged into one Theological Institution. These departments of Divinity had been run by the Church Missionary Society and the Wesleyan Methodist Mission respectively.

These missions in line with the missionary method of that period, established Elementary and Secondary Schools at the beginning of their evangelistic propaganda in Nigeria. But from about the 1880's the European missionaries who supervised these missions lost interest in them. The major reason was that the schools were not serving their evangelistic purpose. The missionaries had hoped that the brightest of the students would offer themselves for employment as Church workers. Unfortunately, from the missionary perspective, however, the most brilliant of the scholars concentrated more on secular education than the religious one.

Consequently, the missionaries became lukewarm about Elementary and Secondary Schools and decided to concentrate more on establishing Training Colleges where church personnel: evangelist/teachers might be trained specifically to help in the propagation of the Gospel. This change of policy was crucial because at the time the missionaries were losing their lives rapidly on the mission field and those who survived the climate had their own problems: it was difficult for the Mission Boards to maintain them satisfactorily away from home. Thus the idea of establishing training institutions for training local personnel was advantageous. In consequence, the C.M.S. established the Oyo Training Institution in 1896, later known as St. Andrew's College[1] and the Wesleyan Methodist Missionary Society also commenced Wesley College, Ibadan in 1905.

Prior to the establishment of the Oyo Training Institution, Africans who served the Church Missionary Society in Nigeria, were trained in Sierra Leone. Most of them were trained as school masters and catechists. Among them were Thomas King and T.B. MaCaulay who also had additional training in England. Later both men were ordained into the ministry of the C.M.S. at Abeokuta in 1854.

The first attempt to establish a local Training Institution by the C.M.S. in

---

1 E.A. Ayandele, *The Missionary Impact on Modern Nigeria 1824-1914. A Political and Social Analysis* (Longmans), p. 294.

Nigeria, was made in 1853 when the *Ake Institution* was established in Abeokuta,

> ... not to educate a few young gentlemen but to make a model, self supporting educational Institution by combining industrial labour with book learning.[2]

The first three Principals of this institution did not remain for long at their post to give the institution the desired character. Mr. Paley, the first Principal appointed in January, 1953, died in April; the Rev. T.B. MaCaulay, the second Principal 1853-1855 was removed in 1855 bcause "the instruction he gave the students was too academic".[3] The third Mr. William Kirham, 1855-1856, died within a year.

But from 1857 to 1864 when the next Principal, the Rev. G.F. Buhler, served the institution, the original purpose for establishing the school was partly implemented. Buhler neglected the industrial aspect of the training and concentrated mainly on general and theological education as illustrated in this report:

> I lay particular stress upon Scripture History to give them a good and practical knowledge of it; in general History, they were taught the History of Rome to Constantine; in Physical Geography, Europe; in Bible Geography, St. Paul's Missionary Journeys; in Arithmetic, fractions and application thereof; in reading, translation of verses or portions of whole chapters from English to Yoruba and vice versa.[4]

As the result of the thoroughness of Buhler's training, the following distinguished themselves (among others) as Nigerian Anglican Clergymen: Bishops Isaac Oluwole and Charles Phillips.

In 1864, unfortunately, Buhler died and once again the life of the institution began to decline due to lack of an effective replacement. Three years later, in 1867, the *Ake Institution* ceased to exist because the missionaries had to leave Abeokuta due to the persecution of the Christians.[5]

When the missionaries returned after the persecutions the institution was reopened in Lagos and designated the *C.M.S. Training Institution, Lagos.* The students went out first as teachers or catechists. After some period of service those who were found by the missionaries to possess a genuine vocation were selected as the need arose, and given additional training towards ordination into Holy Orders. Some of them were trained either in England at Islington or Highbury or in Freetown at Fourah Bay College. Others were trained locally at Sunday Schools or in a Mission House,

---

2 J. Olumide Lucas, *A History of Anglican Ministerial Training in Nigeria being an Abridged Edition of a lecture presented at the first Session of eighteenth Synod at Ijebu-Ode in May 1971*, p. 10.
3 *Ibid.*, p. 11.
4 *Loc. cit.*
5 Ayandele, *op. cit.*, pp. 9-10 includes further references on p. 9 footnote 1.

while they were "carrying on active service in the church and could be kept under observation".⁶

Bay 1890, the training had yielded substantial results: there were 40 Anglican ordained ministers, trained mainly in Sierra Laone and Nigeria as follows:

> Five at Islington, one at Highbury Training College; fourteen had been to Fourah Bay for longer or shorter periods; two to the Freetown Grammar School; six possessed no more than primary education; two went only to Sunday School. Besides the three products of the Abeokuta Training Institution, only two others had been trained wholly in Nigeria. One was Edward K. Buko, the son of Possu, from Golmer's boarding school at Badagri; the other was Daniel Olubi who had a few terms at the Abeokuta Training Institution but was trained mostly in the household of the Hinderers. And only these two last mentioned were not emigrants or sons of emigrants.⁷

The period 1891 to 1896 was one of extension for the C.M.S. mission in Nigeria. The Yoruba and Niger Missions merged in 1893 as the Diocese of Western Equatorial Africa after Crowther's death in 1891. As a result of the expansion of both Missions, there was the feeling that the Training Institution in Lagos should be expanded. Lagos, however, was too congested for that purpose. Consequently, a new site was acquired at Oyo, plans were made for the buildings to be put up and by the end of 1895 the *Lagos Institution* was closed down. The new institution, the *Oyo Training Institute*, commenced its life early in 1896.

The first period of the *Oyo Training Institute* extended from 1896 to 1919. The Principal during these 24 years, was the Rev. Frank Melville Jones. During the period he organized the institution in two sections: the normal section for the training of school teachers and the Theological division for the training of Church personnel—ministers and catechists. Generally, those who entered for the catechist training had poor educational background. In order to help them improve their educational standard, the catechists were separated from the ministerial candidates. A new catechists' training centre was opened at Akure where the students were trained to sit for the General Certificate of Education Examination as preparation towards their candidature for the ordained ministry.

The Divinity or Theological department at Oyo then became concerned with the training of only ministerial candidates. The course lasted two or three years depending on the academic standard at which each candidate was admitted. The curriculum followed included: Old Testament, New Testament, Theology, Church History, Traditional Religion, English Language, Greek, Christian Worship, Pastoralia, Ethics, Islam and Evangelistic Methods.

---

6 J.F.A. Ajayi, *Christian Missions in Nigeria 1841-1819: The Making of a New Elite.* (Longmans 1965).
7 *Loc. cit.*

At the end of their studies, the students took the Deacon's Orders Examination conducted by the Bishop's Examining Chaplains. The successful candidates were first admitted to the Diaconate by the Bishop. This was followed by a period of at most two years' probation after which they took another examination for admission into the priesthood.

The regime of Mr. Jones, as Principal of the *Oyo Training Institution*, ended in 1919 when he was appointed Bishop of Lagos at the end of that year. In appreciation of his devoted services as Principal and that of his wife, the students of the institution styled themselves Franciscan's (Frank & Frances).

During the next period, 1920-1947, the *Oyo Training Institution* made some significant changes. In the first place, the Rev. George Burton, the Vice-Principal since 1907, was appointed the new Principal. He was loved by most Africans among whom he worked because of the respect he, unlike some of the other expatriates, accorded them. As a practical demonstration of his respect for the African, he was ordained in 1908 by an African, the Rt. Rev. Isaac Oluwole, assistant Bishop of Lagos in St. Paul's Church, Breadfruit, Lagos.[8] The second change made was that the Divinity or Theological section of the institution was named Melville Hall in about 1927 in commemoration of the first Principal's, the Rev. Frank Melville Jones', devotion to the department.

Another significant change was that Melville Hall became affiliated with Durham University so that degrees could be offered locally in Arts and Theology on the same lines as Fourah Bay College in Sierra Leone. After the affiliation the Durham Licence in Theology was taken at Oyo and was followed with two academic years' course at Fourah Bay College leading to the award of an Arts degree in Theology. Those who took full advantage of the scheme were D.O. Awosika and G.A. Jadesimi. Both of them spent two years, 1928-1930 at Oyo for the Licence in Theology and 1930-1931 at Fourah Bay College. Later Awosika became the Bishop of Ondo and Jadesimi Assistant Bishop and Vicar General of Ibadan. The others D.R. Oyebode and I.O.S. Okusanya were at Oyo from 1929-1931 and at Fourah Bay College from 1931-1932. After their training Oyebode became Bishop of Ibadan and Okusanya succeeded Awosika as Bishop of Ondo.

After 1932, however, the scheme could not be continued because Durham revised its regulations and separate courses were offered for Licence in Theology and the Bachelor of Arts Degree respectively.

This change did not disrupt the ordinary ministerial training offered at Melville Hall. In 1937, however, Melville Hall, that is the Divinity or Theological department of the *Oyo Training Institution*, was transferred to Ondo under the care of Bishop Akinyele for one year because Burton

---

8 Other European missionaries would go back to England to be ordained by European Bishops.

went on leave during that period. In the following year, 1938, the work of the Principal was reorganized. He was no longer to be the head of the Divinity Department. Accordingly, a new head, Rev. S.J. Baggott was appointed and the post was designated Warden. This was the first time that the head of the Divinity department was so styled. With the appointment of the Warden at Oyo, Melville Hall was moved back from Ondo and it continued there until the end of the year, 1938.

In the following year, however, the ministerial training was suspended for the whole year because during the first half of the year the Warden was away on furlough. When he returned to the institution during the second half of the year, he was appointed the Acting Principal when Burton also went away on leave.

By 31st January, 1940, things became normal: the Principal, who had returned from furlough and Baggott had reverted to their posts respectively and Melville Hall was reopened with ten students. The ministerial training continued at Oyo until 1943 when the Warden the Rev. S.J. Baggott resigned.

The exact circumstances leading to the resignation have not been articulated in the records. But it is clear from the documents used that the resignation was sudden and troublesome to the Diocese. For example, between May 10 and 16, 1943, the third session of the Eighth Synod of the Diocese of Lagos met at Lagos. The Bishop gave a charge during which the problem of Baggott's resignation was enunciated in these words:

> The resignation of the Rev. S.J. Baggott from the Wardenship of Melville Hall has therefore come at a very awkward time for us. It is hardly likely that a successor will arrive before the end of the year and meanwhile we felt that training could not be delayed. Accordingly, we have moved Melville Hall to Lagos.[9]

So ministerial training was once more located in Lagos. The lectures were given by some of the ministerial staff in Lagos and the Rev. H.N. Hunter acted as the Bursar.

Meanwhile another Ministerial Training Centre was opened at the *Awka College* in the East. This was motivated by the fact that, at that time, the large Diocese of Western Equatorial Africa was divided into two: the Diocese of Lagos and that of the Niger. The new training centre at Awka was therefore established to cater for the training of ministerial candidates in the Niger Diocese. The centre was run along the lines of Melville Hall. In the course of time, however, it was united with the Methodists and Presbyterians to form a United Theological Training College at Umuahia, designated Trinity College.[10]

---

9 Melville Hall, "Log Book, Starting January 1941", p. 13.
10 The history of this institution will not be pursued because a detailed study of a joint Anglican and Methodist with Presbyterian Training in Ghana, Trinity College, Legon, has been discussed elsewhere in these studies.

The distinctive Anglican training continued in Lagos until the end of 1946. In 1947, the training was transferred from Lagos to Ibadan because the University of Ibadan was being established and this inspired the Anglican Church to move their Ministerial Training College to the University environment.

The site selected was the Kudeti Church Compound which had been used as the C.M.S. Headquarters in Ibadan. The transfer to this location "thus gave the Hall the distinctiveness of being on its own site and located in a University town with its academic atmosphere".[11]

The story of the *Wesleyan Methodist Section of Immanuel College* may be summarised as follows: unlike the Anglicans, the Wesleyan Methodist mission did not provide any institution for the training of teachers and evangelists in Nigeria in the nineteenth century. In 1900, however, Mr. Findlay, the secretary of the W.M.M.S. visited the Nigeria District. He commented severely upon the absence of training institutions in the District. As a result of his recommendations a Methodist training institution, *Wesley College, Elekuro*, was opened in Ibadan in 1905.

The original purpose was to train teachers who would teach in the schools after having passed the Government Teacher's Certificate Examination. At the initial stages, no evangelists were trained in the institution. But in 1923 a department for the training of catechists was introduced by the Principal, the Rev. E.G. Nightingale B.D. to train men who would be,

> capable of conducting the little village school during the week and of leading the worship of the congregation of Sunday and supplying its religious wants. They [would] be pastors and school masters in one....[12]

This department was further enlarged when a Divinity class was added to prepare candidates for the ordained ministry. Thus Wesley College, Ibadan, was developed into an Institution, rendering to the Methodist Church, "the service which the CMS St. Andrew's College at Oyo [was] performing so efficiently for the Anglican Church of the Lagos Diocese."[13]

The foundation students of the Divinity department were D.O. Kanmi Ologunde, J.O.E. Soremekun, A.T. Ola Olude, A.O. Orekoya, Samuel Ekundare and Samson T. Solaru.

By 1923 when Wesley College, Ibadan, celebrated its 21st Anniversary, the College was able, for the first time in its history, "to have school teachers, catechists, subpastors and ministers, all in training at the same time".[14] The staff were satisfied "to find that the normal students as well as those

---

11 J. Olumide Lucas, *A History of Anglican Ministerial Training in Nigeria. An Inaugural Lecture.* (The Nigerian Baptist Theological Seminary 1971) p. 13.
12 Rev. Edgar, W. Thompson and Sir Arthur Black, *Wesleyan Methodist Mission in West Africa.* Report of Official visit 1921-1922 (WMMS. Lon. n.d.) p. 27.
13 *Loc. cit.*
14 Methodist Church Nigeria, *Annual Report* 1926, p. 15.

marked down for Evangelistic work [were] showing great enthusiasm for carrying the Gospel to the heathen".[15]

After 1925 the Divinity department of Wesley College grew from strength to strength until by 1934 the organization of the Theological department became distinctly marked out into three: Divinity class for the ordinands, teacher/catechist class and the subpastors' class.[16]

In 1935 the Principal of Wesley College the Rev. E.G. Nightingale retired and was succeeded by the Rev. W.E. Hodges. Under him also,

> the work of training ministers, subpastors and teachers [went] steadily forward with a very fair measure of visible success.[17]

The theological students pursued the traditional theological subjects together with school method since most of them would precede their ordination with teaching.

Under Mr. Hodges there was steady and uninterrupted growth except that in 1952 training in the Divinity class was suspended and the two students in residence were transferred to Umuahia in the East because their tutor, the Rev. Roberts, had left Wesley College for good in 1951 and he was not replaced immediately. The students D.O. Babatope and E.A.O. Idowu remained at Umuahia for two years. In their second year, that is, in 1953, the Rev. C.T. Day succeeded Rev. Roberts and went to teach at Umuahia. In the following year, in 1954, Rev. Day returned to Wesley College, Ibadan and with the new Divinity students admitted for 1954 reopened the Divinity class there. The training for the ministry continued at Wesley College until the end of 1956. In the following year the Divinity students of Wesley College were transferred to Melville Hall at the Kudeti site, Ibadan to join the Anglican students in preparation towards the establishment of a Joint Anglican and Methodist Theological College in Ibadan.

Negotiations had been going on since 1940 between the Anglicans and Methodists for that purpose. The preliminary conversations lasted five years, 1940-1945, during which some far reaching agreements were made. In the first place, the consensus was that the two training institutions should

---

15 *Ibid.*, 1922, p. 12.
16 A note on Subpastors: Subpastors were trained as catechists but they were also taught teaching method and at the end of their four year studies sat a Higher Elementary Certificate Examination. This was the Teachers' Certificate Examination which was first taken by the 1937-1940 subpastors' class. Those who were successful proceeded to a fifth year course to study specifically Theological subjects.

At the time when the Higher College, Yaba in Lagos and Achimota College, Accra, were preparing students for the Inter. B.Sc of London University, Wesley College, Ibadan had already been preparing students for the Inter. B.D. of London University.

The Nigerian lecturers who backed and taught the Inter. B.D. course at Wesley College were the Rev. J.O.E. Seremekun and T.T. Solaru.

The students who derived benefit from the Inter B.D. Scheme included Prof. E.B. Idowu (Patriarch Bolaji), G.O. Orekoya, E.A. Adeolu Adegbola and D.O. Omotunde.
17 Methodist Church Nigeria, *Annual Report*, 1935.

be merged and that the Methodists Divinity students at Wesley College should be moved to the spacious Kudeti side. Secondly, it was agreed that each of the co-operating bodies should provide its own share of the required buildings, equipment, staffing and general maintenance of the institution.

No definite action was taken to implement these agreements until 1952. On 22nd February that year, the Methodist Synod which met in Lagos approved, in principle, the recommendation that Melville Hall and the Divinity section of Wesley College should be developed into a United Theological College as Bishop Neill had suggested in 1950.[18] The matter was then referred by the Methodists to the Anglican Vicar General's Board. Consequently, the negotiations were revived and in 1956, on 13th December, a Joint Theological Committee met in Lagos. They recommended that a meeting should be arranged between the Melville Hall Board and the Methodist Ordination Training Committee to set up a Governing Body for the Joint Theological College.

In response, the Anglicans met in March 1957 and firmly decided:

1. To unite fully with Wesley College (ordination training) from January 1958.
2. To extend the present two-year course to three years from January 1958.
3. To pay an allowance to students from January 1958. £2,000 voted for this purpose for 1958.
4. To have entrance examination week for September. During this period the candidates should reside at Melville Hall for 3 days.[19]

This was followed by a joint meeting of the Anglican and Methodist Ministerial Training Committee. They decided that:

1. The Joint Training should commence in 1958.
2. The proposed Governing Body should be formed and should have its first meeting on 1st August 1957.
3. The Methodists should supply two members of staff and pay half of the cost of building the new College.[20]

The Governing Body met according to schedule and agreed that the College should be called "*IMMANUEL COLLEGE*" (so spelt) although no reason was recorded for choosing the name itself. In addition, it was decided that in order to avoid the idea that one party was stronger than the other, the capital costs should always be borne 50:50; that the running costs should, however, be treated on pro rata basis. This meant that the running costs to be paid by either party would be determined by the number of students belonging to each party.[21]

The next Governing Body meeting took place on 10th October, 1957 at

---

18 Neill, *Report. op. cit.*, 1950.
19 Melville Hall, "Log Book" 1957, March 19, p. 140.
20 *Loc. cit.*
21 This information was given by the Principal in 1976.

Melville Hall, Kudeti. At this meeting, plans to go ahead with the United College were confirmed and a working committee was appointed and charged to find suitable site for the new buildings. The working committee performed its duty without delay and on 31st January 1958 the United College was opened at the Kudeti site with 66 students: 55 Anglicans and 11 Methodists.

The pioneer members of staff were four Anglicans: the Rev. Canon David Anderson, the Rev. E.O. Idowu, the Rev. F.F. Foulkes and the Rev. J. Simonson. The Methodists were two: the Rev. C.T. Day and the Rev. S.G. Williamson.[22]

The Inaugural Service was held in St. David's Kudeti, Ibadan, on 14th February 1958, at 4 p.m. Among the congregation were His Excellency the Governor and Lady H.H. Randkim, the Olubadan of Ibadan, Church representatives, students from the Theological College Umuahia with their Principal and the Rev. Joe Wood and the Professor A.D. Galloway of the University College of Ibadan preached the sermon and the benediction was pronounced by the Bishop of Ibadan. Simultaneously, with the service in Ibadan another service of prayer and thanksgiving was held at the Church Missionary House, London for the success of the new ecumenical venture at theological education in West Africa.

One of the most alarming problems after the inauguration concerned expenditure. In 1959 the cost of running the college surprisingly shot up. In 1958 the running cost was £6,754 but in 1959 it was £8,409 excluding the missionary staffs' salaries. The factors which contributed to this distressing increase were attributed to the following circumstances: the great number of students admitted in 1959, payment of the students' allowances, the transfer of houses and equipment to the new college which became responsible for their maintenance and the rising costs. One way out of this problem was that the principal appealed, in 1960, to the Theological Education Fund (T.E.F.) for funds. The T.E.F. responded favourably and promised to give $2,000.00 worth of new books to the Library to be chosen from a Catalogue compiled by the T.E.F. for the purpose.

In the following year i.e. in 1961, the T.E.F. agreed to give $100,000.00 towards the construction cost of the permanent buildings of *Immanuel College* with certain strings attached. For example, a Savings Account: "Immanuel College Building Fund" should be opened by the Governing Body and an appeal fund should be set up. This fund was set up and inaugurated, at a Garden Party, in the College on 6th April, 1961. Although the weather was inclement and attendance small, the C.M.S. and M.M.S. London promised to give £10,000 each to the building fund.

Another significant problem was that the Kudeti site was found to be no longer suitable. It was not large enough for future expansion of the Institu-

---

22 *Ibid.*

tion. Consequently, a new and large piece of land was leased from the Government at the Ibadan Eduation Zone, adjacent to the University College, now the University of Ibadan. This site was chosen because:

> It was felt that dormitorial nearness to the university would be an advantageous factor, facilitating contact and co-operation with the University.[23]

Having satisfactorily dealt with these problems, the Governing Body authorised the construction of the new buildings at the new site. The work progressed so fast that in September, 1964, the college moved to its present site near the University of Ibadan,

> surrounded by various other educational institutions, including an international Secondary school, a Technical College, a Community Development Women's Training Centre and the Institute of Church and Society of the Christian Council in Nigeria. There are also a Remand Home, Cheshire Home for handicapped children and a Home for the Young Deaf.[24]

This educational climate of the environment has had its impact on the life of the college. For example,

> the academic standard of the college both for admission and at the conclusion of the course, has risen considerably. The course which was formerly a two year course was increased to a three year course. The curriculum, which includes nearly all the subjects prescribed for the Diploma in Theology of London University, (comprises) the following subjects: Old Testament, New Testament, Biblical and Historical Theology, Church History, Christian Worship, the Prayer Book, the 39 Articles, Ethics, Islam, Traditional Religion, Pastoralia, English Language, Evangelistic Methods, Music and simple Accounting.[25]

Subjects such as Greek and Latin were optional for the students who were training just for ordination but compulsory for these who wished to obtain the College Diploma in Theology in addition to the Certificate of Proficiency at the end of the course.

The academic standards of the college have further been enhanced because the college has close links with the University of Ibaban as shown below. The structure of the courses has now been patterned along the following lines: the ordinands' course still lasts three years, the first two years being devoted to the preparation of the ordinands for the External Diploma of the Department of Religious Studies of Ibadan University. Lecturers from UI are also employed as guest lecturers, in some of the subjects such as Philosophy of Religion and Sociology. They also act as external examiners for the College Diploma in Theology. The students' association with the University students' organization and their attendance at the University

---

23 Lucas, *Inaugural Lecture, op. cit.* p. 14.
24 Immanuel College Ibadan, *Prospectus 1970,* p. 10.
25 Lucas, *Inaugural Lecture, loc. cit.*

open lectures may continue to strengthen the academic standard of the College.

During the third year, practical training is emphasised. The students, once in that year, have missions to various areas in the country. The time of the missions is determined by the convenience of both the college and the receiving church. But during the long vacation in August and September the students are distributed normally to their home areas.

In addition to academic pursuit and practical work, the students organize extracurricula activities:

> Two afternoons per week are set aside for sports: there are facilities for volleyball, tenniquoits and football. In-door games, especially table-tennis, are played more often. Occasionally, football or table-tennis matches are played against other institutions in Ibadan. At the annual Sports Day, though track events are impossible, field events and various tournaments are held. All this is organized by the student Sports' Officer in consultation with a member of staff.[26]

There are other spare-time activities such as the student Christian Movement of Nigeria and the Boys' Brigade Officer Company.

This account cannot be ended without reference to the real centre of the life of the College. This is the Chapel. It is here that "Worship expresses and creates the united fellowship"[27] of the institution. Worship is offered every morning and evening in the week. The Holy Communion, the central act of the Christian worship, is celebrated weekly when a sermon is preached. The type of liturgy used is determined by the officiant for each occasion. That is the liturgy used by the officiant's denominational tradition is followed by him.

Other important features of the College worship include the use of hymn books belonging to both co-operating churches, the observance of the Methodist Covenant Service at the beginning of the year, a Valedictory Service for out-going students at the end of each session, a Quiet Day observed each year and normally led by a visiting speaker "with deep spiritual resources" from any denomination.

Finally, the chapel functions to some extent as a Parish Church and provides an opportunity for in-service training under the supervision of the Principal assisted by a staff Chaplian to the chapel and students who serve and observe. The chapel congregation engages in evangelistic work, community development in a neighbouring village and family worship services are held as the need arises.

The inside of the chapel is simple but attractively decorated thus:

> Round the wall of the chapel are eight panels of wood-carving on "The Way of the Cross" executed by one of [the] old students. A plain wooden cross, made

---

26 Immanuel College, Ibadan, *Prospectus 1970*, p. 12.
27 *Ibid.*, p. 10.

from two pieces of wood saved from the CMS house built in Lagos in the Last Century, dominates the internal view of the Chapel.[28]

In addition to these acts of worship in the chapel the students have daily private devotion and Bible study in their rooms, and also run a Sunday School for the College.

We may conclude this story with the following opinion:

> The setting up of Immanuel College and the decision taken from the start to site it adjacent to a University expresses the intention to constitute it a "Theological College." Or, in other words, the founding of Immanuel College in 1958 and its ultimate move in 1964 to the site adjacent to the University of Ibadan must mean for it the rising of theological academic standards from what they were in the early '40s.[29]

In 1964 the College practically demonstrated its intention of up-grading theological education in Nigeria by its transfer to a University Environment. This is a challenge which the training tomorrow will have to reckon with.

---

28 *Ibid.*, p. 11.
29 *Ibid.*, p. 9.

CHAPTER THIRTEEN

AN APPRAISAL

In this chapter an attempt will be made to examine in greater depth some of the basic problems raised in this survey, but not adequately analysed in the historical sections, and then a conclusion will be drawn either justifying or disapproving of the demand that the training of the clegry in West Africa should be reformed.

It has been shown in the preceding chapters that the main objective of the Missions in establishing Theological Institutions in Africa was to train a number of African assistants to help in evangelizing the indigenous population, using exactly the same methods employed in the missionaries' home for evangelizing Westerners. Within the limits of this aim, the training has yielded good results. During a period of over one hundred and twenty-five years many African ministers were ordained. Through sacrifice, obedience and intense loyalty to Jesus Christ, they helped the missionaries to spread the new faith—as the missionaries comprehended it—among the indigenous people. Thus, from very small beginnings along the coast, many mission stations were planted all over English speaking West Africa.

But when we consider that in 1962, using Ghana to represent the general West African situation, each of the 300 active ministers was in charge of approximately 4,000 men, women and children, then it becomes indisputable that the training did not entirely succeed in producing an adequate number of ministers.[1] The seriousness of this ratio is alarming when we recall that in addition to his normal pastoral duties, the minister or priest, during the period of this investigation, was grossly overburdened with the

---

1 These figures were collected from: Kenneth Grubb, *World Christian Handbook, 1962* (London, 1962) and Church Reports for 1962. Grubb's statistics were incomplete in respect of some of the Denominations listed below, and had been supplemented by the relevant statistics recorded in the Annual Reports.

Total Christian Community—(Ghana) in 1962		No. of Ministers
Anglican	50,000	46
E.P. Church	85,802	43
Methodist Church	159,254	91
Presbyterian Church	207,652	83
Roman Catholic	655,138	57
	1,157,846	320*

*allowing about 20 for administrative work, 300 were in charge of congregations.

management of schools in his Circuit or District or Diocese. The position becomes even more disquieting when it is learnt "that in the United States of America and other countries in the West a pastor can expect to serve a Church community of only about 200 souls".[2] The point of all these considerations is that the recruitment of men for theological training in West Africa had not kept pace with the growth of Church membership.

It has been pointed out earlier in this survey, that from the pioneer days of the training, the lack of vocation was one of the major problems which hindered the progress of the Institutions. Two reasons were given as the factors that contributed to the difficulty. As regards the non-Roman Catholic Missions it was mainly the economic attraction of commerce that prevented young men from offering themselves for the Christian Ministry. But concerning the Roman Catholic training the idea of celibacy was the major factor which dissuaded candidates from persevering to the priesthood.

In recent years, however, additional reasons have been adduced to explain why recruitment to the ministry has been declining all over the world.[3]

The A.A.C.C. had grappled with the problem and given one main reason why people have not been offering themselves for the Christian ministry in Africa. According to them recruitment has been declining because "the economic position of the pastor in the community has deteriorated"[4] as a result of the Church's failure to care for her own ministers.[5] This point of view has been confirmed by Dr. Hopewell in these words:

> The problem of financial support of the ministry is therefore equally acute. Whether or not we approve of the concept, the fact persists that the worth of a man and his work is generally measured by the salary he commands.... If the image of the minister is a devalued one, then the support he can expect is equally diminished. The reverse is also true. If a minister receives an inadequate salary, then he can expect his image as a man of value to be recognized only by that small segment in society which knows how to judge a man by less material standards.[6]

The impression given by scholars on the problem of inadequate financial support for the Christian ministry may be summed up thus: "The salary paid him (the minister), while possibly once adequate, now is only a fraction of that paid men of comparable training in Government, Commerce or school teaching".[7]

---

2 James Hopewell, *The Crisis of the Christian Ministry in Africa Part I*, (Enugu, 1965), p. 2. (Hereafter cited as Hopewell), *The Crisis*.
3 Literature enumerated in the bibliography on Ministerial Training confirms that the problem is not peculiar to Africa.
4 A.A.C.C., *The Crisis in the Christian Ministry in Africa*, (Kitwe, 1964), p. 2. Hereafter cited as A.A.C.C., *The Christian Ministry*.
5 *Loc. cit.*
6 Hopewell, *The Crisis, op. cit.*, p. 5.
7 *Loc. cit.*

This assertion might be valid in other parts of Africa and the world; but it did not correspond with the position in West Africa. Reasonable parity had been maintained between the salaries of ministers and men of comparable training for example, in the teaching profession, during the period of inquiry. A few representative non-Roman Catholic instances taken from Ghana might illustrate this point. At the beginning of the Twentieth Century the minimum salary of the ministers in the E.P. Church was £24 (¢48.00) per annum,[8] while that of teachers was about £20-£30 (¢40.00-¢60.00) per annum, according to the grade of the certificate obtained by the teacher.[9] In the 1920's the minimum salary of Methodist Ministers was £80 (¢160.00) for an unmarried man and £100 (¢200.00) married, per annum,[10] and that of teachers was about £100 (¢200.00) per annum.[11] In the early 1960s the salary scale of teachers was revised as follows: Pupil Teachers (untrained Standard VII certificated teachers) £144-£180 (¢288-¢360) per annum; Certificate A (Post Primary) £250-£475 (¢500-¢950) per annum. Certificate A (Post Secondary) £300-£490 (¢600-¢980) per annum, and Senior Teachers, £500-£700 (¢1,000-¢1,400) per annum.[12]

During the same peirod the salary scale of Trinity College trained ministers (their standard of education was equivalent to that of the Certificate A Teachers) was as follows:

Presbyterian Ministers:
Trinity trained   £300-£500 (¢600-¢1,000) per annum.
Graduate   £348-£500 (¢960-¢1,000) per annum.
Methodist Ministers:
Trinity trained   £230-£500 (¢460-¢1,000) per annum.
Graduate   One increment of £20 (¢40) for each year of training beyond the normal three-year theological training at Trinity. Thus a minister entering on his work for the first time with one year post-Trinity training received a minimum salary £250 (¢500) instead of £230 (¢460) per annum.[13]

In addition, the minister's rent, light, conservancy and water were free, in the sense that he did not pay these expenses from his salary. But the teachers did not have any allowances for these items. In view of the evidence it is obvious that the clergy were better provided for than the teachers. The only exception was that the disparity between the salary scale of a lay graduate teacher and that of a graduate minister was so vast that it was

---

8 B.M.A., Salary Scale of African Ministers, revised in 1899. (Kept in an uncatalogued envelop containing miscellaneous papers on the Gold Coast.)
9 McWilliam, *The Development of Education, op. cit.*, p. 47.
10 M.M.S. G.C.D.S.M. 1920, p. 22.
11 McWilliam, *op. cit.*, p. 65. Marriage did not determine the salary scale of teachers.
12 *Ibid.*, pp. 106-107.
13 Trinity College, O.C.M. 40-58, 13th December, 1957. The Roman Catholic ministers' salary has not been discussed since they did not receive salaries.

not surprising that some graduate ministers left circuit work for the teaching profession where the lay graduate had a minimum salary of £680 (₡1,360) per annum.

Thus it might be suggested that the lack of vocation among Post-Primary Certificate A and Post-Secondary Certificate A teachers during the period of investigation was not due entirely to the differences between the salary scales of teachers and ministers. The main deterrent among non-Roman Catholics, was apparently, the irregularity with which the ministers received their stipends. Generally, they collected dues from their members, and from the proceeds paid themselves and other expenses of the circuits, districts or dioceses. If the members did not pay their dues, the ministers did not have their stipends. Sometimes, as mentioned in Chapter VI above, the arreas owed to the ministers made their position precarious. Above all, the meagre pension received by ministers on superannuation was so inadequate that the last days of most retired ministers were spent in abject poverty. Thus it was not easy that this type of insecurity could attract people (they might be very good people) to offer themselves for the Christian ministry.

To the A.A.C.C. suggestion might be added two other factors that contributed to the lack of vocation among young men of good general education in recent years. They were: the poorer educational standard of most of the non-Roman Catholic ministers[14] and the disparaging image some people had been holding about the clergy. In the pioneer days and even until the 1940s the clergyman was one of the most respected personalities in West Africa and the Christian ministry used to be a favoured profession which commanded an enviable prestige. The reason is simple: in those days the recruits for the ministry were among those who received the highest education available in their countries—post-elementary education. They were among the most brilliant and well-behaved boys of their age; it was the prospective candidates who learnt Greek, Latin and Hebrew; and the prospective ordinands were among the very first Africans in modern times who "shared in the prestige and the magic of the new knowledge and power brought in by white men".[15]

But after 1950 this image had changed considerably. To some people it was those "who had failed to get into secondary schools"[16] and wanted to get an employment "above that of a labourer or subsistence farmer but who were not competent to obtain a 'white collar' job",[17] that offered for the Christian ministry. Others thought of the minister as a legalistic and unsympathetic executor of Church Laws. This concept about the minister

---

14 All the students who entered the major seminaries should have done two years' Sixth Form studies and taken the 'A' Level examination in at least two subjects. See Chapters VIII and IX.
15 M. Searle Bates, et. al., *Survey of the Training of the Ministry in Africa Part II* (London, 1954), p. 40.
16 Hopewell, *The Crisis, op. cit.*, p. 4.
17 *Ibid.*, p. 8.

and his work had developed from the exercise of moral discipline by the clergy in the past. At the time that almost all schools were under mission control and supervision, teachers who lapsed sexually were dismissed by the ministers, apparently without much sympathy. There were others whose image of the clergyman had been described by an observer from the Cameroon as follows:

> The pastor is a man who lives outside the current of life; he is the guardian of the legalistic discipline of the Church; the Church itself resembles a European civilization which destroyed African practices. The Pastor is a figure of authority.... He is a man whose personal development has been slower than that of the world around him.[18]

To other observers represented by a critic from Uganda,

> the ordained minister's work seems to be the work for an old man. There is little in the work, as he sees it, to attract a young man. Because of his life, a minister seems to lose contact with the people.[19]

It seems from these examples that the derogatory reputation which the ministry has acquired is not peculiar to West Africa alone. It is irrelevant to question the validity of the impressions quoted. What is important is that they indicate that lack of ministerial prestige, whatever be the cause, can exercise a detrimental effect on the recruitment of the right type of candidates for the ministry.

The factors that had led to the development of the vilifying image of the clergy might be briefly summarised thus:

> The recruitment of men with a low level of education has, in many cases, had a serious detrimental effect on the image of the ministry and has discouraged young educated men from looking further into the ministry as a possible calling of God for them.[20]

It might also be observed that the Denominations themselves had contributed to the lack of vocation. Serious confrontation has not been made by the non-Roman Catholic Churches with the young people in the higher institutions of learning about the need for well educated young men in the Christian ministry. It is in this respect that effective chaplaincy work in the institutions of higher learning cannot be exaggerated. Parents should also be reminded to pray for and encourage their sons to respond to the "Call" to enter into the Christian ministry.

Concerning the question of over coming the problem of the lack of vocation among well educated young men, many suggestions have been made from various quarters. But they may all be summed up briefly in the words of a recruiting team which visited various secondary schools in East Africa:

---

18 *Ibid.*, p. 5.
19 *Loc. cit.*
20 *Ibid.*, p. 4. Citing from comments made in a Conference held in Uganda in 1964 on the recruitment of Candidates for the ministry.

The amount of interest shown in training for the ordained ministry by educated young men in the institutions visited was tremendous, once they realized that the Church needed the service of its members who are of the younger generation. While a strong interest is not the same thing as a real sense of vocation and a willingness to plunge into the ordained ministry in East Africa with all its financial insecurity, this interest cannot be without significance. From seeing it so often and so plainly, I am driven to the conclusion that the Church is just making excuses when it is claimed that the educated younger generation is not interested in training for the ministry.... When one has the experience, for example, of seeing 10% of the boys of one secondary school voluntarily attended four successive meetings in 24 hours, in order to hear about the ordained ministry, one cannot but believe that the real trouble is that the challenge is not presented to them regularly, and that they are not normally told that people like themselves are needed for the ministry of the Church.[21]

These findings are also true of schools in West Africa.

The crux of the matter then seems to be that the Churches through their Chaplains in the higher institutions of learning should make constant and determined efforts to bring the problem of the lack of ministers vis-a-vis the students. A recent example from Achimota School in Accra will reinforce the significance of school chaplains in relation to the recruitment problem.

Achimota is the foremost Government Secondary School in Ghana. Towards the end of our period of investigation its enrolment was over 800 scholars, boys and girls from all denominations in the country. In the academic year 1964/65 there were four Chaplains (an Anglican, a Methodist, a Presbyterian and a Roman Catholic) in the school. One of the Chaplains very much concerned about the lack of secondary students offering themselves for the ministry conducted an experiment with the permission of the Headmaster. Briefly, a local preachers' band was formed and during the years 1964/65 and 1965/66, 16 students, including girls, sat for a local preacher's examination, and three of the boys, one from a lower class and two from the Upper Sixth Form, expressed intense desire to offer themselves for the Ordained Ministry.

It is gratifying to note that the Roman Catholics in West Africa and other parts of Africa had been more ardent in their desire to recruit mainly secondary school scholars for the ministry, and as shown in Chapters VIII & IX their efforts had been rewarding in spite of the drop-outs.[22] The question which the non-Roman Chatholic Churches under discussion in this inquiry should answer without any hypocrisy is as follows: "Did the older men in the ministry sincerely wish to recruit young secondary scholars

---

21 Hopewell, *The Crisis, op. cit.*, p. 8.
22 *Ibid.*, p. 7, points out that in Uganda whereas the Roman Catholics had 250 men in senior seminaries in 1964/65 the Anglicans had only two ordinands studying on the postsecondary school level. In Tanzania 200 Roman Catholics were in senior seminaries, while only 12 ordinands in all the Protestant seminaries were studying at a similar level during the same period.

into their ranks?[23] So much for the result of the training in relation to the expansion of the Church and the adequacy of the number of ministers trained.

The next few paragraphs will now be devoted to assessing the impact the programmes followed had made. The primary task of the training in relation to the content of the curricula was to provide the student (as is done in most seminaries in the Western countries) with the following: adequate education in theology, community formation, that is "the deepening of a man's prayer and commitment and self-knowledge in a way that is integrated with his growing grasp of the theology"[24] and an adequate foundation of practical and professional training. Or in other words it aimed at providing the tools that would enable the students to interpret the Holy Scriptures, the Creeds of the Christian faith and the History of the Church in direct confrontation with the students' personal spiritual life. The subjects taught were not different from those taught in seminaries elsewhere in the world, because as Sundkler has said, theological subjects are neither primarily western, nor conventional, but "they are part of the heritage of the Catholic Church".[25] Thus if theological training in West Africa or elsewhere "is to be faithful to the true interest of the Church [it] dares do nothing less than transmit that heritage".[26] Within the limits of this definition the heritage had been faithfully transmitted to the students trained in the various seminaries by the missionaries.

But this should not mean that the minister, in his attempt to guard the heritage transmitted to him, should "evade the tensions and problems of the society in which he ministers. He must feel the full force of the many bewildering and practical problems which confront the members of his congregation".[27] He should interpret the heritage in the local thought forms, making use of local values to inspire a more intelligible interpretation of the faith. At the same time he should bear in mind the standpoint of the Gospel which should be drastically differentiated from Western interpretations, patterns and accretions if they are present.

It is in this context that the content of the programmes pursued did not make the desired impact. During the over 125 years, that the various

---

23 The following incident may partially illustrate the validity of this question. In 1928, the question was raised in the Synod held by the Presbyterian Church of the Gold Coast, whether younger men should be recruited for ordination as soon as they left the seminary. But "surprise was caused by the question, and with little discussion it was agreed to adhere to the present practice of ordaining only approved catechists chosen by the Synod Committee". Cf. P.C.G., *Scottish Mission Reports*, 1928, p. 59.
24 B.S. Mass, et. al., *Theological Colleges for Tomorrow*, (London, 1968), p. 3.
25 Sundkler, *The Christian Ministry in Africa, op. cit.*, p. 190.
26 *Loc. cit.* But this heritage, Sundkler forgets, could be coloured by the social background and philosophy of the agents giving the training.
27 Norman Goodall and E.W. Nielsen, *The Survey of the Training of the Ministry in Africa Part III*, (London, 1954), pp. 41-42. (Hereafter cited as Goodall and Nielsen, *The Training of the Ministry.*)

theological institutions trained their ministers, the students learnt facts related to the Christian faith and heritage handed down over the years; but they had not been able, as shown below to apply intelligibly the knowledge acquired to West Africa's cultural background and social and political issues.

A few examples will substantiate this point. In talking about the relevance of the curricula the missionaries used in their primary schools David Kimble wrote with reference to Ghana, that

> little attempt seems to have been made to adapt the method of teaching to local conditions; the syllabus, too, was almost entirely [Western] in origin.[28]

This remark about primary education was also true generally, of theological education. The seminaries were controlled by Westerners who transmitted the core curricula with Western interpretation, accretions and prejudices. Indeed, the missionaries who came to West Africa regarded, in the words of Mary Kingsley,

> the African minds as so many jugs, which had only to be emptied of the stuff which is in them and refilled with the particular form of doctrine they, the missionaries, are engaged in teaching. . . .[29]

Moved sincerely by the social and philanthropic aspirations of their age, the missionaries set out with a conviction that they had a divine obligation to save brutal and degraded savages from error's chain.

In pursuit of this goal, most of the missionaries, until quite recently, made persistent efforts to prune African culture and "to assimilate Africans to the assumptions, values and practices of the Christian West".[30]

A few examples may suffice to illustrate how the African ministers and lay men who attempted to exercise personal judgements on cultural and national issues contrary to the expectations of the missionaries were dismissed. In 1894, the Rev. R.S.B. Solomon founded and edited the Gold Coast Methodist Times. Mr. Solomon made the paper quickly become popular by its successful handling of the Lands Bill agitation. In 1897 the Methodist Synod expressed misgivings about the fact that Mr. Solomon concerned himself with temporal affairs. As a result of further pressure brought to bear upon him by the Chruch for his exercise of personal judgement in national affairs Mr. Solomon had to resign. About the same time, at the turn of the nineteenth century, Mr. Yoyovi was dismissed by the Bremen Mission because he wrote about the need for re-examining the polygamy controversy.

---

28 Kimble, *The Political History, op. cit.*, p. 78.
29 Max Warren, *Social History and Christian Mission* (London, 1967), p. 75. Citing Mary Kingsley "The Development of Dodos", *The National Review*, Vol. XXVII (March to August 1896)—March 1896, p. 71.
30 C.G. Baeta, ed., *Christianity in Tropical Africa*, (Oxford, 1968), p. 16.

Dr. E. Amu (a one time Senior Research Fellow at the Institute of African Studies, University of Ghana, Legon) was compelled in 1937 by the Basel Mission to resign as tutor at Akropong Training College because he insisted that the Gospel could be preached by African preachers wearing African dress instead of European attire. Another member of the staff in the same college, Mr. Puplampu, was suspended for publicly criticising the Synod Committee for asking Mr. Amu to resign.

The result of this missionary attitude against the exercise of independent judgement by the African helpers was detrimental: it promoted the fundamental paternalistic attitude of the missionaries and discouraged, threatened, stifled and inhibited the helpers' sense of initiative, originality and creativity. Worst of all, it dissuaded the clergy "from seeing that in the [indigenous] traditions there is a world view and an attitude to life—a theology, in fact—which deserves to be examined seriously and objectively"[31] in the light of the facts of the Gospel.

Thus psychologically, the students accepted as important and worthy of transmission to posterity not only the truth of the Gospel but also "the entire apparatus of European Civilization",[32] values and practices. For an African to be considered a good clergyman he had first to be Europeanised in thinking, in dressing, in his condemnation of the indigenous culture and in upholding only the Western norm of behaviour.

It is in this respect that the programmes did not make the desired impact. They did not enable the students to take a more comprehensive view of the indigenous values which, until the planting of the Church in West Africa were "inseparable from social decency and justice",[33] values which directed and disciplined conduct for centuries.

It is significant to note that the late Dr. S.G. Williamson confirmed, after many years of ministerial training in non-Roman Catholic theological institutions in West Africa, that the programmes failed to make a desirable impact. His impression about the clergy and the leadership of the Church, especially, in Ghana, which follows illustrates this:

> Unable to read the new day realistically, they (the Clergy) retreat from their problem rather than attack it. In addition, there is the recurrent and pertinent question of the Christian faith in its attitude to [African] Culture. While on the one hand the non-Christian [Ghanaian] is led to reject the Christian faith as a European product with no relevant message for his own land, on the other hand, and within the Church, the question is raised how far the Christian faith has become naturalised in the [Ghanaian] setting. The Church for its part suffers from a malaise since, in the form it has assumed, and using an agency and methods inherited from the past, it proves unequal to its task and makes too slight an impact on society.[34]

---

31 J.S. Kingsnorth, "The Changing Role of Missionary Societies in Africa", *Overseas Quarterly*, March 1963, p. 143.
32 C.G. Baëta, *Christianity in Tropical Africa, op. cit.*, p. 17.
33 S. Radhakrishnan, *Religion and Society*, 2nd ed., (London, 1948), p. 10.
34 S.G. Williamson, *Akan Religions and the Christian Faith*, (Accra, 1965), p. XIII.

In Roman Catholic circles also it has been felt by some people that the ministerial training did not succeed in making an acceptable impact especially on the secular aspects of human experience. In Ghana, Roman Catholic students in the higher institutions of learning in Cape Coast, met in the 60's at St. Peter's Seminary at Padu and discussed "The Role of a Priest in our Society Today".[35] One of the students from the University of Cape Coast maintained that the spiritual aspect of the priest's responsibility had been over-emphasised at the expense of the mundane function and this may be true of West Africa generally. In concluding his speech he said that:

> The priest must come down to earth in the present-day society, retaining his sacred function, no doubt, but sharing the social development of the world he must minister to. He suggested that the priestly training should move away from the exclusiveness to which it is bound. 'Heaven means nothing to me' he said, 'if those who direct me spiritually cannot show me how to do good in the various areas of our human experience'.[36]

It may be added that most theological and seminary tutors today may agree with the Rev. John Shaw Banks that,

> the work of the Christian Church is always and everywhere religious primarily and essentially religious. But for a Church to isolate itself competely from the great questions that stir the national heart, and that determine the national safety and honour, is to condemn itself to impotence; and it is a great service to bring [the clergy] into line to all great questions that move the thought of our people.[37]

It seems, from the evidences cited, that the ministerial training in West Africa during the period discussed did not succeed in bringing the clergy into line on all the great cultural, national, religious and sociological questions of the local environment.

We have surveyed over one century and a quarter's gradual development of African Christian Ministry in West Africa. During those years many difficulties were encountered: funds were not always adequate for the support and maintenance of the institutions and the payment of the ministers' salaries; candidates did not offer themselves in sufficient numbers and most of those who offered themselves after the pioneer period did not have good general education. The missionaries who promoted the training also had their difficulties: blinded by the social environment from which they came to West Africa, they rejected the values of the indigenous world view some of which could have been accommodated for the enrichment of the

---

35 "Students Discuss Priest's Role in our World Today", *Standard*, (Cape Coast), No. 45, Nov. 17, 1968, p. 1.
36 *Loc. cit.*
37 "The Synod of 1903—Righteousness Exalteth a Nation", *The Gold Coast Leader* (Accra), March 7, 1903, p. 3.

new faith; they did not find it useful to abandon the fallacious and mythical prejudices Europeans have had about the African mind.

Nevertheless, as the missions discussed have all become autonomous under the leadership of the indigenous clergy, it may be suggested that the ventures have not been in vain. In spite of the difficulties encountered and in spite of any weaknesses scholars of today may detect in the missionaries' attitudes and policies towards the seminarians, the tutors gave good theological education to their students. But what has been said about the failures of seminaries in the U.S.A. may equally be adapted for the seminaries in West Africa:

> The seminaries of our time are not so much failing to educate—even to educate well—for the historic ministry toward the current needs of an explosive social order and an insurgent [nationalism]. The commitment and the energy of serious candidates for the ministry are not being provided with structures that enable them to come to grips with the emergent [cultural revolution which yearns to restore indigenous values to their past significance].[38]

It is in the light of this failure to bring ministerial candidates to grips with their contemporary national aspirations that the demand for a reformation in the Church and in the training for the Christian ministry in West Africa should be taken seriously. Indeed, it has been suggested that

> If the Church in Africa does not make a drastic change in its theological training, and accept the fact that its greatest immediate challenge is relevance, then it will be an even greater instrument in creating Post-Christianity than it has been hitherto.[39]

In the attempt to keep strictly to the purpose of this enquiry, viz, the history of the training of African ministers in West Africa, many other related subjects, which readers would have liked to know more about, have been left out. Such themes may include the following: the nature and pattern of the Christian ministry in the new West Africa; a careful study of the lack of effective stewardship among the members of the Church; the social background of the African ministers, and many other subjects which may occur to the various readers. These may form major themes for further researches which it is hoped this history may inspire.

Notwithstanding these limitations it may be agreed that this investigation has been an invaluable contribution to the history of the Church in West Africa. It has made available, for the first time in the life of the Churches, an integrated historical account of how the clergy were trained in the past; it may direct the Churches in thier attempt to make wise planning for the further training of their clergy and serve as an indispensable guide to the expansion of theological education in West Africa.

---

38 Howard Schomer, *The Seminary as a Christian Community*, (New York, 1967), p. 3.
39 G.O. Oosthuizen, *Post-Christianity in Africa: A Theological and Anthropological Study*, (London, 1968), p. 255.

CHAPTER FOURTEEN

THEOLOGICAL EDUCATION FOR TOMORROW

Two questions must be asked to guide the discussion of the subject of this final chapter. Firstly, what do we want Theological Education to achieve tomorrow and secondly what kind of clergyman can most effectively implement whatever end we may have in view?

As regards the first question most people would agree that Theological Education tomorrow should be able to provide mankind with both physical and spiritual wholeness. The emphasis in the past has been placed mostly on the spiritual wholeness of members of the Church. But this approach is quite different from Jesus Christ's methodology. He paid equal attention to both the physical and spiritual wholeness of people. He healed sicknesses, he gave food to the hungry, he forgave sins and set those who had emotional crisis at ease.[1] In short, he was concerned about the total wholeness of the human personality: physical and spiritual health of people were his aspiration for mankind. This is what he intended all his apostles to be concerned about too. He taught them to feed the soul and the body. That is why when he called the twelve disciples together, he gave them power and authority to drive out all demons and to cure diseases. Then he sent them out to preach the Kingdom of God and to heal the sick. After they had returned from this missionary errand Jesus took the twelve to Bethsaida and they were followed by a crowd. Jesus spoke to the people about the Kingdom of God and healed the sick. When the disciples discovered that the people were hungry they told Jesus to send them away because there was no food for them. But Jesus told the disciples, "You yourselves give them something to eat"[2] and Jesus provided food from a limited stock of provisions and the five thousand people were fed more than enough. All these are practical demonstrations whereby Jesus dramatized the nature of the ministry which the disciples should execute: they should provide both physical and spiritual satisfaction for their followers.

This naturally leads to the second question: what kind of a clergyman can effectively implement this type of ministry? The clergyman of tomorrow should be a very highly educated person whose vocation is genuine and who should have sympathy for his church member's "desire to maintain or regain his appropriate place"[3] as an integrated human being in a highly technologically developed world of hopes, frustrations and uncertainties. That is, the clergyman of tomorrow will be required to perpetuate

---
1 Luke 9:1-2 (Good News Bible).
2 *Ibid.*, verse 13.
3 Diedrich Westermann, *Africa and Christianity.* (Oxford University Press, 1937), p. 185.

a ministry of the word, the sacraments and the wholeness of the human personality.

In the past, during the period under consideration, the seminaries could not have done otherwise than train the African ministers only to administer the Word and the Sacraments. The main concern then was the planting of Christianity among Africans. Even at that time the complexities of the technological era as we know them today did not exist and the missionaries, accordingly, did not have any diversified training which would have enabled them to include in their syllabuses subjects other than the traditional Theological ones Thus they transmitted, principally, the spiritual heritage of the Christian faith·and treated the human body in a puritanical manner. For example, when a child was baptised one of the prayers said (and it is still maintained in the Methodist Church liturgy for the Baptism of infants) was that God might "Grant that all things belonging to the flesh [might] die in *him* and that all things belonging to the spirit [might] live and grow in *him.*"

But now circumstances have changed: some seminaries overseas have already realised that the minister should be concerned about both the flesh and the soul. As a result, most of the seminaries overseas have diversified their theological training in such a way that the minister of today can serve both the bodily and spiritual needs of the flocks entrusted them. This is why Psychology and Counselling are assuming large proportions in many American seminaries. All these are confirming the fact that the minister of tomorrow should have the kind of training which will enable him to minister to both the physical and spiritual needs of human beings.

The first approach to be adopted towards this end is that the seminary curriculum should be amended accordingly. This should be the first step towards the reformation of Theological Education in West Africa. In order to diversify the training meaningfully, certain theological subjects should be retained as *core* subjects. All students will have to study such subjects. It is these subjects which will give the professional training needed to prepare the clergy as leaders of the church. Such subjects may comprise firstly, Biblical studies with emphasis on the principle of Biblical interpretation. The reason is that the Bible message is meant for all ages; but each age will have to apply the teachings of the scriptures to suit the needs of that particular age. So the principles of interpreting the Biblical message should be as important as knowledge of the facts of the Bible. Other core subjects are Theology, Church History, Principles of Teaching because by his very vocation the minister has been called upon not only to read the scriptures in public and preach but also to *teach* (1 Timothy 4:13); Pastoral Psychology, Principles of Preaching, Liturgical Studies, Study of Religions other than Christianity, Church Music, African Culture and Philosophy, Ethics and Research Methods. The twelve areas are of equal importance to me because without an adequate training in them a person cannot be truly described as professionally trained Church leader. In addition to these there should be an area of Electives. It is this area which will give training to each minister according to the special gift he may have and enable him to make his ministry relevant in a special way. The Electives may include subjects such as Music, Counselling, Social Welfare, Philosophy of Religion, Sociology of Religion, Agriculture, Mass Communication, Principles of Faith Healing, Biblical Languages etc.

All these subjects should be dealt with academically but the training must always be kept within the context of the Church. The aim of Theological Education is to provide leadership for the Church. So, whatever be the up-graded academic standard of a seminary, the training should not be secularised; it has to remain always within the perspective of the Church and the aim should always be the training of leaders for the Church. This approach may enable the seminaries of tomorrow to continue to serve the Churches by educating seminarians not merely to provide "a general education for those interested in a diffuse variety of religious studies, personal quests for the meaning of life, social activism and pastorally oriented behavioral science".[4]

The reformation of the curriculum will demand some reformation in the teaching staff position. There will be the need for an adequate number of staff well qualified academically and spiritually to handle the subjects efficiently. The objective can be achieved without much delay by reforming the methods we have employed in West Africa so far in training personnel for seminary teaching; up till now most of the highly qualified West African ministers who teach in the seminaries were trained in overseas universities. This system has both advantages and disadvantages. Elsewhere I gave a detailed discussion of the subject: "The problems of Training African Ministers Abroad",[5] and I need not rehearse the whole matter here. I shall only reproduce verbatim some of the relevant sections dealing with the major problems of training African ministers in the West, for the first degree:

> Some of the most common difficulties which deter people from supporting the idea of Africans studying in the West, especially for the first degree, have been clearly summarised as follows: First, life abroad is so greatly different that the African striving to adapt himself to it and to make his way within it may lose contact with his own people, who are very sensitive to the change in him. Second, problems of marriage or family are critical. Third, expense is a burdensome matter, often untterly unrelated to the man's economic base and future income in Africa. Also from the point of view of mission, the money required to send someone abroad could care for several in Africa.[6]

The most practical approach West Africa should adopt to solve these

---

4 "Fading Big Five". *The New York Times.* Friday March 5, 1976, p. 64.
5 Edward Fashole—Luke ed. *Training for the Ministry in West Africa* (WAATI Publication), pp. 123-134.
6 *Ibid.*, p. 129. See also Begt Sundkler, *The Christian Ministry in Africa* (SCM 1960), p. 272.

problems and especially to accelerate the production of highly qualified African seminary staff is to establish a Christian University in West Africa. It is rather sad that though formal education was introduced to West Africa by way of Christianity, the church has no university of its own where its problems could be handled, without secular pressure, in an atmosphere of reverence and academic freedom.

On the spur of the moment, the church leaders may be frightened by this proposal in view of the enormous funds that may be involved. But the suggestion can be implemented without much sweat. In the first place, two of the existing seminaries may be selected, one in Nigeria and one in Ghana. These may be made colleges of some of the local universities or universities overseas by affiliation along the lines of the Baptist Theological Seminary at Ogbomosho.

> This will enable ministerial candidates who are also prospective university candidates to remain at the seminary and follow the seminary courses to degree level. This has two main advantages: first, it will satisfy the aspirations of competent young ministers who would like to pursue their ecclesiastical studies to university level without necessarily going to Europe or America. Second, it will obviate the problem of transferring seminary students to university campuses to continue their studies. The advantages of training ministerial students in the seminary rather than on the university campus are worth noting here. At the university students are brought up academically. Academic excellence is the avowed aim of university education. But it is not so with seminary training which involves much more than mere academic excellence.
> Take for example, in 1954, the Revs. J.P. Hickinbotham, S.G. Williamson and L.O. Shirley studied and produced a paper on "Ministerial Training in Sierra Leone". Among other things these men divided Theological Education into three aspects, namely: devotional, academic and professional.[7] From this analysis it is clear that the academic, which is the main concern of the universities, is only one third of the demands of ministerial training.[8]

It is because of this that I hold the view that Departments of Religion in our universities are not suitable places for training ministers. Worst of all, these university departments of Religion or Religious Studies are neither concerned with conversion of individuals nor with the life of the church.

All these emphasize the point that the time has come for the Church to think seriously of establishing a Christian University in West Africa.

By adopting the first step towards this end viz. making some of the seminaries Colleges of Universities, the university authorities would vet the seminary curriculum, give accreditation to the seminary academic staff and serve as external examiners. After a period of time one of these colleges may be developed into a fully fledged church or Christian university serving principally but not exclusively West Africa.

---

7 Rev. J.P. Hickinbotham, et al, "Report on Ministerial Training in Sierra Leone". (Mimeographed, Sierra Leone 1954), p. 11.
8 Fashole—Luke ed., *op. cit.,* p. 130.

This scheme will undoubtedly demand drastic changes in the seminaries. First, the entry qualification of prospective candidates will have to be raised generally. The course will have to be graded to suit both the degree and non-degree candidates. For example, there should be courses for students who may not be able to go beyond the basic seminary certificate, another for Diploma students and there should be separate courses for prospective degree students. Certainly, the implementation of this proposal may create numerous problems; but difficulties need not deter the church from giving serious consideration to the scheme. The ultimate advantages to be derived from a judicious and quick implementation of the suggestion will eventually outweigh the initial difficulties.

For instance, the scheme will, in the first place, accelerate the training of the African seminary academic staff. There are brilliant boys in the secondary schools and teacher training colleges who have genuine vocation; but they prefer to go to the university to earn a degree before considering the ministry. Other influences may have their impingement on some of such students at the university and after graduating from the university they may refuse ordination. If the seminaries can offer degrees, such brilliant and convinced boys may prefer or be encouraged to enter the seminary rather than the university and they may not be lost to the ordained ministry after graduating. It will be from among such men that a cadre of prospective seminary lecturers can be established.

Thirdly, with the establishment of an army of good quality African seminary staff, specialists in various theological disciplines will emerge. It is these who will make the diversification of the curriculum, suggested above, possible. By the very nature of the training of such men it is hoped that they will have the initiative and confidence which shall enable them to write textbooks for seminary and church consumption. One of the first steps towards making seminary training and Christianity relevant within the African context is that Africans should write books which will reflect African background in the interpretation of Biblical and allied message.

But Africanising the staff of the seminaries will put greater financial burden on the churches. The reason is that hitherto foreign missionaries employed by the seminaries are financially catered for by their mission boards. If they are replaced by African staff then the local sponsoring churches will have to provide the funds for the maintenance of their staff in the seminaries.

This is not an insurmountable difficulty. Africanising the staff of the seminaries should not necessarily mean non-co-operation with the West in Theological Education in West Africa. Western missionaries and Africans can still work together in training seminarians in Africa and in the West. But the Western missionaries should be given the appropriate re-training which can properly fit them into the reformed climate and aspirations of the seminaries in Africa. Their normal Theological training should be reinforced with relevant African Studies which will prepare them to understand the African way of life and to respect African culture and thought-forms. Having armed themselves with this type of African orientation the western missionaries can properly fit into the Africanisation programme of the seminaries of tomorrow. Thus Africanising the seminary staff does not and should not imply the elimination of western missionaries from Theological Education in Africa. Rather, it should mean retraining them to be African in thought and to accord things African the respect and honour they desire. With this orientation the respective mission boards could continue to send missionaries from the West to Africa when the seminaries demand them. They will continue to be financially responsible for the number of missionaries they will second to the African seminaries. Thus, unlike politics, the seminaries should always remain a veritable avenue where people of different races can co-exist in harmony, concord and love because they all belong to our Lord Jesus Christ, for in Christ there is neither Jew nor Gentile.

The alternative suggestion to the above is that some other Africans think that the Western mission boards should offer the cost of keeping a missionary in a seminary to the Governing Body of the relevant seminary. This amount could then be used locally to subsidise the employment of only African staff for the seminary.

Personally, it is my conviction that we can only insist on this approach if the mission boards overseas refuse to reform their Theological Education along the lines suggested above. "Once the western missionaries can be reorientated to be African in thought and maintain respect for [our] racial heritage as it is expressed in the social institutions and the African style of life",[9] then the ideal thing should be a permanent arrangement whereby African and Westerners can co-operate in the training of Christian ministers in West Africa. Similarly, there should be a reciprocal arrangement whereby African theologians could be employed by seminaries in the West to co-operate in the training of Western ministers. In the church, nationalistic aspirations should not necessarily lead to racial discrimination.

It is hoped that the Church in West Africa will consider seriously and implement these proposals. By so doing, the weaknesses of Theological Education discussed above may be either removed or minimised. Above all, the judicious and a quick implementation of the suggestions will enable Theological Education tomorrow to produce clergymen who will exercise their initiative and vision without fear of molestation. They will no longer isolate themselves completely from the great questions that stir up the national and individual consciousness. They will come to grips with the contemporary national, social, cultural and spiritual aspirations of the people they minister to. Thus, relevance is the challenge of Theological Education

---

9 Westermann, *loc. cit.*

for tomorrow in West Africa. That is, "the training of ministers should be geared toward life and living in the society in which the ministry is to be carried out."[10]

---

10 C.F. Whirley, "A consideration of Curriculum. Matters in Training for the Ministry in West Africa". Typed Address, 1970, p. 7 (Kept in the Library of the Baptist Theological Seminary, Ogbomosho, Nigeria).

APPENDIX I

PLANS FOR ESTABLISHING MFANTSIPIM SCHOOL

1. Richmond College should be removed from Freetown to Cape Coast because Cape Coast was the most central town in the Gold Coast District and, as the Gold Coast had supplied the largest number of candidates to Richmond in Freetown, it was hoped that a greater supply might be expected from the Gold Coast District for many more years.
2. Richmond and Mfantsipim be amalgamated to serve the three West African Methodist Districts or those of them that might agree to associate together.
3. The Home Committee be asked to sanction the building of new blocks at a cost not exceeding £5,000 (¢10,000) including the furnishings.
4. The Home Committee was to be asked to guarantee one-third of the cost of the buildings and plant.
5. Local members were to be taxed 2/- (¢ 0.20) per member per year till the District's contribution be completed.
6. The Chairman of the District and Mr. J.E. Biney (layman) were appointed District Treasurers of the Institution Building Fund.
7. A 14-man building committee was appointed.
8. A site was to be secured on the outskirts of Cape Coast for the buildings which should comprise

   (a) accommodation for the European Principal, the staff and
   (b) dormitories for the candidates for the ministry, the Mission Agents, and the pupils of Mfantsipim School.

Provisional estimates for running the Institution was also drawn up. The estimated capacity of the Theology Department was a maximum of 30 students, five of whom would be candidates for the ministry, and 25 agents. The total estimated cost of running the Department was £980 (¢1,960.00) per annum, analysed as follows:

Food and light £16 (¢32) per man per annuam	£480	(¢960)
Tutors	160	(¢320)
Stationery & Books (ministers)	20	(¢ 40)
Stationery & Books (agents)	75	(¢150)
Washing	36	(¢ 72)
Rates & yard servants	35	(¢ 70)
Sundries	30	(¢ 60)
Total	£836	(¢1672)
Average, about £30 (¢60.00) per man Family allowances for say 12 agents at £12 (¢24) per month	£144	(¢288)
Grand Total	£980	(¢1960)

Agents who would benefit from the scheme would repay half the cost of their training by five annual instalments of £6 (¢12) each. The Gold Coast District was assessed at 7% of the Class & Ticket money to yield £168 (¢336). From the District Extension Fund £200 (¢400) was devoted to the upkeep of the Institution and the Home Committee continued to give its grant of £50 (¢100) for the training of agents.

APPENDIX II

THE ENGLISH CHURCH MISSION REPORT ON THE OPENING OF THE NEW BUILDINGS OF ST. AUGUSTINE'S COLLEGE, KUMASI ON 22ND APRIL, 1928

At the last Easter Vestry meeting, held on Wednesday, the 18th April, 1928, His Lordship the Bishop of Accra announced that Mr. P.D. Quartey and Mr. Kojo Golightly had been appointed to represent Holy Trinity and St. Mary's Churches at the opening of St. Augustine's College, Kumasi.

The Accra delegates, with His Lordship, left by train on Friday, the 20th April, 1928, at 7.30 a.m. At Nsawam delegates from Winneba and Kwanyaku joined them. One delegate also entrained from Koforidua. They arrived at Kumasi at 5.55 p.m., amidst the welcome of a host of Church People and friends. There were 19 delegates in all.

A short description of the cottage buildings would not be out of place here.

As one approaches the College grounds from the old Ejiso road, the College Chapel stands out first and foremost and quite apart from the other buildings. Then follows in a straight line to the Chapel and in the middle of the other group of buildings a cottage containing 3 rooms. They are the lecture room, the library and a spare room for visitors. On the left of this block stands the Rector's Cottage of 3 rooms viz: a bedroom, a dining hall and an office; and on the right, two separate cottages with a bath-house between them for the students. Each cottage has the same number of rooms viz. 3. In this case, however, two are bedrooms and a dining hall in the middle. Each bedroom should accommodate four students, total 16 students, but at present only two in each. The outhouses are on the extreme south and consist of kitchens, boys' rooms, etc.

The buildings are of cement blocks, quite simple and of no artistic taste. With the palatial buildings of the Government Senior Boys' School nearby, it makes a vast contrast. No wonder the Bishop prefers to call them Cottages instead of Dormitories.

Dedication of the Chapel of the new Diocesan Theological College of St. Augustine by the Rt. Revd. the Lord Bishop of Accra, and the formal opening of the College by his Honour Major F.W.F. Jackson, D.S.O., Acting Chief Commissioner of Ashanti:

All the delegates then went up and filed at the steps of the Chancel, and the Bishop charged them to take a report of doings of the afternoon to their people—a correct account of what they saw and heard. It behoved them therefore to look round well. They should impress upon their people to support the College by getting students from all over the Diocese, and it should be the aspiration of every Church family to send a member of the family to be trained for the priesthood.

The Te Deum was sung and the Bishop gave an address from Psalm 118 v. 24: 'This is the day which the Lord hath made; we will rejoice and be glad in it'.

His Lordship said the day was a great day for us.

When a great day comes, first of all, we look back and remember with thankfulness the benefits we have received. In this particular instance, we remember Bishop O'Rorke during whose episcopate our Church came at Ashanti, and who had planned in his heart this College.

We remember the name of Archdeacon Morrison who, with his characteristic foresight and wisdom, selected and purchased the piece of land on which the College now stands.

We remember also the past clergy, one of whom we are happy to have with us here today.

'The Chapel has been dedicated to St. Augustine and St. Peter, and that reminds us of those people in England who had enabled us to put up the structure. The people of St. Peter's Church at Swinton, Manchester, gave the money with which the Chapel was built, and it is only fitting, therefore, that the name of their Church should be linked with it.

'This is a great day, and we look round; and what do you see? you see a Chapel.

'The College buildings cost nearly £5,000 and much of this sum came from Christian people in England. The College is simple, it could not but be simple, but the Chapel is to be beautified and made more glorious. It is not for men, but for God.

'It may be years before we have a cathedral in the Diocese of Accra.

'Cottage life means a great deal. No great dormitories here. Men will live in a simple way in their own cottages. One of the cottages is the Rector's which is exactly the same as the others. There is a reason, and you can grasp it for yourself.

'This is a great day. Look back, look round, look on, and look up. Our Church is just beginning to tackle seriously the problems confronting us, and we look up to God for guidance. As your Bishop, I look up with feelings full of pride and triumph. This is a great day for us'.

The foregoing are some of the salient points from His Lordship's address. He made it quite clear that the success of our Mission depended on the number of African Clergy we trained and produced. After all, Europeans are here for a time, to show us the way. Africans would, in due course, aspire to be Bishops, and the work would be left in their hands. He therefore appealed to the delegates, and through them to their people, to support the College financially and with men, so that in course of time when the Diocese grew and more students were forthcoming, the College buildings, standing on so spacious a piece of land, could be enlarged.

Poverty is no real bar to becoming a student. Time is not limited for a student to be under training, and no promise is held out to anybody who goes to the College that he would be ordained.

After the Bishop's address a procession was formed to each of the buildings of the College. The college was opened by the Acting Chief Commissioner of Ashanti, and blessed by the Bishop. The cottages in order were opened by delegates from Accra, Sekondi, and Kumasi, in terms of the following:

'We, Peter Quartey and Kojo Golightly, delegates from Accra, do hereby open this cottage and bring with us hearty greetings from all our members.'

Then the procession, including a concourse of Church members, spectators, Chiefs and followers of Nana Prempeh, assembled before a platform specially put up. The Rector, Father Bernard, thanked the Chief Commissioner and all who had helped in making the College buildings an accomplished fact.

Mr. H. Van Hien, delegate from Cape Coast, ably supported the motion, the Chief Commissioner replied in suitable terms, the choir sang the Doxology, and His Lordship gave the blessing, which terminated a function most auspicious in the annals of the English Church Mission on the Gold Coast.

APPENDIX III

BISHOP'S £67,000 (¢134,000) APPEAL FUND

On the Spot	£4,000	(¢8,000)	
Bishop Daly's Gift	£ 400	(¢ 800)	(sent before the meeting)
Mr. James Mercer	£1,200	(¢2,400)	(£10 (¢20) p.m. for ten years)
Men and Officers of the Gold Coast Regiment, Accra	£ 105	(¢ 210)	
Anonymous Covenated Subscription	£ 175	(¢ 350)	

The estimated expenditure of the appeal had been recorded as follows:

Reserve against Clergy Stipend	£5,000	(¢10,000)
Clergy back-pay for 1954 Salary Revision (Increases were not paid due to lack of funds)	£1,200	(¢2,400)
The Training of Priests (It was hoped to double the number of African Priests in 10 years.)	£21,800	(¢43,600)
New non-contributory Pensions Scheme for the Clergy	£10,000	(¢20,000)
Advance and Extension of work in Ashanti, N.T.s, Togoland and elsewhere	£25,000	(¢50,000)
Capital Endowment: Province of W.A.	£4,000	(¢8,000)

Every penny of the Appeal had already been exhausted on paper even though all the cash was not in hand. It would embarrass the Church. But the response by the end of the first year was very discouraging. On 28th August, 1957, *the Daily Graphic* reported that the Bishop's appeal fund reached £56,102. 16s. 0d. (¢112,205.60). At first sight it is encouraging but the analysis is heartbreaking:

Gifts in Cash	£ 4,340	12s. 0d.	(¢ 8,681.20)
Promises over 10 years	£51,762	4s. 0d.	(¢103,524.40)
Instalments received	£ 2,293	19s. 0d.	(¢ 4,587.90)

APPENDIX IV

CATECHISTS' INSTITUTE, OSU
TIME-TABLE FOR JULY-DECEMBER 1853

DAY		7-8	8-9	9-10	11-12	12-1	1-2	2-3	3-4
MON	I	Bibcal Theology	Catech.	Catech.	Geogr.		World History		
	II		School	School				Arith.	Ga Exs.
TUES	I		Biblical Theology	Catech.		Break for Lunch			
	II	Bible History	School	School					
WED	I	Biblical Theology					World History		
	II		School	School					Arith.
THURS	I		Biblical Theology	Catech.	Geogr.		World History		
	II	Bible History	School	School					
FRI	I		Biblical Theology	Catech.	World History			Bible History	Ga. Exs.
	II		School	School					
SAT	I								
	II	Bible History							

APPENDIX V

EWE PRESBYTERIAN CHURCH—THEOLOGICAL SEMINARY 1933
TIME-TABLE—HO

TIME	MONDAY	TUESDAY	WEDNESDAY	THURSDAY	FRIDAY
a.m. 8.00-8.50	Relg. Prelim.	Relg. Intr.	O.T.	O.T.	Rel. S. School Tg.
8.55-9.45	Cor. I	N.T.	Native Customs	Native Cus.	Ethics
10.00-10.50	Homiletics	Ethics	Cor. I	N.T.	N.T.
10.55-11.45	Ethics	Church Dogmatics	Symbolics Dog.	Symbolics	Ewe Grammar
a.m. p.m. 11.45-12.45			HARMONIUM		
p.m. 2.40-3.30	Private Studies		Copying	Ewe Harmonium	
3.30-4.20	Bremen Misn. Hist.	Missions History	Church History	Homiletics	
4.30-5.30			GAMES		
7.00-9.00			PRIVATE STUDIES		

N.B. 6.00 a.m.-Morning Prayers by the Weekly Snr.
6.45 a.m.-7.00 a.m.-Manual Labour
9.30 p.m.-Bedtime
12.00 noon-2.00 p.m.-Town Leave. Also 5.00-6.00 p.m. Motto: Miwɔ ɣeyiɣi nuti do blibo! (Be thrifty with time)

APPENDIX VI

VOLTA REGION SHOWING GERMAN TOGOLAND-1919

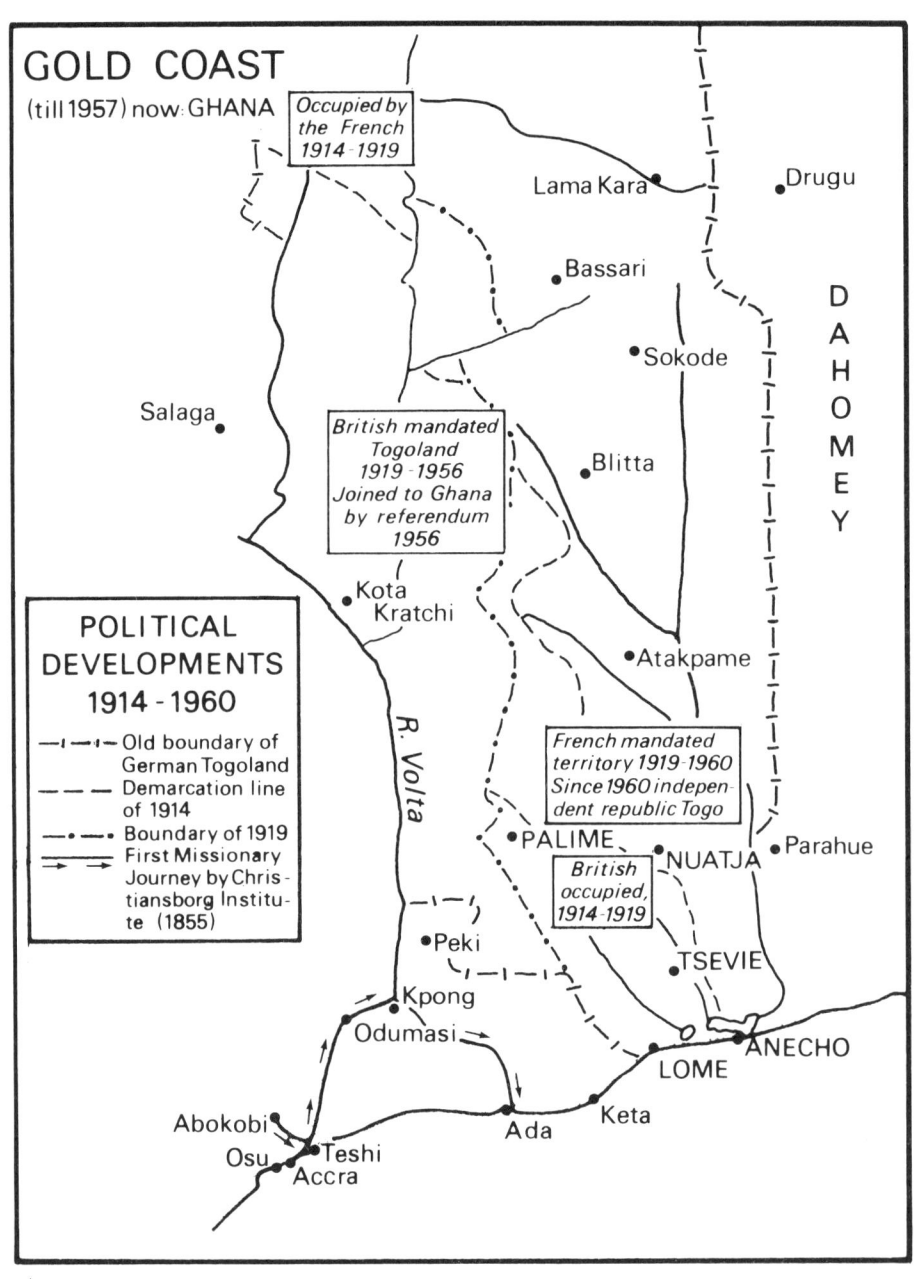

APPENDIX VII

LIST OF AFRICAN MINISTERS TRAINED FROM 1842 to 1965 (GHANA)

The figures at the beginning of the lines mark simply the year in which each Minister entered on his work. The years correspond with the date of ordination in respect of the Anglican, Presbyterian and the Roman Catholic Communions. But the Methodist until 1960, used to ordain their ministers four years after the date of entry and since 1960, three years after.

The names have been compiled from the various Annual Reports belonging to the non-Roman Catholic Churches. As regards the Roman Catholic Church, the names were supplied by the Bishops of the six Dioceses in Ghana.

METHODIST CHURCH MINISTERS

1843	William de Graft	1894	W.S. Forson
	John A. Martin		F.J. Nelson
1845	John Hagan	1896	J.R. Addo
1851	John Ossei Ansah		E. Butler
	George P. Brown		J.B. Graham
	Joseph Dawson		John A. Quayson
	Timothy Laing	1898	T. Marshall
1852	J.A. Solomon	1901	A.W. Stanhope
1854	E.J. Fynn	1902	J.A. Hayford
1856	John Plange	1904	Christian E. Barnes
	H.F. Morgue	1905	I.A. Assan
1857	Fred France	1906	F.E. Ekuban
1873	J.D. Hayford		J.C. Mensah
	J.R. Hayfron	1908	J.J. Mettle
	A.W. Parker	1909	D.M. Bruce
1877	F.E. Wood	1910	E.O. Lartey (Lartson)
1884	R.M. Acquah	1911	M.L. Portuphy
	Isaac Anaman		A.M. Wright
	I.A. Graham	1912	G.R. Acquaah
	R.G. Jones		J.W. Acquah
1886	J.O. Hammond	1913	H. Bart-Plange
	I.H. Hayford	1914	J.E. Appiah
	J.A. Markin		J.G. Koomson
1887	K. Egyir Assam		Joseph Oppan
	(William F. Penny)		T.S. Quarshie
1888	Henry Anaman	1915	J.T. Clegg
	Ernest Bruce		S.C. Dodd
1889	S.R.B. Attoh-Ahuma		F.C.F. Grant
	(S.R.B. Solomon)		B.A. Markin
1890	Jacob Anaman	1916	F.A. Acquaah
	J.J. Reynolds		J.E. Addo
1892	J.B. Baiden		A.B. Dickson
1893	A.E. Brew		Moses Enin
	E.A. Sackey		F.A. Markin

1917	Robert Acquah	1950	Charles Kittoe
	C.H. Bartels		J.C. Koomson
1919	K.A. Blankson	1951	J.K. Andoh
	S.Q.G. Ghartey		Y. Adu Badu
1921	S.D. Nate-Kodsi		Joseph K. Baiden
	J.E.A. Pappoe		Jacob S.A. Stephens
1923	J.S. Aidoo	1952	Robert Evans Ackaah
	J.E. Wi-Afedzi		Henry G. Ayerakwa
1924	C.C. Ohene		Allen N.K. Sackeyfio
	J.B. Wilson	1953	Lawrence H.S. Osae-Addo
1925	S.B. Akyeampong		F.A. Esar
	I. Amonoo		John K. Owusu
	Eben. Brown		I.K. Asuamah Thompson
	S. Butler	1954	A. Osei Asibey
	G.J. Nyarko		J. Yedu Bannerman
1927	T. Asare		J. Kweku Kyereboah
	Jos Wilson	1955	Emmanuel L. Adjetey-Adjei
1928	I.B. Affram		Solomon K. Debrah
	H.V.A. Baddoo		E. Amuah Ebonyi
	E.W.O. Tetteh		A. Emmanuel K. Orgen
1932	M.K. Debrah		Joseph G. Williams
	J.E. Mensah	1957	John K. Agbeti
1933	F.E.K. Ekuban		F. Mensah Akyea
	E.G. Quantren		Charles C. Andoh
	W.Q. Quartey		J.E. Ebe-Arthur
1935	F.J. Bart Addison		Kwesi A. Dickson
	Charles Graham		D.B. Ofori Rockson
1937	J.A. Hammond	1958	George E. Acquah
1939	T.W. Koomson		Paul E. Awuah
1940	Godfrey A. Apatu	1959	Philip R. Anderson
	S.Y. Brew		Ebenezer K. Baiden
	P.K. Dagadu		Kofi A. Boateng
	J.K. Otoo		Charles W. Dickson
1941	Charles K. Yamoah		Isaac D. Ewoodzie
1942	S.G. Nimako		Daniel K.M. Okwaisie
1943	William C. Cudjoe		Samuel E.A. Quarm
	K.B. Ellis		E. Okyere Twum-Baah
	Charles A. Pratt	1960	Gideon K. Agordome
1945	Joseph K. Clegg		Charles O. Aryee
	S.B. Essamuah		Ebenezer K. Dadson
	J.E. Yarquah		John K. Foh-Amoaning
1947	Samuel K. Abruquah		Kodjo Hazel
	Napoleon K. Donkor		Nahum A. Mensah
	S.A. Dzirasa		R.E. Kwesi Sagoe
	S.T. Ofei	1961	John E. Ackeifi
	Ebenezer Allotey-Pappoe		Jonathan L. Acquaah
	John O. Tawiah		Justice K.N. Ansah
1948	Frank E. Adams		Jacob H. Obresi
	S.K. Akesson		
	Joseph W. de Graft Johnson		
1949	Paul Adu		
	W.G.M. Brandful		
	J. Appiah Yankson		

1962	Joseph Ampiaw	1964	Samuel K. Acquah
	John C. Amponsah		Emmanuel K. Ampiah
	Nathaniel A. Arhin		John E. Arhin
	John K.A. Arko		Samuel H. Biney
	Solomon K. Baiden		William K. Dadson
	William K. Bekoe		Nicholas B. Gyamerah
	Joseph K. Markin		John K. Nketsia
	John K. Morris-Mensah		Martin L. Sintim
	George K. Neizer	1965	I. Maxwell Appiah
	Alfred Priddy		Jacob Arhin
1963	Josiah E.A. Akushie		Samuel K. Asamoah
	Micah E. Annor		Emmanuel A. Ashitey
	Albert B. Appiah		Joseph K. Bassaw
	Sampson A. Assan		Alphonse Etsibah
	Isaac Barnes		Samuel K. Hodasi
	Paul Cobbina		Peter K. Mensah
	Noah K. Danquah		Walter G. Obeng
	K.B. Micah Edu-Buandoh		Nathan Williams
	I. Freeman Konadu		Joseph K.M. Wilson
	Fredrick G.O. Lartey		
	Albert K. Mensah		
	C. Harry Ohene-Bekoe		
	Emmanuel D. Okyere		
	Joseph E. Prah		
	J.M. Kofi Yankson		

PRESBYTERIAN CHURCH OF GHANA MINISTERS

1862	David Asante	1895	Joseph Labi
1867	A.W. Clerk	1897	Emmanuel Wentum
1872	Theophilus Opoku	1898	Daniel Awere
	Karl Reindorf		S. Boateng
1874	Simeon Koranteng	1899	Joseph Aye
1875	Jeremias Engmann		Henry R. Ofosu
1877	Nathaniel Date	1900	Timothy Mensah
	Timothy Mullings	1902	Ludwig Richter
1878	Peter Hall	1906	Samuel Kumi
	Carl Quist		Charles Martinson
1880	William Hesse	1908	Christian Fleicher
1881	Jeremias Anoba		Martin Adade
	Nathaniel Asare	1909	Gottfried Agyakwa
	Emmanuel Obeng		Samuel Kwafo
1883	Esau Ofori	1910	Joseph Asante
1884	S. Daniel Saba		Andreas Saki
	Edward Samson	1912	Daniel Akwa
1885	Peter Anteson		James Birikorang
1888	Nicholas Clerk	1913	George Akwa
1890	Philipp Kwabi	1914	James Afari
1892	Daniel Ablo		W. Odjidja
	William Kwatei		William Quartey
1893	Martin Amah	1915	Thomas Hall
	Benjamin Ntow	1916	Thomas Dampte
	Samuel Ofei		

Year	Name	Year	Name
1917	Peter W. Anaman	1937	B.F. Ansong
	Benjamin Martinson		E.T. Koramoa
1918	Charles M. Adu		S.W. Mamphey
	Esau B. Amaning		J.D. Mmireku
	H.L. Anang		Wilfred Tete
	Paul G. Djoleto	1938	J.B. Afro
	Henry E. Ofori		H.A. Boateng
1919	Frederick Ashie		P.D. Denkyem
1920	David Sam		J.R. Kisiedu
1922	Samuel Agyei		F.C. Mante
	Robert A. Doku		C.S.T. Owuo
	C.F. Fleischer		B.R. Seku
1923	M. Agyemang	1940	H.E. Addae
	David R. Asong		P.E. Addo
	H. Keteku		S.A. Adow
	C. Saba	1941	S.E. Birikorang
1924	C.W. Agadzi	1943	B.E. Dua
	E.M. Asiedu		L.N. Kuafo
	C.E. Opoku		E.R. Anno Kwakye
1925	M.V. Gyang		J.K. McCarthy
1927	H.N. Anang		T.H. Sintim
	T. Dankyi	1944	J.O. Kisiedu
	J.K. Sam		E.M. Mensah
1929	G.O. Apronti	1945	I.A. Amaning
	M.A. Obeng		S.M. Akita
	T.J. Osei		A.L. Kwansa
1930	E.V. Asihene		S.A.A. Saki
	T.H. Boadi	1946	E.A. Afriyie
	J.E. Hall		R.O. Danso
	H. Hammond		R.F. Mante
	S.E. Obeng		I.J. Tawia
	H.R.S. Saforo	1947	F.W.K. Akuffo
1931	S.V. Amoa		E.K.O. Asante
	M. Apea		G.R. Badu
	C. Hesse		E.R. Gyampo
	N.A. Kwakye		T.A. Kumi
	S.S. Odonkor		S.E. Kwaa
1933	I.G. Apea		E. Gyako-Mensah
	R.M. Amoako		T.K. Okuno
	A.L. Asare	1948	W.V. Ofori
	D.R. Essah		S.R. Ntiforo
	J.P. Kofi		G.K. Sintim Misa
1934	B.K. Anyang	1949	B. Okyere Aboagye
	W.D. Asamani		L.S.G. Agyemfra
	C.R. Boateng		D.A. Konotey Ahulu
	A.A. Holm		E.A. Ansah
	John Teye		M.H.A. Henking
	J.W. Twum		E.D. Kitcher
1935	I.M. Akoto		S.E. Agyei Mante
	T.W. Ansah		Asare Mfoafo
1936	A.C.T. Apo		T.A. Osei
	E.M. Bodu	1950	J.F. Asa
	S.A. Gyansa		E.N. Abboa-Offei
	J.A. Padi		

1951	B.B. Addade	1961	W.J. Akyeampong
	D.K. Antiri		M.L. Awuku
	Kofi Asare		K. Obiri Boateng
1952	C.C.P. Mohenu		B.A.K. Lokko
	E.M. Lartey Odjidja		C.J. Natoma
	E.N. Okyere		N.A. Kuma-Ollenu
	C.N.T. Tawiah	1962	M.A. Addo
	F.J. Wiredu		Mafo Ahenkora
1954	M.E. Addo		S.D. Amaning
	B.S. Antwi		H.O. Ankrah
	G.S. Kumi		D.T. Padi
	H.B.A. Osei		S.F. Nii Padi
1955	E.D. Amakye	1963	S.O.Y. Adade
	W.H. Kwakye		E.C. Adu
	S.K. Kwabena Ofei		I.H. Frempong
	A.K. Sah		P.M. Kodjo
	I.A. Sowah	1965	W.H. Addai
1956	B.D. Teyegaga		E. Ansa-Akyea
1957	E. Ansah Akyea		A.E. Bannerman
	J.K. Asiedu		H.T. Dako
	A.E. Ohene Okae		S.O. Karikari
	S.D. Tetey		K.A. Ofosuhene
1958	E. Cole-Agbetawokpor		C.W. Osei
	E.D. Asante		J.E. Graham
	S.O. Ayim		E.N. Korley
	D.A. Koranteng		J.F. Kotei
	J.A. Kyereme		G.N. Kuma
	S.K. Ofei		L.P. Nyakor
	J.M. Opare-Pensang		E.E. Obeng
1959	B. Ottopa Kisiedu		plus 24 ordained
	E.S. Mate Kojo		5th September, 1965
	E.A. Misa		at Akropong
	A.R. Secu		
1960	S.L. Agyemang		
	J.W. Amoa		

E.P. CHURCH MINISTERS

1882	Rudolf Mallet	1923	Petro Alomenu
1901	Adolf Lawoe		Benjamin Amegashie
1910	David Besa		H. Nyalemegbe
1911	Robert Kwami	1925	S.D. Buatsì
	Theodor Sedode	1926	Daniel K. Adinyina
1912	Elia Awuma	1927	Jonas M. Kwabena
1914	Paulo Ntumitse	1928	C.B. Gati
1915	Nehemia Akude	1930	Robert M.K. Affor
	Edmund Ayikutu		Theodor Anku
	Simon Peter Kwist	1934	Solomon Anku Motte
1916	Timotheo Ametowobla	1935	Elias W. Tamaklo
	Albert Binder	1936	Christian Baëta
		1938	T.K. Afenyo
			M.W. Akama

1939	C.J. Obeko	1953	S.K. Agbiey
1940	S.K. Akude	1954	S.K. Dankwa
	G.K. Ampofo		J.K. Dose
	B.K.T. Banibensu	1955	P.Y. Agboka
	E.A. Banini		S.K. Yuia
1941	G.K. Ababio	1956	O.D. Martin
	D.K. Ametefee	1957	J.K. Dzato
	S.K. Bensah	1958	T.K. Bruku
	W.D. Gbolonyo		A. Agobo
1942	G.K. Alifo		E.T. Obro
	C.K. Mensa	1959	D.K. Do
1944	G.B. Ansre		E.Y. Tawia
1946	C.H. Ababio	1960	C.K. Agbola
	W.E. Adinyina		D.K. Mensah
	E.K. Galevo	1961	C.Y. Adzanku
1947	G.D. Acolatse	1963	J.K. Addey
	G.K. Agbodza		G.O. Anku
	F.R. Ametowobla		G.K. Ansre, Jnr.
	F.H. Buatsi		R.B.K. Dovlo
1949	J.A. Awafia		N.K. Dzobo
	M.K. Avotri		T.K. Gbodzo
	F. Gabusu		W.K. Kwawu
1950	C.K. Dovlo		A.Y. Wurapa
	G.K. Lotsu	1964	T.W.K. Ankude
	T.K. Setse		S.E.K. Anipa
1951	E.T. Adiku		R.F. Agawu-Kakraba
	E.Y. Forson		P.G. Komladzei
	J.D. Wampah		B.M. Opoku
1952	A.K. Abutiate	1965	Martin Gelli
	O.B. Kunu		Benjamin Tettey
	W.D. Kumordzie		

ANGLICAN PRIESTS

1916	E.D. Martinson	1932	R.A.A.C. Ankrah
	H.T. Mensah		A.K. Nelson
1922	Kwamina Annan-Sey		D.K. Poku
1924	C.H. Elliot		A. Ben-Smith
	O.M. Renner		J.K. Yebuah
	J.R.C. Yalley	1936	I.S.M. Lemaire
1928	J.F. Appiah		S.B. Pennie
	A.M. Asare		V.K.A. Saifah
	T.E.F. Asiedukofiawua		J.E.B. Welbourne
	S.A.C. Lutterodt	1941	A.C. Agyemang
	B.T. Quartey		Joseph Adeseko
	W.E.C. Yalley	1942	J.W. Ben-Acquaah
1931	J.N. Armah	1947	R.E. Ashitey
	J.B. Arthur	1948	A.D. Ahmoah
	J.P.A. Labi		G.T. Anim
	G.E.F. Laing		T.A. Annobil
	J.A.Q. Okwabi		I.F. Baidoe
	S.E. Quarm		A.E.B. Sackey
	J.K. Quartey	1952	A.E. Brient
	K.P. Sakyiama	1953	A.C. Obodae
	T.D. Ward		A. Ofei-Kwatia

1955	E. Yeboah	1962	G.M.S. Ampah
1956	D.O. Adeloye		R.J.A. Adjaayi
1957	A.B. Agordekpe	1963	W.S. Awuma
1958	K.E.Y. Arkorful		A.W.Y. Mensah
	B.B.O. Bewaji		P.D. Aggrey
	J.K. Dadson		P.S.D. Martinson
	S.B. Erskine	1964	M.K. Ntow
	C.A. Obeng		F.W.B. Thompson
	A.G. Opoku	1965	T.S.A. Annobil
	J.K.A. Sam		W.A.A. Okai
1959	E.T. Mends		R.G.A. Okine

N.B. During the period of investigation the following men
    S.R.C. Nicholas, and
    John Prempeh
were trained as Anglican Priests in Nigeria and Mauritius respectively. As they served mainly outside Ghana, their names are not included in the general list of Ghanaian Anglican Priests.

ROMAN CATHOLIC PRIESTS

1922	Athanasius O. Dogli	1956	Dominic Andoh
1934	Gerald Fini		Rudolf Apietu
1935	G. Ansah		*J.B. Asoedena
	F. Menyah		*Evarist Kuwulong
1942	J.A. Essuah		J.K. Owusu
	Killian Kpatakpa	1957	M. Ackerson
	Bernard Y. Mensah		J. Akono
	Paul Y. Simpini		*Bernad Ato
	R. Yankah		V. Damuah
1943	S.W. Van der Puije		M.K. de Graft
1946	*A. Abatey		J. Mochia
	F.K. Buah		Albert Opong
	F. Couston	1958	*G.Y. Anoa
	C. Lejeune		*Francis Baghre
	P. Louis		A. Mensah-Brown
1949	J.K. Amissah		G. Mensah
	Philip Bonto		F.B. Ocran
	John Mensah	1959	J.K. Osei
1950	J.K. Adams		Peter K. Sarpong
	*R. Akanlu	1960	*J.W. Apuri
	*R. Pwamang		Gabriel K. Asare
1951	P.K. Akoi		J.B. Baidoo
	*Peter Dery		*Irenaeus Songliedong
	*Lawrence Kyemalo	1961	J.B. Amissah
1952	M.K. Adjaye		*J. Awia
1953	T.W. Darku	1962	Joseph T. Addy
	J. Ennoo		James K. Anokye
	Joseph Kpeglo		F. Eboyi-Anza
1954	F.M. Baffoe		Richard Asomantsi
	Joseph K. Yeboah		Joachim Eleeza
1955	*K.P. Avereyire		*Gregory Kpiebaya
	*Alfred Bayo		Matthias Kumesi
	*Hippolyte Putiere		

1963	Robert M. Abrampah	1965	R. Aboteyuure
	Philip K. Boateng		Joseph Amoako-Adusei
	A.Y.K. Bomah		Simon Agboso
	Stephen Danso		C. Akabote
	A. Ghansah		Donatus Akpeity
	Emmanuel Quasigah		Wynand Amewowor
	Hilarius Senoo		Emilio Asie
1964	A.M. Asamoah		Pius Deng
	P.X. Assamoah		A. Kazaresam
	J.G. Asuah		Henry Frempong-Manso
	J. Awuah		G. Sentu
	J Kofie		Romano Tampah
	Francis Lodonu		

*Represents students from St. Victor's Seminary.

APPENDIX VIII

REGISTER OF IMMANUEL COLLEGE OF THEOLOGY STUDENTS, IBADAN, NIGERIA 1958-1965

The figure at the beginning of each group of students in the Register indicates the year in which the students completed their studies.

1958

1. Julius Oluwadare Arifalo Adedipe
2. Moses Oluwayemi Adejumo
3. Ezekiel Sakede Akerele
4. David Adebayo Alao (went to Uni. College)
5. Raphael Sunday Alao
6. Michael Akinola Aluko
7. Gabriel Akinlolu Fagbolagun
8. Gabriel Kolawole Falusi
9. Elkanah Olurinde Folorunso
10. Benjamin Amgbo Kato
11. Nathaniel Dangana Kolo
12. Michael Olajide Ogunleye
13. Emmanuel Olatubosun Ogunseyiju
14. Ezekiel Adewolu Ogunsusi
15. Joseph Adejumo Oni
16. Daniel Osanyin Atitebi Olomu
17. Samuel Sunday Oluwole
18. Joseph Adebowale Ojomo
19. James Oladosu Olojo
20. Gabriel Adedeji Ogunyimika
21. Emmanuel Oluwayemi Sewo
22. Samuel Alilu Yuseph
23. Samuel Ladipo Fawole (External Student)
24. Timothy Osairinmwian Uwogbiren
25. Titus Lakpini Kofo Waniko
26. (Sic)

1959

1. Aratunte Samuel Adegboyega (Captain)
2. Adebayo Samson Ajewole
3. Adejimi Samuel Adegoke
4. Adesun Samuel Afolarin
5. Agbonze John Otasowie
6. Alieu Emmanuel Ayodele
7. Ajayi James Emila
8. Akinboro Ezekiel Oreolu
9. Enitilo Zacchaeus Awoyemi
10. Fesobi Robert Ekundayo
11. Idowu Michael Oluwanwo
12. Imoroa Gabriel Uzinigbe
13. Ogunmilade Joel Johnson
14. Ohida Samuel Ogbadayin
15. Olaoye Samuel Ayatunde
16. Olowokure Jacob Olabode Kehinde
17. Oluwatola Ezekiel Osiola
18. Omokogbo James Oriloye
19. Oyelade Olaife Solomon
20. Owolabi Joseph Oladunjoye
21. Sotunde Victor Olufowora (spent 3 terms at overseas)
22. Tsuzom Alfred Afum Onimola
23. Wemida Caleb George Osedayo
24. Ukwuoma Theophilus Ahe
25. Efunboade Timothy Oderemi

1960

1. Frederick Olakanmi Aderibigbe
2. Samson Olusola Adesina
3. Albert Aduloju Agbaje
4. Jeremiah Olagbamigbe Ayewumi Fabuluje
5. Buddah Samuel Garbah
6. Ayoola Oludayo Kuforiji
7. Samuel Morolayo Odedele
8. Gabriel Babalola Olomiyo
9. Joshua Olayele Omosola Omoseibi
10. Augustus Omotunde Taiwo
11. Abraham Akinsola Ademibiayan

1961

1. Richard Adekunle Aderogba
2. John Bamidele Adewale Ajayi
3. Cornelius Alaiki Akanya
4. Daniel Alao Akinola
5. Jacob Ilesanmi Akinyele
6. Moses Rotimi Alabi
7. Jonathan Oloruntomi Alemika
8. Matthew Babafemi Awe
9. Peter Ofobukueta Ereh
10. Moses Akinlose Fatukasi
11. Samuel Ojo Jegede
12. Joshua Olumide Kayode
13. Emmanuel Oladipupo Macaulay
14. Samuel Omosanya Ogunsanya
15. Isaac Onasola Oguntuyo
16. Isaac Oladenusi Olupitan
17. Gabriel Omotayo Omonijo
18. Joseph Akinyele Omoyajowo
19. Samuel Akinola Osatuyi (Left the College Oct. 1961)
20. Ezekiel Bankole Osunlusi
21. Samuel Olufunmilayo Shidi (Left June 1962)
22. Matthew Chidiegwu Oraegbulam
23. James Aliu Yisa

1962

1. Adeagbo Afolabi Joseph
2. Adebiyi Robert Adekanbi (deceased)
3. Adenuga Adebanjo Zacchaeus (deceased)
4. Ado Idowu Thomas
5. Ajayi Olarewaju Cornelius
6. Ajayi Oluwawemimo Isaac
7. Ajayi Babadayisi Samuel
8. Akinyemi Oyeleye Jude
9. Amadi Noel Justin Onukwuforobi
10. Bisuga Adeite Timothy
11. Bolaji Ipadeola Olaniyi Timothy
12. Esho Daniel Adedayo
13. Christopher Okafor Ezeonyeodu
14. Fagoroye Samuel Akin
15. Familua Ojo Moses
16. Christopher Folowoseye Itamakinde
17. Olaonipekun Obayomi Joseph
18. Obianwu Nwabueze Ernest
19. Odusina Gideon Olusola
20. Ogunro Moses Akinola
21. Christopher Abiodun Ogoigbe
22. Olagundoye Olafioye Moses
23. Oluwadare Moraninyo Isaac
24. Omonije Oyelade Joseph
25. Oni Omoniyi Amos
26. Oni Omatayo David
27. Oparah Godson Ekeamadi
28. Osinubi Olukayode Julius
29. Oyatoye Igbayiloye Adeyemi John
30. Oyekusibe Oluwambe Joseph
31. Owadayo Oluwaremilekun Matthew
32. Oyeleye Ogundele Joseph
33. Taiwo Oladele Joseph

1963

1. Abiona Olatunji Isaac
2. Adekanmbi Olutola John
3. Adeleye Adewumi Amos
4. Adubi Oyewole Daniel
5. Akinyele Olusegun Akinola
6. Alabi Moshobalaje Odunola John
7. Apata Adepoju James
8. Asaolu Orire Zacchaeus
9. Awe Olaniran Simeon
10. Babatayo Olatunde Titus
11. Bowaje Adedayo Joshua
12. Faluyi Taiwo Samuel
13. Jayeola Oluwatayo Joseph
14. Kufeji Oluseyi Babatunde
15. Karau Peter
16. Ojo Ademola Samson
17. Omosola Oyewole Thomas

1964

1. Kolawole Oladapo Idowu
2. Mark Boloje Forae

3 Jacob Babalola Faroki
4 Ruese Urwierairho Emekakao
5 Israel Ojo Komolafe
6 Rowland Kolupo Kusanu
7 Joseph Olusegun Ogunlade
8 Jonathan Aradion George Ilevbare
9 Ephraim Ayodele Ogundipe
10 Michael Oluwole Babarinsa
11 Wilfred Adebayo Titilayo Akinwale
12 Clement Oluwole Adetula
13 Ebenezer Opeoluwa Dosumu
14 Slemanu Likita Bamai
15 Monday Nkemakolam
16 Michael Dada Dare
17 Josiah Ademola Okubanjo
18 Joshua Alakinde Adediran Adebamiwa
19 Vincent Omashele Muogbereh

1964 (September)

1 James Ovebanji Adegboye
2 Jimmy Adeoye
3 Ebilola Olusegun Ajayi
4 Timothy Akinloye Akinlade
5 Samuel William Olatubosun (Pratt Doherty)
6 Nathaniel Akporoyabe Enuku
7 Emmanuel Olugboyega Ladipo
8 Joshua Oni Olawumi
9 Theophilus Ajaja Oni
10 Godwin Chukueloka

1965

1 Joshua Iluyomade Adeoba
2 Samuel Abiodun Adewale
3 Emmanuel Ogundeji Adeyelu
4 Solomon Akanji Akindele
5 David Adebayo Alabi
6 John Ibikunle Asaolu
7 Jacob Monday Daodu
8 James Adegbola Fadipe
9 Michael Agosu Job
10 Emmanuel Shody Ogunyemi
11 Abraham Sunday Oluwole Olowoyo
12 Samuel Oladipo Oluwatusin
13 Emmanuel Olusola Osilaja
14 Eric Olusegun Williams
15 Jeremiah Idowu Bamigboye (One year course)

APPENDIX IX

REGISTER OF TRINITY COLLEGE STUDENTS LEGON, GHANA 1943-1965

The Register of Past Students of Trinity College with the Rate of Growth of Student Body 1942-1965.
The figures at the beginning of each line in the Register indicate the year in which the students completed their studies; but in the Rate of Growth they indicate the year in which the students were admitted.

1943 Gilbert Bansa Ansre
1944 Joseph Kwao Clegg
Samuel Benyarku Essamuah
James Emml. Yarquah
1945 Isaac Adu Amaning
Albert Lawrence Addae Kwansa
Allen Nei Kwei-Mensah Sackeyfio
Samuel Augustus Ahuate Saki
1946 Christian Kobla Dovlo
Samuel Kwesi Abruquah
Francis Richard Ametowobla
Napoleon Kwaku Donkor
Stephen Allen Dzirasa
Sampson Titi Ofei
Ebenezer Allotey-Pappoe
John Osam Tawiah
1947 Griffith Dixon Acolatse
Frank Ebenezer Adams
Samuel Kwao Akesson
Frederick William Kwesi Akuffo
Edmund Kwaku Osafo Asante
Martin Ntow Badu
Felix Humphrey Buatsi
Jeremiah Chi Kangsen (British Cameroons)
Thomas Amu Kumi
Samuel Emml. Kwaa
Emml. Agyako Mensah
1948 Gottfried Kwadwo Sintim Misa
Paul Adu
Manasseh Kwame Avotri
William George Mensah Brandful
John Victor Graham Ham
Seth Richardson Ntiforo
John Appiah Yankson

1949 Ebenezer Atuah Ansah
Asare Mfoafo
Lawrence Samuel Gyang Agyemfra
Michael Herman Henking Anyang
Charles Dawson Kittoe
James Cantamantu Koomson
Gotlieb Kwame Lotsu
Timothy Augustus Osei
Theophilus Kwadzo Setse
1950 Laurence Hardy Shewland Osae Addo
Ehrenfried Tongo Adiku
Joseph Kwesie Andoh
Jeremiah Festus Asa
Yaw Adu Badu
Elias Yaw Forson
Ernest Benjamin Stafford (The Gambia)
Jacob Seth Adamah Stephens
Ebenezer Nelson Abboa-Offei
1951 Benjamin Bekoe Adade
Robert Evans-Ackaah
Daniel Kisiedu Antiri
Kofi Asare
Henry Gyan Ayerakwa
Aaron Su (British Cameroons)
1952 Seth Komla Agbley
Joseph Edmond Ebe-Arthur
Francis Annan Esar
John Kwasi Owusu
Peter Ebot Tabi (British Cameroons)
Collins Asuamah Thompson
Kwesi Abotsia Dickson
(Left for the University)

1953	Jospeh Yedu-Bannerman	1960	Christian Yawo Adzanku
	Seth Henry Kwasi Dose	Dec.	
	Johnson Kweku-Kyereboah	1961	John Enos Ackeifi
	Abraham Osei Asibey	July	Jonathan Lino Acquaah
1954	Emmanuel Lawrence Adjetey-Adjei		Justice Kwasi Nunoo Ansah
			Martin Larbi Awuku
	William Kwasi Agbenyega		Nii Amaa Kuma-Ollennu
	Solomon Kwasi Debrah		Christian Jedua Natoma
	Ebenezer Amua Ebonyi		Jacob Hughes Obesi
	Samuel Kwabena Ofei	1962	Mafo Ahenkora
	Albert Eml. Kwamina Orgen		Samuel Danso Amaning
	Joseph Gladstone Williams		Joseph Akyene Ampiaw
1955	Andrew Kwami Abutiate		Humphrey Opare Ankrah
	John Kwesi Foh-Amoaning		Michael Ansgar Addo
	Adolf Kwaku Sah		John Kow Ampiah Arko
	Ishmael Ayi Sowah		David Tawia Padi
1956	John Kofi Agbeti		Samuel Frederick Nii Padi
	Edward Ansah Akyea	1963	Samuel Osafa Yaw Adade
	F. Mensah Akyea		Eugene Charles Adu
	Charles Christian Andoh		Noah Kwame Danquah
	Jacob Koranteng Aseidu		Kobina Badu Micah Edu-Buandoh
	Modi Ebenezer Essoka (British Cameroons)		
			Isaac Hudson Frempong
	David Bruce Ofori Rockson		Peter Mangbi Kodjo
	Sampson Damptey Tetey		Rederick Gorge Odame Lartey
	David Famiye Yankey		Albert Kwesi Mensah
1957	George Edward Acquah		Charles Harry Ohene-Bekoe
	Jonathan Adde Kyereme		Joseph Essilfie Prah
	Paul Ernest Awuah		Seth Edward Quarkwei Quartey
	Ebenezer Kwesi Baiden		Nathan Williams (left 1964)
	Charles William Dickson		Albert Yao Wurapa
	Isaac Crampa Ewoodzie		Peter Barker, B.A. (European)
	Daniel Agyei Koranteng	1964/65	
	Osmund Bainn Kwesi Morrison		Four-Year Course Introduced in October 1961
	Jacob Mathews Opare-Pensang		
	Ian Cuthbert Roach (The Gambia)		E. Ansah-Akyea
			I.M. Appiah
	Emml. Otchere Twum Baah		J. Arhin
1958	Gideon Kwao Agordome		S.K. Asamoah
	Philip Robert Anderson		E.A. Ashitey
	Charles Oswold Aryee		J.A. Badu
	Kofi Akyeampong Boateng		J.K. Bassaw
	Emml. Anyamesem Misa		A. Etsibah
	Daniel Kwesi Mensa Okwaisie		S.K. Hodasi
	Samuel Evans San Quarm		P.K. Mensah
	Andrews Ramseyer Secu		W.G. Obeng
	Emml. Sakite Mate Kojo		J.K.M. Wilson
	Richard Godson Tettey		K.A. Ofosuhene (B.A. Hons.)
1959	Samuel Lawrence Agyemang		Ben. K. Tettey (B.A. Hons.)
	Ebenezer Kwadwo Dadson		
	Kwadwo Hazel		
	Daniel Kwaku Mensah		
	Nahum Ansah Mensah		
	Richmond Enoch Kwasi Sagoe		
	Samuel Kwasi Ofori Sey		

APPENDIX X

TRINITY COLLEGE, KUMASI, GHANA
RATE OF GROWTH OF STUDENT BODY

YEAR	ENTRANTS				
	E.P.	G.P.	M.	CAM.	GAMB.
1942	—	—	4	—	—
1943	1	3	—	—	—
1944	2	—	6	—	—
1945	2	5	2	1	—
1946	1	1	4	—	—
1947	—	9x	2	—	—
1948	3+	1	4	—	1
1949	—	3x	2	1	—
1950	1	3x+	4+	1	—
1951	—	1	4+	—	—
1952	1	1	5	—	1
1953	—	2	1	—	—
1954	—	3	6x	1	—
1955	1x	3	8	—	1
1956	—	4x+	6	—	—
1957	1	2x	5	—	—
1958	1	3	4	—	—
1959	—	7x+	2	—	—
1960	1	4	8	—	—
1961/62	—	4x+	10	—	—
Totals	15	59	87	4	2

```
         x     One for one year only
         +     One for two years only
E.P.     =     Evangelical Presbyterian Church
G.P.     =     Presbyterian Church of Ghana
M.       =     Methodist Church, Ghana
CAM.     =     Presbyterian Church, Cameroons
GAMB.    =     Methodist Church, Gambia
```

YEAR	NO OF STUDENTS IN EACH CLASS		
	1st Year	2nd Year	3rd Year
1942	4	—	—
1943	4	4	—
1944	8	4	4
1945	10	8	4
1946	6	10	8
1947	11	6	10
1948	9	9	6
1949	6	9	9
1950	9	5	8
1951	5	8	5
1952	7	5	6
1953	3	7	4
1954	10	3	7
1955	13	9	3
1956	10	12	9
1957	8	9	12
1958	8	7	8
1959	9	8	7
1960	13	9/8	7 Graduates 2
1961/62	12	13	7

Total of all entrants: 167
Total staying 2 years: 7
Total staying 1 year: 10
Total staying 3 years: 150

YEAR	TOTAL NUMBER OF STUDENTS			
	E.P.	G.P.	M.	TOTAL
1942	—	—	4	4
1943	1	3	4	8
1944	3	3	10	16
1945	5	8	8	22 (1 Cam.)
1946	5	6	12	24 (1 Cam.)
1947	3	15	8	26 (1 Cam.)
1948	4	9	10	24 (1 Gamb.)
1949	3	11	8	24 (1 Gamb.)
1950	3	6	10	22 (2 Cam., 1 Gamb.)
1951	1	5	10	18 (2 Cam.)
1952	2	3	12	18 (1 Cam.)
1953	1	4	9	14
1954	1	6	12	20 (1 Cam.)
1955	1	8	14	25 (1 Cam., 1 Gamb.)
1956	—	10	19	31 (1 Cam., 1 Gamb.)
1957	1	8	19	29 (1 Gamb.)
1958	2	6	15	23
1959	2	10	11	24
1960	2	14/13	14	30/29
1961/62	1	13	20	34

APPENDIX XI

THE PHASINGS OF TRINITY COLLEGE PLAN, LEGON

PHASE I

	£	ȼ	
Student accommodation (for 60):	35,544	(71,088)	
+ furniture:	2,550	(5,100)	
Classrooms 4 × 24:	9,957	(19,914)	
+ furniture (for 60):	360	(720)	
Lecture Assembly:	6,565	(13,130)	
+ furniture (for 60):	300	(600)	
Teaching Staff Accommodation × 5:	26,610	(53,220)	
+ furniture:	1,300	(2,600)	
Administration Accommodation:	16,913	(33,826)	
+ furniture:	510	(1,020)	
Administration (omitting Bursar's Office & Clothing Store):	3,248	(6,496)	
+ furniture:	117	(234)	
Fencing:	750	(1,500)	£104,724 (ȼ209,448)

PHASE II

	£	ȼ	
Library:	3,494	(6,988)	
+ furniture	300	(600)	
Common Room:	1,517	(3,034)	
+ furniture: (for 60)	180	(360)	
Chapel (including furniture):	16,038	(32,076)	
Covered Ways	5,426	(10,852)	
Outside W.C.	503	(1,006)	
External Lighting	750	(1,500)	£28,208 (ȼ56,416)

PHASE III

	£	ȼ	
Staff Room:	1,644	(3,288)	
+ furniture:	150	(300)	
Student Accommodation (for 25):	14,810	(29,620)	
+ furniture:	1,700	(3,400)	
+ furniture for classrooms:	150	(300)	
+ furniture for Lecture Assembly:	125	(250)	
+ furniture for Common Room:	75	(150)	
Garages:	965	(1,930)	
Workshop:	400	(800)	
Main Gate:	294	(588)	£20,313 (ȼ40,626)
			£153,235 (ȼ306,470)

PHASE IV

Would provide for full expansion for 100 students, and playing fields.
The house for the sixth member of staff should be added as part of Phase II.

APPENDIX X(C)

TRINITY COLLEGE NEW BUILDINGS: PHASE I
ACTUAL COST

Ghana Churches	£47,000	(c94,000)	6 House + Furniture	£29,250 (c58,500)
Trust Foundation	35,000	(c70,000)	2 Dormitories + Furniture	34,450 (c68,900)
Interest	1,250	(c 2,500)	4 Classrooms	
Local Church Promises	10,000	(c20,000)	Library	
Missionary Societies	12,000	(c24,000)	Lecture Hall	15,000 (c30,000)
			Furniture	3,000 (c 6,000)
			Administration	7,980 (c15,960)
			Dining Hall & Kitchen	1,225 (c 2,450)
			Furniture	995 (c 1,990)
			Kitchen Equipment	1,100 (c 2,200)
			Electricity & Water	3,600 (c 7,200)
			Roads	1,750 (c 3,500)
			Boys' Quarters (8) + Toilets	6,000 (c12,000)
			Professional Fees	1,000 (c 2,000)
			Cost of Land	
			Legal Fees	150 (c 300)
			Building Permit	500 (c 1,000)
Total	£106,000	(c212,000)		£106,000 (c212,000)

APPENDIX XII

THE STAFF OF TRINITY COLLEGE, GHANA
1943-1965

Member of Staff:	1943-1965
Rev. D.S. Elder, M.A.	1943-1945 Vice-Principal
Rev. R.S. Morris, M.A.	1943 (seconded from Wesley College, Feb.-April)
Rev. S.G. Williamson, M.A.	1943-1950 Principal
Rev. P.C. Richter	1944-1947
	1948-1949
Rev. C.K. Yamoah, B.D.	1945-1948
	1956-1961
Rev. J. Noel Smith, M.A., B.D.	1946-1950 Vice-Principal
Rev. E. Asamoa, M.A.	1947-1948
Rev. J.W. de Graft-Johnson, B.A., B.D.	1949-1952
	1950-1952 Vice-Principal
Rev. C.K. Dovlo, B.D.	1950-1952
Rev. H.E. Thomas, B.A., B.D.	1950-1951 (seconded from Wesley College)
	1955-1961 Vice-Principal
	1961 Principal
Rev. W.A. Stamm	1951-1961 Principal
Rev. G.T. Eddy, M.A., B.D.	1951-1954
	1953-1954 Vice-Principal
Rev. F.J. Dankwa, M.Th. (1966)	1952-1955
	1957-1962
	1961-1962 Vice-Principal
Rev. J. Beech	1954 (seconded by Methodist Church, Sept.-Dec.)
Rev. G.K. Sintim Misa, B.D.	1955-1957
Rev. C. Graham	1955-1956
Rev. J.K. Andoh, B.D.	1961-65ff
Rev. P.G. Ritter, B.D.	1961-65ff
Mr. R.P. Nyako, B.D.	1961-1962 Tutor-Student
Rev. J.F. Asa, B.D.	1962-65ff
Rev. E. Grau, B.Th., Ph.D.	1964-1965 (Part-time)
	1965 (Full-time)
Rev. H.V. Huppenbauer, D.Th.	1965ff

Principals:	
Rev. S.G. Williamson, M.A.	1943-1950
Rev. W.A Stamm	1951-1961
Rev. H.E. Thomas, B.A., B.D.	1961-65ff

BIBLIOGRAPHY

1. PRIMARY SOURCES

   A. UNPUBLISHED

   1. CHURCH ARCHIVES
   C.M.S. Sierra Leone Letter Book Vol. 13:
   Box G3 AI/L13, 1900-1907 and
   Box G3 AI/L14, 1908-1920
   Evangelical Presbyterian Church:
   Bremen: Seminary Reports and Papers,
   File Nos. 66, 67, 69, and 101(b)
   Textbooks written in Manuscript for the use of the Amedzofe Seminary, 1894-1914
   (In Ewe Language).
   HO: Files: CH/3, Statistics CH/10, Steps Towards Ordination.
   Minutes of Synod Committee, 1941-1952.
   Methodist Church, Ghana:
   MMS, London: Gold Coast District Syhod Minutes
     (i) Box (1842-1866)
     (ii) Box (1867-1879)
     (iii) Box (1880-1890)
     (iv) Box (1891-1897)
     (v) Box (1898-1906)
     (vi) Box (1907-1911)
   Accra: Gold Coast District Synod Minutes, 1912-1957.
   Ghana District Synod Minutes, 1958-1961.
   Ghana Conference Minutes, 1962-1965.
   Presbyterian Church of Ghana:
   Basel:
   File, Afrika, 1851-1853.
   File, Goldküste Ausschuss und konferenzen 1938-1942,
   Afrika Inspectorat.
   Roman Catholic, Cape Coast
   Heesewijk, John "St. Theresa's Seminary, Admisano
   Notes". Cape Coast, Bishop's House, n.d.

   2. SEMINARY AND COLLEGE DOCUMENTS

   Anglican Seminary, Kumasi:
     St. Augustine's College, Visitors' Book 1947.
   MGC. Mfantsipim School, Log Book 1900-1910.
   Roman Catholic Seminaries:
     St. Peter's, Pedu, Log Book, 1955 following.
     St. Teresa's, Amisano, Diary, 1930-1954.
     St. Victor's, Tamale, Log Book, 1946 following.
     Private Papers:
     Asamoa, P.K., "Notes on the History of St. Victor's Seminary, Tamale".
     Wouters, M.P., "Particulars on St. Teresa's Seminary, Amisano, Gold Coast and Liberia, 1938".
   Trinity College, Legon:
     Daily Records Book, 1943-1965.
     Governing Body Minutes, 1961 following.
     Joint Committee Meeting Minutes, 1940-1960.
     News Letter. New Series No. 2, September 1964.
     Oversight Committee Meeting Minutes, 1940-1960.

Staff Meeting Minutes, 1943-1965
Visitors' Book, 1965 following.
Private Papers:
The Presbyterian Church of Ghana. "The Holy Ministry", Mimeographed, n.d.
Methodist Church, Ghana. "Memorandum on the Advisability of Establishing a Theological Faculty in Connection with the Proposed West African University. I. Statement on the Methodist Approach to the Training of the Ministry and the Present Practice". Mimeographed, n.d.
Nickles, A., "Recruitment and Training for the Anglican Ministry in Ghana", Mimeographed, n.d.
Wesley College, Kumasi:
Log Book, 1924-1942.
Records, 1924-1942.

3. ADDRESS AND REMINISCENCES

Dowuona-Hammond, A.J., "Address delivered to the Fourth Annual Conference of the Methodist Church of Ghana at Winneba, August 1965", Mimeographed.
Hopewell, J.F., "Address delivered at the Dedication of Trinity College, Legon, 23rd January, 1965". In manuscript.
Reminiscences of Past Students.
Letters:
Amu, E. to Agbeti, J.K., 2nd Aug., 1969.
Dogli, A.O. to Agbeti, J.K., 13th Feb., 1969.
Sarpong, P. to Agbeti, J.K., 28th Jan., 1968 and 23rd June, 1969.
Oral Information:
Elliot, C.H., "The Informal Training of the Five Pioneer Anglican Priests", Cape Coast 1968.
Laing, G.E., "A Brief Biography of G.E. Laing", Accra, 1969.

4. DOCTORAL THESES

Carter, F.V., "Education in Uganda 1894-1945", London, King's College, Ph.D. 1965.
Gaba, C., "Anlọ" Traditional Religion: a study of the "Anlọ" Traditional believer's conception of and Communion with The 'Holy'", London, King's College Ph.D. 1965.
Grau, E., "The Evangelical Presbyterian Church: A Study in European Relations Affecting the Beginning of an Indigenous Church in Ghana". Hartford, U.S.A., Hartford Seminary Foundation, Ph.D., 1958.

B. PUBLISHED

5. REPORTS:

Amissah, J.K. et. al. *Libation*, Cape Coast, 1958.
Bates, Searle M. et. al. *Survey of the Training of the Ministry in Africa Part II*. London, 1954.
Busia, K.A., *Report on a Social Survey of Sekondi-Takoradi*, London, 1950.
C.A.C.T.M. *Training for the Ministry*, Westminster, 1948.
C.M.S. *Intelligencer*, 1892.
Goodall, N. & Nielson, E.W., *Survey of the Training of the Ministry in Africa Part III*, London, 1954.
Goudie, W., *Report of Visit to West Africa*, London, 1915
I.M.C. *The Life of the Church*. Tambaram Series, Vol. IV, London, 1939.
M.M.S. *Reports*, London, 1838-1942
  Missionary Notices, London
    (i) Vol. VIII 1835-1838
    (ii) Vol. IX 1838-1841
    (iii) Vol. X 1842-1844
    (iv) Vol. XI 1845-1847
Methodist Church Ghana. *The Gold Coast Annual*, Cape Coast, 1885-1922.

Moss, Basil S., Canon et. al *Theological Colleges for Tomorrow.*, London, 1968.
N.B.M.A. "Seminary Reports", *Bausteine.* "Amedzofe" Seminary Jubilee Report". *Monatsblatt,* 1914
N.C.C.C. *The Seminary as a Christain Community, New York,* 1967.
Neill, Stephen. *Survey of the Training of the Ministry in Africa Part I.* (East and West). London 1950
Sarpong, Peter, "Traditional Beliefs". *GATRK, Annual Report,* 1966.
S.P.G. *Reports.* London, 1900-1965.
Stockwell, B. et. al., *The Christian Ministry in Latin America and the Carribean.* London, 1962.
Welch, F.G., *Training for the Ministry in East Africa,* Limuru, 1963.

6. REPORTS FROM GOVERNMENT CIRCLES

Gold Coast Gazette
Gold Coast Year Book, The, 1964.
Ministry of Education, Ghana. "A Brief Sketch of the History of Education", Accra, n.d.

7. NEWSPAPERS

African Times, The (Lagos). 1867.
Catholic Voice, (Cape Coast). 1934.
Christian Messenger, The (Accra). 1965.
Daily Graphic, The (Accra). 1957 and 1965.
Ghanaian Times, The (Accra). 1965 and 1969.
Gold Coast Aborigines, The (Cape Coast). 1899.
Gold Coast Independent, The (Accra). 1928.
Gold Coast Leader, The (Cape Coast). 1903, 1914, 1917, 1926.
Gold Coast Methodist, The (Cape Coast), 1886.
Gold Coast Methodist Times, The (Cape Coast), 1894.
Gold Coast Times, The (Cape Coast), 1930.
New York Times, 1967.
Standard, The (Cape Coast). 1968.

II. SECONDARY SOURCES

1. BOOKS:

Abbo, J.A. and Hunnan, J.D., *A Concise Presentation of the Current Disciplinary Norms of the Church,* Vol. II. (Canons 870-2414), 2nd ed. trans. London, 1960.
Ajayi, F.J.A., *Christian Missions in Nigeria 1841-1891: The making of a New Elite.* London, 1965.
—and Espie, I. eds., *A Thousand Years of West African History.* Ibadan, Nigeria, 1965.
Allen, Yorke, Jnr., *A Seminary Survey.* New York, 1960.
Almedingen, E.M., *Dom Bernard Clements,* London, 1945.
Armytage, W.H.G., *Four Hundred Years of English Education,* Cambridge, 1964.
Austin, Dennis, *Politics in Ghana 1946-1960.* London, 1964.
Ayandele, E.A., *The Missionary Impact on Modern Nigeria 1842-1914: A Political and Social Analysis,* London, 1966.
Baeta, C.G., *Prophetism in Ghana,* London, 1962.
—ed., *Christianity in Tropical Africa: Studies Presented and Discussed at the Seventh International African Seminar at the University of Ghana.* Oxford, 1968.
Bane, M.J., *Catholic Pioneers in West Africa,* Dublin, 1956.
Bartels, F.L., *The Roots of Ghana Methodism,* Cambridge, 1965.
Beaver, Pierce, R., *Christianity and African Education,* Michigan, 1966.
Beetham, T.A., *Christianity and the New Africa,* London, 1967.
Blyden, E.W., *Christianity, Islam and the Negro Race,* London, 1887.

Bourret, F.M., *The Gold Coast: A Survey of the Gold Coast and British Togoland*, 1919-1951., 2nd ed. London, 1952.
Busia, K.A., *The Position of the Chief in the Modern Political System of Ashanti.* London, 1951.
Clark, G. Kitson, *Guide for Research Students working on Historical Subjects*, Cambridge, 1965.
Coolsey, J.J. and McLeigh, A., *Religion and Civilisation in West Africa*, London, 1931.
Cordasco, F. and Garter, E.S.M., *Research and Report Writing*, New York, 1964.
Crowder, Michael, *West Africa under Colonial Rule*, London, 1968.
Danquah, J.B., *The Akim Abuakwa Handbook*, London, 1928.
Debrunner, H.W., *The Church in Togo: A Church between Colonial Powers*, London, 1965.
— *A History of Christianity in Ghana*, Accra, 1967.
Ellis, A.B., *The Ewe Speaking Peoples of the Slave Coast of West Africa*, London, 1890.
Fage, J.D., *Ghana: A Historical Interpretation*, Wisconsin, U.S.A., 1966.
Field, M.J., *Search for Security: An Ethnopsychiatric Study of Rural Ghana*, London, 1960.
Findlay and Holdsworth, *The History of Wesleyan Methodist Missionary Society*, Vol. IV (Five Vols.), London, 1922.
Forster, Philip. *Education and Social Change in Ghana*, London, 1965.
Grove, C.P., *The Planting of Christianity in Africa*, Vols. II and III, (Four Vols.), London, 1948-1954.
Gold Coast Government, *The Gold Coast Handbook*, 1928, London, 1928.
Good, C.V. and Scates, D.E., *Methods of Research*, New York, 1954.
Grubb, Kenneth, *World Christian Handbook*, 1962, London, 1962.
Hargreaves, J.D., *Prelude to the Partition of West Africa*, London, 1966, reprint.
Hastings, Adrian, *Church and Mission in Modern Africa*, London, 1967.
Hollis, Michael, *Paternalism and the Church: A Study of South Indian Church History*, London, 1962.
Jones, J.J., *Education in Africa*, New York, 1922.
Kemp, Dennis, *Nine Years at the Gold Coast*, London, 1898.
Kimble, David, *A Political History of Ghana: The Rise of Gold Coast Nationalism*, 1850-1928, Oxford, 1963.
Keller, James, *The Priest and a World Vision*, New York, 1946.
Laing, E.F., *Dom Bernard Clements in Africa*, London, 1944.
Ledochowski, Wlodimir, *The Choice and Formation of Native Clergy in the Foreign Missions—a Letter Addressed to Superior of the Mission of Kiang-Nan, China, from Rome, August 15th, 1919,* New York City, n.d.
Marshall, James, *Reminiscenes of West Africa and its Missions*, London, 1885.
Mason, R.J., *British Education in Africa*, London, 1959
Melo (De), M.C., *The Recruitment and Formation of the Native Clergy in India—16th-19th Century: An Historical-Canonical Study*, Lisbon, 1955.
Metcalfe, G.E., *Great Britain and Ghana: Documents of Ghana History*, 1807-1957, London.
Moss, B.S., *Clergy Training Today*, London, 1964.
Oliver, Roland and Atmore, Anthony, *Africa since 1800*, Cambridge, 1967.
Oliver, Roland, *The Missionary Factor in East Africa*, Longmans, 1952.
Oosthuizen, G.O., *Post-Christianity in Africa: A Theological and Anthropological Study*, London, 1968.
Parrinder, G., *African Traditional Religion*, rev. 2nd edn., London, 1962.
— *West African Psychology*, London, 1951.
Parsons, R.T., *The Churches and Ghana Society 1918-1955*, Leiden, 1963.
Pfann, H., *A Short History of the Catholic Church in Ghana*, Cape Coast, 1965.
Radhakrishnan, S., *Religion and Society*, 2nd ed. London, 1948.
Reindorf, C.C., *The History of the Gold Coast and Asante*, Switzerland, 1889.
Schlatter, W., *Geschichte der Basler Mission 1815-1915*, Vol. III Basel, 1916.
Shipman, S.A., *The Missionary Child*, London, 1846.
Smith, Noel, *The Presbyterian Church of Ghana, 1835-1960*, Accra, 1966.
Southon, A.E., *Gold Coast Methodism: the First Hundred Years, 1835-1935.* Cape Coast, n.d.
Stacey, John, *About the Ministry*, London, 1967.
Taylor, J.V., *The Growth of the Church in Buganda*, London, 1958.

Teitelbaum, H., *How to Write Theses*, New York, 1966.
Tempels, Placide, *Bantu Philosophy*, Paris, 1959.
Todd, J.M., *African Mission—A Historical Study of the Society of African Missions*, London, 1962.
Ward, W.E.F., *A History of Ghana*, rev. 4th edn. London, 1967.
Warren, Max, *Social History and Christian Missions*, London, 1967.
Williamson, S.G., *Akan Religion and the Christian Faith*, Accra, 1965.
Veuillot, P., *The Chatholic Priesthood Bk. I—Papal Documents from Pius X to Pius XII*, 2nd edn. Dublin, 1962.
— *The Catholic Priesthood Bk. II—Papal Documents of Pius XII*. Dublin, 1964.
Wiltgen, R.M., *Gold Coast Mission History*, 1471-1880, Illinois, U.S.A., 1956.
Wise, C.G., *A History of Education in British West Africa*, London, 1956.
Wolfson, Freda, *Pageant of Ghana*, Oxford, 1958.

2. PAMPHLETS

AACC. *The Crisis in the Christian Ministry in Africa*, Kitwe, Northern Rhodesia, 1964.
Agyeman, F.M., *A Century with Boys: the Story of Middle Boarding Schools in Ghana 1867-1967*. Accra, 1967.
"Akropong Presbyterian Boys' Middle School: Centenary Celebration 1867-1967", Accra, 1967.
Baeta, R.D., *The Development of Native Leadership*, Bremen, 1924.
Binder, J.C., *Bericht der Evhe-schule und das letzete, Niger—Missionsfest in Westheim*, Bremen, 1900.
Elliot, C.H., *Some Historical Events of the Diocese of Accra from 1752-1937*, Cape Coast, n.d.
E.P. Church, *Keta Ewe Kristo Hame: Fe Alafa Deka Nutinya 1853-1953*, Accra, 1953.
— *E.P. Church Year Book, Ho*, 1960-1965.
Gunn, G.G., *A Hundred Years, 1848-1948: the Story of the Presbyterian Training College, Akropong*, (Cyclostiled) Akropong, 1948.
Harris, W.T. and Parrinder, E.G., *The Christian Approach to the Animist*, 2nd ed., London, 1962.
Hopewell, J.F., *The Crisis of the Christian Ministry in Africa, Parts I and II*, Nigeria, 1965.
Keteku, H.J., *The Revs. Theophilus Opoku and David Asante*, Accra, 1965.
Maycock, Edward A., *The Vocation of an African Priest*, London, n.d.
Schott, O.A., *A Retrospect on Fifty Years of Mission Work*, Basel, 1879.
Verstraelen, F.J., ed. *Christians in Ghanaian Life*, Accra, 1968.
Wiegrabe, P., *Ewe Mission Nutinya 1847-1936*, St. Louis, U.S.A., 1936.

3. PERIODICALS

Adelaja, B.A., "The Christian Faith and African Culture (Conference at Accra)", *East and West Review*, April, 1956, pp. 34-41.
Allen, D.W., "Fewer Ordinands", *Church Quarterly Review*, Vol. 167, July/Sept., 1966, pp. 322-8.
Allison, S.F., "The Vocation of the Ministry", *Churchman*, June 1950, pp. 69-75.
Armstrong, C.B., "Training of the Clergy of the Church of England: is there an alternative?", *Theology*, April, 1960.
Asamoah, E.A. "The Conflict between the Christian Church and African Heritage", *International Review of Missions* (IRM), July 1955, pp. 292-301.
Bates, Searle M., "The Training of Christian Ministers in Non-British Africa", *I.R.M.*, July 1954, pp. 294-300.
Bethune, Roderick, "Selection and Training of Candidates for the Ministry of the Church of England", *Expository Times*, Vol. 73, July 1962, pp. 308-311.
Beck, George Andrew, Bishop of Salford, "*Training of Priests* (R.C.), *Wiseman Review*, Spring 1962, pp. 35-42.
Black, Matthew, "Ministerial Training and Vocational Needs", *Expository Times*, January 1951, pp. 100-103.
Brothers, Joan, "The Priest's Role" (R.C.), *New Society*, 1st Oct. 1954, pp. 10-11.

Busia, K.A., "Has the Christian Faith been adequately presented", I.R.M. Vol. 50, Jan. 1961, pp. 86-9.

Barry, F.R., "Selection and Training of Candidates for the Ministry: A New Deal in Training", *Expository Times*, Vol. 74, Nov. 1962, pp. 43-46.

Carstairs, G.M., "A View from the Shrine: The Rural Priests in West Africa and India", *Listener*, Vol. 65, 2 March 1961, pp. 387-389.

Central Advisory Council of Training for the Ministry (CACTM), "The Clergyman's Training: has it moved with the times?" (Review of the purpose and scope of clergy training published for the Central Advisory Council of Training for the Ministry.) *Times Educational Supplement*, 25 Nov., 1949, p. 821.

Christians Asleep. 4. "Something is badly lacking in the training of the clergy", *Times*, 21 May 1966, p. 9.

Cobham, J.O., "Advocating greater use of readers and deacons (in the present emergency due to the shortage of trained clergy)", *Theology*, April 1953, pp. 122-130.

Concillium: "Liturgy No. 1(a)", *An International Review of Theology* Vol. 2, No. 1, Feb. 1965.

Crane, Paul, "The Catholic Church in Changing Africa", *Africa*, October 1960, pp. 197-260.

Crane, William H., "Indigenization in the African Church", *I.R.M.* Vol. 53, Oct. 1964, pp. 408-422.

Crowder, Felix E., "The colonial clergy Act 1974 and the overseas and other clergy (Ministry and ordination) measure 196". *Church Quarterly Review*, Vol. 167, Oct./Dec. 1966, pp. 479-487.

Culkin, Gerald, "The English Seminaries" (Comprehensive account), *Clergy Review*, February 1951, pp. 73-88.

Cunliffe-Jones, H., "Selection and training of candidates for the Ministry: the right perspective in ministerial training" (Congregational Church). *Expository Times* Vol. 74, Oct. 1962, pp. 4-6.

Dammers, A.H., "Training for the Ministry in Africa and Asia", *I.R.M*, July 1958, pp. 312-315.

Davies, G. Henton, "Selection and training for the Ministry: the Baptist Churches in Great Britain", *Expository Times*, Vol. 73, May 1962, pp. 228-230.

Davies, Horton, "Ministers of tomorrow: their duties and training", *Hibbert Journal*, April 1950, pp. 226-230.

Derby, Archdeacon of, and Richardson, Alan, "Training for the Ministry", *Church Quarterly Review*, Vol. 156, No. 321: 367-71.

Drewett, John, "Recruiting: an appraisal of the present situation", *East and West Review*, Jan. 1952, pp. 21-27.

Eagleton, Terry, "Priesthood and Paternalism", *New Blackfriars*, Vol. 47, Dec. 1965, pp. 141-157.

Evans, Stanley, "Selection and training of candidates for the Ministry: new essays in ordination training", *Expository Times*, Vol. 74, March 1963, pp. 181-182.

—"Selection and training of candidates for the Ministry: the Church of England", *Expository Times*, Vol. 73, April 1962, pp. 181-211.

Foreign Field, The (WMMS), 1910-1930.

Frost, Stanley B., "Selection and training of candidates for the Ministry: post-graduate theological training", *Expository Times*, Vol. 74, Jan. 1963, pp. 112-114.

Golden Shore, The (Anglican), 1925-1965.

Hastings, Adrian, "Christianity and African Culture", *New Blackfriars*, Vol. 48, Dec. 1966, pp. 127-136.

Harris, Peter, "Are Seminaries Essential", *Herder Correspondence*, Vol. 5, No. 5, May 1968.

Hanssen, Olav, "A dynamic and flexible form of Ministry", *I.R.M.*, Vol. 53, Oct. 1964, pp. 423-433.

Hindmarch, Roland, "African culture and the West:

(a) "Protestant and self-discovery", *Blackfriars*, Vol. 45, Jan. 1964, pp. 14-22.

(b) "Western cultural engagement in Africa", *Blackfriars*, Vol. 45, March 1964, pp. 111-120.

Hodgson, Leonard, "The training of the Clergy", *Church Quarterly*, July-Sept. 1953, pp. 282-291.

Hopewell, James, F., "Mission and Seminary structure", *I.R.M.*, Vol. 56, April 1967.

Horton, Robin, "The High God: a comment on Father O'Connell's paper", *Man*, Sept. 1962, pp. 137-140.
Hughes Lachlan M., "Priestly Formation", (R.C.), *Month*, Vol. 218, Sept. 1964, pp. 149-151.
Huxtable, John, "Thoughts on ministerial training", *Congregational Quarterly*, April 1955, pp. 141-150.
Kingsnorth, J.S., "The Changing Role of Missionary Societies in Africa", *Overseas Quarterly*, March 1963.
Knapp-Fisher, E.G., "Training for the Ministry", *Theology*, February 1959, pp. 58-64.
Kuse, W.F., "What the African Ordinand is thinking", *Theology*, Vol. 64, Aug. 1961, pp. 329-330.
Lash, Nicholas, "The place of the priesthood" (R.C.), *New Blackfriars*, Vol. 47, Aug. 1966, pp. 564-571.
Litton, John, "The training of junior clergymen: a systematic approach", *Theology*, Vol. 69, Nov. 1966, pp. 502-506.
Matthew, David, "The training of an African clergy", *Africa*, October 1960, pp. 197-260.
Mitton, C. Leslie, "Selection and training of candidates for the Ministry: a new deal in training", *Expository Times*, Vol. 73, March 1962, pp. 177-179.
Moss, Basil S., "The proposed new Theological College", Theology, Vol. 64, Feb. 1961, pp. 57-9.
Moxley, C.E. and (2) Pritchard, B., "Training for a prophetic ministry (correspondence on Ghraham Noville's article in August 1958)", *Theology*, Nov. 1953, pp. 465-466.
Neill, Stephen, "The Indigenous Church in self-governing countries", *East and West Review*, April 1954, pp. 35-42.
Neville, Graham, "Training for a prophetic ministry: (some criticism of present methods in the Church of England)", *Theology*, August 1958, pp. 324-327.
Nunn, H.P.V., "The Advantages of a classical training as a preparation for the Ministry", *Evangelical Quarterly*, Jan. 1949, pp. 49-70.
O'Connell, James, "The withdrawal of the High God in West African religion; an essay in interpretation", *Man*, May 1962, pp. 67-69.
Parrinder, E.G., "The religious situation in West Africa", *African Affairs*, Vol. 59, No. 234, pp. 38-42.
Paton, David M., "Theological training in the Younger Churches", *East and West Review*, Vol. 26, No. 4, pp. 125-127.
Paton, M.J.M., "Promises (made by clergymen at their ordination which they are unable to keep)", *Theology*, Sept. 1954, pp. 335-339.
Paul, Geoffrey, "An Ecumenical Theological College?" *Ministry*, Spring 1968, pp. 14-15.
Phillips, John, "Vocation of the Ministry", *Theology*, July 1950, pp. 242-245.
Potts, W.M.A., "Finding and fostering vocations", *Theology*, August 1950, pp. 329-332.
Rossman, "The breaking in of the future: the problem of indigenization and cultural synthesis", *I.R.M.*, Vol. 52, April 1963, pp. 129-143.
Shelton, Austin J., "On recent interpretations of Deus Otiosus; the withdrawn God in West African Psychology", *Man*, Vol. 64, March-April, pp. 53-54.
Shepherd, R.H.W., "Indigenous evangelism in Africa", *World Dominion*, Nov.-Dec. 1951, pp. 363-368.
Stacey, David, "Processing Parsons", *London Quarterly and Holborn Review*, July 1965, pp. 221-224.
—"Concerning the Ministry—three addresses to ordinands:
   (i) "Vocation", *Expository Times*, Vol. 75, May 1964, pp. 264-266.
   (ii) "Ordination", *Expository Times*, Vol. 75, June 1964, pp. 264-266
   (iii) "Vows", *Expository Times*, Vol. 75, July 1964, pp. 292-294.
Stockwood, Mervyn, "A dwindling Ministry", *National and English Review*, May 1951, pp. 284-286.
Stourt, William, "The Ordained Minister in the Indian Church", *I.R.M.*, Vol. 52, April 1963, pp. 144-154.
Taylor, J.V., "Problems of Training Men for the Ministry in Equatorial Africa", *East and West Review*, October 1954, pp. 103-109.
Tauton, Francis, "Post-ordination Training", *Theology*, Vol. 65, July 1962, pp. 273-6.
Taylor, C.L., "Selection and Training of Candidates for the Ministry: the Training of American Ministers", *Expository Times*, Vol. 73, Sept. 1962, pp. 363-366.

Thomas, M.M., "Indigenization and the Renaissance of Traditional Cultures", *I.R.M.*, Vol. 52, April 1963, pp. 191-194.
"Vatican seeks way to get more priests", *Times*, 1st June 1962, p. 11.
Waal, Victor de, "A Shortage of Vocations" *Theology*, Vol. 65, Dec. 1962, pp. 488-494.
Waish, M.J., "Approach to Africa: the Problem of Adaptation", *Dublin Review*, No. 482, pp. 324-336.
Walsh, Richard, "The Outlook for Catholic Education", *Africa*, Oct. 1960, pp. 197-260.
Williams, R.R, "The Reformed Pastor in the Twentieth Century", *Churchman*, March 1950, pp. 28-35.
Williamson, S.G., "Missions and Education in the Gold Coast", *I.R.M.*, July 1952, pp. 234-236.
Welbourn, F.B., "Tent makers (The problem of the provision of an adequate supply of Ministers)", *International Review of Missions*, Oct. 1951, pp. 421-425.
Worlock, Darek, "V for Vocations (urgent need for more priests)", *Clergy Review*, June 1953, pp. 321-328.
Ziegler, Jesso H., "Selection and Training of the Candidates for the Ministry; Education in Pastoral Theology; Some American Approaches", *Expository Times*, Vol. 74, Dec. 1962, pp. 69-72.

4. UNPUBLISHED THESIS (M.A.)

Agbeti, J.K., "Missionary Enterprise, Education and Nationhood in Ghana since 1928", New Haven, Yale Divinity School, U.S.A., S.T.M. Project, 1967.

Index

AACC, 197, 199
Abadoo, D. Myles, 25
Abakrampa, 124
Abban, Emml., 144
Abbo, John A., 130n
Abeokuta, 74-75, 184, 186; High School, 76; Training Institution, 186
Abetifi, 41, 43, 45-47, 66
Abiriw, 41
Abokobi, 38, 52
Abuagdie, Kwadzo Ayity, 122
Aburi, 33, 44, 48, 124, 151
Abutiate, Christian, 59; Rev. A.K., 105
Accelerated Development Plan of Education, 137
Accra, 28, 46-47, 65, 88-89, 100, 107, 110, 141, 151, 173-174, 177; Boys' school, 14; circuit, 22; community centre, 109; Training Institution, 18
Achimota, 112; Link road, 170, 172
Acquaah, Gadiel, 27
Aquaah, G.R., 29
Acquaah, W., 27
A.D.A., 113
Adaklu, 51
Addison, Rev., Edward, 16
Addo, J.R., 22
Adegbite, S.A., 75-77
Adegbola, Adeolu, E.A., 190n
Adeseko, Joseph, 104-105
Adiembra, 103
Adesadel, 144
Adukrom, 161
Adzaklo, Ludwig, 59, 62
Afraboadzi, 122
African, *passim*; Anglican priests, 78-88, 115, 135; Assistants, 5, 57-59, 62-63; candidates for the ministry, 11; Christian ministry, 205; Church music, 85; Clergy, 87, 97, 99, 104, 116, 127; helpers, 7; ministers 30, 33-34, 89, 100, 106, 206, 208; pastors, 84; Personality, 85; priests, 97-98, 100-101, 112, 116, 122, 151-152; Priesthood, 90; Roman Catholic Priests, 120; Traditional Religions, 82n; training of, ministers, 11
Africanization of staff, 85
Agbeti, J.K., 3, 65n, 86n, 125n, 132n
'Agbomosho', 74
Aggrey, J., 128
Aggrey, Philip, 114
Aglionby, 89, Rev. John Orfeur, D.D. M.C., 88
Agogo, 161
Agona, 124

Agyeman, Andrew, 104
Agyeman, Fred M., 39
Ahama, Gottfried, 36
Aidoo, J.S., 31
Ajayi, J.F.A., 7, 26, 186n
Ake Institution, 185
Akim, 37, 72
Akingbala, E.O., 77
Akinyele, Bishop, 187
Akinwumi, G.O., 77
Ako, Adjei, Okyeame (Linguist), 174
Akoi, Patrick, 140
Akpey, D. Glover, 153
Akrah, 13-14, 18; Institution, 17; Mission House, 13
Akropong, 39-47, 67, 70-72; Middle School, 40
Aku, Andreas, 53, 63
Akuafo Hall, 171
Akure, 186
Akuete, Isaak, 36
Akwamu, 51
Akwapim, 37, 72
Akwapim, Ridge, 48
Akyeampong, Solomon B., 32
Algiers, 120
Alifodzi, Christian, 59
Allen, York, 120n-121n
Allotey-Pappoe, J.E., 30
Almedingen, E.M., 88n, 98n
Amakom (Ewe and Asante), 161
Amedzofe, 52, 55, 58, 61; German Zone, 60
American, 48, 77
Ametowobla, Timothy, 56, 59, Rev., 168
A.M.E.Z., 165
Amisano, 121-124, 128-129, 132-149; Anglican members, 113, Diary, 134, 147n; Seminary students of New Site, 129
Amissah, John K., 140, 151; Roman Catholic Archbishop of Cape Coast, 134
Amonoo, Ishmael, 32, Mr., 131
Ampofo, Rev. G.K., 72
Amu, E. 65 n, 204
Anang, Gottlieb, 36
Anderson, Rev. Canon David, 192
Andoh, Rev. J.K., 182
Andrew, John, 124
Anglican, 35 and *passim*; African Clergy, 111; Christian community, 117; Church, 105; ordained ministers, 185; ordinand (1958), 114; ordination, 108; Priesthood, 101; training, 189
Anglicans, 169, 189
Anglicans and Methodists, 190

Anglo-Catholic, 108
Aŋlɔ, 51-52
Annan, J.S., 170
Annobil, T.A., 106
Annobil, Theophilus, 114
Annual Session, 76
Ansah, George, 125
Anum, 41, 48
Anyako, 49-52
Appiah, B., 22
Appiah, J.E., 29
Apo, A.C.T., 153
Apostolic Succession, 108
Archbishop of Canterbury, 88
Archbishop of Cape Coast, 151-152
Archives, Basel Mission, 9; North Bremen Mission, 52, 59
Armah, Bernard, 114
Armah, Rev. J.N., 100
Armstrong, C.W., 32
Asamoah, P.K., 142n, 144n
Asante, David, 39, 44
Asase Yaa, 5
Asesieso, 41
Ashanti, 41, 51, 61, 65, 72, 88, 93, 100
Ashanti-European Wars, 93
Ashanti Wars, 51-52
Ashun, Papa Andrew, 128
Asihene, E.V., 168
Assam, Egyir F., 21
Assam, Kofi, 19
Attee, R., 21
Audio-Visual, 85
Auer, Rev. J.G., 39-40
Australian, 48
Avatime, 52
Awka, College, 188
Awosika, D.O., 187
Axim, 100, 131
Ayandele, E.A., 184n-185n
Ayerinde, J.T., 75-76

Babatope, D.O., 190
Bachelor, of Arts Degree, 187; of Religious Education, 82; of Theology Degree, 72-78, 80, 82
Baeta, C.G., ix, 3n, 20n, 204n; Dr. C.G., 180-181
Baeta, Robert, 56
Baglo-Buem, 125n
Balme, Mr. D.M., 168-169
Balmer, Rev. W.T., 24-26, 30
Baptist: Academy, 75, 77; American Mission, 77; Chapel of Osupa, 74; Church, initial classroom, 74; College and Seminary, the, 76; Foreign Mission Board, 74, 79; Ijaye Church, 75; life in Nigeria, 79; Seminary, 77n; Southern Convention, 74; Southern Theological Seminary, in Louiseville, Kentucky, 77, 79; Theological Eduation 74; Theological Seminary, 77n; in Nigeria, 85; at Ogbomosho, 210; Training College, 75
Baptists, 10
Barker, Peter A., 180
Barnes, 170n, G.E., 24
Barret, Robert, 140
Bartels, C.H., 29
Bartels, F.L., 11, 14, 25
Basel, 38, 40; Mission Archives, 37; Mission, Cameroons, 165; Mission Field, 65; Mission in Eweland, 63; Mission Seminaries, 50; Missionary Society, 44, at Abetifi, 65; Missionaries, 36-38, 46-47, 52
Bates, Searle, xiv, 119n, 199n
Beaulieu, J.M., 146
Beckers, Fr., 134
Begoro, 41
Bekoe, Jonathan, 39
Bekwai, 100, 161
Bel, Le, 142
Belgium, 148
Bendor, 51
Bentle, Miss Muriel, 109
Berg, Fr. V., 124
Bethsaida, 207
Beveridge, W., 170
Beyer, E., 146
Bihler, 51
Binder, Pastor, 52, 54-56, Rev. C., 53; Jnr., 54; Mrs., 53
Binder's Farewell Report, 56
Binders, the, 55
Biney, J.E., 25
Binly, Joe, 124
Binly Michael, 122
Bishop of Ondo, 187
Bishop's Special Appeal, 113-114
Bismarck, 60n
Black, Sir Arthur, 31
Blengo, 65
Boating Company, 27
Bodewes, Fr. Corn, 139
Bodi, 100
Bogg, Mrs., 93
Bohn, Joshua, 59
Bonni III, Nii Kwabena, 135
Bontomoroso, 103
Botsio, Kojo, 107n
Boumans, Fr. Walter, 129
Bourret, 150n
Bremen: Missionaries, 36, 52; Evangelical Mission, 65
Bresillac's, Bishop de, 151
Briant, Adolf, 36
Britain, 64-65, 108, 113
British, 37, 52, 64, 112; Administration, 37-38, 46; Cameroons, 158; East Africa, 121; Foreign Office, 46; Government, 46; Methodist Conference, 166; Rule, 135;

INDEX 253

Zone of Eweland, 60; West African Colonies, 104
Bronk, Fr. Andrew van den, 132
Brown, 27
Brown, J.P., 18, 21
Brown Ebenezer, 32
Buah, K., 140
Buatsi, H.H., 170
Buhler, Rev. G.F., 185
Buko, Edward K., 186
Bullen, Fr. John, 139
Bürgi, 59, 63, Rev. Ernest, 56, 61
Burton, 187
Busia, Dr. K.A., 4, 94n
Butler, Solomon, 32

C.A.C.T.M., 117
Calabar, 65
Cambridge School Examination, 133
Cameroon(s), 84, 165, 200; students, 165
Cape Coast, 27-29, 86n-87, 100, 121-128, 133-140, 151, 205; castle, 11, 13-14; castle school, 20; Institution, 21; Training Institution, 17-18
Carson, W.H., 76
Carstairs, G.M., 5
Castle, 38
Castle School, 12-13
Catechists' training, 43
Cathedral, 152
Catholic Priests, 130
Certificate(s): Advanced, 81-82; Agricultural, 45; Catechists' Training, 69; Courses, 83; General certificate of Education, 81, 186; Higher Elementary, 81; in Religious Education, 80; in theology, 81; London Matriculation, 166, 171; Senior Cambridge School, 134; Trinity College, 167; West African School, 137
Chairman, of the District, 25, 168; of the Gold Coast District, 25; of Methodist Church, 25
Champagne, Lord Bishop, 144
Chandran, Rev. Dr., of Bangalore, 180
Charway, Mr. D.S. (draughtsman), 174
Christian: Church, 57, Subversive of Democratic and public good, xii; community, 52; Council, xii, 168; discipline, 51; Faith, 6, 52, 80; Gospel, 72; ministers in West Africa, 85; ministry, xii, 19, 83, 197, 199, in Africa, 82; of the Gold Coast, 2; ministries, 81; Natives, 12; University in West Africa, 210
Christiansborg, 36-38, 41n, 44, 50; Osu, 37
Christianity, 6, 28
Church, 7-8 & passim: Anglican, 110, 117, 119; Anglican, in Ghana, 116, in the Gold Coast, 11, in Lagos, 189; Baptist, 74; Catholic, 204; Christian, xii, 57; in Ghana, xi, in West Africa, xi, in Eweland, 56; disloyalty to the State, xii; Evangelical Presbyterian, 9; Ewe, 62-63; Ewe Presbyterian, 60, 63, 71-72, 157, 165, 175, 198; Methodist, 11, 153, 164, 168, 175; Methodist and Presbyterian, 171, 177, 181; Missionary House, 192, 194; Missionaries, 18; Organization, 8; overhaul, xi; Presbyterian, xii, 73, 87, 153-154, 164, of Cameroons, 164, of Ghana, 9, 175; St. Cyprian's, 92; St. Mary's Horse Road Accra, 96; St. Paul's Breadfruit, Lagos, 187; Union, 108
Churches' censure, 6
Circuits, 29; Akrah, 34; Anomaboe, 28; Anomabu, 34; Cape Coast, 28-29; Dominasi, 34; Elmina, 28; Kumasi, 34
Cleland, William, 36
Clements, Fr. Bernard, 58, 96, 98, 100, 105, 116-118
Clerk, Charles, 68
Clerk, C.H., 168
Clerk, Nicholas, 44
Cocoa Hold-up, 99-101
Cockers, 125
College, 24, 29, 132, & passim: Aburi, 32; Achimota, 190n; Achimota Training, 71; Adesadel, 99; 102; Akropong, 48, 71; Akropong Teacher Training, 69; Akropong Training, 162, 204; Elekuro, 189; Evangelical Training, 53; Fourah Bay, 26, 31, 58, 87; Ibadan 184, 189-191; Immanuel, in Nigeria, 184-195; Inspection Report in 1964, 183; Joint, 162; Joint Theological, 35; Methodist, 158; Richmond, 24-25, 27-30; Rural Training, 70; St. Andrews, at Oyo, 189, foundation students, 189; St. Augustine's, 58, 90-91n, 92, 95, in Kumasi, 58, 89ff., rector of, 96-99; Teacher Training, 70, 72; Theological, 11, 36, 72; Theological Training, 10, 35; Training, 130, 132; Trinity, 7n, 8, 15, 19n, 154, 158n, 161n-163n, 165n-183; Trinity, Legon, 73, 178, grounds, 177; Trinity, at Umuahia, 188; Wesley, 155, 157, 162, Aburi, 32, Elekuro, 189, Ibadan, 184, 189-191, in Kumasi, 11, 31-32, 133
Collett, Dom Martin, OSB, 88-89
Colonial Acting Secretary, 46
Colonial Chaplain, 19
Colonial Secretary, 47
Committee:
Advisory, 109; E P Church Synod, 71; Executive, 156; Foreign Mission, 66, 165; Home, 9, 40; Home Board, 66; Missionary, 11-12, 22, 26-27, 29; Ordinands Advisory, 9; Synod, 9
Compere, 75
Congregation of the Propagation of the Faith, 121

Connolly, Fr. John M., 150n
Continuing Education Conferences, 82n
Coomasie, 88, 90
Cote, Rev. Pere H., 150n
Crankson, 48
Crowther, S.A., 13
Crowther's death, 186
Cruts, Fr. P., 134, 139

Dadson, Rev. Joseph, 114
Dagadu, P.K., 170
Daly, Bishop, 111, 169n
Danes, 36-37
Danyame, Fr., 128
Dartey, Nicholas, 115
Dauble, Rev. G., 61
David, Rev. W.T., 74
Davies, Peter, 152
Davies, Dr. W.H., 77
Dawson-Ahmah, A., 106
Day, Rev. C.T., 190, 192
Deacon's Orders Examination, 187
Debrunner, H., 41n, 42, 52n, 56n, 58n, 62n
Dedicatory Service, 180, 182
Deed of Conveyance, Amisano, 122
de Graft, Johnson, J.W., Snr., 21
de Graft, Johnson, Rev. J.W., 168
de Graft, William, 11
Departments of Divinity, 184, 190
Department of Religion, 210
Department of Religious Studies, Ibadan University, 193
Derick, Fr., 131
Dery, Peter, 152
Dieterle, Rev., J.C., 39
Diploma, course(s), 83; in Religious Education, 83; in Theology, 83
Director of Education, 45
District:
 Anwiaso, 100; Chairman of the, 21; Commissioner, 47; Denchera, 100; Minutes, 21; Reports, 23
Divine Word Fathers (SVD), 120
Divinity Department, 111, 178n
Divinity of Theological Department, at Oyo, 186
Djoleto, Mr. P.G., 66
Doctoral Degree, 152
Dodowa Road, 172
Dodu, Mr. E. Max., 173
Dogli, Fr. A.O., 125
Dominic, Fr., 90
Donath, A.C., 76-77
Dunkwa, 100
Durham, 68
Durham Licence in Theology, 187
Durham University, 187
Dzelukofe, 50, 132n
Dzokpe, 52

Earth Goddess, 45
Ecclesiastical Province, 151
Eddy, Rev. G.T., 171-173
Education Department, 43, 96
Efiduase-Ashanti, 161
Eikwe, 131
Ejisu-Akyinakrom, 161
Ekuban, Ernest, 132
Ekuban, Frederick Emmanuel, 24
Elbers, Rev. Fr.Corn, 139
Elder, Rev. D.S., 72, 153
Elliot, C.H. 86n, 87-88n, Fr., 105
Elmina, 121-122, 124-126, 128, 130, 132, 151
Emisa, Kobina, 122
Encyclical, in the Gold Coast, 127-128
England, 88, 98, 102, 104, 108-109, 111-112, 184; at Islington or Highbury or in Freetown, 185
English University, 112
Ennoo, Rev. F.J., 121, 140, 157
Europe, 210; Some Negro Youths in, 52; a 14 year old boy to, 53; trained in, 53; training in, 55; students' stay in, 55
European Archdeacon, 93
European Civilization, 204
European Community in Accra, 102
European Culture, 56
Evangelical Mission, 65
Evangelistic route, 38; tour, 38; work, 94
Evangelists, 26
Evangelists' School, 42
Evans, Fr., 100
Esuman, Joseph Anu, 128
Essilfie, 132
Essuah, J.A., 140, 152
Ewe, 59, 62, 65, 70; boys, 53; Bremen Church, 64; Church, 58-59; Hymn Book, 62; language, 53; ministers, training of, 64; Presbyterians, 157; School in Westheim, 56; students, 72; young men in Germany, 57
Eweland, 49, 52, 57, 63, 72; African minister in, 57; Partitioning of, 65, Seminary Work in, 55, 60

Faculty of Theology, 171
Fadipe, Mr., 74
Falkenhayn, Alsace and Claver of Madam, 148;
Fanti, 90; Public Schools Directors, 25; Public Schools, Ltd., 25
Fashole-Luke, Edward, 209n
Field Education, 83
Field, M.J., 5
Fifth Year, 69-73
Fifth Year Ewe, 71-72
Final B.ED. Examination, 163
Findlay, Mr., 189
First Anglican Ordinands in Accra, 94-95

Fisher, Fr., 96
Fisher, J., 125
Fletcher, Rev. James, 21
Flothmeir, 54
Foh-Amoaning, J.K., 164
Foreign Field, 28
Foreign Mission Board, 74
Forman, Charles, 175n
Foulkes, Rev. F.F., 192
Fourah Bay, 189, College, 111, 185, 187; Scheme, 20; Training College, 29
Francis, Dom, Acting Rector, 91
France, 64, 120
Franciscans (Frank & Frances), 187
Freetown, 24, 26, 30, 87
French Colonial Africa, 120

Gã, 36, 113, 115; Grammar book, 37; Language, 37; student, 39
Gaba, Christian, 4
Gagnon, Fr., 142
Galloway, Prof. A.D., 192
Gambia, 107, 109, 165, 182
Gambians, 109
Garden Party, 192
General Certificate of Education, 149
General Council of Basel and Scottish Missions, 155
General Ordination Examination, 106; GOE, 108
General Superintendent, 46-47
German, 45-46; Mittleschule, 40; new policy in Africa, 60n; Province, 146
Germans in Togo, 64
Germany, 53, 55-56; trained in, 53, 60-65; pastors in, 57, 147; Eastern, 147
Geurts, Fr. James, 132
Ghana, 65, 84, 86, 111, 116, 149-151, 153, 196, 201, 205, 210
Ghartey, S.P.Q., 29
Gibson, S.J., 28, 31
Gidigago, Afeni, 123
Girls' High School and Training Home, 25
Goeller, Fr., 123
Goerner, Dr. Cornel, 78
Gold Coast, 12, 19, 23-28, 33, 37-38, 44-49, 53, 63, 65-66, 71, 86-89, 91, 94, 96, 98, 100, 102, 104, 108-110, 112, 120-121, 130, 151, 153-154, 157, 164-170; Colony, 52, 64; District, 18, 25, 28, 30, 31; District Synod, 13; Government, 137; Methodist Times, 34, 203; Mission, 65
Golmer's Boarding School, at Badagry, 186
Goodall, Norman, 202n
Governing Body, 180, 182, 193, of Trinity College, 175, 177; and the Standing Committee, 179; for the Joint Theological College, 191

Government, and Mission Assisted Schools, 59; Education Act, 1882, 20; Grants, 22; Inspectors, 22; invitation of the, 65; New Education Act, 59, 112; Service, 96; Standard VII Examination, 68; Teachers' Certificate Examination, 189
Grant, Francis, 14
Grant, F.C.F., 29, 34
Grau, 47, 50n; Dr. E., 182; E., 49, 51n-53n, 65, 57n, 60n; Mrs., 47
Great Britain, 60n, 77
Greaves, L.B., 32
Green, Dr. George, 75
Green Latice Lane, 124
Griffin, Rev. W.R., 28-29
Grubb, Kenneth, 196n
Gudeti, Solomon, 50
Guggisberg, Gorden, 32
Gunn, 39, 42n-43n, 45n, 47, 72n
Gydem, 44

Hagan, John, 34
Half Assine, 131
Hammond, S., 21
Hamlyn, Bishop, 86
Hannan, Jerome, D., 130n
Hanson, William, 14
Hargrieves, J.D., 60n
Harker, F.D., 153
Harrison, 170n
Harrison, R.A., 25
Haruisch, Rev., 40
Harward, Rev. W.G., 102
Haskew, Fr. P., 142
Hastings, Adrian, 149
Hauger, Fr., 128
Hausa, soldiers at Keta, 52
Hauser, 51
Hauser, Johann Conrad, 49
Hayford, Ernest, J., 19
Hayford, J., 24
Heesewijk, John van, 121n-122n, 124n-126n, 128, 140n, 147-148n
Heilbronn, 53
Henking, H., 48
Herman, Bishop, 130, 132n
Herskovits, 86n
Hess, Gottlieb, 49
Hickenbotham, Prof., J.P., 169, 210
Hinderers, the, 186
High, 79-80, 84n; Dr., 84
High, Thomas O'Connor, 74n
Highbury Training College, 186
Ho, 49-50, 52, 57, 61, 70, Districts, 64; station, 57
Hodges, Rev. W.E., 189
Hohoe, 125
Holgate, Mr. K., A.R.T.B.A., 176
Holland, 139

Hollis, Michael, 150n
Holm Neils, 36
Holy Eucharist, 136
Holy Orders, 57, 111, 178n, 185
Holy Rosary Guild, 109
Holy Trinity Cathedral, 95
Holy Trinity Church, 95, 102
Hoof, H.V., 140
Hopewell, 199n; Director of the Theological Fund of the World Council of Churches, 181; Dr., of the T.E.F., 96n; Rev. Dr., J.E.F., 180, 197n
Hopper, Mr. J., 128
Hout, Fr. Antony van, 139
Hubbard, Mr., 168-170n
Hulsen Rev. Fr., Corn, 140
Hummel, Bishop Francis Ignatius, 122, Father, 124-125
Hunter, Rev., H.N., 188

Ibadan, 184, 189
Ibadan Education Zone, 193
Ideal College, 154-155
Idowu, E.A.O., 190
Idowu, Prof. E.B., 190n
Idowu Rev. E.O., 192
Ignatius, Bishop, 118
Independence, 112
Indigenous World View, 2
Influenza Epidemic, 66
Inspectors' Examination, 21
International Missionary Council, ix
Institution, 22, 24, 27-29; Aburi, 31; at Akrah, 16; Cape Coast, 21, 28, 31; Central, 24, 26; Central Theological Training in West Africa, 26; Wesley Training, 31
Islam, 72
Islamic Studies, 82n
Islington, 186

Jackson, Major, C.M.G., 93
Jadesimi, G.A., 187
James Fort Prison, 102
Jehle, Rev. A., 46; Principal, 47
Jenkins, James, 20
Jenkins, Paul, 116
Jerusalem, 52
Johnson George, 50, 59
Joint Committee, 154, 162, 165, 167-168, 174-175, 178; Methodist and Presbyterian, 164-170
Joint Executive Committee, 157
Joint and Oversight Committees, 179
Joint Provincial Council of Chiefs, 116
Joint Training, 111, 155
J.T.C., 153-154, 156-157, 163-164; students' offices, 161
Joint Theological College, 153, 157ff, 170; pioneer students, 157; Trial Period, 157; Committee in Lagos, 191

Jones, Rev., Frank Melville, 186; Mr., 186
Jong, de Father, 126
Jost, F., 48
Jubilee, 63

Kelham, 111-112, 114; first prospective students of, 111
Kelly, Fr. Maurice, 128; Fr., 130-131
Kenya, in East Africa, 84
Keta, 49-50, 52, 60, 66, 125-126, 130, 132, 157
Kete Krachi, 64
Keteku, H.J., 44n
Keteku, Paul Staudt, 39
Kimble, D., 86n, 203
King, Noel, 111
Kingsley, Mary, 203
Kingsnorth, J.S., 204n
King, Thomas, 184
King Tom's Point, 18
Kirham, Mr. William, 185
Knight, Mr. Alan J., 101
Knight, William, 7
Knüsli, 52
Koforidua, 100, 149
Kohlhammer, 49
Kok, F. Adrian de, 139
Koomson, T.W., 170
Kooy, Fr, John, v.d., 139
Kowu, Reinhold, 53
Kpalime, 61-62, 125
Kudeti, 190-192
Kudeti Church Compound, 189
Kumasi, 32-33, 43, 61, 86, 88-89, 92, 94-95, 98, 100, 106, 113, 116-119, 136, 151, 153, 155, 157, 167, 175, 177, 180, 182; Wesley, 161; Ramseyer, 161
Kwaku, Ernest Winard, 53
Kwami, Aaron, 50
Kwami, Fredrich Larson, 50
Kwami, Isaac, 50
Kwami, Robert S., 59-60
Kwami, Stephano, 59
Kwansa, A.L., 170, Rev. A.L., 174

La Mantse, 174
La Stool, 174
Lagos, 28, 74, 111, 121, 185-186; Bishop of, 187, 188-189
Laing, E., 21
Laing, Provost, 118
Laing, Rev., G.E.F., 105, 117, 169
Laing, Rev. Timothy, 20
Lalemand, Fr., 142
Lamaire, Rev., 114
Land, for Trinity College, 173
Lang, A. & Co., 176
LaRoache, R., 145
Lavigerie, Cardinal, 120
Lawoe, 58

Lawoe Adolf, 57
Leaders' Meeting, 8
Legislative Assembly, 142
Legon, 110, 112, 114-115, 168-169, 173, 180, 182-183
Legon Hall, 171n., 181
Lichtenstein, 53
Lieben, Fr. G., 140
Life, 1-2, 4, 6
Little Legon, 170, 172
Local Accra Committee, 113
Local Committee of Missionaries, 43
Local Missionary Committee, 50
Lodholz, 51
Löenstein, 53
Lokko, C.D.K., 170
Lome, 57, 62, 64, 125
London Bachelor of Divinity Degree, 112
London, B.D., 112, 114, 180
London B.D. Examination, 166
London, B.D. Intermediate Examination, 168
London Diploma, in Theology, 115
London Intermediate B.D., 33
London Matriculation, 112
London University, 193
Lorenzo, Brother Fr., 144
Louise, Mary, Her Royal Highness the Princess, 93
Lower Volta, 132
Lucas, J. Olumule, 185n, 189n, 193n
Lungling, 51
Lutheran Orders, 44
Lyons Missionaries, 120

MaCarthy, Sir Leslie, 113
MaCaulay, T.B., 184-185
MacKay, Neil, 65
Maclean, Dr., 76
MacMillan, 157
McCormick, H.P., 76
Maddry, Dr. C.E., 77
Mader, Rev. Mr., 45
Major Seminary, 126; at Pedu, 137, 148
Mallet, first Ewe Minister, 57
Mallet, Rudolf, 57
Mallet, Timothy, 56
Malm, Jonas, 36
Manoing Road, 177
Manderville, Rev. Maurice, 115
Markin, Benjamin, 34
Mathew, Archbishop David, 140
Martin, Dom, 89
Martin, Fr., 122
Martin, John, 11, 15
Martinson, 88
Martinson, Fr. E.D., 86-87, 96, 169
Mary, Blessed Virgin, 88
Matriculation, 31
Mayera, 52

Meelberg, Fr. Wilh., 126
Meelberg's Preparatory Seminary Students, 126
Melville Hall, 187-188, 190-191; Kudeti, 192
Mensa, Gebhard, 59
Mensah, Hutton, 86, 88
Mensah, Joseph C., 59
Menya, Francis, 125
Methodist, 35, 153; Covenant Service, 194; Doctrines, 117; Education, 18; ministers in West Africa, 24; Headquarters, 174; Standing Committee, the, 162; ministers, 198; Training School, 18
Methodist Missionary Society, 13-16, 19, 25, 165, 175, 192
Methodist, xii, 157; and Party Politics, xii; Elementary School, 19; Family, 105; Work, 12
Methodist/Presbyterian Co-operation, 106; members, 177
Mexadzi, Aaron, 59
Miller, Paul H., 75n, 79n
Minister(s), 26
Ministerial Training, 30, at Legon, 171, centres, 188, College, 189, Committee, 191; in Sierra Leone, 210
Ministry, 22
Ministry in Africa, ix
Minor Seminary, 126; St., Teresa's, Amisano, 137
Misa, Rev. Sintim, 166
Mission, Anglican, 9; Assisted Schools, 59; Authorities, 41; Baptist, 74; Basel, 6, 36, 38, 41, 44, 46, 49, 56, 65, 158, 176; Bell, 61; Bremen, 6, 23, 57, 59, 63, 65; in Eweland, 61; Field in Eweland, 58; Elmina, 126; English Church, 48, 51, 86, 89, 93-94, 97-98, 100, 103, 105, 110; Evangelical, 44; House in Basel, 44; Inspector, 57, in Bremen, 54; Scottish, 65-66, 67n, 176; Station at Ho, 52; Wesleyan, 9; Wesleyan Methodist, 7
Missionary Diocese, 110-111; Field Conference, 161; Garden Party, 177; Secretaries, 13; Strategy, 88; supervision, 58
Missionaries, 36, 39, 62-63; African, 120; English, 88, 100; European, and *passim*; German, in Eweland, 63
Missionary Society, 18, 55, 179
Missionary Societies, *passim*
"Mittel" Schule, 6, 39
Moffat, Mrs., 65
Mohammedan, Head in Kumasi, 93
Monninger, 47
Moone, Fr. L., 139
Moreau, Fr. Auguste, 151
Morgan, John, 125n
Morris, Rev. R.S., 157
Morrison, Peter, 127n

Morrison, Rev. Greshman Wynter, M.A., 86, 88n
Mountford, Rev., M.W., 20
Murray, W.G., 65
Muslims, 70, 121

Nate-Kodsi, S.D., 30
National Eucharistic Congress, 136
National University of Ireland, 140
Native Agency, 7, 12, 14, 16, 18
Native Agents, 36
Navrongo, 143, 145, 151
Navrongo Senior School, 142
Neil, Rt. Rev. Stephen, xi, 107, 116, 168, 191
Nelson, Fr., 102n
Newell, Samuel, 57
Nkrumah, Redeemer (Osagyefo) Messianic Majesty, xii
Nickles, A., 10
Nickles, Rev. Fr., 109-110
Nickles, Rev. Fr., Albert, 119
Nielsen, E.W., 202n
Niger, 188
Nigeria, 65, 74, 77, 84, 103, 121, 123-125, 186, 189, 210
Nigerian Baptist Convention, 77, 84; Ministerial Board of, 81
Nigeria Baptist Seminary, 78
Nigerian Method, 121
Nigerian Society, 80
Nigerian Theology, 79
Nightingale, Rev. E.G., 189-190
Nimako, S.G., 157
non-Roman Catholic African Ministers, 153
Northern Ghana, 121, 142, 177
North Road, 157
Northern Students, 142
Northern Students (transfer from Amisano), 142
N.T's Council, 150
Northern Vicariate, 142
Nothwang, E., 40n, 47n
Ntumitse, Paul, 52
Nylo, Geo. J., 32
Nyako, R.P., 180
Nyamasro, Joshua, 50
Nzimaland, 131

Obobi, Christian, 36
Odartei, 27
Odjidja, Rev. 173, Rt. Rev. Eml. 174, 177
Odumasi, 48, 153
Oecumenism, at Bossey in Switzerland, 114
Ogbomosho, 74-77
Ofori, Mr., 66
Oforikai, Wilh., 44
Ofosuhene, A.K., 182
Ohene, C.C., 31

Okine, O.K. Robert, 114
Okoto, Kwadjo, 45
Okpoti, Manche (Chief), 174
Okusanya, I.O.S., 187
Okwabi, Canon, 113
Olaleye, Mr. A.M., 77
Ollennu, Mr. Justice Nii Amaa, 174
Olubi, Daniel, 186
Oluwole, Bishop Isaac, 185, 187
Omotunde, D.O., 190n
Ondo, 187-188
Onipayede, Benjamin, 63
Oosthuizen, G.O., 206
Opoku, Theophilus, 44
Ordained Ministry, 201 & *passim*
Ordinary Levels, 149
Orekoya, G.O., 190n
O'Rorke, Bishop, 87, 89, 116, Bishop of Accra, 88
Osei, Joseph Owusuansah, 152n
Oshea, Fr., 135-136
Osu, 37
Osupa Baptist Church, 74
Oyebode, D.R., 187
Oyerinde, Rev. N.D., 75-76
Oyo, 76-77, 111, 186-188
Oyo Training Institute, 186
Oyo Training Institution, 184, 186-187
Ouellet, 142
Oversight Committee, 154, 158, 161, 165-167, 177-178
Oxford, 106

Pageault, M., 145
Paley, Mr., 85
Pan-Anglican Thank-Offering Fund, 89
Parking, W.E., 153
Paris Peace Conference, 64
Parrinder, E.G., 25
Paton, Nico, 140
Patterson, 76
Patterson, A. Scott, 77n
Pawelzik, Mr., 182
Pearson, 48
Pedu, 137, 139n, 140, 146
Pfann, Helen, 120n, 151n-152n
Peki, 49, 65; boys to Abetifi and Akropong 1916-1923, 65n
Pellat, Rev. Father Prefect, 125
Pershore, Brotherhood, 88; men, 89; (Nashdom Abbey), 98
Peters, Fr., 88
Phillips, Bishop Charles, 185
Picot, James, 19
Pietersen, W.E., 21
Pius XI, Pope, 127
Pobee, John, 114
Pool, Elizabeth Routh, 74n-75n, Mrs., 84n
Pool, Rev. J.C., 76-77
Pontifical Orders, 147

Pope, 151
Porter, Archbishop, 152
Portuphy, 27
Presbyterian, 35, 153
Presbyterian Agents, 70
Presbyterian Church in Ghana, 73
Presbyterians, 36
Presbyterian System, 72
Presbyterian Training, 23
Pre-Ordination, 110
Pre-Ordination School, 109
Preparatory Seminary, 122, 124; at Amisano, 125
Principal, of the University, 171; of Trinity College, 170
Pronk, Nico, 140
Provincial Training College, 111
Provost, 172; of the University, 172

Quaidoo, P.K.K., 172-173n; Cabinet Minister, 172
Quao, G.A., 106
Quarterly Meeting, 8
Quatei, Thomas, 37-38
Quiet Day, 167, 194
Quist brothers, 50, 59
Quist, Samuel, 52, 58-59, 62

Radhakrishnan, S., 204n
Rapp, Dr., T.E.L., 153
Rapp, Theo, E.L., 70
Rankin, His Excellency the Governor and Lady, 192
Rankin, Rev. J.W., 65
Reformation, in the Church, xii
Reindorf, Carl, 36, 38n, 41n, 44
Reindorf, Joseph, 59
Reith, 66
Reith, G., 65
Renner, O., 87-88
Reports: Annual, 1848, 44; Inspection, 45
Rhode, N., 48
Richard, Fr. A., 142
Richter, P.C., 153, 157
Robbens, Fr., E., 128
Roberts, Rev. 190
Rochester, John, 39
Rockson, J.K.A., 182
Roman Catholic, African Priests, 125; African Priests in Ghana, 121; Celibate Priesthood, 127; Church, 150, 151-152; Circles, 205; converts, 121; priest, 125; Province of Ghana, 148, 151; Seminaries, 148; teacher, 125; Training, 197; work, 151
Roman Catholics, 10, 35, 122, 136, 151
Rome, 136
Rooseveare, 111
Ross, Miss I. P., 65

Royal Air Force, 138
Russian Concentration Camp, 147

Sackey, E.A.B., 106
Sadler, Rev. Dr. G.W., 76
Sah, A.K., 164
Salbach, John, 21
Sam. W., 25
Samson, Rev. W., 65
Sampson, Magnus, 116
Sanny, Joseph, 125-126
Sarbah, Mensah, 25
Sarpon, Peter, 5, 149n, 152n
Schlatter, 39n
Schlatter, Wilhelm, 36, 42n-45n
Schlunk, 57-58, 62
Schlunk, M., 55
Schön, Rev. J.F., 13
Schoeder, Dr. H., 125
Schoen, Fr. Henry, 139
Schols, Piet, 140
Schomer, Howard, 206n
School: Achimota, 109, 121n, 201; Cape Coast High, 24; Collegiate, 21, 25; E.P. Church, 11; High, 20; Higher, 49; Mfantsipim, 25, 27, 29-30; 66n, 86n; Middle, 39, 67-68
Scotland, 66, 70
Sea View House, 28
Secretary of State for the Colonies, 47
Sects, xiv
Sedode, Christian Alifodzi, 53, 62
Sedode, Theodore, 59
Seeger, 52, 58
Sefwi, 110
Sekondi, 96n, 100, 126, 129, 131
Seminary, 13, 40, 44, 50 and *passim*: absence of, ix; Akropong, 44, 46; American, 208; Amisano, students of 1932, 131, of 1933, 131-134; authorities, 68; at Abetifi, 42-43, 66, 68; at Abokobi, 39; at Akpafu, 71; at Amisano, 121-122; at Ogbomosho, 77-78; at Wiagha, 121; Baptist at Ogbomosho, 75n; Basel Mission, 41; Bigard in Nigeria, xiii; Bremen Mission, 50, 63, seminary training, 63, 66-67; Christiansborg, 39; Louiseville Kentucky, 75n, 78; Major, Amisano students of 1932, 131, of 1933, 131-134; Minor, 10, at Amisano, students of, 1932, 131-142, in Ghana, 149; Notre Dame, Navrongo, 149; Presbyterian, 8, at Amedzofe, 52, 58, 59n, 60, 63, at Keta, 49, HO, 71-72; St. Charles, Tamale, 149; St. Francis, Wa, 149; St. John's, Koforidua, 149; St. Mary's, Lolobi, 149; SS Peter and Paul, in Nigeria, xiii; St. Peter's, Pedu, 205; St. Peter's Regional, 137, 140, 148; St. Teresa's, 121n, 126n, 132n, 148; St. Victor's, Tamale, 142-146,

148, 150; teacher-catechists', 37; Theological, 40
Seremekun, Rev., J.O.E., 190n
Shaki, 75-77
Shipman, S.A., 13-15
Shirley L.O., 210
Sierra Leone, 18-20, 23-24, 26, 29-30, 84, 87, 111, 184, 186-187
Signatories of Amisano, 1892, 122
Simonson, Rev. J., 192
Slater, Sir Ransford, His Excellency, Governor, the, 128, Governor and Lady, 97
Smith, 42n, 46n-48, 65n, 68n, 75n
Smith, Rev. Mr., C.E., 74, 75n
Smith, John Fletcher, 122, 124
Smith, M.G., 172
Smith, Noel, 36
Smith, W.C., 65
Smith's, Mr., 171
Sneath, Rev., Alec A., 28-29
Society for African Mission (SMA), 120, 151
Society for the Propagation of the Gospel (SPG), 81, 100, 104, 113
Solaru, T.T., 190n
Solomon, John Ahoomah, 14
Solomon, Rev. S.R.B., 34, 203
Somerville, William F., 23
Southern Baptist Convention, 74
Southern Nigeira, 28
Southon, 12
S.P.C.K., 113
Srogbe, 50
St. Alban's Church, 115
St. Andrews' College, 111, 184
St. Augustine, 93
St. Augustine's, Day Celebration's Re-Union, 98; Secondary, School, 133-135, 138; Training College, 128
St. David's Kudeti, Ibadan, 192
St. Nicholas Grammar School, (Adesadel), 101
St. Peter, 93, the Apostle of Holland, 130, 148, Claver Solidarity, 130, the Apostle, 131
St. Teresa, of the Child of Jesus, 130
Stamm, Rev. W., 70, 153, 167-168, 177
Stauffer, John, 125-126
Steemers, Hans., 140
Stool, 4
Stool Elders, 174
Stoughton, R.H., 172-173
Strebler, J., 125-126
Strebler, Fr., 130-132
Stricker, Rev., 47
Students, admitted outside the Gold Coast, 164
Suame, 161
Subpastors, note on, 190n

Sudan, 121
Sundkler, 26
Sundkler, Bengt, xiv, 117-118, 209n
Supreme Being, 4, 6
Surry, 125
Sutter, Abbe, 148
Suykerbuyk, Fr. Andrew, 139
Swaniker, Thomas, 36
Swinton, Lord, 104
Swiss, 46-47, 58, 63
Switzerland, 49, 70
Synod(s): African members of, 65-66; Committee, 67-68, 112, 204; District, 16; districts into, 58; First under U.F.C.S., 65; Gold Coast District, 17, 23, held at Cape Coast, 18, of 1894, 22; the Gold Coast, 24, of 1909, 26, of 1910, 26, of 1911, 28, of 1913, 25, of 1916, 29; 1919, 30, 66-67; 1921, 30; 1931, 69; 1937, 153; 1952, 108; Methodist, in Lagos, 191; Minutes, 108; Standing Committee 111.

Tafo, Kuma, 161
Takoradi Harbour, 94
Tamakloe, 70
Tamale, 121, 139n, 142n-143, 146, 150, Mission, 139n, 150
Tanzania, 201n
Targett, M., 146
Tarkwa, 87, 100, 105-106
Teacher-Catechists, 68
Teachers', 26, Certificate, 43, Course, 68, Training School, 40
T.E.F., 176, 178, 180
Tema, 110, 115
Tempels, Placide, 1
Ten Anglican Ordinands in Higher Institutions, 115
Termeulen, 122
Teshi, 38
Tetteh, B.K., 182
Theological: College, 110, 167, 169; course 69; course in West Africa, 211; Department, 20, 190; Education Fund, ix, 179, 192, 207; Fifth Year Tranining, 69; History of Theological Education xi; Institution, 14-16, 22, 26, 87, 89, 101, 107, 184; Institution of Mfantsipim, 22; Schools, 45; Seminary, 68; Survey, 107; Training Institution, 12, 21, 52, 88, 186
Theodor, Heinrich, 50
Thomas, from the Gambian Diocese, 106
Thomas, Rev. Hugh E., 166-168n
Thomas Rt. Hon. J.H., 94
Thompson, Rev. Edgar and Black, Sir Arthur, 189n
Thompson, Rev. Edgar W., 31
Togo, 64, 84
Togoland, 64, 165; British, 64; French, 64; schools, 60; The Government of, 57

Topo, 21
Training, Bremen Mission, 59; Colleges, 155, 184; Institution, 22-23, 28, 115
Tremblay, R., 145
Trial Period Review Committee Members (1945), 163
Tryers, Fr., 150
Tupper, H., 77n
Twenty Ewe boys trained in Germany, 52-54
Twenty-fifth Jubilee, 61
Twi students, 39

Uganda, 121, 200, 201n
U.K., 114
Umuahia, 190, Theological College, 192
United Church of Christ in the USA, 176
United College, 192
United Free Church of Scotland, 65
United Theological, College, 154; training, 154; training college, 191
U.N.O., 147
University, 112, 114-115, 174, 204; at Legon, 183; Architect, 170; campus, 171; College, 107, 109-110, 112, 168-169, 172-174; at Achimota, 166; Council, 171-172; Examination, 165, 167; of Cape Coast, 205; of Ghana, 171n-172n, 175, 181; of Ghana, Legon, xii, 14; of Legon, 180; of Ibadan, 189, 193; of Rome, 140; site, 169; the Gold Coast, lll, 116; the University, 167-168
Usher, Governor, 18

Valedictory Service, 194
Vatican, 120
Venn, Henry, 7
Vermülst, Fr. E., 129
Vernacular Course, 81
Veuillot, Pierre, 127n
Vicariate(s), 151, of Africa, 120, of Keta, 125
Vice-Principal, 186, of the University College, 170
Vietor Trading Company, 51
Vocation(s), 84
Vögelin, Rev. Mr., 50
Volta Region, 125
Volta River, 38

Wa, 145, Bishop of, 152
Wallace, Miss G.M., 65
Wanner, G.A., 46
Ward, 38n, 44n, 75, 93n, 110n, 135n
Warman, the Rev. N.L.P., 176
Warren, Max, 203n
Watkins, Rev. B., 15
Waya, 49-50
Weatherspoon, Dr., J.B., 77
Webster, 30

Weijden, Rev. Fr. G.v.d., 125n, 132n
Well's Theological College, 114
Wesleyan Methodist, Church, 18, 28; Missionary Society, 12, 18, 28, 30, 184; WMMS, 189, Mission, 34, 184, 189
Wesleyan Mission House, 38
West African, 23, 30, 85, 90, 104, 107, 121, 192, 196-199, 200-206, 209, 213; Districts, 23-24, 31; Methodist Teachers and Preachers, 18; Ministers, 196; School Certificate Examination, 108
West Africans, 6
Westheim, 53-57
West Indian Immigrant, 44
West Indians, 39
West Indies, 18
Western Equatorial Africa, 186, 188
Western Germany, 181
Westermann, Diedrich, 207n, 212n
Westminster, Abbey, 88
Weyhe, 51
Wharton, Henry, 16
Whirley, Carlton, F., 85, 213n
White Fathers' (WF), 120-121; of Navrongo, 142
Wiagha, 142-143
Widman, Rev. J.G., 39
Wiegrabe, 51n-52, 61n-62n, 70
Wiegrabe, Paul, 7
Wilhelmsdorf, in Würtemberg, 53
Wilkie, 66, Rev. & Mrs. A.W., 65, Rev. A.W., 65
William, from the Gambia Diocese, 106
Williamson, S.G., 156-157, 166, 168-169n, 192, 204, 210
Willingham, Dr. R.J., 75n, 77n
Wilson, Dr., 109
Wilson, J.B., 31
Wilson, M.H., 117n
Wilson, S.H., 31
Winfield, T.W., 20
Winneba, 100
Wise, C.G., 11
Wolfson, Freda, 13
Wolsey College, 106
Women's Department, 82-83
Wood, Rev. Joe, 192
World Church, 181
World Council of Churches, 116, 175
World Roman Catholic Ecclesiastical Communities of Priests, 120
World War I, 45-46, 50, 62-64, 70, 73, 87
World War II, 71, 120, 134, 138
Wouters, Mathew P., 132n-133n, 138n-139n
Wulff, Theodore, 36
Wurtemberg, 39, 50

Yaba, 190n
Yalley, J.R.C., 87, 102

Yamfu, Ekroful, 124
Yebuah, Rev. J.K., 100
Yendi, 64
Yirenkyi, William, 39
Young Pioneers, Founded 1960, xii; condemned publicly by the Church, xii
Youth Work, 154
Yoruba, 74, 80, 103-105, 185
Yoruba and Niger Missions, 186

Yoyo, Herman, 53, 62
Yoyovi, Mr., 203

Zahn, 55, 57; Inspector, 58
Zimmermann, J., 36-39
Zone, English, 66
Züundel, 50, Rev., 51
Zürcher, G., 47-48

```
BV                    35044
3540
.A35    Agbeti, J. Kofi
1986       West African church
v.2     history.
```